THE BRITISH MUSEUM **Pocket Dictionary**

ROMAN ARMY

Richard Abdy

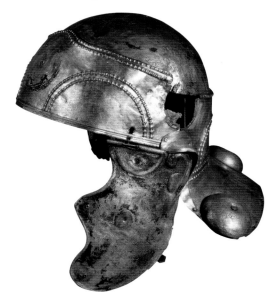

THE BRITISH MUSEUM PRESS

First published in 2008 by
The British Museum Press
A division of The British Museum Company
Ltd, 38 Russell Square, London WC1B 3QQ

www.britishmuseum.org

Richard Abdy has asserted the right to
be identified as the author of this work

ISBN: 978-0-7141-3126-9

A catalogue record for this book
is available from the British Library

Designed and typeset by
HERRING BONE DESIGN
Printed in China by
South China Printing Co. Ltd

ILLUSTRATIONS

Unless listed below, all photographs are
© The Trustees of the British Museum and
have been taken by British Museum
Photography and Imaging.
p.6 akg-images / Peter Connolly; p.7 Vale and
Ridgeway Project, the University of Oxford /
Ian Cartwright; pp. 8, 9 (below), 11, 31 (below),
33, 38 Sam Moorhead; p.10 Reinisches
Landesmuseum, Bonn; p.12 Grosvenor
Museum, Chester City Council; p.14
Hunterian Museum and Art Gallery, University
of Glasgow; p.17 T.W. Potter; p.23 Colchester
and Ipswich Museums; p.24 Museum of
Antiquities, University of Newcastle; p.25
(above) The Vindolanda Trust; p.25 (below)
Hadrian's Wall Heritage Ltd / Roger Clegg.

CONTENTS

A-Z Glossary of Roman Military Terms

adlocutio	'address' (commander's pep talk)
ala	'wing' (cavalry unit equivalent to infantry cohort)
aquilifer; signifer	standard-bearer
armillae	armlets (decorations)
ballista	catapult
caligae	hobnail sandals
canabae	civilian town next to a fortress
cassis	helmet
castellum	fort for a smaller army unit (e.g. cohort)
castrum	legionary fortress
cataphractus	completely armoured cavalryman (e.g. Sarmatian)
centurion	commander of a century
century	unit of 80 men
classis	the fleet, navy
cohort	unit of *c*.480 men (six centuries)
contubernium	section of eight men
cornicen; tubicen	horn-blower / trumpeter
corona	crown (various military decorations)
decimation	ritual execution of one in ten men of a unit
decurion	commander of a *turma*
duplicarius	junior officer on 'double pay'
gladius	short-sword
hasta pura	untipped spear (decoration)
legatus legionis	commander of a legion
legion	army of about 5000+ infantrymen (ten cohorts including one double cohort)
lorica hamata	chainmail body armour
lorica segmentata	segmented body armour
lorica squamata	scale body armour
miles gregarius	soldier 'of the herd' (i.e. private)
optio	deputy centurion
phalerae	'harness' of medal decorations
pilum	javelin (throwing spear)
praetorians	bodyguards
praetorium	commander's house in a fort
prefect	Commander (e.g. of a cohort)
primus pilus	'first-spear' – senior centurion of a legion
principales	staff officers
principia	headquarters building in a fort
sagittarius	archer
scutum	shield
sesquiplicarius	junior officer on 'pay-and-a-half'
signifer	standard-bearer
singulares	horseguards
spatha	long-sword
tesserarius	adjutant
testudo	'tortoise' (battle manoeuvre)
tribulus	(caltrop) spike to throw in front of enemy horsemen
tribunus angusticlavius	aristocratic officer with 'narrow-striped' toga (indicating equestrian rank)
tribunus laticlavius	aristocratic officer with 'broad-striped' toga (indicating senatorial rank)
turma	cavalry squadron of thirty-two men
vexillum	flag / banner
viaticum	enlistment payment (three gold coins)
vitis	vine rod – centurion's stick

ntroduction

Roman cavalry defeat barbarians. 2nd century AD frieze reused in the Arch of Constantine in Rome.

n AD 117 the Emperor Hadrian inherited from the all-conquering Trajan an empire richer and larger than ever before. It contained about a quarter of the earth's population in an area stretching from Scotland to the Red Sea.

They were mostly civilians whose wealth and potential as slaves were eyed greedily by Rome's enemies beyond the frontiers. The Roman Empire required constant defence, which was provided by a tax-funded army of about 300,000 men. Most were permanently deployed in the distant borderlands and never saw Rome, which seems peculiar as their organization, tactics, equipment and culture were inherited from the early inhabitants of the city that lay at the heart of the empire.

The ranks, weapons and everyday life of the army at the empire's greatest extent — roughly around Hadrian's lifetime — form the subject of this book, and we begin with how the Romans fought. It should be remembered that Roman art (of the kind displayed in the British Museum) shows the conquest of the non-Roman 'barbarians' in a glorious way. The unromantic workaday reality of soldiers is rarely featured.

Romans versus Barbarians

A letter of the second century AD reveals the secret of the Roman army's success: tactics and organization. The letter, written by Flavius Arrianus, governor of a province in Asia Minor, to the Emperor Hadrian, reports his victory over the Alanoi, a tribal grouping of the nomadic people known as the Sarmatians.

Artist's impression of Arrianus's description of the battle. Note the high ground in the distance confining the action. A good Roman commander chose a battlefield carefully to make sure the enemy attacked head on, with no ambushes, so that his soldiers could work as closely as possible to a pre-arranged plan.

The Frilford brooch, 2nd century AD bronze disc brooch recently excavated in Oxfordshire. It shows Roman infantry breaking an enemy cavalry charge – with the help of Jupiter's eagle.

As expert metal–workers as well as fierce warriors and horsemen, the Sarmatian cavalry were covered in armour and were like the tanks of the ancient world. Most Roman soldiers fought on foot and Arrianus knew that his own lightly armoured cavalry could not match the Sarmatians directly. Instead he formed most of his infantry shoulder to shoulder, ten rows deep. When the Sarmatians charged the front row they were blocked not just by one man but by a bank of soldiers four deep, all brandishing spears. Behind these blocking men he drew up four rows of javelin throwers, archers and mounted archers. Finally, behind these ranks Arrianus had positioned catapults. In this way the Sarmatians were first halted and then pelted by missiles. Afterwards, the light Roman cavalry darted in to catch the fleeing survivors ensuring that as few Sarmatians as possible escaped to fight another day. Organization and tactics had prevailed.

The Private and the Section

The basic rank of the Roman army was the *miles*, the equivalent of the private soldier in a modern army. A young man joined for a term of service that lasted twenty-five years and could expect a hard life of strict discipline, severe punishments, exhausting physical work and great danger. There were also times when there was little to do, yet leaving barracks to visit family was probably rarely an option.

Although some soldiers were forced to join (conscripted), most did so voluntarily, attracted by the pay, which was more regular than most common civilian work, which usually involved seasonal agricultural labouring. A new soldier traditionally received an ample bonus of three gold coins to see him to his unit and his first payday, of which there were only three each year. The modern word 'soldier' comes from the late Roman and medieval word for gold coin, *solidus, solde*. Food, shelter and arrangements for retirement, none of which could be relied upon in the ancient world, all made military service an attractive career. To increase pay, there was also the chance of gaining loot through wars of conquest or of achieving promotion.

Barracks room at Caerleon, South Wales. The whole section (eight men) would have lived in the front room (where eight people are pictured standing), and the back room (behind them) was probably for storing equipment (see p. 11 for a view of the whole block).

The Roman private was known as the *miles gregarius* (soldier 'of the herd'). Even when not fighting he was forced to live in very close contact with seven other 'mess-mates'. This eight–man section was known as a *contubernium*, and even today the basic unit of the British Army is usually eight men. At barracks the *contubernium* would have lived and slept in one small room, while on campaign they shared one tent and one mule to carry their shared domestic equipment.

Gold *aureus* (coin) of Hadrian (AD 117–38).

Legionaries on parade – a troop of re-enactors perform at the British Museum.

Centurion and Century

Ten eight–man sections grouped together were called a 'century', although it numbered eighty men, rather than the hundred that the name suggests.

Monument to Marcus Caelius Rufus. Rufus, at the age of fifty-three the senior centurion of the 18th Legion, went missing in action after a notorious defeat of the Roman army in Germany in AD 9. He was presumed killed, and the inscription asks that his bones be buried there if ever found. The two busts either side of Rufus were his slaves who became freedmen on his death; they put themselves in the picture when they set up the memorial.

Barracks at Caerleon. The great fortress of Caerleon in South Wales has the clearest foundations of Roman barracks in Britain. The suite of rooms in the foreground was the centurion's house (see p. 8 for a view of the common soldier's quarters).

TACTICS AND BASIC ORGANIZATION

Probably in the early pre-empire days the unit was made up of a hundred men and the name stuck when it was re-organized. The officer in charge was called a centurion. He had to be brave because he led his men into battle and tough enough to control eighty soldiers. The usual image of a centurion shows a man covered in military decorations carrying a rod cut from the springy wood of a vine. It was a badge of office like a modern officer's 'swagger stick', but it also had a more sinister purpose.

The ancient writer Tacitus tells of a centurion called Lucilius who was known to his men as *cedo alteram* (meaning 'give me another'). Cedo Alteram would beat any soldier who displeased him until his vine rod broke. But it was not the end: 'give me another' he would cry and the beating continued. It is not surprising that he was eventually murdered in a mutiny.

One reward of being a centurion was increased pay compared to a private soldier. He also had his own house, which was much larger than the neighbouring communal rooms provided for each section. There, aided by servants, he could bring up a family, whereas ordinary soldiers in this period were not allowed to marry. The centurionate was not one rank but a class of officers. During his career an able centurion might rise through several grades to the top rank of senior centurion, or *primus pilus* (the 'first spear' of his regiment).

Centurion's Staff and Other Specialists

Each centurion was assisted by a number of staff officers (*principales*). They enjoyed higher pay than privates, earning either double pay (*duplicarius*) or pay-and-a-half (*sesquiplicarius*).

Principales The man with the biggest stick in the unit was not the centurion but his deputy, or *optio*. The *optio* took up position at the rear of formation, making sure that everybody kept up when marching (see p. 20), and during battle he used his long staff to push the century into straight lines. If soldiers tried to back out of the fighting they could expect a much more forceful use of the stick.

Tombstone of an *optio* from Chester. The tombstone shows Caecilius Avitus, of the 20th Legion. He was from Merida in Spain and lived to the age of thirty-four. As well as his *optio's* staff, he holds a writing tablet to indicate his administrative role.

A group of trumpeters. Detail of the battle scene frieze shown on p. 5.

One man called a *tesserarius* carried out an administrative role (adjutant), which included setting passwords on writing tablets (*tesserae*). Another man who engaged in administrative work (such as supervising the unit's pay) was the *signifer*, or standard-bearer. During battle he carried the unit's banner and acted as a rallying point for each unit. The standard-bearer was among the first to advance and therefore had one of the more dangerous jobs in the army (see pp. 14–15 for regimental standards).

Immunes The many other soldiers with specialist skills needed in the army were called *immunes*. They were rewarded not with more pay but, as their name implies, with immunity from the more boring duties (e.g. guard duty). *Immunes* included many types of craftsmen and the trumpeters that were vital to relay instructions above the din of battle.

Cohort and Legion

Centuries were grouped into larger units, with six centuries forming a cohort of 480 men.

Sometimes the cohort (or double cohort) was the standard size for support units such as cavalry or support infantry (see pp. 24–5). However, the backbone of the Roman army was the legion. Each legion comprised about 5,300 men divided into

ine cohorts and one double-strength cohort. Legion' was a byword for a huge number of people. In the Bible Jesus confronts a man possessed by a multitude of demons. 'Our name is legion', they inform him, 'for we are many!' Under the Emperor Hadrian the army included around thirty legions.

Each legion had their own symbol and their own regimental standard bearing a Roman eagle – a form of corporate identity familiar in modern army regiments. The eagle' (*aquila*) embodied the honour of the legion and was much revered (its loss was a terrible disgrace). The man privileged to bear the legion's eagle standard was called the *aquilifer*, or eagle-bearer, and was on the staff of the senior centurion of the legion.

Gold coin (2nd century AD) showing standards. The legion's eagle standard (*aquila*) is in the centre, flanked by two century standards (*signae*).

Unless a legion fought a major war in their home province, the men of a legion were often dispersed for various temporary duties in cohort or century groups called '*vexillations*'. From the Latin *vexillatio*, they would identify themselves with a flag, *vexillum* (e.g. see the Emperor Hadrian's warship, p. 27). An emperor on campaign would usually prefer to assemble *vexillations* from various legions, rather than uprooting an entire legion from its home province. This would have been very disruptive and happened only on rare occasions. Two of the three legions in Britain at the end of the Roman occupation had been there since the invasion in AD 43.

2nd century AD building slab of the 20th Legion. The legion's *aquilifer* bows to allow the goddess Victory to decorate his eagle standard. The legion's badge is the running boar below.

Legions and Fortresses

Like many modern regiments, the Roman legions were identified by a name and number.

The 30th Legion, for example, was also called *Ulpia*, the Emperor Trajan's family name. *Legio XXX Ulpia* was therefore named in a way a British regiment might be called 'the king's own'. There was no logic to the numbering system, with some numbers missing and others repeated. Legions 17, 18 and 19 were lost in the disastrous German expedition of AD 9 (see p. 10) and the unlucky numbers were never used again. Other legions used the same number, so the name was also needed to identify them. Thus there was *Legio II Augusta* (Augustus's own) and *Legio II Traiana Fortis* (Trajan's strong legion).

3rd century AD coin with badge of *Legio II Augusta*. Capricorn was the birth sign of the Emperor Augustus (27 BC–AD 14).

e *principia* (headquarters) at Lambaesis in North Africa.

soldier of one regiment would be quite at home in the base of any other
roughout the empire, as all of them were built to a similar design. Both fortresses
or legions) and forts (for cohorts) were laid out in grids (like towns) and usually
t within playing card-shaped walls. The walls of the fortress were light defences
ompared to medieval castles – the Roman army expected to meet the enemy in
e field. A fortress had many of the facilities of a Roman city: amphitheatre, baths
d even a hospital. Where the two main streets crossed at the centre was the
eadquarters (*principia*) with the commander's house (*praetorium*) behind. Each
ntury's barracks were arranged around these within their cohorts. The first
ohort was the most senior – it was double strength and was home to the
nior centurion.

Aristocrats in the Army

As an experienced professional soldier, the senior centurion could expect to rise one further step to the position of prefect of the camp (*praefectus castrorum*), who ran the fortress.

The other senior posts were the preserve of aristocrats who mixed stints of military service with political roles in Rome and the other cities of the empire.

The empire had two ranks of aristocrats based on wealth and inherited status. The most privileged were known as senators. They numbered only a few hundred men (in an empire of millions) and were mostly based at Rome. A young senator would hold the rank of senatorial tribune (*tribunus laticlavius*, meaning 'broad stripe' from the purple stripe of a senator's toga).

s second-in-command of the legion they ranked
bove the prefect of the camp, even though they
robably lacked any military experience. The
eneral in charge of the legion was the legate
egatus, meaning the emperor's representative).
f the province had only one legion he would
ormally also be the provincial governor,
gatus Augusti, in addition to *legatus legionis*.

he lesser aristocrats were called equestrians. Their
reater numbers were reflected by the presence of
he five equestrian tribunes (*tribuni angusticlavii*, with
arrow purple-striped togas) attached to each legion.
hey had no fixed commands in the legion but
robably led detachments of cohorts when needed,
nce the equivalent rank was also found as the
ommander (prefect) of cohort-sized support units that
ere separate from the legions (see pp. 24–5).

n aristocrat's sword scabbard (1st century
). It is highly decorated with gilded bronze
nd would have cost a lot to make. It might
ven have been the gift of an emperor. The
cene at the top shows the Roman emperor
iberius (reigned AD 14–37) symbolically
resenting his military victories to the seated
mperor Augustus (reigned 31 BC–AD 14).

nd/3rd century AD altar dedicated by Gaius
ornelius Peregrinus. Peregrinus was a town
ouncillor and equestrian from Bejaia, Algeria,
ho served as a cohort commander near
adrian's Wall. He was praying to 'Fortune
e Home-Bringer' so he may not have been
nd of his cold northern posting.

The Emperor and his Guards

The Roman emperor was the commander-in-chief of the Roman army. It was the source of his power and authority, but also his greatest problem.

When the army supported a rival contender for emperor it usually led to the downfall of the current one. Successful emperors followed the habits of all good military commanders through the ages by inspiring the troops to train hard and maintaining their loyalty. The emperor had to make sure the troops were paid regularly and encouraged with financial bonuses and decorations. As a result the Roman army possessed many of the successful qualities desired by modern armies.

Coin showing the Emperor Hadrian (AD 117–38) leading soldiers on a route march. Sharing military discipline was a way to be popular with the soldiers. Three standard-bearers follow the emperor; at the back (in his usual position) is an *optio* (centurion's deputy) with a rod.

MAIN UNITS AND COMMANDERS

The Praetorian Guards. Roman commanders had a long tradition of keeping a bodyguard stationed at their residence (*praetorium*). In Hadrian's lifetime nine cohorts were kept back from the frontiers to act as the emperor's bodyguard and enforce his will over the aristocrats. Praetorians led a much more privileged life than the frontier troops, being an elite force with fancier uniforms and the chance to enjoy life in Rome when the emperor was in residence. Horseguards also formed part of this force and gradually developed into a unit called the *singulares*.

Coin showing the Emperor Nero (AD 54–68) addressing a praetorian cohort (*adlocutio coh*) at their fort, the *castra praetoria* in Rome. On duty in Rome praetorians did not usually wear defensive armour.

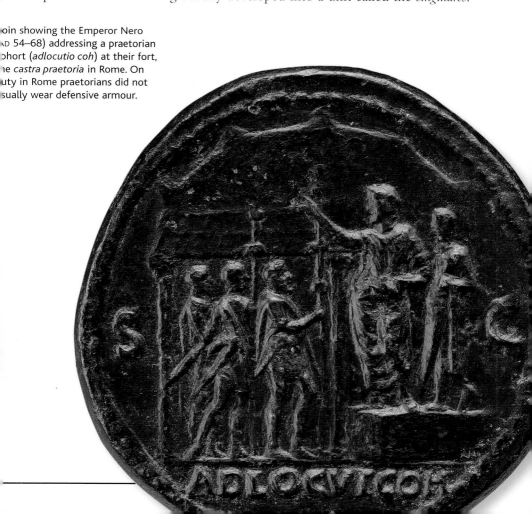

Cavalry

Most Roman cavalry were lightly equipped and armoured, which enabled them to perform various supporting duties where speed and range were useful.

In major battles the cavalry were usually deployed towards the end, after the infantry had turned away the enemy. They were used to rout and pursue the retreating army. While it might not seem very noble to kill people who were running away, the role was often considered suitable for emperors and kings in ancient times.

The Emperor Trajan (AD 98–117) as a cavalry officer. Performing the cavalry's usual role, he rides down a terrified and fleeing foe.

Bronze figurine of a Moorish cavalryman (his horse is missing). It dates to the 2nd or 3rd century AD and was found in London. The people of the Roman province of Numidia in North Africa were considered excellent horsemen and saw much service in the Roman Army.

Cavalry were grouped into units called wings (*alae*) rather than cohorts, a term reminiscent of modern airforce. Instead of centuries, a wing was divided into squadrons (*turmae*) of thirty-two horsemen. The officer in charge of a *turma* was a *decurion*. The cavalry did not form part of a legion (although legions themselves had a small number of horsemen to act as scouts). In fact they were considered to be of a lower standing than legionaries and, like other army support units, recruited men who did not enjoy the legal status of Roman citizens. They were, however, the elite of their kind, ranking above other types of support soldiers, and were paid an equal amount to legionaries.

1st century AD tombstone of the cavalryman Longinus Sdapeze from Colchester. Another helpless foe is shown routed by this junior officer (*duplicarius*), who died at the age of forty after fifteen years' service. He was originally from the lower Danube area, nowadays in Bulgaria.

Auxiliaries

The cavalry were part of a branch of the Roman Army called auxiliaries or support units. They offered less privileged members of the empire the chance to serve in the army (only full Roman citizens could join the legions).

Pay was lower than the legions (except for those in the cavalry), but in return, after twenty-five years' service, an auxiliary soldier was awarded Roman citizenship, which conferred higher legal and social status and made his sons eligible to join the legions.

Tombstone of an archer from Housesteads on Hadrian's Wall. He is armed with knife, axe and bow. His pointed helmet is eastern in style – 'Hamian' archers (from the Middle East) were highly prized by the Roman army for their skill.

Vindolanda fort near Hadrian's Wall. In the decades around AD 100 this fort was used by the 9th Cohort of Batavians (area of the lower Rhineland), a part-infantry and part-cavalry unit, and then became home to the 1st Cohort of Tungrians (from south of Batavia), a double-strength infantry unit. The group of buildings in the upper left is the civilian town.

Most auxiliaries were light infantry. They were usually employed in various battle roles that involved supporting the heavy infantry of the legions. However, Tacitus tells us of one incident where auxiliaries made such a good job of tackling an enemy army in Scotland that there was no need for the legions to be deployed. Both infantry and cavalry auxiliaries were also put to work on more routine policing activities and were often stationed right at the border or sent in detachments for security duties in provincial cities.

Some auxiliary units also provided specialist services such as archers, slingers and artillerymen.

Hadrian's Wall. Although built by the legions, the forts along the Wall were mainly garrisoned by auxiliaries.

The Navy

The Romans did not consider themselves to be a great seafaring nation. In fact the ships of Hadrian's day had changed little from those used by the Greeks and Carthaginians.

This is probably because the Romans had not gone to war with a seafaring enemy since they had opposed these two peoples in the third and second centuries BC. Most Roman naval duties involved policing the sea against pirates who threatened the coasts and Roman merchant ships. To guard against pirates, naval bases were established throughout the seas that bordered on Roman territories. The most famous of these was at Misenum, near Naples, which was instrumental in the attempts to rescue the citizens of Pompeii and Herculaneum during the eruption of Vesuvius.

Tombstone of Titus Valerius Pudens (1st century AD). Pudens was once a marine based at the port of Ravenna but, along with many of his comrades, he joined *Legio II Adiutrix* in Britain (a legion in which the young Hadrian served). He died at the age of thirty and his tombstone is appropriately decorated with dolphins and Neptune's trident.

The main weapon of a Roman war galley was the ram, making the ship itself a missile propelled by its oarsmen. The ram was located at the front of the ship, low enough to pierce an enemy craft below the waterline. This was the only practical weapon, as ships could not carry artillery big enough to sink another ship. The only other method of attack was to board the enemy; the marines on Roman ships were essentially infantry who fought on the decks of ships and who could easily transfer to land-based roles.

Coin showing the Emperor Hadrian's warship. It is flying the flag (*vexillum*) of the fifth cohort of praetorians, his onboard bodyguard.

Tile with a sketch of a Roman lighthouse (1st–4th century AD). A Roman lighthouse of similar shape can still be seen at Dover.

The Sword

The main armament of both the infantryman and cavalryman was the sword.

Roman swords fall into two basic types — long and short. Perhaps surprisingly, the heavier infantry, the legionaries, used short swords. This was because short swords suited the way they fought. In close combat order, with the enemy bunched up

The Fulham sword and scabbard (1st century AD). An example of a legionary's sword found in the River Thames. The pommel did not survive.

efore their shields, the legionary only needed to stab a little way in
ont with his oversized dagger. The Roman sword has a large
ommel, the grip at the end of the handle, which acted as a
ounterweight to the blade. But more gruesomely it also
elped to pull the blade from a human body, which
equires a great deal of pressure. A major battle could last
om dawn to dusk, which would have been another
ood reason to carry the lightest sword possible.

/ith other forms of fighting the greater
each of a long sword was required. For a
avalryman a long sword was essential to
each the enemy from a mounted
osition. The sword was carried
eathed in a scabbard which
ould be highly decorated
it belonged to an officer

(see p. 19). Legionaries carried
their swords on the same side as
their sword arms (right-hand side),
as it was easier to draw when fighting
in close ranks. This did not apply to
officers or cavalrymen who had more
space to comfortably draw their swords
from the opposite side.

A Roman long sword from Hod
Hill in Dorset (1st century AD).

Other Weapons

The Romans possessed an arsenal of weapons in addition to the sword.

The spear was used to repel an enemy attack or to provide a cavalryman with a longer reach. It could also be thrown as a javelin and for this purpose the Romans developed an ingenious form called the *pilum*. This had a long thin metal shaft on top of a pole so the point could pierce a shield and continue on into the man behind it. The shaft was designed to bend if it missed its target, which ensured that it could not be thrown back. Other Roman missiles ranged from lead bullets fired from a simple sling to catapult bolts – giant arrows – that could pierce any armour and might even pass through several men if they were in close ranks.

Caltrop – a nasty spiked metal device that was placed in the path of enemy horsemen to stick in hooves. When thrown, it always lands with a point upwards.

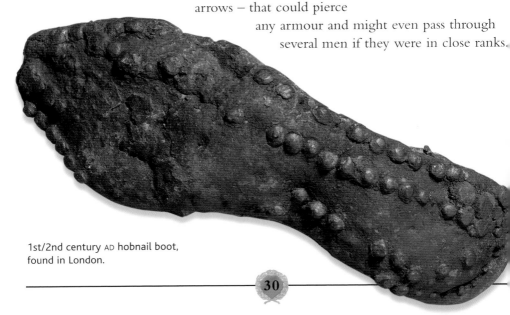

1st/2nd century AD hobnail boot, found in London.

Perhaps the legionary's most basic weapons were his boots (*caligae*). The soles were covered in metal hobnail tacks and could be used to stamp to death injured foes who had fallen beneath the advancing line of legionaries.

Catapult bolt head.

Re-enactors prepared to fire a replica catapult.

The Shield

The shield appears at first to be one of the simplest items of army equipment. In fact it was vital for the legions' battle-winning tactics.

The legion fought rather like a modern police riot squad. Big shields acted as an ever-advancing wall to contain an opposing force. The Romans' enemies were squashed up to prevent weapons such as spears, long swords or axes being swung properly. The Roman short sword then needed very little reach to stab the vulnerable bodies squashed before the shield.

Boss for a legionary shield (early 2nd century AD). The wooden part of this shield did not survive but the bronze boss mimics its original shape (as used by the re-enactors pictured in this section performing the *testudo*). It is highly decorated and even bears the owner's name, Junius Dubitatus of the 8th Legion. To ensure it was looked after, the cost of equipment was stopped against wages, and then the legionary 'sold' it back at the end of service.

e-enactors
erform the
studo.

nields were made of wood, probably built up from laminated strips for extra
ringiness under the blow of a weapon. This was then encased in leather and often
chly decorated with regimental insignia. At the centre a piece of metal called the
oss was shaped as a dome around the grip to give protection to the hand. The
nield boss had another function in that it could be used to give a very nasty
unch, while the edge of the shield could catch an opponent on the vulnerable
ot under the chin. The typical legionary shield was oblong with a cylindrical
rofile that curved protectively around the body. This had another benefit to solders
erforming a manoeuvre called 'the tortoise' (*testudo*). This was a sort of Roman
nk where shields were held so as to give an advancing column all-round
moured protection, and the curve allowed the leading men forward vision. Other
oops such as the auxiliary cavalry and light infantry used flat shields, which were
obably more manoeuvrable and suited their own fighting style. Flat shields are
ually round or oval to eliminate easily damaged corners.

Chainmail and Scale

The main concern of personal armour in the Roman army was to protect the vital area of the torso.

Leg armour (greaves) and arm armour (vambrace – often worn by gladiators to protect the sword arm) were optional items of military equipment. One form of body armour was a tunic (a long shirt that reached the upper thighs) of chainmail (*lorica hamata*). Chainmail looks like knitted iron wire from a distance, but in fact it was made from thousands of interlinked iron rings. It was heavy and usually needed a belt to help spread the weight on the shoulders but it was also very flexible. Although it probably would not stop a direct hit, the wearer could make use of his flexibility to dodge out of the way and chainmail protected against most glancing blows and cuts.

Fragments of scale armour found in Somerset (1st/2nd century AD). These are made of bronze but iron could also be used. Some scales have traces of tinning surviving on the surface for a silvery appearance (which could then be alternated with what would have been bright bronze coloured ones for decorative effect, as shown here).

nd century AD relief e-used in the 4th ntury Arch of onstantine in Rome). ree soldiers are own in the foreground tening to the nperor's speech. Left right, they wear ainmail, a segmented irass (see next section) nd a scale cuirass.

Chainmail was very intricate. It took a long time to make and needed specialist tention to repair. An alternative to chainmail was to stitch overlapping platelets nto a leather tunic. These platelets were held on with wire and resembled fish-scales, hich would have shimmered if polished. Because they overlapped (protecting the ea where it was wired to the tunic), each scale could be quite thin; it was also less borious to make than chainmail and could be swiftly repaired. However, scale mour (*lorica squamata*) was less flexible and seems to have been preferred by valrymen who did not need the same freedom of movement as infantrymen.

Segmented and Muscle Cuirass

Neither chainmail nor scale armour was a Roman invention and both had long been in use in the ancient world. The ancient Gauls and Britons used chainmail, while scale armour was popular in the Middle East where it is thought to have been invented.

A uniquely Roman invention of body armour was the segmented cuirass (*lorica segmentata*). It resembled the armour of an armadillo, being composed of overlapping strips. It offered its wearer some of the flexibility of chainmail combined with the protection of solid plate. Extra plates ran across the shoulders to protect against downward slashing blows from an axe or sword. However, it was only in use during the first three centuries AD (the earliest examples were found on the German battlefield of AD 9), probably because of the complexity and cost of its production and maintenance. Although the design was simplified over time, many straps and fittings were required, which were vulnerable in battle. As the more delicate hooks and washers usually had to be made of bronze, they must have been prone to cause corrosion while in contact with the steel plate armour.

The only other form of metal body protection was the muscle cuirass. This was a steel breastplate beaten into the form of an impressively muscled torso. It seems that few could afford the 'superhero' look, as only senior officers and emperors are ever shown wearing them.

Coin (early 2nd century AD) showing a muscle cuirass.

The Helmet

Roman helmets offered as much protection to the head as was possible without obstructing the field of vision or covering the ears (it was essential to hear orders).

To this end, helmets tended to be metal bowls to cover the crown of the head plus an expansion for the back of the neck. To protect the face, two broad cheek pieces were fixed below the bowl on hinges to get the helmet on and off comfortably. On the ends eyelets were provided to fasten the helmet on securely. Other fittings on the helmet bowl provided strengthening and ornament. A crest of dyed horsehair could be fitted to the top to add imposing height or to enable officers to be quickly distinguished in the confusion of battle. Crests usually looked like 'Mohican' haircuts, but those worn by centurions faced sideways.

Gold coin showing the Emperor Postumus (AD 260–9) wearing the sort of helmet used by aristocrats; it is an ornate version of a classical Greek design.

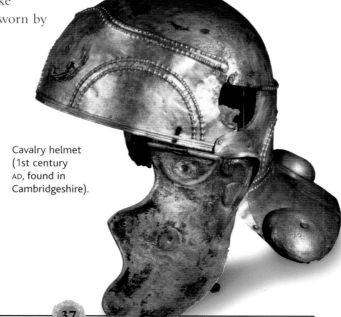

Cavalry helmet (1st century AD, found in Cambridgeshire).

Punishments and Awards

The Roman army had many punishments to ensure discipline. Beatings (see p. 11) were commonplace, as were extra duties of a boring or unpleasant nature such as guard duty.

Dishonourable discharge and even execution were also possible. If an unfortunate soldier on guard duty fell asleep he could expect to be clubbed to death by those he left unguarded. The army was always swift to punish desertion or cowardice and execution could include crucifixion or death in the amphitheatre.

DISCIPLINE, REWARDS AND SPECTACLE

Gold coin showing military decorations
1st century BC). A gold wreath and *phalerae* set
as seen on centurion Rufus, p. 10) are divided by
nother award, the *hasta pura*, or untipped spear.

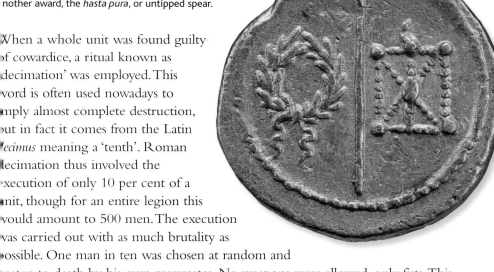

When a whole unit was found guilty
of cowardice, a ritual known as
decimation' was employed. This
word is often used nowadays to
mply almost complete destruction,
but in fact it comes from the Latin
decimus meaning a 'tenth'. Roman
decimation thus involved the
execution of only 10 per cent of a
unit, though for an entire legion this
would amount to 500 men. The execution
was carried out with as much brutality as
possible. One man in ten was chosen at random and
beaten to death by his own messmates. No weapons were allowed, only fists. This
ensured that the victim died slowly and that the survivors experienced death so that
they would never forget how close they had come to the ultimate punishment.

The Roman army took as much care to reward the brave as it did to punish the
disobedient and cowardly.

n addition to promotion, which resulted in higher pay and immunity from certain
duties, a brave soldier might be rewarded with a gift of money. However, some
soldiers preferred an outward symbol of valour that gave them status among their
comrades. Such adornments were called *dona militaria*.

The amphitheatre of the legionary fortress of Caerleon. This was
probably often used as the venue for the legion's public punishments.
xecution, by the sword, or by exposure to wild beasts provided both
ntertainment for some and a warning to everybody.

Punishments and Awards

Another tale told by Tacitus concerns a brave cavalryman who was denied an award of gold armlets on the grounds that he was a non-citizen and an ex-slave. He refused offers of money but was delighted instead with armlets made only of silver. It is often the case that the intrinsic value of the award was irrelevant. Indeed, it was said that the Romans originally needed only their battle-scars as ornaments.

Thus, the golden wreath was the lowest of the wreaths awarded for valour. More valued were the gold crowns shaped like walls that were awarded to the first over a fort or city rampart (seen on the Ribchester helmet). But most highly prized were the oak wreath with its acorns for saving a comrade (worn by Centurion Rufus on p. 10) and the wreath of humble grass for rescuing a besieged army.

The Ribchester helmet (1st to 2nd century AD) used for cavalry sports (see p. 42). The decoration includes a rampant crown just above the brow.

Silver-plated *phalera* decorated with a bust of Jupiter (2nd century AD).

Other decorations can be seen on Centurion Rufus: a harness set of medals (*phalerae*), armlets and two torques hanging around his shoulders. The last indicate how such awards developed – as the looted decorations from fallen barbarians that took on a symbolic value.

Parades and Triumphs

It has always been important for soldiers to practise working as a team and to carry and use their equipment in preparation for fighting. Parades were one way of doing this.

They also made an impressive spectacle, encouraging the men to take pride in their 'performance'. The most impressive Roman army display was a sporting event put on by the cavalry, where two competing sides fought a mock battle. Armour was no doubt polished and any awards worn. Streamers would be flying and other ornaments were used including fanciful mask helmets. (It has been suggested that mask helmets might also have been employed in battle to frighten the enemy or hide the wearer's fear.)

Two cavalry sports helmet masks (1st/2nd century AD). They represent two opposing sides – a Greek warrior (right) and an Amazon (above).

42

DISCIPLINE, REWARDS AND SPECTACLE

Hadrian himself was a fan of such spectacles as the cavalry sports. He is recorded at Lambaesis (see p. 17) noting how they 'wheel right in close formation, they … manoeuvre in close array … fired stones from slings and fought with javelins'. He also appreciated 'the beauty of their horses and the splendour of their weapons'.

A special parade was occasionally put on in honour of a victorious commander. This was known as a triumph and was reserved for the emperor or his relatives. The successful army would march through Rome with their spoils and prisoners in tow. The latter came to an unfortunate end – traditionally garrotted in the temple of Jupiter as a human sacrifice. The triumphant commander would ride in a ceremonial chariot to accept the adulation of the crowd, his face painted red in imitation of Jupiter.

Terracotta panel showing chained prisoners paraded in triumph (1st/2nd century AD).

Building Work and Daily Duties

Roman soldiers walked — a lot. It took over two months to march from Rome to the key frontier city of Cologne in Germany.

The roads on which they marched, and their forts and camps, were all built by the legions themselves. In fact, when they were marching into enemy territory, they constructed temporary forts from turf each night, which they then destroyed before departing in the morning. This made for slow progress, but helped to protect them from ambush. Naturally, if an enemy city was to be besieged, forts were built outside and systems of counter defences were laboriously constructed. All this building prompted one Roman general to assert that the Romans won battles with the *dolabra*, or pickaxe.

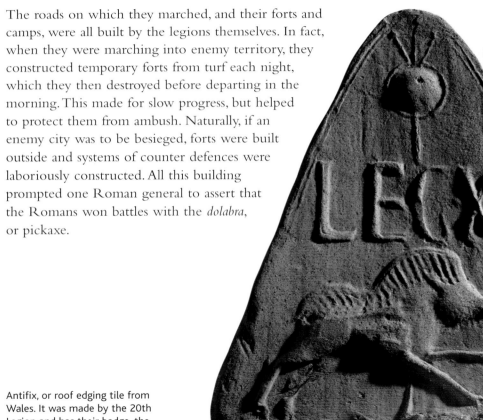

Antifix, or roof edging tile from Wales. It was made by the 20th Legion and has their badge, the running boar (2nd/3rd century AD).

Two sets of fragile documents, from opposite ends of the empire, provide us with evidence of daily life in a Roman fort. The waterlogged soils of Vindolanda, near Hadrian's Wall, and the dry sandy conditions of Egypt have both helped to preserve organic writing materials. Rosters tell us of soldiers' duties while unit-strength reports tell us why personnel could be absent from barracks.

A soldier could expect guard duty a couple of times a week, when he would be stationed at a gate, on a watchtower or rampart, or at the *principia*, or protecting the revered standards of the unit. Other daily postings might involve policing the local market or even a flogging. 'Latrines' and 'street cleaning' were probably the least relished tasks. Documents also record peacetime fatalities such as 'killed by bandits' or 'drowned'. One day at Vindolanda eleven soldiers were dispatched to collect the unit's pay from York, but ten were taken ill with eye inflammation – no doubt caused by guarding the windswept northern frontier!

dolabra (with modern wooden handle), found in Dorset (1st–4th century AD). Such a tool is also shown on the tombstone on p. 26.

Domestic Life in the Forts

Roman army bases were not exclusively male or even adult environments. Officers of the rank of centurion or above could marry and raise families, meaning that there could be up to seventy-four families in a legionary fortress.

There were also civilians living just beyond the walls of the camp who provided the economic impetus for the formation of towns called *vici* or *canabae*. Many ordinary soldiers would have kept girlfriends and unofficial families in these settlements.

When an emperor resided with his legions during a campaign, the imperial family came too. The empress even bore the title 'mother of the army camps' and seems to have had a role in leading some of the ceremonial life in the base.

Invitation to a birthday party from Vindolanda.

he activities of empresses have long been known from the history books. Much
ore recently, the Vindolanda tablets have provided us with information on the
ivate lives of ordinary officer's wives. One famous tablet is a birthday invitation.
 about AD 100 Claudia Severa, the wife of an officer in a neighbouring base
erhaps Corbridge) sent Sulpicia Lepidina, the wife of Vindolanda's commander
avius Cerialis, an invite to her birthday party. A scribe wrote most of the letter
t Severa herself signs it and adds an extra message in her own hand. This is the
rliest piece of writing by a woman in Britain. Amazingly, a second tablet survives
at contains Lepidina's letter of acceptance.

any of the other Vindolanda tablets concern the ordering and transport of
pplies. We hear of the foodstuffs that went into army rations and the sort of
othing soldiers required. One letter
ls of the sending of socks and
derpants, which must have been
uch appreciated on Rome's
ost northerly frontier.

nbstone of a soldier's
ughter (2nd–4th
tury AD). She is shown
a banquet. Her name
 broken off, but she
 the daughter of a
itary standard-bearer
ed Crescens.

Discharge

The legionary's reward for twenty-five years' service was a retirement bonus, the freedom to marry (if he had been below the rank of centurion/decurion) and the opportunity to return home.

However, many stayed on in the nearby town to be near their friends and unofficial 'families'. Others even re-enlisted if they were fit enough. For the auxiliary soldier discharge was an especially important event. At this point he was awarded Roman citizenship, which carried legal and social benefits that were also inherited by his children if they were born after the time of the award. He received a diploma as proof of this status – to impersonate a Roman citizen was punishable by death.

Retirement diploma of Decurion Reburrus, of the 1st Pannonian Ala, dated AD 103. Although his regiment was originally from Hungary, Reburrus himself was Spanish. It is doubtful that he retired to his homeland: this diploma was found in Malpas, Cheshire.

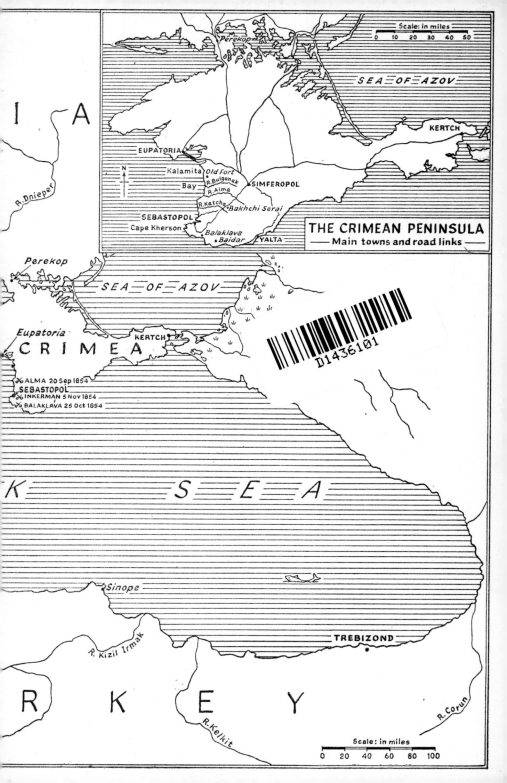

THE CRIMEAN PENINSULA
— Main towns and road links —

Scale: in miles
0 10 20 30 40 50

Perekop

SEA OF AZOV

KERTCH

EUPATORIA

Kalamita
Bay
Old Fort
R.Bulganak
R.Alma
R.Katcha
SIMFEROPOL
Bakhchi Serai

SEBASTOPOL
Cape Kherson
Balaklava
Baidar
YALTA

I A

R. Dnieper

Perekop

SEA OF AZOV

Eupatoria

CRIMEA

KERTCH

ALMA 20 Sep 1854
SEBASTOPOL
INKERMAN 5 Nov 1854
BALAKLAVA 25 Oct 1854

K   S   E   A

Sinope

TREBIZOND

R. Kizil Irmak

R K E Y

R. Kelkit

R. Corun

Scale: in miles
0 20 40 60 80 100

'Little Hodge'

'Little Hodge'

being extracts
from the diaries and letters of
Colonel Edward Cooper Hodge
written during
the Crimean War, 1854-1856

EDITED BY
THE MARQUESS OF ANGLESEY

Leo Cooper · London

First Published in Great Britain 1971 by
LEO COOPER LTD
196 Shaftesbury Avenue, London W.C.2.

© *1971 by The Marquess of Anglesey*

ISBN 0 85052 070 3

Printed in Great Britain by
Clarke, Doble and Brendon Ltd
at Plymouth

Contents

Illustrations

Editor's Note

The annals of the Crimean War are enriched by numerous letters and diaries written by members of the British army. Many of these personal records have been published, but large numbers remain in the hands of their writers' descendants, or in regimental and other museums.

In the course of my researches into the history of the British cavalry in the 19th century, I have been fortunate enough to come across many such unpublished first-hand accounts. By far the most complete of these is that of Lieutenant-Colonel Edward Cooper Hodge, who commanded the 4th Dragoon Guards throughout the war, except when temporarily in command of the Heavy Brigade.

His grandson, in reply to a letter from me which appeared in *The Sunday Times* in 1961, requesting just such material, very kindly allowed me to borrow his grandfather's papers. Amongst them are two well-preserved Letts Diary volumes for the years 1854 and 1855. In these, on every single day of those two years, Hodge made an entry, sometimes of considerable length, more often of about 80 to 90 words, but rarely less.

His papers also include fifty-five letters which he wrote to his mother during those two years, as well as eighteen written in the first part of 1856. Taken together the diaries and letters provide one of the most comprehensive pictures ever painted of the life and doings of a British regiment and its commanding officer on active service.

Hodge was not a great man. Nor, though he ended his career as a full general, was he a particularly outstanding soldier. He had little enough opportunity to become one, since only once was he effectively engaged with an enemy. Like most heavy cavalry officers of the time he almost certainly did not expect ever to have to take the field, except in the limited sense of aiding the civil power at home. He was perfectly suited to command of a regiment in peace time. Meticulous, conscientious and hard-working, he was completely reliable. Possessed of the highest Victorian virtues, he was very different from so many of the aristocratic officers, such as Lord Cardigan. When he found himself unexpectedly plunged into war, the basic humility of his character, linked to his lack of ambition, prevented him from assuming the bombastic, false self-confidence of some of his contemporaries, like, for example, Lord George Paget of the 4th Light Dragoons (my own great-great uncle). Conscious of his ignorance of the art of war, he was prepared to learn and ready to take advice. Being without any desire to 'cut a figure', and without any thoughts of posthumous publication, he writes down, in his diaries and letters, exactly what he sees and feels. The ring of truth unadorned is there.

Though he nowhere gives his reasons for keeping a diary, it seems likely that his exceptionally tidy mind wished to have a record to refer to, both, in the short term, from a professional point of view, and, for his later years, as a means of recollecting what turned out to be the most important, and certainly the most interesting, phase of his career.

His letters, on the other hand, were designed to give his mother and sisters an up-to-date account of his doings and thoughts. They, for the most part, repeat what the diaries record, but in some instances they dwell in greater detail upon personal matters.

The correspondence of Hodge's second-in-command, William Forrest, has also survived, and is now in the National Army Museum. I have drawn upon this to supplement Hodge's narrative. Forrest quite often refers to his commanding officer, generally in not very flattering terms, while Hodge becomes increasingly critical of 'the Major'. Since their temperaments were very different, this mutual enmity is not surprising, particularly after Mrs Forrest arrived in the Crimea and the married couple occupied one half of Hodge's hut. Himself a bachelor, he strongly disapproved of officer's wives on active service, especially if they brought no female servant with them. The tussle between these two men, carried on in a coldly polite manner, adds rich comedy to Hodge's daily chronicle of the weary months which preceded the fall of Sebastopol.

Extracts from the letters home of another, very junior, officer of the 4th Dragoon Guards, Cornet E. R. Fisher, were privately printed in 1907.[1] From these, too, I have quoted. They add a lively, gaily malicious touch to the writings of the two older, more sober men. Fisher was twenty-two years old in 1854, and had bought his commission in the regiment the previous year. Soon after the war was over he suffered a severe hunting accident which made it necessary for him to leave the service. In 1865 he married Hodge's niece.*

* * *

From a military history point of view, Hodge's papers do not add any startling new facts. Nevertheless the correspondence which he carried on in the 1860s with some of his officers (and the account, also hitherto unpublished, of the Colonel of the Royals, from part of which I have quoted), concerning the charge of the Heavy Brigade at the battle of Balaklava (see p. 45), do throw some highly interesting fresh light on the part taken by the 4th Dragoon Guards and the Royals in that engagement.

So many accounts of the Crimean War, both from original documents and from the pens of historians, concentrate, naturally enough, upon the three major battles of the Alma, Balaklava and Inkerman and upon the horrors of the winter. All these happened in the space of about five months, while the war itself lasted for two whole years. Hodge's writings cover virtually the whole of this period, and give, therefore, an unusually well-proportioned idea of what the war as a whole was like for those, such as Hodge, who remained in the theatre throughout its duration.

* * *

There are no paragraphs in the diaries and few in the letters. In neither is the punctuation more than vestigial. I have therefore added both arbitrarily. I have also standardised the spelling throughout.

* * *

For allowing me unrestricted access to his grandfather's papers and relics, for not complaining when I kept them for very long periods, and for much helpful advice and background information, I am deeply indebted to Mr Frederick R. Hodge.

Amongst other persons and institutions for whose help in preparing

---

*The only child of Hodge's eldest sister, Anna Maria Adams, who died in 1871. Three years later Fisher married a daughter of the Earl of Ravensworth.

this book I am particularly grateful are Mrs L. S. Bickford; Mrs Pat Brayne; Mr Roger Fulford, C.V.O.; Mr R. G. Hollies-Smith, F.R.G.S., F.S.A.Scot.; Mr D. W. King, O.B.E., F.L.A., Chief Librarian of the Ministry of Defence Library; the London Library; Mr Boris and Mr John Mollo; the National Army Museum; Mary, Countess of Pembroke, C.V.O.; Mrs H. St G. Saunders; Mrs B. Walker-Heneage-Vivian, and Captain V. M. Wombwell.

I should also like to thank the Humanities Research Center, University of Texas, for permission to reproduce illustrations nos 10, 18 and 19; the Victoria and Albert Museum for illustrations nos 2, 4, 5, 7, 8, 12, 13, 14, 22, 23, 24, 25, 26, 27 and 33; and the Museé de L'Armeé, Paris, for illustrations nos 6a, 6b, 9 and 30a, b, c, d, e and f.

The references, numbered throughout each chapter, refer to the source notes on page 157.

A.

Plas Newydd,
Anglesey,
August, 1970.

Prologue

Edward Cooper Hodge was born at Weymouth on 19 April, 1810. He was the only son of Major Edward Hodge of the 7th Hussars, who was killed, aged 33, at Genappe on the day before the battle of Waterloo.* He was brought up, therefore, from the age of five, without a father's influence. His mother was the youngest daughter of Sir Edmund Bacon, baronet, of Raveningham Hall, Norfolk, while his father came from yeoman stock in the West Country.

Hodge was sent at the age of seven to Dr Pearson's School at East Sheen, where he stayed until July, 1822, when he went to Eton College. In the previous year, King George IV, honouring Hodge's father, had made the eleven-year-old boy one of his extra Pages of Honour at the Coronation.

At Eton Hodge's classical tutor was Richard Okes, who later became Provost of King's, while the 'Dame' of his house was Miss Sophia Angelo, who, when she died in 1847, at the age of 88, was described as 'the oldest and most celebrated dame at Eton'. She was probably a daughter of Domenico Angelo, the famous fencing master.[1]

Little is known of Hodge's career at school, though his small stature made him, almost inevitably, into a rowing cox. At the age of sixteen he was only five feet, one inch in height. It is certain that he steered the *Victory* longboat at Eton, for A. W. Kinglake specifically

---

*A painting of Major Edward Hodge by R. Dighton, showing him in the extravagant uniform of the 7th Light Dragoons in 1805, is reproduced with accompanying article by W. Y. Carman in the *Journal of the Society for Army Historical Research*, XLII (1964), 1.

'Correspondence concerning the Death of Major Hodge, 7th Hussars, at Genappe, 17th June, 1815' edited by the Marquess of Anglesey and Frederick R. Hodge, appeared in *JAHR*, XLIII (1965), 80.

The Diary of Captain Edward Hodge (7th Light Dragoons) kept during the Corunna Campaign, October, 1808 to March, 1809, which was recently presented by Mr F. R. Hodge to the Regimental Museum of the Queen's Own Hussars at Warwick, has been transcribed with notes by Mr J. M. Brereton.

mentions the fact in his *Invasion of the Crimea*. (See p. 48). In 1866, Kinglake wrote to him asking for information about the charge of the Heavy Brigade: 'Dear Hodge, I hope you will not think I am taking an undue liberty in omitting the "General", but I write thus in order to prevent your giving me the "Mister", having a theory that when "old Eton fellows" have once renewed their acquaintance, it is hardly natural for them to be ceremonious.'[2]

In the spring of 1826, Hodge left Eton and went to Paris to join his mother who was living there for the benefit of her daughters' education. Four months after his sixteenth birthday, in August, 1826, the Duke of York, who was Commander-in-Chief of the Army, 'most kindly', according to Mrs Hodge, 'gave Edward a Cornetcy in the 13th Light Dragoons, then in India'.* Four months later, through the interest of his father's old friend, Sir Herbert Taylor, Military Secretary at the Horse Guards, he was exchanged into the 4th Dragoon Guards, with which regiment he remained for thirty-three years as a regimental officer, and for a further twenty in old age, as Regimental Colonel. (A Note on the history of the regiment is appended at p. 153.) He did not, in fact, join the regiment till September, 1827, because he spent a year's leave in 'a French house at Abbeville to improve himself further in the French language'.[3]

---

*Hodge was promoted (by purchase) lieutenant on 3 July, 1828, captain on 19 December, 1834, major on 3 December, 1841, and lieutenant-colonel on 3 October, 1848. (See p. 57).

Chapter 1

1853 – 7 July 1854

The first glimpse we get of Edward Hodge from his own writings is in the piping time of peace. His mother being far from well, he accompanied her and two of his sisters to Malta in November, 1853. Having left them safely in the hands of friends, he went off on a short sight-seeing tour in southern Italy, before returning home.

In mid-December, following a spell in the south of France, he arrived in Paris. There it was 'snowing and freezing and beastly'. In his hotel he sat 'close into a low fire, which has no effect in these rooms, which though very small are all doors and windows. I shall be off to London as soon as my linen comes from the wash. They say that war is inevitable, and that a French and English Army will go to Constantinople.'

On Boxing Day, back home and staying with his elder married sister at Sydenham, Hodge's forebodings were reinforced. He had had news that 'a Cabinet Council sat for five hours' on Christmas Day. 'I fear', he wrote, 'that war is inevitable.' To his diary, early in January, 1854, he confided his feelings at the prospect of war: 'Like England,' he wrote, 'I have nothing to gain and much to lose.' This was not, perhaps, the proper sentiment for a regular soldier, but it was refreshingly unlike that of so many people in England at the time.

On 11 January, Hodge returned to Ireland to join his regiment. At 8.45 in the evening he left London on the mail train for Holyhead. Before the days of sleeping cars, he had learnt how to make himself snug. 'I have had 3 sticks made, connected with pieces of web to go between the 2 opposite seats in the railway carriage, and most comfortable have I found them.'

Arrived at Dundalk, where the regimental headquarters were stationed, he 'found two louts of Captains and four Cornets there and many things all wrong. I am full of trouble: no Adjutant, no Riding Master, no Regimental Sergeant Major, and I have no servant.'

> **16 January.** Major Forrest [the next senior regimental officer after Hodge] evidently does not look after matters in my absence. He actually did not know that the subaltern officers had never attended drill in my absence.

Major William Charles Forrest, son of a lieutenant-colonel in the service of the Hon East India Company, had joined the 11th Light Dragoons in India, as a Cornet, in 1836 aged 16. There he had served for eight years, reaching the rank of Captain in 1841. For most of his time in that regiment (which returned home in 1838 after seventeen years in India), he had the misfortune to be commanded by Lord Brudenell, later Earl of Cardigan. On a number of occasions he, like all the officers who were not complete toadies, fell foul of his impossible commanding officer. The last time this happened, in 1843, Cardigan refused Forrest extended leave when his wife, Annie, (of whom we shall hear much more later) was seriously ill at her first confinement. Forrest nevertheless took the leave, and was supported in the violent quarrel which followed, by the Duke of Wellington, the Commander-in-Chief. In a memorandum, Wellington rebuked Cardigan thus:
'The Duke considered that nothing could be more fair and proper than that Captain Forrest should apply for leave to escort his wife to her friends under the circumstances of her approaching confinement. . . . The Duke must observe that in the whole of his experience he has never known the time of the staff of the Army to be taken up in so useless a manner as in the present instance.'
Finding it impossible any longer to remain in the 11th, Forrest exchanged into the 4th Dragoon Guards in 1844. Four years later he became a major, and in effect Hodge's second-in-command.[1]
In 1877 Forrest was promoted to Lieutenant-General. He became Colonel of the 8th Hussars in 1880, and, ironically, of the 11th Hussars six years later. He died, aged 82, in 1902.

> **8 February.** Drilled the officers at packing a valise, rolling a cloak, putting together a saddle, etc. Such ignorance as they

displayed! Not one of them knew by sight the lower part of the breastplate.

17 February. Instructed the officers in putting a saddle together, and packing a kit. Many of them seemed to be dreadfully bored by it, especially my new Adjutant, Webb,* who is quite ignorant, but has not, I fear, much wish to learn.

26 February. Pine [the regimental surgeon. See p. 92] has received an official [notification] from the Director General of Hospitals informing him that the 4th are going on service immediately. I hope it is not so. I do not think that we are efficient enough. We have too many 4 year old horses—53. This is far too many, and we have so many of the old big men, some 13 and 14 stone weight. I cannot take these.

God grant if it be true that we may acquit ourselves well and return in safety to England.

27 February. Heard that we are selected to proceed to Turkey after the 8th [Hussars] and 17th [Lancers]. If I was to say I like going, I should say what was not true. I can gain nothing and have everything to lose. My whole fortune is invested in my commission and I shall now never get back the money that I have paid. [See p. 57].

6 March. Had an inspection of the swords of the regiment, and found them in very good order. [By contrast, see p. 49 for comments on the Greys' swords at Balaklava, made by their Colonel.]

14 March. Received the orders. Now begins a life of neither profit nor pleasure. I expect no more peace, comfort or happiness in this world. I will however do my duty to the utmost in my power, and I humbly pray to God to give me health and strength to fulfil my calling.

21 March. We are to take 250 horses. Where I shall get these I know not. Also 295 men.

23 March. Went to Lord Cardigan† [in command of the Light

---

*John MacDonnell Webb; cornet in the regiment, 1847; retired Sept. 1855.
†James Thomas Brudenell, 7th Earl of Cardigan, KCB (1797–1868); cornet, 8th Hussars, 1824; Lieut.-Col., 15th Hussars, 1832; commanded 11th Light Dragoons (later Hussars), 1836–47. He became Inspector-General of Cavalry in 1855; Lieutenant-General, 1861. He died as the result of a fall from a horse. The best accounts of Cardigan's extraordinary character and unattractive behaviour are to be found in Woodham-Smith, Cecil, *The Reason Why*, 1953, and in Wake, Joan, *The Brudenells of Deene*, 1953, 349–445.

Brigade] to find out all I could. He was very civil. He received
his order of Brigadier-General when I was with him. I learnt
much that was worth knowing. I see an infinity of bother before
me.

28 March. War is now to be declared.

Britain and France both declared war on this day. The background
to that fateful decision was the fear of the supposed expansionist
aspirations of Russia, which so preoccupied Western European
statesmen throughout the century, and came to be known as the
'Eastern Question'. 'Any aggrandisement,' Lord John Russell had
told the Commons in 1852, 'which disturbs the general balance of
power in Europe . . . could not be a matter of indifference'[2] to
Britain. This was, and long remained, the corner-stone of British
foreign policy. Only once in the ninety-nine years which followed
Waterloo did it get knocked awry. The result was the Crimean
War.

By the 1850s the Turkish Empire, after three centuries of domination of much of the eastern world, seemed on the point of dissolving.
Its rulers appeared no longer capable of ruling and defending their
vast territories. Russia, it was supposed, was set on filling the
imminent vacuum. Neither the British, nor the French (who had
Near Eastern ambitions) were prepared to remain impassive in face
of such a threat.

The immediate cause of the war between Turkey and Russia which
had broken out in 1853, was a dispute between the Roman Catholic
and Greek Orthodox Churches respecting the custody of certain
shrines in Jerusalem, which was, of course, within the Turkish
Empire. Napoleon III of France championed the Catholics;
Nicholas I of Russia, the Greeks. The Russians demanded a general
protectorate over the millions of Christians living under Turkish
rule. The Turks, rather than negotiate, rejected these demands
outright. They believed, rightly, that Palmerston, the most powerful
member of the British cabinet, would persuade his colleagues to
stand by them.

In June, 1853, a British fleet, supported by a French squadron, was
posted outside the Dardanelles. In July, the Russians invaded
Turkish Moldavia.

Though Lord Stratford de Redcliffe, the influential and usually
pro-Turk ambassador in Constantinople, advised the Sultan to

accept an offer of mediation by a council of ambassadors, the Turks refused to do so. Even now war, as Churchill put it, 'was not yet certain. The Czar, alarmed at Turkey's resistance, sought a compromise with the help of Austria, but by September Aberdeen [the Prime Minister] and his Cabinet had become so suspicious that they rejected the offer. On October 4 the Sultan declared war on Russia, and soon afterwards attacked the Russians beyond the Danube. Such efforts as Aberdeen and Stratford could still make for peace were extinguished by a Russian onslaught against the Turkish Fleet off Sinope, in the Black Sea. Indignation flared in England, where the action was denounced as a massacre. . . . Thus England drifted into war.'[3]

* * *

The British army at home was in almost every respect ill-prepared to fight a war in Europe. The greatest difficulty was experienced in trying to scrape together an expeditionary force of some 27,000 officers and men, with 26 guns. To find thirty-one infantry battalions at war establishment it was necessary to draft large numbers of volunteers from other battalions into those chosen for service.

The same applied to the cavalry. The maximum force which could be put into the field was one heavy and one light brigade. To produce the twenty squadrons of which these were made up, ten regiments were required to furnish two squadrons apiece. Each of these 'Service Squadrons' consisted of only about 155 of all ranks, with 140 horses, yet extraordinary measures had to be resorted to to find even that modest number.

> **4 April.** Colonel Clarke, A.Q.M.G., came down, and transferred 15 horses from K.D.G.s [King's Dragoon Guards] to me, and 5 are to come from the 3rd Dragoon Guards. I gave them 20 young ones—as great a set of brutes as ever I saw. I felt quite ashamed of the transaction.

Each regiment was ordered to leave at home two troops to form a recruiting depôt. In fact, some of the regiments, for example the Royal Dragoons, left behind far fewer men than the number stipulated.

The mounted force which left the shores of Britain between mid-April and mid-July, numbered, at the most, 3,100 officers and men, and 3,000 horses.

It was at first proposed to march the cavalry across France and to embark them at Marseilles.

5 April [*Letter*]. I do not like the idea at all. We shall have much trouble I am sure with the men. The weather will be terribly hot. The brandy is plenty and cheap. We shall knock up many horses, and as no one can speak the language but some two or three of the officers, the trouble and annoyance we shall experience will be very great indeed.

Your surmises are quite correct as to the force of cavalry going out: the 4th & 5th Dragoon Guards, Inniskillings [6th Dragoons] & Royals [1st (Royal) Dragoons], under Col. Scarlett;* the 8th [Hussars], 11th [Hussars], 13th [Light Dragoons] and 17th [Lancers] under Lord Cardigan. Lord Lucan† commands the whole. He is brother-in-law to Lord Cardigan, and they do not speak. How this will answer on service I know not.

I have got a capital servant to replace Ryan, a man who has campaigned and is very understanding. I have bought another horse [for £80],‡ and a small stretcher bed, very light indeed. I mean to have a tent, two portmanteaus, a canteen and cooking apparatus in one. They make them packed into a leather bucket, with a little grate, soup pot, gridiron, frying pan, cups and saucers of iron lined with china; plates the same, and very nice they are. I shall take two waterproof sheets—they are capital to lie on if the tent is not up. I shall also take a gutta-percha bottle that will fit a holster, and a gutta-percha basin. They are very light.

Even before he reached the Crimea, and after only a few weeks in camp on the Bulgarian coast, the Colonel had radically revised his

---

* The Hon Sir James Yorke Scarlett, GCB (1799–1871), 2nd son of 1st Baron Abinger, Lord Chief Baron of the Exchequer; cornet, 18th Hussars, 1818; lieut-col commanding 5th Dragoon Guards, 1840–1854; in command at Aldershot in the 1860s; general, 1870.
† George Charles Bingham, 3rd Earl of Lucan, GCB (1800–1888); ensign, 6th Foot, 1816; lieut-col commanding, 17th Lancers, 1826–37; witnessed the 1828 campaign in the Balkans, attached to the Russian staff; Field-Marshal, 1887.
‡ At the end of November, in the Crimea, Hodge had to have this horse shot. 'He has contracted a disease in his fetlock (off hind)', he wrote in his diary, 'which is caused by cold and exposure to weather, and of which I cannot cure him, not having any stable to put him in. Thus £80 is gone.'

views on kit. On 6 September he wrote to his mother: 'People coming out here should not bring gutta-percha bottles or things of that manufacture. In five minutes the sun will destroy them. Vulcanized India rubber answers, and the blow-up beds and pillows answer, but the India rubber pails do not answer so well. They require great care in using. Stout leather bags, lined with waterproof canvas I recommend. They are better than portmanteaus, which will not give to the pressure, but are apt to be torn off the packsaddle. The Turkish packsaddles are infamous. No one should bring them. The French are good, and the English one, of the Ordnance pattern, but made smaller, is not bad at all. Saddlery soon rots and goes to pieces here, as it is always exposed to the sun, dust and rain. Woollen clothing of every description we wear even in the hottest weather.'

8 April [London]. Went to the Horse Guards where I met Duke of Cambridge,* [commanding the 1st Infantry Division (Guards and Highland Brigades)] Lord Lucan and others respecting this odious march through France.

9 April. Bid adieu to my dear sister [Mrs Mayow Adams]. I hope it may please God that we may meet again. If not, His will be done. The chances of war, fever, and starvation may be too much for me, but I trust I shall do my duty.

10 April. I hear today that this march through France will not take place.

21 April. I shall be ruined for want of money, so I have written to my uncle, Sir Edmund [Bacon, baronet], to ask him for a loan of £100.

From Newbridge, where the regiment was now assembled, Hodge kept his mother informed of his preparations:

22 April [*Letter*]. I have procured all my kit. I take out flannel shirts. They are recommended. I thank you so much for the filter. I will carry it as long as I can. I hear that the water is very bad all over Turkey. My present puzzle is the mode of

---

* H.R.H. Prince George William Frederick Charles, 2nd Duke of Cambridge, KG, KT, KP (1819–1904), only son of 1st Duke, 7th son of George III; served in Hanoverian army, 1836; General and Commander-in-Chief of the Army, 1856–95; Field-Marshal, 1862.

attaching my mosquito curtains. I do not see my way there,
my bed having no cross-bars above.

My Field Allowance will be 4/6 a day, and I believe they
give us our horse rations for nothing on service. I hope therefore to be able to live upon a little more than my pay; not that
I intend to save, for I shall make myself as comfortable as
circumstances will enable me to do.

We are all in the dark as to how we are to manage. No
orders are given to us, but Colonel Shirley has just published
a little book upon the treatment of horses on ship board, which
contains much that is good, and comes most opportunely.
I shall make every officer buy one and read it, if I can.[4]

I see *The Times* is crying out about the delay in sending
the cavalry. All this sounds correct, but it is far better to fit
up the ships properly than to send us to sea but half found.

On 10 April *The Times* complained that merchant seamen were
'engaged at an immense cost, and then they are at Woolwich or
Southampton for weeks, and no horses or men ready for them'.
Nine days later, a leader asked, 'What is being done with our
cavalry? Are they really to go or are they to stay? If the army is to
be kept waiting for them, why are they here? Why are their commanding officers still in London?'

28 April. Saw the 11th Hussars pitching tents. We have much
to learn.

4 May [*Letter*]. Newbridge.

Anna Maria & Mayow [Adams, her husband] have given
me a beautiful double glass & a very excellent German map
of Turkey. Eleanor & Caroline [his younger, unmarried sis-
ters] have given me my canteen, you a filter—in fact I have
had so many presents I shall not, I think, require the Bart's
money.

My servant is not a private servant. He is a dragoon, and
an active little fellow. He understands washing linen, cooking,
can repair my saddlery, has made many little things for me
already, and will be, I hope, of very great use to me.

I have had a long field day on the Curragh and am quite
hoarse with shouting at the stupid officers I have.

I have an order to buy fifty more horses, and we have an
increase of 100 men.

6 May. Went down to Kingstown [now Dunlaoghaire] to see the transports of the 11th Hussars. They are fine ships, and very well fitted for both horses and men and officers. They will be off immediately. Now is our time near.

11 May. The following transports are named for us:

Burmah	718 tons 52 horses 2 spare stalls	
Sir Robert Sale	741 tons 54 horses 4 spare stalls	
Libertas	602 tons 48 horses 2 spare stalls	
Palmyra	749 tons 48 horses 2 spare stalls	
Deva	1033 tons 60 horses 4 spare stalls	
William Jackson	956 tons 58 horses 6 spare stalls	

The first three from London, the last three Liverpool.

16 May [*Letter*]. I cannot think what our horses will do out in Turkey for food. Animals like ours that have been accustomed always to such good fodder will, I fear, soon fall off, even before leaving Constantinople.

22 May. Bought a bât-horse, 7 years old, much fired [cauterized] about the hocks, but very strong indeed. I gave £60.

23 May [*Letter*]. Mrs Cresswell, the wife of Capt C. of the 11th has gone out with a complete suit of leather, a brace of pistols, and intends to ride throughout the campaign. [She] was a Gordon-Cumming, sister to the Lion Man.

This refers to Miss Adelaide Gordon-Cumming (d. 1870), a daughter of Sir William Gordon-Cumming, 2nd baronet, and sister of the African lion hunter, Roualeyn Gordon-Cumming. He was a man of great physical stature and strength, who made his name and a fortune from a book called *Five Years of a Hunter's Life in the Far Interior of South Africa*, and from lectures and exhibitions of lion skins.

His sister married, in 1852, Captain W. G. B. Cresswell of the 11th Hussars, who died of cholera on 19 September, 1854, aged 25[5]. She accompanied him to Bulgaria, and after some difficulty found a passage to Balaklava, only to hear of his death.

Mrs Duberly (see p. 104), another wife who went campaigning with her husband, who was in the 8th Hussars, wrote of Mrs Cresswell in a letter home: 'We heard wonderful stories of her before she arrived—"tremendous woman"—dead shot—brilliant rider—*very* fast. . . . They put in an Irish paper that "when her husband was killed she would lead the troops into action". At last

we determined to put on our most *feminine* get-up and go and call. . . .
We expected something rather fashionable and brilliant—but after
waiting some time a woman came from among the troop horses—so
dirty—with such uncombed, scurfy hair, such black nails, such a
dirty cotton gown open at the neck, without a sign of a collar or
linen sleeve. Oh, you never had a kitchen maid so dreadful. She
calls the officers "boys"— and addresses them as "Bill and Jack"—
talks of nothing but her horse—found fault with my saddle. . . .
Told me I was "a fool" to have a marquee, a bell-tent was quite
good enough for anyone—that my husband would vote me "a bore"
if I didn't cook his dinner—that I was foolish to wear collars and
sleeves as they were unnecessary—and that if I wished my husband
to like me, I should always the night before a march strike my tent,
and sleep either wrapped in a cloak or "anywhere". . . . I do not
exaggerate when I say that her neck and bare arms were earth
colour with dirt—among her plates for dinner was a very old hair-
brush with the handle broken off. . . . Mrs Cresswell allows no
woman near her tent—so who empties her slops—or how she
manages about etc. etc.—I can't divine. I suppose the soldier
servant does it!'[6] This was, in fact, what later happened in the case
of the wife of Hodge's second-in-command, Major Forrest, (see
p. 116).

25 May. Went to Kingstown and embarked a large portion of
Forster's* Troop in the *Maori* transport. We got the horses in
very well indeed.

29 May [*Letter*]. I have, I believe, paid every debt I have,
except a £10 subscription to the Duke of Wellington's testi-
monial,† and this I shall pay ere I go.

　　Sir Edward McDonnell, the Lord Mayor of Dublin, has
kindly taken charge of all my baggage.‡ He will put it into an

---

*Francis Rowland Forster, joined the 4th Dragoon Guards in 1840;
captain 1847.

† The Duke had died in 1852. Over £100,000 was subscribed for a national
memorial to him, which took the shape of a college near Sandhurst for the
education of officers' sons.

‡ Sir Edward McDonnell (1806–1860), was a paper manufacturer. He was
chairman of the Great Southern and Western Railway of Ireland, and was
knighted on the opening of the railway to Cork in 1849. His son, Christopher,
was in the 4th Dragoon Guards, which he had joined in 1852, and went
right through the Crimean War, becoming a captain in 1856.

empty room, and will have fires in it in winter. I shall send home my best plain clothes to Anna Maria in a large carpet bag.

I have insured my horses pretty largely, as I fear we cannot help losing some—the 17th Lancers have been most unlucky. [This regiment had lost 26 horses on the voyage to Constantinople.]

The *Himalaya* has embarked the whole of the 5th Dragoon Guards on board of her, and a detachment of the 68th [Foot]. You must try and see her [when she calls at Malta]. She will be a wonderful sight. She has 325 horses on board.

This was a larger number of men and horses than had ever before been carried in one ship.

The *Himalaya*, 3,438 tons, was one of the earliest screw-propelled steamships of the P. & O. Line. She arrived in the Bosphorus after a voyage of only sixteen days from Queenstown [now Cobh], including a call at Malta. When she was launched she was the biggest steamer in the world, but the Company operated her at a loss. Consequently the Admiralty's purchase of her as a troopship came as a welcome relief. She was eventually sunk by German bombers in the Second World War whilst serving as a hulk in Portland Harbour.[7] She also transported the whole of the Scots Greys, which left later than the 5th Dragoon Guards. The 4th Light Dragoons, (not to be confused with the 4th Dragoon Guards), which was the last of the ten regiments to sail, were carried by the P. & O. steamer *Simla*, of 2,400 tons. She had only been completed earlier in the year. Later she was to carry the 4th Dragoon Guards from Varna to the Crimea (see p. 28).

I like my ship [the sailing ship *Deva*] and the Captain seems a very civil fellow. Captain Scott, the Admiralty Agent, a funny old brandy-faced cove, has given me up his cabin. It is more in the centre of the ship than mine, and will, I think, be less *moveable*. We arrange to pay 7/6 a day for our living. That is to include 4 meals a day, and a pint of wine.

Letters from England to Turkey under ¼ of an ounce will be conveyed through France for 3d, and under ½ an ounce, 6d.

1 June [*Letter*]. I want a pint of spirits of wine put into a strong bottle, to light my boiling pot, a sort of little Etna that I have for heating soup or coffee.*

2 June. Marched from Dublin at 8 and embarked. We slung our horses on board, 61 in number, and completed the embarkation in 2 hours and a half, without an accident.

Such a confusion as our decks are in! Quantities of people are here bidding us goodbye. I can hardly expect that the men will do much towards putting away their things. It was not known in the garrison that we were going away this morning, therefore we had no bands to play us out.

3 June. At 9 we commenced slinging the horses. We put the slings under them so that if any of them should fall they will be caught in them. My charger was very nervous at being put into the slings.

At 5 minutes to 5 p.m. we commenced leaving the quayside. Two steamers took us in tow and worked us clear off to Howth. When there they let us clear off. We hoisted sail and with a strong breeze from the N. East we sailed away.

I got very seedy towards evening and was obliged to take to my bed.

Poor old Ryan, who has been my servant for 20 years, left me today. He came to arrange my cabin for me, and when I shook hands with him on parting I felt I had lost a really good friend and servant.

Hodge had taken great trouble to try to obtain a position for Ryan in his old age. 'I think I have got old Ryan', he wrote to his mother on 31 May, 'a place as servant to two old ladies at Cheltenham.' This, however, seems to have come to nothing, for in late November, Hodge wrote from the Crimea to his mother in England: 'I really think old Ryan would answer you well. He will never want to go out. You may find him slow, but I am certain that he will serve you faithfully. You must not put him *into shorts* [knee-breeches]. His legs are dreadful.'

6 June. Cape Finisterre south west 112 miles from us.

Cleaned out the ship, shifted horses, got up many tubs of manure from below.

---

*Also sometimes called an *aetna*; so named from the volcano. A vessel for heating liquids, consisting of a cup fixed in a saucer in which alcohol is burned.

At 11¾ p.m. a horse was reported as being down. The men worked well at it, but the animal was so injured that we could not get it up. We therefore threw him overboard after knocking him on the head. It was a fine and good horse.

Saw porpoises and Mother Carey's chickens* about the ship.

7 June. We have run to within 12 miles south of Oporto in 3 days and 14 hours.

12 June. I cannot help being struck with the vulgarity of Mr Gunter's manners. He is dreadful, I think: very consequential, eats with his elbows on the table, and makes pert remarks to the Captain. The old story of the silk purse and the sow's ear.

Robert Gunter had joined the regiment in 1851, and was a Captain in 1855. He was a son of the famous confectioner, who was also called Robert, and who died in 1852. In April, 1855, Hodge told his mother that Gunter, who had gone home sick, was on his way back to the Crimea. 'You could hardly expect much manners from "the nobby pieman". I am sure that he would have brought a box for me.'

17 June. Finished reading Dumas's *Mâitre d'Armes*—an amusing little book.†

Our feeding is pretty good, fresh bread and fresh meat nearly every day. I cannot manage the butter, but the cooking is tolerable, rather greasy, and the dirt I am getting accustomed to. The men are all on salt provisions, but I hear of no complaints.

19 June. I felt seedy all day but I managed to dine. Read *The Bride of Lammermoor* [published by Sir Walter Scott, in 1819] all day.

22 June. Made Malta at 5 a.m. I got on shore as soon as I could, and went to see my dear mother and sisters, whom I found pretty well.

Lunched with my family, and at 2 bid adieu to those I love dearest on earth, perhaps never to see them more. God bless and preserve them.

---

* The common name for small petrels of several species, especially the stormy petrel. Mother Carey is a corruption of *mata cara*, dear mother, which was the superstitious exclamation with which sailors used to greet the sight of stormy petrels.

† *Mémoires d'un Mâitre d'Armes* by Alexandre Dumas, the Elder, was first published in 1840.

23 June. The Regimental Sergt-Major of the Inniskillings and 11 of their men who were burned out of the *Europa,* have been put on board our ship. Poor Willoughby Moore, the Vet Surgeon, 4 Sgts and 12 men are lost in her, two women and 57 horses. Had the sailors behaved properly every man would have been saved. There was nothing saved at all.

24 June. I have been questioning the Sergt Major of the 6th [(Inniskilling) Dragoons]. The *Europa* caught fire at 10 p.m. on 31 May, 123 miles west of the Scilly Isles. The two mates and three able seamen at once deserted the ship in a boat. The rest of the crew took to their boats. The soldiers behaved well.

27 June. Very hot at night. No air. The horse hold and men's decks like ovens. Ther 82 [F.] in my cabin.

5 July [*Letter*]. In the Dardanelles.

I went on shore and visited the Fort in which are some of those large guns that throw stone shot. We saw a few women covered up to the eyes. There seemed little occasion for it, as they were fearfully ugly as far as I could see.

5 July. A very strong current of nearly four miles an hour runs here. Byron must have had a good swim. [In 1810, Byron had swum the Hellespont from Sestos to Abydos in emulation of Leander.]

6 July [*Letter*]. I met a young man of the artillery, I think a Mr King, who was at Malta (I remember Caroline danced with him at St Antonio). He has been to Tunis to buy horses, and has purchased about 250. Some are large fine looking beasts. They cost he says about £16 on an average. He is now taking some of them in a steamer in our company, and towing two ships, in one of which is Cresswell of the 11th and his wife. She is burnt as brown as a berry.

6 July. At 5 p.m. Constantinople was well in view, and at 8 we cast anchor under the large barrack at Scutari, the view of the Seraglio, &c. &c. most lovely.

The view by moonlight very lovely, but I have no heart to enjoy it. I feel I am going into this business quite ignorant of what I have to do. I have no baggage horses, no native servant, and I do not like the things I have brought to carry my baggage in.

7 July. Steamed away all day through the Black Sea. The gay dresses, pretty lights, boats and painted houses, make the Bosphorus a very beautiful scene.

At the end of May it had been decided that the British and French expeditionary forces should move to the Bulgarian port of Varna, 160 miles by sea from Constantinople, and from there make a demonstration in support of the Turks. The Russians had at this time crossed the Danube and were investing Silistria, fifty-five miles north of Varna.

Chapter 2

---

9 July – 24 October 1854

[Letter to Mrs Hodge, whose departure from Malta for England was announced to Hodge in a letter which he received on arrival at Varna.] **9 July.** We quitted Constantinople at 7 a.m. on the 7th and were towed right up to Varna, where we arrived yesterday morning very early. I immediately went on shore. Such a scene as it is! Imagine an arid sandy shore, the thermometer at 90 in the tents, the shore covered with horses and soldiers picketted and encamped all about it. 12 men lie in a tent; the saddles are in the open air; the burning sun is on the horses all day, and for one hour in the evening there comes a plague of cockchafers from the land side that regularly drive the horses mad.

The greatest part of the troops are encamped about twenty miles from here. There is no town nearer than Varna from [the camp], so that everything that has to be bought, men must go 20 miles to Varna to fetch. The Commissariat is infamous.

The baggage arrangements are dreadful. They order us to carry certain things. They do not provide us the means of the transport, and they will not allow more than the regulated number of baggage animals to accompany the troops. I have had to reduce my baggage very considerably.

How we shall ever get accustomed to the bad living I know not. It is, I hear, all bacon and eggs, nothing else, and very little of that; no bread. The water at the camp at Devna is, I hear, good, but it is two miles off. This will be dreadful work to have to fetch every drop.

9 July. Dined with Lord Lucan. A moderate feed, very.

11 July. We have now all the ships arrived, except the *Palmyra*, in which are all my staff. I wish they were here. I work from 5 a.m. till dark, in the sun all day with the ther. at 100 in my tent. The horses are picketted in the broiling sun, and in deep sand which is scorching hot. At nights the dew is cold and heavy. There are many dead horses lying about the shore, the stench from which is awful.

12 July [*Letter*]. My tent is in the middle of the camp. The noise is very great, as I have 250 wild Turkish Horse within thirty yards.

There are about 45,000 French troops in and about Varna; they look very businesslike, and I hear that their commissariat is well arranged. We can buy nothing but a very little milk, and the commissariat do not send us any food before 11 a.m. Our horses will have to eat barley and chopped straw.

Lord Cardigan has been away towards Silistria with some cavalry. He was absent 17 days and it was thought he was lost. They sent two parties of cavalry to look for him; one marched sixty miles a day. They went in sight of the Danube. Many of their horses are quite done up.

Hodge here refers to what came to be called the 'Soreback Reconnaissance'. When Lord Raglan.* the Commander-in-Chief of the British force, learnt that the Russians had raised the siege of Silistria and were retreating in disorder, he ordered Cardigan, commanding the Light Cavalry Brigade, to carry out a reconnaissance to find out where the enemy was. For this purpose a squadron of the 8th Hussars and another of the 13th Light Dragoons were selected. In complete marching order, such as they would have worn in England, and encumbered with much unnecessary lumber, this little force marched relentlessly on from dawn to dusk, in very great heat. Five horses died and seventy-five were rendered useless for

---

* Lord Fitzroy James Henry Somerset, 1st Baron Raglan, GCB (1788–1855), son of 5th Duke of Beaufort; cornet, 4th Light Dragoons, 1804; aide-de-camp to Sir Arthur Wellesley (later Duke of Wellington) in the Peninsular War and Netherlands campaign, 1805–15; lost his right arm at Waterloo, 1815; secretary to Wellington when he was Master-General of the Ordnance, 1818–1827; Military Secretary at the Horse Guards, when Wellington was Commander-in-Chief of the Army, 1827–52; Master-General of the Ordnance, 1852; General and Field-Marshal, 1854.

ever. Many others were never again really fit. A number of men collapsed, but none, luckily, was permanently disabled. The results of the reconnaissance were negative. 'You have ascertained for me', wrote Raglan rather indulgently to Cardigan, 'that the Russians have withdrawn . . . and that the country . . . is not only clear of the enemy, but is wholly deserted by the inhabitants. These are important facts.'[1]

> My horses have arrived all well. I hope they will continue so, for the loss of a horse here is dreadful. They cannot be replaced. Those officers who have lost their horses must walk.
> **12 July.** The population [of Varna] looks all French or English. There are many shops, or rather stores, kept by the former, and some Greeks, chiefly provision stores.
> **15 July.** Up at 5. We have many prisoners in the Guard Room. If I can I will stop this work.

A Sergeant-Major of the Royals said that there was at this time 'a great deal of grumbling among the men [of the Heavy Brigade] about one thing or another, but when the Brigade gets all together the grumbling will be taken out of them, as several men of the other Corps have been flogged and a little would do some of our fellows good'.[2]

> Went to Lord Lucan early about these drunkards, and about other matters, but I could not get any answer to my application. He is of a violent temper and an unreasonable man to deal with.
> Saw a boat come on shore to sell rum to the men. Made a rush at it and seized the whole crew and cargo and took it up to Lord Lucan, who caused the spirits to be spilled, but let the crew go. I would have burned the boat, and flogged the crew.
> **18 July** [*Letter*]. Camp at Devna.
> I rise at $4\frac{1}{2}$, then I roll up my own bedding and make as much as I can of a toilet (not much); then I have to look after some breakfast, give out orders, &c. &c. My servants have 7 horses [to attend to] between them, so I do not get much assistance from them, as the horses must be taken to water three times daily $1\frac{1}{2}$ miles.
> Our rations are $1\frac{1}{2}$ lbs of black bread. I am getting used to it, for we cannot get any other; also 1 lb of thin mutton.

1. Lieutenant-Colonel Edward Cooper Hodge, Commanding Officer, 4th Dragoon Guards. Oil Painting by F. Salabert, 1850.

2. *Photograph from William Simpson's sketchbook. The inscription in his handwriting reads, "Balaklava, 1854. This was Photo'd on first occupation of Balaklava, and shows what the place was like before it was changed by huts, tents, etc."*

3. *Punch. 25 November, 1854.*

A TRUMP CARD (IGAN).

Lord Lucan has this the same as we do. Our cooking is not first rate, and I have not time to go and forage.

My horses have suffered much. They are coughing, and two have very bad eyes, caused by the glare and the dust.

The thermometer is 102 in my tent.

We have a large French army and Marshal St Arnaud* in Varna. Their commissariat is very superior to ours. I never go into Varna without seeing large trains of fine mules laden with corn, &c. &c. going to the camp. Our commissariat is infamous. Here we are on the sea shore, with several fine transports doing nothing, whose boats might land our rations in camp. Instead of which we have to send at 7 a.m. into Varna for them and the forage, and it often takes 6 or 7 hours to obtain it. The bread has to be baked when it is applied for. It is disgraceful to our country, all this. Here is a fine army as ever was seen, but they make so much fuss about transport that I doubt much whether the men's tents will be carried. They tell us we must have orderly room tents and books and papers, but they provide no animal to carry this, and they say they will not permit any animals beyond the regulated numbers to be in the line of march.

The Duke of Cambridge came into camp some days ago. He was outside our lines with Lord Lucan, and I went up to him. He spoke to me in the most cordial manner, quite making Lord Lucan open his eyes. Lord Raglan also has been most civil. He wanted me to dine with him some few days ago, but I excused myself in consequence of the distance at night that we are from Varna.

The country is pretty. It has a parky look, the whole of which is fast disappearing under our axes. We have to get all our cooking wood in this way.

They serve out the coffee to the men *unroasted* and *unground*, and we have nothing but a spade to roast it on, and two stones to grind it with by smashing it up.

---

*Armand Jacques Leroy de Saint Arnaud (1801–54) had made his name in Algeria as a remorselessly ambitious, unscrupulous and brave commander. He had assisted Louis Napoleon in the savage coup which brought him to power as Napoleon III in 1851. The next year he was made a Marshal of France, and in 1854 was given the command-in-chief of the French army in the east.

> We know nothing of what is going on here beyond what we
> read in the English papers.

A good deal had, in fact, been going on. After raising the seige of
Silistria, the Russian commander had been routed by the Turks,
without the aid of their allies. By mid-July his army was in full
retreat north-westwards. Before long it had evacuated Wallachia
and Moldavia. The declared objects of the war seemed to have been
gained. But few people in Britain or France cared a fig for the
official *casus belli*—the saving of Turkey. Only a crushing military
defeat, it was felt, would teach Russia—'this barbarous nation', as
Lord Lyndhurst called it in the House of Lords—the lesson she deserved. So the war went on.

> **18 July.** The horses from the *Palmyra* were landed. They have
> lost 7 which makes our [regimental] loss 14 in all.
>   A council of war was held today at which both the
> Admirals and the Generals were present.
> **19 July.** I hear that Sebastopol is likely to be the place we are
> to go to. I hope not. I cannot say I wish to go to the Crimea.
> It will be bad work, I know.
> **20 July.** Brigade Field Day. Lord Lucan commanded, and
> gave such words of command as were never invented. We could
> not understand him.

The almost unanimous view of the Earl of Lucan's incapacity for
command of the Cavalry Division was summed up by Major Forrest,
Hodge's second-in-command, who on 27 August told his wife:
'We have not much confidence in our Cavalry General and only
hope he will allow the Brigadiers to move their own Brigades. . . .
Lord Lucan is no doubt a clever sharp fellow, but he has been so
long on the shelf that he has no idea of moving cavalry, does not
even know the words of command, and is very self-willed about it,
thinks himself right. He has had a lot of very indifferent Field Days,
which we only hope may have taught him and his staff something,
for certainly nobody else has learnt anything.
'If he is shown by the drill-book that he is wrong, he says, "Ah, I
should like to know who wrote that book. Some farrier I suppose. . . ."
'I trust Scarlett will be allowed to manoeuvre his own brigade and,
then all will go well with the heavies; but I write this in order that
if any mishap should occur to the cavalry, you may be able to form
a correct idea how it happened.'[3]

22 July. Field Day under Lord Lucan. He was quieter today. Somehow I manage to get on with him, though his temper is very violent.

The 44th Regt [of Foot] passed here yesterday. They are gone to make gabions and fascines for some purpose or other. We hear all sorts of rumours.

23 July. Attended the Service at 6 with the men. The clergyman is a terrible old slow coach, and not at all impressive or likely to do good to any of us.

The wind sets in strong from the sea, consequently many dead horses have been washed up, annoying the camp extremely by their stink.

24 July. Lupton of 'F' [Troop] died of cholera. We are to move our camp tomorrow, which I am glad of.

26 July. [The move was postponed one day.] Up at 3. Got the tents down, and baggage animals packed, and we managed to struggle out of our camp by 6½, the poor horses loaded with hay, barley, picket ropes, camp kettles, &c. They allowed us an araba* a troop to carry the axes, shovels, &c. &c. At 9 we reached our new ground on the hill, a fine airy situation west of Varna, with a good supply of water.

27 July. Saw Omar Pasha and a curious guard of fellows with him.†

30 July. The Inniskillings have 46 men in hospital, and we have 12 men. Our horses are beginning to fall off terribly. All the food they are getting is 12 pounds of barley a day.

31 July. We changed our camp and went to a spot overlooking

---

* A heavy wagon or cart, usually without springs, common in the middle east.
† Omar (or Omer) Pasha (real name: Michael Lattas) (1806–1871); born in Croatia; fled to Bosnia, 1828, and became Mohammedan; defeated the Russians at Oltenita, 1853; in command of the Turkish troops co-operating with the French and British in the Crimean campaign, with, at first, 7,000 men, but in 1855 with much greater numbers; marshal, 1864.

He got on very well with Raglan, and was much admired by the British troops. 'He is a capital fellow', said Nigel Kingscote, one of Raglan's aides-de-camp. 'Quite different to the Turks in general, hates all display, and the energy he must have is wonderful. . . . He is a sporting looking fellow and sits well on his horse in a plain grey frock coat and long jack boots.' (Quoted in Hibbert, C. *The Destruction of Lord Raglan*, 1961, 28.) Cornet Fisher of the 4th Dragoon Guards found that he was 'very ugly, and looks worn; very different from our fat old Generals'. (24 Apr, 1855).

the sea, very pretty but bad ground, a long way from water.
I think this change bad.

1 August. Spain of 'E' Troop died of cholera, after a few
hours' illness. In default of a clergyman, I read the burial
service over him. An excellent sober good man.

The sad record of deaths from cholera continues nearly every day
for some weeks to come. The disease had first broken out in the
adjoining French camp in mid-July. It quickly spread to the
British. By 19 August, the 4th Dragoon Guards had buried 23
men. Hodge remarked that 'it was difficult to find a spot here where
burying has not been'.

5 August. I was all the morning on this Board about the
Ambulance Corps, which is quite inefficient. Large wagons
with large harness, with heavy old Pensioners riding little
ponies of the country are expected to draw these machines.
Anything so shameful as the way this corps has been sent out
cannot be conceived. It has been sent out a mere claptrap to
please the newspapers and House of Commons.

8 August. We have sad drunkenness amongst our men. The
fools drink raw spirits, get horribly drunk and then wonder
that they are ill. They do not give themselves a chance.

9 August. We got some milk today, quite a treat. The greater
part is water, I know, but still it is a luxury.

Drunkenness is still rife. I have applied for two Courts
Martial on men for getting drunk on duty.

Fisher wrote home some days later that the men were 'behaving
very badly, and our Colonel', he added, referring to Hodge, 'is not
fit to manage them. Privates and N.C.Os get drunk on escort duty,
and the N.C.Os are not broken, or the privates flogged.'[4]

10 August. A terrible fire raged all night in Varna, burning
the bazaar and a large quantity of stores. This was without
doubt the work of incendiaries, Greek I doubt not, to prevent,
if possible, the proposed expedition to Sebastopol. The fire had
a brilliant effect from our camp. At 12 p.m. a Staff Officer
came up, and ordered out a strong picket of 200 cavalry under
me to patrol round the town.

12 August. I rode to the French Artillery camp, and then to the camp of Bashi Bazooks, a rare wild set.* They had no regular tents, merely a cloth put up over a stick, the horses little wild-looking animals. They had quantities of pistols, a heavy rifle, a sword and a long lance.

My servant, James, taken very ill with cholera. Poor fellow, he is a delicate subject. He sent for me at 9 p.m., gave me some money to send to his wife, and told me that he was dying. It is sad to see some ten men in a tent, all lying ill of this awful disease.

13 August. Wrote to my mother, God Bless her. I hope it will please the Almighty to spare me to see her once again, but when I see all my men wasting away and good men carried suddenly off in this way, I feel I must be prepared.

14 August. My poor servant died. Now I must look for another. Followed James to the grave.

17 August. I do not think that the army is fit to go to Sebastopol. The men are not the men they were, and we have some hundreds of sick.

Further, as Sergeant-Major Cruse of the Royals told his wife, 'most of the men are getting barefoot, and how they will get reshod I do not know'.[5]

18 August [*Letter*]. I wanted coal for my farriers to heat the horse shoes with. I was told that I could not have it from the commissariat but that I must get it where I could, as the commissariat coal belonged to government. It so happens that the only coal to be got is from the commissariat, as it is not to be found here. Therefore the cavalry are not to be shod, because John Bull, who pays for both cavalry and commissariat, has got all the coal in his possession. I offered to pay for the coal, but nothing could be done. Officers commanding regiments

---

* Bashi-Bazouk (Turkish: *bashi-bozuq*, one of disordered [vicious] head), an irregular Ottoman soldier, generally horsed, notorious for lawlessness, but useful for patrolling. The British government wanted Raglan to take bodies of these men into service, trained by Colonel Beatson, the distinguished organiser of Indian irregular cavalry. He refused to have anything to do with them, as the atrocities which he saw them perpetrating upon the Bulgarians around Varna reminded him too vividly of the unspeakable treatment meted out to French prisoners during the Peninsular War.

must, they said, buy it for their regiments where they could. Was ever such a system heard of?

All the shops in Varna are destroyed. Several French merchants had established stores where we got tea, sugar, brandy, rice and such things. These with our ration of meat and bread constitute our food, and the destruction of these stores is most inconvenient to us, as is that of the barley.

My officers are all in good health, but the men have been sickly. They drink a villainous compound called *raki* [a coarse Turkish drink made from grain-spirit], which maddens them for a time. This, combined with exposure to the sun, brings on fever, which has caused us many deaths.

The clergyman who came to perform the service for us this morning had a pair of fixed steel spurs on, and a fine muslin turban wound about his shovel hat. I conclude he wears the former because he is attached to the Cavalry Division.

19 August. We dine daily at 2 p.m. We always have our ration of beef well boiled into soup with rice, pepper and vermicelli in it. Then we have boiled rice mixed with some brown ration sugar and milk if we can get it. Our breakfast consists of tea, boiled rice, fried bacon or sardines, biscuit and sometimes an egg, but not often.

22 August. Called at Lord Raglan's. He is looking well. He was consulting a map of Turkey in Asia. Why so? Hem! Is Sebastopol a blind?

28 August [*Letter*]. Lord Raglan has paid me a compliment which I think I hardly deserve, and a compliment that I receive with pain, as it tends to throw discredit upon one of my best friends, Brigadier-General Scarlett. The 5th Dgn Guards have been visited severely with cholera: 3 officers and 35 men have died. Colonel Le Marchant* has throwed up the command and gone home ill, and they have become, to use Lord Raglan's words, quite disorganised. Lord Lucan reported them, and Lord Raglan went to see them, and the latter in a long letter

---

*Thomas Le Marchant (1811–1873), 4th son of Major-General John Gaspard Le Marchant, the distinguished cavalry general, whose projects for schools of instruction for officers were the germ from which the Military Academy at Sandhurst grew, and who was killed leading the famous charge of the Heavy Brigade (which included the 5th Dragoon Guards) at Salamanca in 1812.

has ordered them to be attached to the 4th Dragoon Guards, and he further says that he has no doubt that Lieut-Colonel Hodge will use his utmost zeal to restore the regiment to its former state. They call me the commander of the 9th (5 & 4)! I know that you like to hear all that occurs to me, or I should not mention this, as it has annoyed me much, on account of Gen Scarlett, who is Lt-Col of it, though he does not command it personally now. Captain Burton, a very gentlemanly young officer, but too young, is in the command. They have lost their surgeon, vet surgeon and Captn Duckworth dead.

In my tent as I am now writing, the thermometer is 95, and the dust is blowing through the tent and filling everything, especially my ink bottle, the contents of which are as thick and muddy as can be.

Great preparations are still going on for this Sebastopol affair. Six batteries of artillery have embarked. The infantry are to go this week, and I expect that about tomorrow week the expedition will sail. My idea is that if they effect a landing, they will send the artillery transports back for the cavalry. It is only 36 hours by steam from this. I hear that the spot that was selected for the army to land on has now a large Russian force encamped upon it. For this we may thank *The Times* newspaper, who has informed the Russians long ago of all we *did*, or rather *did not*. I see in *The Times* of the 5th a long account of our departure from Varna for Sebastopol, and many other lies of equal magnitude. Believe nothing you read in the 'Morning Lie' or the 'Daily Liar' or any other papers.

28 August. Nobody goes with any pleasure on this expedition. Heavens knows I don't. What is the use of CBs and rank? I have yet to learn the use that will be to one.

30 August. There was a great sale of horses and effects, the property of officers who have died in the 5th [Dragoon Guards]. Their horses fetched nothing hardly. Some of the things sold very well, such as shirts, and things wanted immediately.

We hear that Field Officers are only to be allowed to take 2 horses with them. This will be a great sacrifice to us.

2 September. Very weak and seedy. My Adjutant also ill. He has been drinking champagne—poisonous kind of liquid at best. It will not do to play these tricks out here.

From the earliest days of the war, there had been an assumption that the capture of Sebastopol was a desirable objective, both politically and militarily. This assumption crystallized in the last days of June, when Raglan was informed that the cabinet and the French had decided upon a siege of that great naval base. Very reluctantly he agreed to undertake it. Marshal St Arnaud, the ailing French commander, with equal misgivings, concurred. Consequently, orders were given for a survey of possible landing places; a vast fleet was assembled in Varna Bay, and before the end of August, as has been seen, embarkation was well under way. 'Hurrah for the Crimea!' exclaimed Cornet Fisher. 'Take Sebastopol in a week or so, and then into winter quarters.'[6] His commanding officer was less sanguine:

5 **September** [*Letter*]. The first division of the expedition, including the Light Cavalry sailed this morning. Nobody here approves of it, even Lord Raglan I hear. I suppose that the order comes from Lord Aberdeen [the Prime Minister], and I think he is crouching to public opinion and *The Times* newspaper.

I fancy they know but little of the Crimea, and I imagine they intend passing the winter there. I hope they will find us something better than these thin tents, which are already getting very chilly at night. Then our men have no clothing fit for winter. The flannels and things they brought from England are nearly worn out, and all our stores are at Constantinople; as to the clothing, I think a fortnight in wet weather and mud will make nice figures of us all, as where we halt, there we must lie down.

For the last two months we have been in sand and dust, more resembling the links at Yarmouth than anything I know. Do not believe all the stories you hear or read in those lying letters from Varna. The men have been very well fed. I think they get too much meat. They give us $1\frac{1}{2}$ lb a day, more than they ought to have in this country, where people say that no beef is wholesome. Then we have $1\frac{1}{2}$ lb of very hard biscuit, rice, sugar, rum and coffee. They do not provide water skins or anything beyond some little blue water kegs to put [water] in, and these kegs are rotten old things that have been in store since the last war [i.e. 40 years] and are fast breaking to pieces, so that when we require them they will not be forthcoming.

Where exactly we are going to, or what we are to be allowed to carry with us, we do not yet know. The officers on landing are merely to take what they can carry and three days' salt beef and biscuit. I fancy we are not going to storm or even attack Sebastopol; the occupation of the Crimea is, they say, the thing now. I hope this may not prove a second Walcheren affair.* The season is too far advanced and we must be dependent upon a very stormy sea for feeding the army. As to the horses, what they will get, I cannot tell.

We have our newspapers from London to 18 August. I cannot understand why our Funds keep up so high. The City men must have great faith in our prowess. Fancy what a tumbledown there would be if they heard of our failing at Sebastopol.

9 September. Rain continuing in torrents. My tent luckily has stood it as yet. About 1 p.m. the rain began to give over. Looked thro' the lines of horses. The poor brutes had scraped away the sand and were all standing in canals of muddy water, their coats staring, themselves shivering, and looking only fit for the dogs. The saddlery lying saturated with wet. The men are soaked to the skin, one and all, and the wind has turned very cold, from which I am suffering much.

I have no warm clothing, not a winter waistcoat of any kind, and but thin worsted socks. I have no warm gloves, and but one pair of warm drawers. All my warm things are down at Scutari. If I knew at all what was going to become of us I would get some of it up from there. I much fear I shall never be able to stand the cold. It makes me quite ill. I am unfit for anything, and if my bowels become affected by it, and dysentery sets in, I know not what I shall do, ill in a thin tent, and no servant, for Reade is no servant to me. I do more than half my work myself.

14 September. Tasted some Bulgarian bread, unleavened and baked on the coals. It was sweet, but heavy, better than our ration bread.

20 September. The army have landed without opposition

---

* The British expedition to the island of Walcheren at the mouth of the Scheldt in 1809. Having achieved virtually nothing, it ended disastrously, with enormous casualties as a result of what came to be known as 'Walcheren fever'.

[this news first reached Varna on 17 September], and have been well received by the inhabitants, who have brought them provisions. They are moving towards Sebastopol.

On 13 September the fleet carrying nearly all the British and French troops, excepting the Heavy Cavalry Brigade, had come to rest off the Old Fort in Kalamita Bay, some twenty miles north of Sebastopol. The following morning most of the infantry landed unopposed. The local Tartars were discovered to be more friendly than the Bulgarians had been at Varna.

In spite of means adequate to carry only a part of their essential supplies, the armies marched off on 19 September. That afternoon some of the Light Cavalry Brigade and Horse Artillery had their first skirmish with the enemy on the Bulganak river—a very minor affair.

Back at Varna, Hodge reported that:

the steamers and transports [which had taken the Light Brigade to the Crimea] are arriving. Our stay now is very limited indeed.

22 September. We arrived on the beach at $7\frac{1}{2}$ a.m., and immediately commenced embarking on board the *Simla*, a fine steamer, 350 feet long, and which is to carry the whole of the 4th Dgn Guards and 26 of the 5th Dragoon Guards. I got on board at 2 and managed to get 5 horses on board for myself. We have 230 Troop horses, 47 officers' horses and 17 baggage horses.

23 September. None of the subalterns or staff are able to have a baggage pony at all. I know not what they will do.

Felt very unwell, with pain in my stomach, and dysentery, but I was forced to be out in the sun all day and superintending the embarking and stowing away of the horses, baggage, &c. &c.

24 September. The stamping of horses over our heads is beyond anything. We have an awful crowd on board, and the place where the men live is pitch dark. Disease must break out if we are kept very long in this way. The Captain tells me that he has but 8 days' supply of forage and water on board.

25 September. Fomented my stomack several times, which seems to do me good. They talked of sending us away today, but we moved not.

'We are uncommon jolly here,' wrote Cornet Fisher on this day. 'You never saw such good living—every possible luxury. It is a beautiful ship.'[7]

26 September. In my bed all day. Much purged and very ill.

About 6 p.m. we took [in tow] the *Pride of the Ocean* transport with a portion of the 6th [Inniskilling] Dragoons on board, and a collier with coals for the Fleet. It came on to blow a heavy gale of wind with torrents of rain in the night. We parted from both ships, and rolled fearfully, knocking down several horses, some of which died.

28 September. Very ill all day. Kept my bed, as I cannot get up. If I do I run off at once.

30 September. Passed the entrance to Sebastopol, where we saw the *Terrible* steamer trying the range of her guns upon the batteries.

We passed a large fleet of Men of War, and steamed along a pretty coast till we came to Balaklava, a small indented bay and town some 7 or 8 miles to the South of Sebastopol.

We cast anchor and are, I hear, to disembark tomorrow. To me this is the most serious disappointment that has ever happened to me. I lived a life for this time, and now I am prevented [by illness from] taking advantage of the honours that will be conferred, and another will reap all the benefit that naturally accrues to an officer in command of a Regiment. However, God's will be done. He does everything for the best.

1 October. We commenced getting our horses on shore. Many were found to be injured, and our loss in them is great.*
I was much annoyed at the supine manner in which the officers did their duty. Half the day they were eating and chattering

---

*The other heavy regiments suffered worse; those, like the Royals, which were carried in sailing ships, particularly badly. The Royals, indeed, as their commanding officer wrote, were reduced to 'a single squadron. On that fearful night [of 26 September] the regiment lost more horses than at Waterloo. . . . Total loss, 150.'(Oct, 1854, MS letter of Lieut-Col. John Yorke, 1st Royal Dragoons).

In all, the Brigade lost 226 horses on its passage to the Crimea. The remainder, according to Lucan, were 'in such a condition that I should scarcely have recognized them, from what they had suffered at sea'. (*Report of the Board of General Officers appointed to enquire into the Statements contained in the Reports of Sir John McNeill . . . Chelsea*, 1856, 47.)

in the cabin, especially the Major [Forrest], who seems to think he is to do nothing. The subalterns of 'A' Troop he allowed to sleep on board, instead of on shore with their Troops. This is courting popularity, which I cannot do.

Hodge, in giving evidence to the Crimean Commissioners, who were sent from England in March, 1855, to inquire into the 'Supplies of the British Army', stated that 'the men landed without their valises, and had only the following articles in addition to what they wore, viz., one shirt, one pair of drawers, one flannel vest, and one pair of socks wrapped in the blanket.'[8]

> This cove of Balaklava is a wonderful place to get ships into. It is quite land-locked, and the entrance cannot be seen from the sea. The town is small and runs up the hillside.
> **2 October** [*Letter*]. I am still in bed.
> There has been, I hear, a splendid battle at Alma, in which the Russians have been totally defeated. The conduct of our troops was, they say, wonderful. When they came to a rise with the whole Russian Army drawn out on the top, the French turned their flank and the English went right at them. We had not cavalry enough to send at them, or more would have been taken or killed. The loss has been very great on our side.

The battle of the Alma, here so laconically described by Hodge, had taken place on 20 September, when Raglan and St Arnaud attacked the enemy's position on the river of that name. Prince Menschikoff, the Russian commander, had chosen the obvious place from which to destroy the invaders. Properly defended, the six miles of his position must have proved all but impregnable. Over-confidence, however, bred carelessness.
After a period of astonishingly heroic fighting (particularly on the part of the British infantry), the Russians gave way and retreated in confusion. The British suffered some 2,000 casualities, the French only 550, and the Russians about 5,700.
Throughout the battle Menschikoff had allowed his 27 squadrons of cavalry to remain inactive on his right. Opposite them there were only the Light Brigade and two troops of horse artillery. Raglan had the greatest difficulty, towards the end of the battle, in restraining Lucan and Cardigan from attacking this large body of enemy horse. 'His object all day', he said, 'had been to "shut

them up", the enemy's cavalry being so superior in numbers.' It was fortunate that he succeeded. Lucan was furious.

It was not until four days after the battle of the Alma that the allies came in sight of Sebastopol. The French, who were responsible for this unfortunate delay, now refused to attack the almost defenceless town from the north without a proper siege train. The Russians did not neglect this welcome breathing space. First of all Menschikoff sank ships in the harbour mouth, thus effectively closing it. Next, he decided to withdraw his main army from Sebastopol towards Backchiserai so as to maintain communication with the interior, and to be able to threaten the allied rear. This flank march of the Russians coincided with the more famous flank march of the allies. Faced with the obstinacy of the French, Raglan decided, audaciously, to march round to the south of Sebastopol—the supposedly less well defended side, and from there assault the town, at the same time securing the ports of Kamiesch and Balaklava.

By great good fortune the two marching armies only just made contact, for the allied troops, spread out in columns of route over a number of miles in almost trackless scrub country were very vulnerable. As it was, the allies came across nothing more than the extreme Russian rearguard; but Lucan leading the Light Brigade at the head of the army, lost his way, and it was Raglan, himself, who actually first saw the enemy!

On 26 September, the British army entered the port of Balaklava, against almost no opposition. The French, who had followed the British, moved further west and established their sea base at Kamiesch.

They are now getting the guns into position in front of Sebastopol, and as soon as they are placed they will go at it.

I am ill off for a servant but there is no use in private servants at present. They are not allowed to be with the army. A good man would hardly condescend to the discomforts that they must have here—no tents but those in which the men live, and they are crowded—no means of cooking or carrying anything but what he could put in a pair of saddlebags on the country pony he would ride. Few decent servants will stand this, and others take to drinking.

3 October [*Letter*]. I heard that the *Sans Pareil*, Sidney Dacres's ship, had arrived in Balaklava to disembark guns,

&c., so I wrote and told him of my situation. He immediately
sent for me, and I am a wonderful deal better today.

Captain (later Admiral Sir) Sidney Dacres was a relation of Hodge's
eldest sister's husband. For two years he had been in command of
the steam man-o'-war, *Sans Pareil*, 70 guns. She had been used
recently to embark the sick and wounded after the Alma. Her
Captain, before that, had been beach-master at the Kalamita Bay
landing.

We have on board a Captain Baring of the Coldstream
Guards, who lost his left arm at the shoulder by a round shot
at the battle of Alma. He is in the same cabin with me, and it
is beautiful to see the way in which he behaves. I have never
heard him utter a groan or a sigh. He is pretty free from pain
and says he sleeps at night.

[At the Alma] The Duke of Cambridge led on his Brigade
[Division] with great gallantry. This will not be lost sight of in
England. The people will be pleased, and I hope he will be
made much of for it. I hear that he is looking very well.

3 October. Sidney [Dacres] met Lord Raglan at dinner. S.
told him that I was very ill on board his ship. Lord R. told him
he was indeed sorry to hear it, that he could ill spare my
services, that I was a good officer. I trust I may be able to fulfil
this opinion of me.

At 10½ we got out of Balaklava by dint of most beautiful
seamanship, there being just room to move the ship. In
company with Capt Carnegie in the *Tribune*, Capt Power in the
Vesuvius, also three French ships, all under the command of
Rear Admiral De Charner in the *Napoleon* of 100 guns, we
started under easy steam.

4 October. Off Yalta at an early hour. A lovely bay with
high rocks rising gradually almost to mountains. In the
valleys were beautiful villas and parks, one of Prince
Woronzoff's, a gem, all in white marble. Another belonging
to the Empress, a present from the Emperor, very beautiful
indeed. We could observe the people packing up their things
and running away into the country. About 9 a.m. the boats
landed. All quiet, nobody was found but a few Germans, who
said they had been robbed by the Tartars to prevent their

things falling into our hands. No cattle were found, a little bad flour and some wine in the Empress's villa. This the French intend taking. The church is a very pretty building. A guard of English marines was sent to protect this. The sailors remained on shore all day. They got but little, but nearly all got drunk. Dacres much annoyed.

5 October [*Letter*]. I think this place was visited by Oliphant, who lately wrote a book about this country. If my sisters can get the book they will see about it.*

Lord Cardigan is always in front I hear. He is indefatigable. I suppose Mayow [Cardigan's Brigade Major and a relation of Hodge's brother-in-law] is with him, and now I am laid by the heels when what I have lived for was within my grasp. Thank God I am better today.

5 October. Another expedition was sent off to try to obtain bullocks, but they got none. The French robbed a General Poniatowski's villa of some wine, and the English got some coals which an English steward of Prince Woronzoff's swore were the Prince's. Receipts were therefore given.

I am much purged and griped and very weak indeed.

7 October. Arrived and anchored off Sebastopol at 9 a.m. A lovely morning. The sight of the fleet very imposing. We can see the Russians firing away at the French who are disembarking guns.

Marshal St Arnaud is dead of cholera. Canrobert† therefore commands their army.

9 October. What a noisy thing a ship is night and day! People are stumping up and down on the poop deck over my

---

*Laurence Oliphant (1829–1888), the famous novelist, war correspondent and mystic, had published *The Russian Shores of the Black Sea and a Tour through the Country of the Don Cossacks* in 1853.

In 1855 he accompanied Lord Stratford de Redcliffe to the Crimea, (see p. 102) having just published a pamphlet called *The Trans-Caucasian Provinces the Proper Field of Operations for a Christian Army*, 1855.

Later in the year he joined the Turkish army under Omar Pasha as *Times* correspondent, and wrote, on his return to England, *The Trans-Caucasian Campaign. . . . A Personal Narrative*, 1856.

† François Certain Canrobert (1809–1895). Like St Arnaud, he had been active in the *coup d'état* of December, 1851; up till now he had commanded the French 1st Division; in May, 1855, he was succeeded in the chief command by General Pélissier (see p. 107); marshal, 1855; commanded the Army of the Rhine, and taken prisoner at Metz, 1870.

head, and the row of ropes and blocks is eternal. They seem
always at something.

11 October. A Court of Inquiry was held on Dacres today
because his ship touched the ground when going in, cleared
for action, to assist in landing the troops near Alma. He was,
of course, acquitted of all blame, but this is no encouragement
to men to do their duty fearlessly. Half the Captains of the
Fleet came here today to call. They all condemn Admiral
Dundas's* supineness. He does nothing. The army are suffering
from want of fresh provisions. Plenty are to be got by sending
to Sinope or Trebizond, and there are plenty of steamers doing
nothing, but he makes no effort to get any.

12 October. I have not heard one word of or from the regiment
since I left them, and very anxious I am to do so.

What the regiment was doing is well chronicled by Cornet Fisher.
Writing home on this day, he says: 'We are still about 15 minutes
from Balaklava, guarding the rear of the army, who are working
night and day to drag the guns into position. . . . We are turned out
and mounted at 5.0 every morning, and remain under arms till
8.30 or 9.0; the early morn is the time for attack.'

'I have heard nothing of the Colonel [Hodge] since we landed, and
do not care how long it is before he joins us again. . . .

'They give us double rations of rum now, which is a great comfort
and beautiful drink. The Cossacks keep us alive, but don't trust
themselves very near us. . . .

'Horses have got coats like sheep, and are never groomed.'[9]

14 October. I have been amusing myself reading some of
Macaulay's essays, on Warren Hastings, Machiavelli, Sir
William Temple, von Ranke's *History of the Popes*, and about
my great ancestor Lord Bacon, who it seems to me, never did
a good action in his life. What a pity that so learned a man
was obliged to work for his bread. Had he but possessed a
sufficient fortune, and but been known for his works, how

---

* Sir James Whitley Deans Dundas, GCB (1785–1862); entered navy,
1799; Commander-in-Chief, Mediterranean, 1852; Admiral, 1857. An
excessively cautious man, whom Raglan found difficult and obstructive.
His second-in-command, Sir E. Lyons (see p. 35), who, though even older
than Dundas, was a dashing, energetic man, held him in scarcely concealed
contempt. Lyons succeeded him in January, 1855.

4. *Sir Colin Campbell, sketched at his quarters, Balaklava, Camp of the 93rd Regiment, 14 March, 1855. From William Simpson's sketchbook.*

5. *Prince Edward of Saxe Weimar, 1 May, 1855. From William Simpson's sketchbook. (see page 62.)*

6. *(a) A corporal of the 4th Dragoon Guards in foraging order before 25 October, 1854; camp before Balaklava. Sketch by Général Vanson. (b) Heavy Cavalry Troopers. Sketch by Général Vanson.*

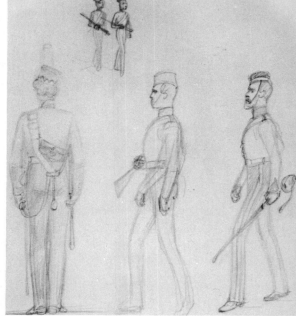

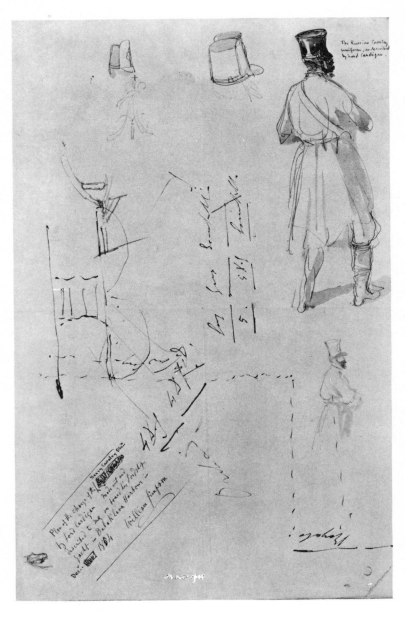

7. Top Right: '*The Russian Cavalry Uniform as described by Lord Cardigan*'. Bottom Left: '*Plan of the charge of the heavy Cavalry Div* [sic] *by Lord Cardigan. Made out and described to me on board his Lordship's yacht in Balaklava Harbour in December 1854. William Simpson*'.

unsullied would have been his great name. Warren Hastings, too, tho' he saved India for England, was a most unmitigated villain.

15 October. Went round the ship. The loaves of white bread for the midshipmen made me quite envious. I believe in camp we get nothing but biscuit and salt beef or pork.

16 October. The orders came to go in and engage the batteries tomorrow. All day long they were knocking down the cabin bulkheads and removing the books and furniture below, till at last we were nearly clear.

I have no purging. Am doing well internally.

17 October. Naval action off Sebastopol.

The guns from the lines of the army began firing at $6\frac{1}{2}$ a.m. and kept up a most tremendous fire. This ship was early cleared for action. All the bulkheads and cabin fitments taken down, and at $\frac{1}{4}$ past 1, we up anchor, and followed the *Agamemnon* [91 guns (steam)], Sir E. Lyons's* ship, into action. At $\frac{1}{4}$ to 2, the *Sans Pareil* fired her first gun at some 2000 yards. The shot fell short, but the Russian batteries which were raised on high ground kept firing over us, and now and then striking the ship. As we got nearer the batteries and the lower deck guns began, the smoke got so thick I could see nothing. I therefore went below and wrote letters in Mr Anderson's [the *Sans Pareil*'s first Lieutenant's] cabin. Every now and then a shell would burst close to me, and on three occasions I heard the alarm of fire close to the magazine under the cabin where I was. The ship was close under the Constantine Fort, and continued firing away most gallantly till $5\frac{1}{4}$, when Admiral Lyons ordered her out of the action, as the batteries had her range, and were throwing shell into her every minute. I fear the loss is very great. I saw many dead and a large number brought down wounded. Sidney Dacres has fought his ship most ably and bravely, and the crew behaved most nobly.

---

* Sir Edmund (later 1st Baron) Lyons, GCB (1790–1858); entered navy, 1803; minister plenipotentiary to various countries, 1835–1853; Second-in-Command, Mediterranean, 1853–55; Commander-in-Chief, Mediterranean, 1855–8. He and Raglan were close personal friends, and were often together at Raglan's headquarters, a fact which Dundas, when he was commander-in-chief, much resented.

The sight between decks was very sad—blood everywhere. I felt how odd that I should be on board a line of battle ship in such a fight.

I fear that the damage inflicted on the Russians is not equal to that our ships have suffered. The range was too great. 1200 yards makes no impression on batteries like Sebastopol in casemate buildings, and on guns raised so much above the ships. The appearance of the decks after the action was dreadful: wreck from the bursting of the shells; blood; wet, from the ship having been 3 times on fire, and the stench awful from the sulphur, and the wounded. We got some cold meat in the ward room, and I had my cot laid down on the cabin floor, but I could not sleep, I was too excited. My brave friend Sidney had a narrow escape. A round shot knocked him down, but he rose again without any injury. The French did not go in well, and the Turks kept firing away at a respectful distance.

18 October. The loss in the ship is frightful: 1 midshipman killed and 11 men; 2 lieutenants and 58 men wounded. The ship, too, is terribly knocked about, many shells having burst in her side. The cabin windows smashed and woodwork damaged; masts and rigging much damaged. They fired 1500 shot & shells. What a sad thing it is to think of all this waste of life and destruction of our shipping, and all to no purpose. On the contrary the ships being forced to withdraw so early will give confidence and courage to the Russians. The loss on board the *Albion* [91 guns (sail)] also is very large: 11 k. and 70 wounded. In Admiral Dundas's ship [*Britannia*, 120 guns, (sail)] they have only two wounded. He took care not to expose himself. Oh, that Sir E. Lyons had commanded the force! Dundas is a disgrace to it.

The *Rodney* [90 guns (sail)], Captn Graham's ship was ashore a long time close under the batteries. Two steamers tried to assist her off. She broke two cables and the jerk of the second carried her off, and the other steamer lashed alongside of her, carried her off with a loss of only two men wounded. We saw her as we came out of action, firing away from both sides.

19 October. The loss of the fleet in this foolish affair has been 2 lieuts killed, 2 midshipmen killed and 47 men killed, 3 lieuts and 263 men wounded. [The official figures are 44 killed and 266 wounded.][10] That of the French I have not heard. The *Albion*, a 90-gun ship, is nearly a wreck. She is to be sent to Malta to refit. The *Arethusa* [50 guns (sail)] is so cut up that they are going to Constantinople. This ship has several large holes in her side, which would quite prevent her going to sea, and nearly all the ships, English and French, are with topmasts down repairing & refitting.

The conduct of the crew of the *Albion* seems to have been very bad. They got rather peppered going into action, some shells burst between decks. An alarm of fire was raised. The men quitted their guns and some tried to quit the ship. They did not fire 100 rounds.

The original plan for the bombardment and assault of Sebastopol on 17 October had been for the guns of the army and for those of the navy to open up together at 6.30 a.m. The combined cannonade was to lay the town open to assaults by the allied infantry.

The French admiral, however, the previous evening, told Vice-Admiral Sir James Dundas, Commander-in-Chief, Mediterranean, that he did not intend to start firing until 10.30 a.m., since he had not enough shot to keep going for very long and the enemy might think him beaten off if he ceased firing early. Dundas weakly agreed and ordered his own ships to conform.

Even worse, at 7 a.m., half an hour after the land guns had opened up, the French decided that their ships, contrary to the agreed plan, were to be anchored over 1,200 yards from the shore, which was well outside the limits of effective fire. They demanded that the British ships should do the same. Dundas had no alternative, at so late an hour, but to agree to what he considered a 'mock battle'.

The 'Inshore Squadron' alone, under Rear-Admiral Sir Edmund Lyons, of which the *Sans Pareil* was one of the ships, was to stick in some measure to the original plan. This had been for the steamers to be placed on the starboard side of the line of battle sailing ships, and to tow them down the north shore, where they would anchor ready to open fire on the forts.

What in fact happened was that the French artillery on land failed, unlike the British, to put out of action the Russian guns opposite their batteries. Further, their gunners had been demoralized by two lucky Russian shots, one of which blew up a magazine, killing

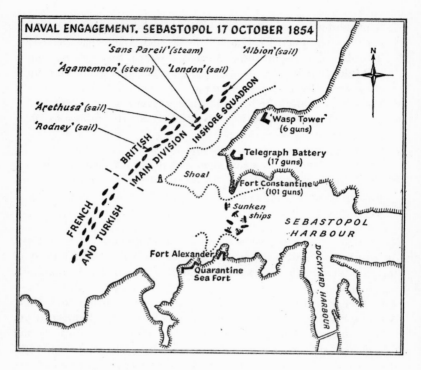

NAVAL ENGAGEMENT, SEBASTOPOL 17 OCTOBER 1854

over fifty men, the other an ammunition dump. The French stopped firing at 10.30 a.m.

Though the way was clear for an assault from the British lines, Raglan felt that he could not go ahead alone, and so the assault never took place. By the time (2 p.m.) that Lyons was anchored off Fort Constantine, and had opened fire, the intervention of the navies had become totally futile. The assaulting columns of British infantry were actually 'falling out' at the moment when the naval guns started their cannonade.

As a result of the 3 hours' naval bombardment, only 6 guns in all the Russian forts were dismounted, 11 men killed and 39 wounded. The allied fleets' casualties were 520 killed and wounded. 'If', remarks Kinglake in his *Invasion of the Crimea*, 'this was the heaviest sea cannonade that, up to that time, had been known, it was also, in proportion to its greatness, the most harmless one ever delivered.'[11]

*   *   *

19 October. The English papers are teeming with lies about the capture of Sebastopol. The French and German are also. We are, I fear, a long way from it, and a bloody business it will be when it, if it ever does happen [*sic*].

20 October. I fear the cavalry are not doing well. The French, they say, went at the Russians a day or so back, but the English did not show. This must be Lord Lucan's fault.

This probably refers to 7 October, when, according to an officer of Horse Artillery, 'the finest opportunity for thrashing the Russian cavalry, was *thrown* away'[12] by Lucan. A large number of enemy horsemen had cavorted about on the plain of Balaklava, seeming to invite a charge. Lucan, probably with wisdom, as there were enemy infantry and artillery in support, refused to charge. It was as a result of this day's work that Lucan acquired the punning nickname of 'Lord Look-on'.

21 October. I am so much better that I intend going down to Balaklava today, if I can get an opportunity. I think I have no right to remain here any longer.

22 October. At 9 a.m. went on shore, wrote to the camp to have my horses sent down to me. Paid Lord Cardigan a visit on board his yacht, the *Dryad*, where he seems very comfortable. This is the way to make war. I hope he will take compassion on me sometimes.

The *Dryad* had arrived in Balaklava harbour on 13 October. Cardigan, 'the Noble Yachtsman', as he at once became known, 'having received Lord Raglan's permission to live on board and do duty from thence',[13] on account of being very unwell with diarrhoea, slept aboard his yacht, having dined upon delicacies prepared by his French chef, for some weeks to come.

Went to our hospital en route to the camp, got my tent pretty comfortable, and my bed up, dined at 2 o'clock with Pine, as formerly.

My horses are looking moderate, one lame and very ill looking. They say he has worms. The Troopers [Troop horses] look but moderate. I hear they are hard worked

and not over-well fed. Tomorrow I must see and hear
more.

22 October. [*Letter*]. Balaklava.

I came down last night in the *Beagle*, nasty dirty little steamer
commanded by Lieut Hore. Hore is in camp with the Navy
Brigade, so I slept in his cabin.

The Naval Brigade consisted of some 3,600 seamen and marines who
had recently been landed from ships, with 29 naval guns. It was a
notable contribution to Raglan's beseiging force.

Cornet Fisher thought the sailors 'most wonderful fellows. They
come along singing and shouting [whilst dragging up their guns],
harnessed to an araba. As they come opposite [our camp] they are
received with loud cheers, which they return with a power of lung
quite extraordinary.'[14]

I find that out of 11 cavalry regiments, I shall rank no. 3.
Lord George Paget [see p. 59] and Shewell* will be the only
two before me. I am senior in the heavy brigade.

The extra command of the 5th [Dragoon Guards] gave a
little extra trouble but not much. General Scarlett was
constantly in their lines, and I, of course, interfered as little as
possible, from delicacy to him.

The weather continues very fine.

23 October. I got myself pretty comfortable today, but I feel
weak and unable to do anything. I did not go out with the
men this morning. They parade at 5 a.m. every day.
Robertson† brought me my bag from Constantinople. I am
so glad. I have now both warm and waterproof things.

There are many double-humped camels used here in draft
in the arabas. They draw by the neck, by a cross beam. I think

---

*Frederick George Shewell, CB (1809–1856); cornet, 8th Hussars, 1827;
Lieut-Col., 1847. He was a very strict and religious man. He rose from his
sick bed on 25 October to lead his regiment in the battle of Balaklava. When
he was seen galloping up to take command, one of his troopers exclaimed:
'Well, I'm d——d if it isn't the Colonel; what do you say to the "old woman"
now?' ('The Charge . . . by one who was in it', Murray R. H. *The History of
the VIII King's Royal Irish Hussars 1693–1927*, 1928, II, 435.)

†Arthur Masterton Robertson; cornet in the regiment, 1846; captain,
1852.

them very graceful, with their small heads and hairy necks. I take them to be the same as the Bactrian camel.

24 October. Slept very well, but during the night we had some ugly gusts of wind. The troops have passed another quiet day.

Chapter 3

25 October – 31 December 1854

While Hodge had been recuperating aboard ship, the army ashore had had to attend not only to the siege of Sebastopol, but also to the defence of Balaklava. For this latter purpose the cavalry was kept perpetually on the alert.

On 14 October, Sir Colin Campbell,* a brigadier in the Highland Division, was placed in command of the defences of Balaklava. Until that date, Lucan, much senior in rank to Campbell, had been entrusted with these, such as they were. Campbell was willing to serve under Lucan, but it was said that Raglan did not trust Lucan to defend the port, so Campbell was given a separate command. The two men in fact co-operated very well.

Beside some large guns placed immediately above the harbour, the resources devoted to its defence consisted of the British cavalry, with a troop of Royal Horse Artillery, some 500 men of the 93rd Foot (later part of the Argyll and Sutherland Highlanders), one battery of foot artillery and about 2,500 indifferent Turkish infantry. These last were stationed in the forward defences, which consisted of redoubts constructed on six high points along the Causeway Heights on the crest of which ran the vital Worontzoff road. In

---

* Sir Colin Campbell (later 1st Baron Clyde) KCB, KSI (1792–1863); son of a Glasgow carpenter; ensign, 1808; served with distinction in the Peninsular War; lieutenant-colonel, 1832; major-general, 1854; commanded the Highland Brigade, under the Duke of Cambridge, at the Alma; succeeded the Duke in command of the 1st Division, 1854; returned home (see p. 135), 1855; Commander-in-Chief, India, 1857–60; suppressed the Mutiny; General, 1858; Field-Marshal, 1862.

the four most easterly of these redoubts had been placed nine 12-pounder position guns.

On the evening of 24 October a spy had reported that an attack was imminent. Raglan merely acknowledged the message, and took no further action. He saw no reason to exhaust his overworked infantry, as he had done four days previously when a similar report had proved untrue, by marching them down from the trenches before Sebastopol and back again next morning. This time, however, the report was true.

At 5 a.m. on 25 October General Liprandi, a Russian commander of high reputation, moved forward with some 25,000 men and 78 guns from the direction of Tchorgun to attack the redoubts.

The British cavalry had turned out, as they had done for many mornings past, an hour before dawn. On approaching the right-hand redoubt (no. 1) the prearranged signs that the enemy was advancing were seen. In a few seconds these signals were confirmed by the Turks in that redoubt opening fire. To this, the Russian artillery accompanying the assaulting infantry, at once replied. The battle of Balaklava had begun.

Hodge's diary entry, though almost the longest for the year, is confined to the barest essentials. It starts thus:

> **25 October.** The Russians in great force attacked the outposts and forts garrisoned by the Turks, who were quickly turned out with a loss of 9 guns.

In fact the Turks, opposed by at least ten times their number, put up an heroic resistance which gave the allies more than an hour's invaluable breathing space. After suffering 170 casualties, they were driven from the first three redoubts. The Russians now poured infantry into these, and brought up to them a number of field-pieces. All this time Lucan could do nothing but make threatening demonstrations whilst falling back before the slowly advancing Russians, and ordering his horse artillery to try to reply to their much bigger guns.

On Sir Colin Campbell's advice, Lucan soon withdrew to the left, so as to be out of the line of fire of both the Russian guns and the 93rd, and in a position to attack the flank of the Russians should they charge the Scottish infantry. This now happened.

> Their cavalry attacked the 93rd, who received them with a volley, and turned them.

Thus, succinctly, does Hodge describe the successful action of Campbell's 'thin red streak' (converted by Newbolt into the famous 'thin red line'). The 'left column' of Russian squadrons which attacked Campbell was only a small part of Liprandi's mounted arm, perhaps 400 in number. Almost immediately after its defeat,

> a large body of cavalry came into the plain and were charged by the Greys and the Inniskillings. We were in reserve, and I brought forward our left and charged these cavalry in flank. The Greys were a little in confusion and retiring when our charge settled the business. We completely routed the hussars and cossacks, and drove them back.

A more pithy description of the charge of the Heavy Brigade does not exist. The 'large body of cavalry' numbered about 2,000. As it had advanced along the North Valley, Campbell and Lucan could not see it because the Causeway Heights intervened, nor could the Russian horsemen see the British. Thus it happened that when, before long, the Russians wheeled to the left and began to cross the heights, they found themselves very close to part of the Heavy Brigade, to the surprise of both sides.

What had happened was that Raglan up on the Sapouné Heights, at least half an hour's ride distant, and able to see all that was taking place in the plain, had despatched an order to Lucan which had the effect of removing the cavalry as far west as possible to await the arrival of the infantry (which had, of course, been sent for the moment the battle started). There now arrived a second order which desired Lucan to detach eight of his ten squadrons of heavies towards Balaklava to support the wavering Turks. By the time this order was received the Turks had long since fled. Lucan nevertheless, in compliance with the order, ordered Scarlett to march westwards. This he duly did, in open column of troops with the 5th Dragoon Guards leading, and the Greys and the Inniskillings following. Hodge, with the 4th, was ordered to follow, while the two squadrons of the Royals were left behind.*

---

*Kinglake states that the men of the 4th 'had been advancing with their swords in their scabbards. . . . Colonel Hodge, I believe, had a theory that the practice of marching with drawn swords was only fitted for peace-time.' (Kinglake, A. W. *The Invasion of the Crimea*. . . . V, (6th ed.), 145.)

Scarlett's squadrons were threading their way through vines and orchards when Lieutenant Alexander Elliot,* one of his A.D.C.s, happened to 'cast a glance', in Kinglake's graphic words, 'towards the ridge on his left, and saw its top fretted with lances. Another moment and the sky-line was broken by evident squadrons of horse.'¹ Elliot pointed these out to his chief, whose short-sightedness made him at first doubtful. When he had been convinced, he decided at once to charge.

Before he could do so, some time-consuming manoeuvres were necessary, not only connected with wheeling into line, but also with avoiding a vineyard wall. When these had been completed, the squadrons calmly went about their business of dressing, their officers supervising with their backs to the enemy.

The Russian commander, when he first topped the ridge and saw the Heavies, took ground to his left (possibly to avoid the vineyard wall). He then resumed his advance down upon Scarlett—but for only a short distance before he came to a halt. He then ordered the prolongation to his right and to his left of his first two ranks, providing thereby two all-enveloping pincer arms.

Meanwhile, when he was satisfied that all was ready, Scarlett himself led off, riding well ahead. He and his staff then forced their way into the centre of the Russian mass, who were either still halted or advancing at a walk, and were well enfolded by the enemy cavalry before the Greys and one squadron of the Innskillings (Tennyson's 'three hundred') had picked their way over the pegs, ropes and vines in their path, and had come, in their turn, to grips with the enemy.

At the moment of impact the extended Russian wings began to close in from both flanks. While this was happening the remaining seven British squadrons came successively into action, all within a few moments of each other.

From the left rear of the Greys, the 5th Dragoon Guards charged into the main mass of the enemy. Into the inward-swinging Russian left wing charged the 1st squadron of the Inniskillings,

---

*Alexander James Hardy Elliot, KCB (1825–1909), grandson of 1st Earl of Minto. He had served with distinction in the Bengal Light Cavalry and in responsible administrative positions, until ill-health forced him to leave India, and start at the bottom in the British army. Lieutenant, 5th Dragoon Guards, 1850. Elliot painted the picture of the Charge of the Heavy Brigade used on the dust-jacket of this book.

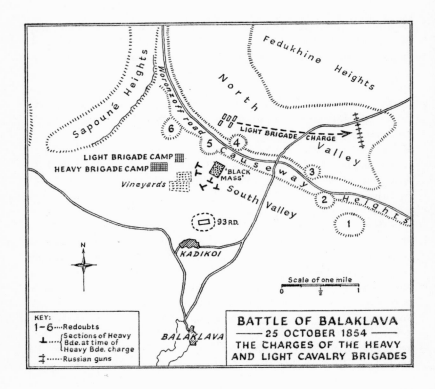

which had been the leading squadron of the brigade column at
the time of the surprise.

A little later, the 4th Dragoon Guards entered the fray.* Writing
to Hodge ten years later, Captain Forster who commanded the
regiment's 1st or Right Squadron, remembered that 'when we
moved down by the side of the vineyard to attack the Russians, we

---

* In a memorandum book which Hodge kept in 1855, occurs the following:
   'On the 25th of October, 1854, at the Battle of Balaklava, the 4th Dragoon
Guards had mounted in the Field:

2 Field Officers	Lt-col Hodge, Major Forrest
4 Captains	Captains Forster, McCreagh, Webb, Robertson
4 Subalterns	Lt McDonnel, Fisher, Muttlebury, Deane
202 N.C. Officers and Men	
also: 1 Surgeon,	Dr Pine.'

were in column of troops or squadrons left in front. At the bottom of the vineyard where we wheeled to the left, we were certainly in column of troops, as I remember perfectly your ordering me, when my squadron had passed through some broken ground at the end of the vineyard, to front-form my squadron, and charge immediately on the flank of the Russians, and that you would bring up the second squadron after me.'[2]

General Richard Dacres (brother of Captain Sydney Dacres), who 'saw it all from the Hill' (i.e. the Sapouné Heights) told Hodge's mother that 'the 4th came up at a very slow trot, till close to [the enemy], when they charged them in flank at a gallop and sent them to the right about. It was well and nobly done and Edward showed himself every inch a soldier by the way he did it, and got much commendation for the same.'[3]

Major Forrest, the regiment's second-in-command, thought that the pace at which the 4th charged was 'little better than a trot; but', he wrote home two days later, 'we had very bad ground to advance over, first thro' a vineyard, and over two fences, bank & ditch, then thro' the Camp of the 17th [Lancers], & we were scarcely formed when we attacked, & had but very little ground to charge over. Still we did not go in at so good a pace as we might have done. Once in, we did better, but the confusion was more than I had expected. The men of all regiments were mixed & we were a long time reforming.'[4]

Forrest's thoughts 'just as we were in the act of charging', were of his wife. 'When once in amongst them', he later wrote to her, 'I scarcely saw anybody—that is to recognize them. One could not look about much until the Russians began to run.'[5]

Kinglake,* who discussed the whole matter at some length with Hodge in 1866, wrote that, after giving his orders to Forster, 'Hodge went on in person with his left squadron; and soon, both that and Forster's squadron were wheeled and formed up with their front

---

* Alexander William Kinglake, MP (1809–91); barrister, 1837; published *Eothen*, 1844; accompanied St Arnaud's flying column in Algiers, 1845; went to the Crimea as an observer and witnessed the battle of the Alma. Lady Raglan asked him to write the history of the campaign up to her husband's death; the resulting work in eight volumes, *The Invasion of the Crimea*, appeared between 1863 and 1887. He and Hodge had been at Eton together. (See p. xiii).

towards the enemy's right flank. The operation by which the whole
regiment thus fronted to its right with each squadron at once in its
place, was made easy and quick by the circumstance that it had
been moving "left in front".

'The enemy made a hasty endeavour to cover the flank thus threatened by an evolution from the rear of his masses; but the troops
which he moved for the purpose were too late to complete their
manœuvre, and Colonel Hodge had the satisfaction of seeing that
although Russian horsemen engaged in this attempt were inter-
posing themselves between him and the flank of the column, they
might be struck in the midst of their effort by the charge of his
4th Dragoon Guards.

'In the days of his boyhood when Hodge steered the *Victory,* there
used to be a terse order which readily came to his lips as often as
the boat crossed the river; and now when he had come to be so
favoured by Fortune as to find himself at the head of his regiment
with no more than a convenient reach of fair galloping ground between him and the flank of the enemy's column, the remainder of
the business before him was exactly of such kind as to be expressed
by his old Eton word of command. What yet had to be done could
be compassed in the syllables of: "Hard all across."*

'. . . Having burst his way into the column, [Hodge] was driving
fast through it from flank to flank—driving through it without losing
men—and so faithfully working out the old precept of "hard all
across!" as to be already on the point of emerging from the mass of
the Russian cavalry at a spot opposite to the one by which he had
entered it.'[6]

Both Hodge and Forster, at this stage, made efforts to get their
squadrons into order again, 'Seeing some Russians assembling in
force on our left front,' wrote Forster, 'I tried to get some of our
men to rally and reform.'[7] Of Hodge's attempt to rally his men,
Kinglake says: 'Almost at the instant of emerging from the depths
of the column—he came out of it panting and vehement as though
fresh from violent bodily effort—Colonel Hodge had laid his commands on the two first trumpeters he could see, and caused them
to sound the rally.'[8]

---

*The direction given by the steerer to the crew of an Eton longboat when
about to cross the river. [Kinglake's footnote.]

Lucan in his despatch, and elsewhere, claims to have ordered the 4th to effect the flank charge, but Hodge specifically refutes the claim. 'I do think', he wrote to his mother on 6th December, 'that Lord Lucan might as well have given me the credit of our flank charge, and not have told such a falsehood about it in saying that he ordered it, when he never gave any orders to us at all.' On 10 April, 1855, he told his mother that the flank charge 'was quite my own idea'.

The Royals, though left in reserve, seem to have come forward, on their own initiative, following behind the 4th, and to have taken some small part in the action. Their Commanding Officer wrote that 'the Greys and Inniskillings did all, the 4th and 5th nothing more than us';[9] but, though it seems that the enemy horsemen began to break in places even before the 4th's flank charge, it was probably that charge, following closely on that of the 1st squadron of the Inniskillings on the right, which made sure of the total retreat of the enemy cavalry, only (according to Lucan) some eight minutes after Scarlett had first ridden into it.

There are conflicting accounts of the way in which both British and Russian horsemen actually fought in the *mêlée*. An officer who took part in the charge said 'it was just like a *mêlée* coming in or out of a crowded theatre, jostling horse against horse, violent language, hacking and pushing, till suddenly the Russians gave way'.[10]

The casualties on both sides were not very heavy. The heavies' swords, according to the Colonel of the Greys, were very defective. 'When our men made a thrust with the sword, they all bent and would not go into a man's body.'[11] There is evidence, too, that the Russian swords were also far from sharp. One of the four 'slightly' wounded troopers of the 4th Dragoon Guards had fifteen head cuts, 'none of which was more than skin deep'.[12]

It is impossible to say what the losses incurred in the charge amounted to. The Heavy Brigade's total casualties for the day were 10 killed and 98 wounded, but most of these were probably inflicted in passively supporting the Light Brigade later on. The Russians may have had 300 killed and wounded, but this figure is probably an exaggeration.

Hodge's diary continues:

They retired, and then Lord Raglan should have been satisfied. The Russians retired to a strong position, a valley with batteries on the heights in front and on each flank. There was a battery of 9 guns [in fact, there were probably eight]* in front of us, and a body of cavalry, and all these batteries on the heights [either side of the valley].

Lord Raglan ordered the light cavalry to charge these guns and cavalry. They did so in the most gallant manner, but at the sacrifice of nearly the Brigade. The guns played upon them at about 200 yards from the batteries in front and flank. They advanced, took the guns, and charged the cavalry, who met them well. They were so knocked to pieces by the guns that the cavalry overpowered them, and they were obliged to retire having lost in every regiment some two 3rds of their men and officers. We advanced to cover their retreat, but the batteries got our range and began cutting us up terribly. I was not sorry when we were ordered to retreat.

Except for the facile way in which the blame for it is unhesitatingly placed upon Raglan, this is a surprisingly accurate outline of the famous Charge of the Light Brigade. The truth is that the infantry coming down from the Sapouné Heights had been extremely dilatory. Had it not been so, Raglan would not have needed to employ the Light Brigade (the only troops available), to exert the slight pressure which he realised was all that was required, after the success of the Heavy Brigade, to force the enemy out of the three captured redoubts. Though his orders were not a model of clarity, it was much more Lucan's than his fault that the Light Brigade was sent off against the distant guns at the end of the valley, instead, as Raglan obviously intended, towards the redoubts.

Once the horrifying blunder had been made, Lucan slightly re-deemed himself by making what was undoubtedly a wise and courageous decision. As the Light Brigade went forward to its destruction, the Heavy Brigade followed it at some distance in support. In fact the Greys and the Royals, in the lead, suffered more casualities at this stage of the battle than during the Heavy Brigade's charge. Remarking that the heavies 'were sufficiently

---

*It is of interest that Hodge writes of nine guns, as most writers say that there were twelve. The figure of eight guns is arrived at after exhaustive research by the present editor into the accounts of the most reliable authorities and eye witnesses.

8. *A photograph by Roger Fenton of the camp of the 4th Dragoon Guards.*

9. *Heavy Cavalry Troopers at Varna, 1854. Sketch by Général Vanson.*

10. *Photograph by Roger Fenton of Colonel Hodge's hut and part of the camp of the 4th Dragoon Guards.*

11. *A watercolour by Simpkin, probably done from the photograph above.* (see page 102.)

close to protect the [remnants of the] Light Cavalry should they be pursued by the enemy' on their return, and that he 'could not allow them to be sacrificed as had been the Light Brigade', he ordered the heavies to halt.[13]

Hodge concludes his diary entry thus:

> The Russians did not follow, or quit their strong position, and we remained on the ground till 8 p.m., when we were ordered to return to our camp, and to go to the rear some two miles, which we did.
>
> Both my servants got brutally drunk, and I found them lying on their backs, and with difficulty I was enabled to save my baggage. I got up my bed in Forrest's tent and slept there.
>
> Our loss today was 1 killed (Ryan), 1 severely (Scanlan) [who died soon afterwards] and 4 slightly wounded.
>
> Many officers of the Light cavalry were killed, and a number slightly wounded. There were no infantry early in the morning, and when they did come they were not engaged. The light cavalry were murdered in doing work, when infantry should have been first engaged, and artillery were indispensable. A very fine, warm day.

After the charge of the Light Brigade, Raglan, it is believed, wished to re-capture the three lost redoubts. He certainly had to hand a sufficiently strong force of infantry to do so successfully; but Canrobert dissuaded him, on the grounds that to hold them it would be necessary to weaken the already inadequate force besieging Sebastopol.

The chief immediate result of the battle, therefore, was that the Woronzoff road was denied to the British for communication between base and siege camp. Neither Raglan nor Canrobert, it seems, fully appreciated the importance of the road. Without it only rough and sometimes precipitous tracks were available, and these were to form the bottleneck which so aggravated the cruel hardships of the winter ahead.

The moral effect of the charges of both cavalry brigades in the Battle of Balaklava was considerable. It is probable that, in Kinglake's words, 'for a long time afterwards it would have been impracticable to make the Russian cavalry act with anything like confidence in the presence of a few English squadrons'.[14]

E

26 October. I find my rascally servants not only got drunk, but they committed robberies upon the officers' stores. They have lost my tent, and I only wonder that I have any kit left. I am most uncomfortable with such blackguards as these about me. I am far from well today. I am much purged and griped.

Captain Methuen of the P. & O. Co's ship *Columbo* has kindly relieved me today of a black bag, large black valise and a Russian sword that I got in the fight yesterday. My baggage is still rather bulky, more than I like a great deal.

28 October. About 11½ p.m. last night we were alarmed by one of our pickets galloping in saying that there was a large body of cavalry advancing in the plain. We then heard guns in the direction of Balaklava, followed by musketry, and soon afterwards Captn Webb and his whole picket came in at full gallop to the camp in a most disgraceful manner. The whole of the cavalry turned out. I thought that the Russians were upon us, and we put out all the lights. The reports from the front showed all quiet, and Webb was sent out with his picket again, with positive orders not to return on any pretence.

At 3 p.m. we changed our camp, retiring more into the lines near Sebastopol. We are now quite on the top of this hill, very exposed to the wind and cold and a long way off from both wood and water. The whole cavalry Brigade are together.

29 October. I banked up my tent inside and out to try and make it warmer and drier.

The firing on the town has been languid all day. They say we are waiting for the French. I hope they will not wait long, as this cold wet weather is killing our horses. I know not how we shall stand it much longer.

30 October. The Major [Forrest] has insisted upon my taking up the messing from today again. I never saw any man who so much consulted his own comforts as he does and that in a purely selfish manner.

Webb has been before a Court of Inquiry. They acquit him, and say that he received orders to retire. I by no means acquit him. If he received orders to come in, he should have done so quietly skirmishing with the enemy, but in his case there was none to skirmish with.

This refers to Hodge's entry on 28 October (see above). Lucan, rightly it seems, agreed with Hodge in dissenting from the Court's finding. He issued an order in which he said Webb had conducted himself 'in a way to deserve the severest punishment that a General court martial can award. The Lieutenant-General feels that he is taking a great responsibility upon himself in not preferring charges against that officer. . . . It is true that Captain —— [Webb] alleges that he acted on the authority of a general officer: that officer denies ever having given any such authority; and, moreover, it should be well known to an officer of Captain ——'s standing, that the general could give no such authority; for a picket placed by a divisional general cannot receive orders from any inferior officer whatever, but solely from the divisional general himself, his staff, or the field-officer of the day.'[15]

Sent Bucknall to his duty for being drunk and being in danger of losing our baggage. I have taken Little, a young soldier, in his place.

31 October. The horses and effects of the officers who were killed in the action at Balaklava were sold today. They realized quite fabulous prices. I saw an old pair of warm gloves sold for 33/-.

3 November. At 2 I got an excellent dinner of hashed beef, onions and rice and sugar. Our rations are ample. We have nothing beyond it, and I think we live well.

Rode to the French lines and to the hill overlooking Sebastopol. They are within 100 yards of the batteries and their riflemen keep down the fire of the Russian works. In the French camp there was an appearance of plenty and comfort. They have brought wooden sheds for their Commissariat stores. They have ovens, and three times a week their men get bread. Their tents are walled round and they have good mats on the ground. Officers even are, in some cases, lying on the ground without bedsteads. Neither our officers nor theirs know how to encamp. A very fine day, warm sun.

I enjoyed my ride extremely, but I wanted a companion. I fear the Russians are in some force in front of our position, and as we have only Turks on our right who will run away and may plunder our camp, I want to move about half a mile to the rear, but I fear that obstinate mule Lord Lucan will not

do it. There is a sheltered valley close to water, and a little
wood in it.

4 November. Recommended Troop Sergeant Major Harran
to Lord Raglan for a cornetcy without purchase in the
regiment with a view of getting him the Adjutancy,
which Webb is quite unfit for, besides being absent in ill
health.

The Russians have received very large reinforcements, and
they say the Grand Duke Michael* is come. We have waited
too long. We shall scarcely save our army if they increase in
numbers in this way.

5 November. Under cover of a thick mist and fog the Russians
attacked our pickets in front of the 1st Division and in part all
along the line [the Battle of Inkerman]. We turned out without
any breakfast and remained sitting on our horses till after $12\frac{1}{2}$
o'clock. Lord Lucan then allowed us to go to our lines, but
before I had time to get anything I was ordered to take a
squadron of the 4th, one of the Greys and the Royal Dragoons
to the front in support of the Horse Artillery. We arrived when
the business was just over, and I met Lord Raglan, Genl
Canrobert, the Duke of Cambridge, &c. &c. coming in about
5 p.m. I ordered the Heavy Cavalry to return to their lines,
and Forster and myself rode to the field of battle. The sight was
dreadful. The ground was covered with dead and wounded
Russians, but very few dead English. I saw Genl Bosquet†
there, and one of his Zouaves‡ held our horses. A man of the
41st [Foot] took them from him, and carried them off, so we
had to trudge on foot to the camp of the Light Dragoons
where Mayow kindly lent us horses to ride home upon. Immediately sent the Provost Sergeant in search of our horses,
and about 2 a.m. he brought them in, minus my pistol and

---

* Mikhail Nikolaevich (1832–1909), 4th son of Nicholas I; became
commander-in-chief of the Russian cavalry in 1881.
† Pierre Jean François Bosquet (1810–1861); commanded a division at the
Alma and with especial distinction at Inkerman; wounded in the assault on
the Malakoff, 8 Sep, 1855; senator and marshal, 1856.
‡ Zouaves: French light infantry recruited, originally, from the Algerian
Kabyle tribe of Zouaoua. Their uniform is peculiar. It consists of gaiters,
very baggy trousers, short and open-fronted jacket, and a tasselled cap or
turban.

canteens. Still I feel most grateful to the Lord for the recovery
of my horse, my entire kit, cloak, blue coat and sheepskin
being on the horse.

6 November. After dinner I rode to the 41st's camp and there
I found out the man who had carried off our horses, and from
him I recovered the greater part of my things. [Hodge
nowhere says what happened to this man.]

7 November [*Letter*]. A severe lesson the Russians got [at
the Battle of Inkerman on 5 November], but the loss they have
inflicted upon us is, I fear, very great, especially amongst
the officers. The Duke of Cambridge showed me the sleeve of
his coat, which had been torn by a musket ball. He is always
very civil to me somehow.

I rode to the front today. The sight of the field of battle was
very dreadful; the dead and wounded Russians were very
numerous. Their soldiers are well clothed and armed, and have
fought with great bravery. I thought that the cavalry we beat
back on the 25th of October met us very gallantly. Our loss is
put down at 96 officers, killed and wounded, and 2,000 men at
least *hors de combat*; that of the Russians at 10,000 at least,
they say.

At Inkerman the Russians, with very superior numbers, had tried
and failed to overwhelm the British right. The rocky, confined
nature of the ground made it impossible for cavalry to operate,
though the remnant of the Light Brigade was present, and for a
time under fire. The battle, which consisted largely of a series of
separate, heroically fought infantry combats, lasted eight hours. It
was the bloodiest slogging-match since Waterloo. Though the
Russians were everywhere repulsed with enormous casualties (which
they could well afford), the battle, from the Allies' point of view,
was negative. After it, there seemed even less hope of an immediate
storming of Sebastopol, particularly as over 2,000 of the army's
best men had been killed or wounded. It became certain after
Inkerman that the winter would have to be spent in the Crimea.

7 November. Our men were endeavouring to pick up the
Russian wounded below our position today, so the brutes
shelled them for their humanity. I do not like our position
here at all. The Russians are daily getting more numerous,

whilst we are getting daily weaker. I pray daily to God to preserve me from danger amongst these horrors.

At 9½ Lord Lucan had us all to his tent. He found fault in a most unreasonable manner with the dirty state of the men of the cavalry. He ordered us all to get our men's kits for them, and also pipe-clay and oil. It is no fault of ours that the men have no kit. They ordered us to leave all the valises on board the *Simla*, and many of the men have now been 5 weeks in the same clothes. They are too far from water to be able to wash either themselves or their clothes, and they are continually under orders to mount at a moment's notice. At 1 p.m. the Boots and Saddles sounded, and the men remained ready to mount till 3. They then had to go for water for their horses, and it was dark ere they returned. Now, what time have they had today?

10 November. The lines are a foot deep in mud and slush. The saddles are all lying in the middle of it, and Lord Lucan expects that under circumstances like these the men will turn out smart and clean.

Rode to the camp of the Second Division to see General Pennefather,* who was delighted to see me. He lives comfortably, and feeds his staff as a General Officer should do, not like that screw of a General of ours [Lucan] who does not even feed his own son [George, Lord Bingham, later 4th Earl of Lucan, who was an A.D.C. to his father].

11 November. Last night we had much drunkenness in the camp. The men have been paid some money and this is the only use they have for it.

13 November. The state of our camp is beyond anything beastly. The mud is a foot deep all round the horses. The rain beats into our tents. How man or horse can stand this work much longer I know not.

---

*Sir John Lysaght Pennefather, GCB (1800–1872); cornet, 7th Dragoon Guards; commanded 1st Brigade, 2nd Division (Sir De Lacy Evans) at the Alma. At Inkerman, Evans being ill and absent till late in the battle, Pennefather commanded the division with great bravery and skill. He succeeded to command of the division later in the month; general, 1868.

He was much respected by officers and men in the Crimea. In January, 1855, Forrest wrote: 'Poor old Pennefather, who is now ill, is about the best man in command out here.'

I was very unwell from diarrhoea all last night. I wish I had my £12,000* safe in my pocket, and that I was safe in a good lodging in foggy, murky London.

14 November. About 7½ a.m. it began to blow a hurricane from the North West which blew down nearly all the tents in the brigade. About 9, mine went, the pole smashing in two pieces. I had taken the precaution to pack up all my things, my bedding excepted. That I covered with a waterproof cover. It blew fearfully, and the snow and sleet came down in showers. Everything that could be blown away was blown away. The miserable horses got nothing all day. Nothing could be got for them, or given to them if got. The lines are knee deep in mud and slush. I lay under the canvas of my tent, which rolled and flapped about in a dreadful manner, till near 4. It snowed most of the time. At 6½, the doctor who had got his tent up, invited me in there, which I accepted, and after eating a dry biscuit and drinking a glass of raw rum, I lay down in

---

*This figure must be merely a rough estimate. On a preliminary page of his 1855 diary volume, Hodge, writing towards the end of that year, states: 'My commissions have cost me as follows:

	£
Cornetcy	[blank]
[Hodge was given his first rank free (see p. xiv). If he had had to buy it, it would have cost him £840.]	
Lieutenancy	350
over for do. [This means the sum of money which Hodge paid, over and above the official price]	250
Troop [This means the command of a Troop with the rank of Captain]	2035
over for do.	1200
Majority	1350
over for do.	1435
Lieut-Colonelcy	1600
over for do.	1400
	——————
	9620

(£4285 over)

'By the War Office Warrant dated 23 Octr, 1855, if I am killed or die of my wounds within 6 months of receiving them, my mother or sisters will receive £6,175 [the full *regulation* price of his lieutenant-colonelcy; i.e. £9,620, in the above table, less £4,285 overpayments, plus £840 (being the value of his free cornetcy)]. The absolute loss therefore will be reduced to £4,445 [£6,175 subtracted from £9,620 (the total amount paid for his commissions) is, in fact, £3,445. Hodge may have made a slip of the pen here], which I shall have paid the country for graciously allowing me to serve her.'

my clothes on some sacks, and with my wet cloak over me. I went to sleep but the violence of the wind made me fear every moment that it [the tent] would come down. The rain beat against it all night. I think I have never passed a more miserable day in all my life. A few of these will be as good as a victory to the Russians.

15 November. The troops were not turned out today, and very luckily, too, for I do not think they could have gone out. Their state was miserable. We lost two horses during the night and this morning many men went to the hospital quite paralyzed with cold, and seriously ill.

The roads around are in a fearful state. We are getting very short of supplies, and to add to our mishaps, 11 transports loaded with stores, all the winter clothing for the troops, and, we hear, £200,000 in money, are gone to the bottom.

The greatest single loss in the catastrophic storm of 14 November was the screw-steamer *Prince* which was smashed up on the rocks in the outer anchorage. With her went to the bottom 'everything that was most wanted',[16] including boots for almost the whole army, and 40,000 greatcoats. Even before the 'Great Storm', as it became known, Mr Filder, the Commissary General, had written to the Treasury to say that he was 'full of apprehension as to our power of keeping this Army supplied during the coming winter. . . . In this crowded little harbour . . . we can do little more than land sufficient supplies to keep pace with daily consumption. . . . To add to our difficulties, the road from the harbour to the camp, not being a made one, is impassable after heavy rains.'[17]

Now, after the storm, the supply problems were immeasurably increased.

Our position is indeed becoming most critical. A bloody battle, to perish by the cold or a Russian prison, now seem our only prospects. I like not our position, and most truly glad should I be to hear that war was at an end. I have passed many happy days in England, and truly thankful shall I be to God if he permits me to return once more to my own country and friends.

16 November. The *Retribution*, War Steamer, with the Duke of Cambridge on board, was nearly lost. He was, they say, in a fearful state of excitement.

The Duke had gone aboard the ship for a few days, so as to recover from the nervous strain of the battle of Inkerman. Cornet Fisher had heard that His Royal Highness 'was most undignified, and held the Steward's hands in his bewailing his fate, saying "Oh! Is it come to this? Oh! Oh! We shall be lost." '

> **18 November.** The state of Balaklava harbour is fearful. The wrecked ships present a dreadful appearance. The Horse Board sat [Hodge was President of it], and passed three of Lord George Paget's [horses]. He has taken himself home in a most extraordinary manner.

Paget, a younger son of the first Marquess of Anglesey, who had commanded the cavalry at Waterloo, was in command of the 4th Light Dragoons. He had led the second line of the Light Brigade in its charge on 25th October. He had married only a few days before leaving home, and now, foreseeing no further action for the cavalry, just went off back to his bride in England. This he did with Raglan's and Lucan's approval. They gave it readily enough as Paget had been on the point of leaving the army when his regiment had been ordered overseas, and now, when he got home, he intended to carry out his earlier intention. It is interesting, and perhaps typical of his unusually high sense of what was proper, that Hodge thought Paget's behaviour 'most extraordinary', for, according to a young subaltern of the 8th Hussars, although Paget 'was greatly snubbed at home, everyone here thought him a most sensible man for leaving when he was tired of it; but the English people are such fools'.[18] The weight of public opinion at home, however, was such that Paget felt bound to return to the Crimea. When he did so, he brought his wife with him. Numbers of other less well-known officers, with smaller excuse, remained at home uncommented upon.

> We are obliged to send in to Balaklava for all our grain for our horses. The Commissariat have nothing up here, and very little on shore. As soon as it is landed, they let us carry it off. The French have stores of all kinds. They have large herds of cattle and flocks of sheep roaming thro' the country. Both the Turks and the French are nearly hutted in, whilst we are without any means of doing it yet. At Lord Raglan's they have begun, and their horses are in stables even whilst we are in the open air.

Thank God for another fine day, dry and tolerably mild.
19 November. My hands are so sore and cracked and
chapped from working, and from dirt that I am in very great
pain, and I can hardly manage to write or to do anything, but
I thank God that my bodily health continues good, with the
exception of a slight dysentery at night, which I cannot get
over. I hear laughing and voices in the tents near me. I cannot
join them. I prefer the solitude of my own.
20 November. Remained in my tent nearly poisoned by a
sack of onions I have in it. We are obliged to keep our stores in
this way.

Read the burial service over Private Burbridge by the light
of a lamp. He died of cholera at 4 p.m. He was a terrible old
drunkard.
21 November. Looked over and divided a sack of onions by
way of a nice employment for a Lt-col. of cavalry. Looked
well round the troops. Found much fault with the carelessness
and dirty state of things. What with my Horse Board, my
regimental duties and my domestic duties, I have no time
for gadding about. I prepare all the meals of our mess, and
manage all that.
22 November [*Letter*]. Do not fear that I shall pinch myself.
I buy everything that I want and I have plenty of money. I
never keep much coin about me, and as we are paid in gold
every month, I remit to England all my surplus cash.

There is really *no arrangement* in any department, and
nothing but the fine chivalric feeling of our officers makes them
go through what they do, and the endurance of our men is
wonderful. Nothing has yet been done about hutting the
cavalry or putting us into winter quarters. They intend that we
should remain here [i.e. in the Crimea and not at Scutari for
the winter] and yet Lord Lucan does nothing. He is quite
unfit for his command, and he disgusts everyone with his
mulish obstinacy and his violent temper.
22 November. At night torrents of heavy rain, our men
soaked to the skin, and many of them have no dry things. The
horses in a dreadful state, the appointments ruined. We are
not even allowed to know upon what ground we are to be
hutted. There will soon be none to hut, sickness is fast doing
our work.

23 November. The roads in a terrible state. We have now been three days without hay, and we certainly shall not get any after this tremendous rain. Two horses more died last night. The tents all flooded. How we ever get a dinner cooked is a mystery to me.

24 November. The sick are lying in bell tents on the wet ground, and for all this I have spent my fortune! I wish I was well out of it. One man died today of fever brought on from cold, wet and exposure, and three more are dying.

26 November. Sunday. Employed all day, it being very fine, in trying to dry my clothes and the contents of my tent. I trust however I did not forget to spend one hour in a more proper manner.

27 November. I rode to call on Scarlett, who is hutted under ground [i.e. in a hut for which some excavation had been made]. Wrote to Eleanor [his sister]—sent her some hair. Mine is getting thin and very grey.

28 November. I begin to despair of things now, and I see no hopes of our ever returning home. Our arrangements are all so bad that we cannot get orders or even information as to what they intend doing with us this winter. It is rather late to begin building huts now. The wood is getting terribly scarce and I am sure our men have neither time nor ingenuity to build them.

29 November. Off at daybreak to post the videttes, the roads so bad I could hardly struggle thro' the mud. I found several commissariat carts broken down upon the road, one had a barrel of rum in it, which had been tapped, and drunken infantry soldiers were lying about in every direction, also many men of the Greys on picket were drunk. Some miserable re-cruits of the 97th [Foot] just landed were struggling up the muddy hill, having been prevented going any further by sheer inability to proceed. They had been all night trying to move up but could not proceed they were so overloaded and weak.

30 November. Rode into Balaklava. The roads in a frightful state of mud. They are still landing heavy guns, a useless thing as they never can get them to the front.

On board the *Columbo*, where I got a lunch of fresh bread and cold mutton. What a luxury after my salt pork and biscuits! Bought a ham too.

Lord Lucan tells me they think of moving us into Balaklava.
It looks a perfect pest house. It swarms with sick Turks and the
harbour is in a horrid state of filth.

1 December. I had on duty today: 1 subaltern and 30 men
& horses, on outlying picket till 12; 1 subaltern and 40 men
& horses, on inlying picket, ditto; 1 subaltern and 30 men and
60 horses down in Balaklava, all soaked.

'Our men', wrote Major Forrest next day, 'are suffering very much
from diarrhoea, rheumatism, numbness of the lower extremities
from the constant wet and cold—severe coughs, &c. The infantry
suffer to a greater extent.'[19]

4 December. Had to send an officer and 8 men today to fetch
the mail bags, which the French had brought to Chersonese
[near Cape Kherson]. Amongst other things there was a large
marquee pole and all for Prince Edward of Saxe-Weimar,*
which they could not convey.

5 December. The cavalry are quite *hors de combat*. They are
utterly done for.

6 December [*Letter*]. We have moved away from our very
exposed, cold camp, and I have got the regiment in a snug
valley near Balaklava. The truth was that we could not any
longer feed the horses where we were. The animals themselves
were so weak they would not struggle up the hill with the sacks
of corn. The condition of everything is awful; weather makes
no difference, the horses are always out. They stand knee deep
in mud, and frequently die from being suffocated in it. Some
12 a night generally die in the Brigade, and you cannot form
any conception of what the men are. Their clothing is nothing
but mud-stained rags. They have not time to wash, and are
so far from water that they cannot go to it, and having no
utensils to convey water in, their condition is horrible. I assure
you that I am obliged sometimes to go two days without

---

*Prince Edward of Saxe-Weimar, KP, GCVO, GCB (1823–1902) was
brought up by his aunt, Queen Adelaide. He was a playfellow of Queen
Victoria and of George, 2nd Duke of Cambridge. Ensign, 1841; served with
3rd battalion, Grenadier Guards in the Crimea. He was wounded in the
trenches in October, and later distinguished himself at Inkerman. In June,
1855, he became A.D.C. to Raglan. General, 1879; Field-Marshal, 1897. In
1851, Prince Edward married, morganatically, a daughter of the 5th Duke
of Richmond and Gordon.

washing, even my hands. The violence of the rain and wind has sometimes been such as to prevent my sending for water beyond a sufficiency for my coffee, or to boil our ration of pork in.

I saw George Mayow today, looking very well indeed. He is of course delighted at Lord Cardigan's going away.

A medical board had recommended that Cardigan 'be allowed to proceed to England' as he was suffering from dysenteric diarrhoea and 'difficulty in voiding his urine'.[20]

6 December. The confounded French drums and bugles come and practice in our valley. The noise is frightful.

7 December. They find fault with us, and say that we have not done our duty. It is a lie. We have all done the utmost we could, but the cavalry have been sacrificed and neglected, exposed to wet and cold on the tops of high hills during the most tremendous and tempestuous weather.

8 December. I continue to like our new camp. It is sheltered, and we have not lost a horse since we came down to it.

9 December. Went early into Balaklava, and I brought out a large box of things, some of them most exorbitantly dear: ham 2/2 a pound, butter 2/- a pound, a small North Wilts cheese 15/-, brandy 5/- a bottle, and all in this exorbitant way.

The French are repairing the road and doing it very well indeed. Their men have not the dirty, squalid look that all ours have. All our men look famished and dirty to a degree.

The French have set us a grand example. They have put a whole regiment upon the roads, and in a few hours they have managed to make a vile slough into a passable road. Lord Raglan should see this, but he never leaves his fireside, and knows, I believe, but little of the state of his army.

This was not, of course, true. It was, nevertheless, the general feeling to an increasing degree amongst the officers, though less so amongst the men. Raglan quite often rode about the camps, but since he was greatly embarrassed by the cheers the soldiers gave him when he was recognised, he seldom rode out with more than a single A.D.C., and both would be dressed in the most inconspicuous and unmilitary clothes. Indeed he was on occasions mistaken for a civilian gentleman come out from England to see the fun.

10 December. Lord Lucan assembled all of us COs to inform us that we might hut ourselves in, and try and endure a winter, as here we are to remain. Now, as we have neither men, timber or tools, I cannot see how we are to do this.

11 December. Remained in camp all day, writing to endeavour to obtain the promotion to these augmentation troops of the officers and N.C. Officers of my regiment.

The addition of two Troops had been ordered in November. This was, of course, a paper affair for the moment; but regiments at home were told to raise and train men and horses for the regiments in the Crimea, so as to realise the new establishment as soon as possible in 1855.

12 December. Cooper built us up a famous kitchen today, far too good for the victuals that we have to cook in it.

Was ordered with all other COs to attend Lord Lucan, who informs us that we are to give 500 horses a day to carry the provisions of the infantry to the front. This, then, is to be our end. We are to be carriers to the Commissariat department, and then, when all our men's things are destroyed, saddlery gone, and horses killed, they will tell us that we have neglected our regiments. It is too dreadful to think about.

13 December. Rode to Lord Raglan's to see Col Gordon [Hon Alexander Gordon, Assistant Quartermaster-General, a son of Lord Aberdeen] about getting wood for hutting. He told me that there was none for the officers, that the work must be done by ourselves, and we must find our own transport. This is an impossibility as we have now to carry up the provisions for the army in the front, for which purpose 120 horses and sixty men went today, besides 10 for our own forage, 4 for stores.

14 December. Rode into town to enquire about wood for building a hut, but I could get but little satisfaction. Bought some biscuits and figs, also a pair of blue overalls, and a suit of waterproof things for my servant.

18 December. Rode into Balaklava. The town in a frightful state of mud. I never can do anything when I am there. There is no finding anyone, and the place is so dirty and crowded.

It may appear strange that Hodge had so much spare time. He seems always to be going to Balaklava for provisions for the officers' mess, and for things for himself. Forrest, his second-in-command and now a lieutenant-colonel by brevet, explains this leisure thus: 'The subalterns have hardish work, as one of them has to accompany the party [taking provisions to the front] from each regiment, and one has to accompany another party that goes to fetch the forage. Field officers and captains have very little to do now, as they are not on duty [as Field Officer of the Day] more than once in 8 or 9 days. We have seldom any "stables" to go to, as our horses are employed all day.'[21]

Saw a Gazette in which I see I am a full Colonel of October 12th, on account of having commanded a regt for 3 years.

Writing to his mother on 28th December, Hodge says: 'The danger of being a full Colonel is that it is now in the power of the Commander-in-Chief to make a Major-General of one at any time. I do not suppose that this will occur. If it did, goodbye to my money.' Under the purchase system, which was not abolished till 1871, an officer on promotion to Major-General lost the value of his commission once and for all.
When Scarlett was promoted to Major-General in January, 1855, Hodge commented that he lost thereby 'all his money. He has, however, married a rich wife, and will not feel this.'*

20 December. Began digging out my stable. I look upon this as a hopeless job. I have no labourers. The French made a strong reconnaissance with cavalry and infantry this day in front of our position. We have none to send.

This French sortie occasioned a comment from Captain Shakespear of the horse artillery: 'I must say', he wrote home, 'it was rather humiliating to the British Cavalry on the 20th to see the French Cavalry pass in front of Balaklava and reconnoitre the enemy.'[22] Considering how degrading the role of purveyor to the infantry

---

* An officer who wished to stay in the army, but did not like to risk losing the value of his commission by death, or promotion to Major-General, was able to exchange with an officer on half-pay who wanted to sell out. He received the official difference between the full-pay and the half-pay commissions. For a Lieutenant-Colonel in the cavalry of the line, the difference was £1,533. The seniors of each junior rank who benefited by obtaining a step in rank, would then club together to give the full-pay officer the remaining money which he would have received had he sold out. Hodge was in fact placed on half-pay in 1859.

must have been for the proud British cavalry, both officers and men, seeing the inescapable necessity for it, took the affront to their dignity with resignation, if not with a good grace. Lucan, as was his duty, protested. In mid-January, not for the first time, he represented to headquarters 'the fearful consequence to the cavalry of having to continue in the discharge . . . of duties so totally foreign to their profession. . . . Since the 12th December, no less than 426 horses have died [in the Division]. . . . A cessation of these duties . . . might yet . . . save 400 or 500 or more.'[23]

The method generally used for conveying the provisions was for one horse to be ridden by a man, who led another horse carrying the supplies. There were no pack-saddles available. Had there been, 'nearly double' the weight which the ordinary regimental saddle was capable of bearing, could have been carried.[24]

> **21 December.** A sortie was made from Sebastopol upon our trenches last night and the sentries bayonetted. They were all asleep. This is the second time this has happened. Our men are overworked, and only half fed.

Such incidents as these well illustrate how much better off were the cavalry than the infantry, especially after they had moved down to within a mile or two of Balaklava. They, at least, were not killed off in their hundreds by exposure, gross over-work and under-nourishment. 'We have every reason to be thankful', wrote a sergeant-major of the Royals, 'that our lot is not so bad as the poor infantry in the trenches.'[25]

Hodge nowhere mentions that Christmas is approaching. This is unlike him, for he normally refers to all important religious feasts. It shows, perhaps, how depressed and preoccupied he was at this time. Forrest, on the other hand, tells his wife on 22 December: 'Our camp is beginning to present a quite Christmas appearance as far as eating is concerned. Paddy Webb has got a turkey tied by the leg to his tent. Briggy* has got a couple of geese fastened up in the same fashion.'

In the same letter, Forrest records that 'the little Colonel', as he often calls Hodge, was robbed 'of a lot of his little shirts, etc., on board the *Simla,* where he left a bag of things. The stores [at

---

* Captain George C. H. P. Brigstocke; joined the regiment in 1850; retired, September, 1855.

12. A page from William Simpson's sketchbook.

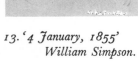

13. '*4 January, 1855*'
    William Simpson.

14.   '*Cavalry Camp, 9 July, 1855*'
                    William Simpson.

15.   *The Railway from Balaklava to Kadikoi.* Illustrated London
                    News, *24 March, 1855.*

Balaklava] are shamefully plundered by Turks and all sorts of vagabonds, as we cannot afford men enough to furnish the necessary guards, and though there are now some mounted police there, they do not appear to be very efficient. They seem to think more of looking like soldiers than of acting like constables.

'The little Colonel requests me to tell you that he hopes you will call upon his mother. . . . He is pretty well now, but has lost flesh. He grew thinner when in Bulgaria and his illness reduced him still more, and he has never picked up flesh again.'[26]

> **23 December.** My hair is getting so thin, it is quite uncomfortable. My dear mother is sending to me a fur coat at £15. 15.
>
> I find that the government are about to issue us coats of sheepskin, also gloves and woollen things. Likewise clothing for our horses.

The men, according to Forrest, writing six days previously, had 'within the last few days all received woollen jerseys, which are a great comfort to them. They were given drawers at the same time, but they are so absurdly small that they are useless for any of our men, as are also the greater part of the boots, and from the same cause, more particularly as our men are suffering much from swollen feet and legs.'[27]

> **24 December.** A dreadfully rainy day, snow and sleet, and with all this much firing and fighting at Sebastopol. We are still months from taking that place, if ever.
>
> **25 December.** Called on the Colonel of the Zouaves to ask for some men to build me a hut. I hope he may grant me this favour. I am making no progress in hutting my horses.

Hodge makes no mention of the fact that it is Christmas Day. Forrest wrote home that evening saying that the men were in great heart and singing lustily. 'I was amused', he added, 'at hearing poor little Hodge say to himself with a huge sigh: "Ah, I wish I was in spirits to sing like those fellows!" He, Hodge, gets very much down in the mouth sometimes, and he has a habit of thinking aloud, and my tent being next to his, I am made an involuntary deposit for all his thoughts. I frequently tell him of it, and he says, "I believe I do always think aloud and talk to myself. I always used to

F

do so in my barrack room, and living so much alone I have got into the habit of it." [28]

> **26 December.** A very sharp frost last night. We had to send today 60 horses to the 4th Division to bring down their sick men. 400 horses in all were sent. About 300 sick were brought down to Balaklava, and on their arrival there were no preparations. They did not even know that they were coming. The want of management in all that concerns this army is truly lamentable.

In a letter written in the middle of January, Forrest describes what this harassing duty entailed. 'The only means of transporting the poor fellows from the front down to Balaklava, is upon Troop horses. One of our officers went in charge of one of these parties a few days since. The day was bitterly cold. When he arrived at the Division to which he was ordered to go, he found that the Medical Officer had received no intimation of the intended removal of the sick. Consequently there was great delay before the different cases could be selected for removal, and when they at last started, these poor fellows had no extra clothing, beyond a blanket to wrap round them, and many of them had no shoes. They were altogether in a most pitiable state: many of these poor fellows actually crying—men who probably had fought at Inkerman. One man was obliged to be left in another hospital upon the road, and another was put into the boat in a dying state.'

Two days later he 'met the sick and wounded being brought into Balaklava. A more distressing sight there could not be. To my feelings it was much more horrible than the battlefield of Inkerman. Many of these poor fellows were scarcely able to sit on the horses, but were leaning down with their heads resting upon the horses' necks. The road was like a sheet of ice, and though our men led the horses of the most helpless, yet occasionally a horse would slip and fall. One poor creature's foot caught in the stirrup and he would have been dragged, but that I caught hold of the horse's head. The poor man wanted to walk the rest of the way, but he could not have walked 300 yards, so we had to lift him on to the horse again.'[27]

> Bought two turkeys on board the *Cormorant*. Gave 8/- each for them.
>
> **27 December.** Our picket now comes into camp at night, a

sensible arrangement. Rode into Balaklava. Bought a pair of boots for £2. Just the things I want. They call them waterproof. That we shall see to.

28 December [*Letter*]. I hear of many ships having arrived with parcels on board for me. You will hardly credit that I am writing with my tent wide open, and that I have had my hair cut in the open air today. The thermometer in my tent is now 45, and it is quite a May morning.

Now if Lord Raglan did right, he would send away to Scutari 8 out of the 10 regiments he has here, to save, if possible some of the horses, but he will not. He sits in a comfortable house, and has no idea that we are quite unprepared to face the cold that always comes in the beginning of the year. I know not what we shall do. We have no huts or stabling. Our men are employed from morning to night carrying provisions to the front and returning with sick men. The road is a ploughed field all the way for seven miles, and in the face of that that donkey General Airey [the Quartermaster-General]* expects us to house ourselves in. Last week 121 horses died from overwork and from exposure. The cavalry have been infamously treated and they want to throw the blame on us Commanding Officers. In the spring we shall have no men or horses if they go on as they do. In fact the army will be sacrificed. We commenced this siege too late and without the requisite means of transport. If they attempt a campaign in the spring without an organised waggon train and a better Commissariat we shall meet with fearful reverses.

The French are good fellows. They assist us in every way. They make our roads, carry our sick and wounded and even carry our shot and shell in their hands to the front. They deserve the greatest praise and the best of treatment from us. I hope the two nations will never again go to war. Their dress which you all despise is far better adapted to campaigning than ours. You can form no idea of what wretched objects our men

---

* Sir Richard (later 1st Baron) Airey, GCB (1803–1881); ensign, 34th Foot, 1821; lieut-col, 1838; military secretary to Lord Hardinge, when Commander-in-Chief, 1852; Quartermaster General, Horse Guards, 1855–65; Lieut-Gen, 1862. President of the 'Airey Committee' on the results of the short service system, 1879–80.

are in their tight coats. They cannot wear warm things under them.

It is shameful the way our things are being treated here. I saw a large barge yesterday full of boxes and packages for the army overset in deep water from carelessness. I only hope my fur coat &c. is not amongst them. Then I hear that 600 parcels belonging to officers were today landed from a steamer, and placed on the beach without cover or guard of any kind.

We all labour, either cut wood or dig out our stables or holes we are going to live in when the frost comes. Mine is not begun I regret to say. I intend trying to get some French soldiers. They are the best hands at these things. I must say I dread the approach of the cold weather. War is very fine to read about, but in the making of it, it is most unpleasant.

29 December. Dined with Lord Lucan. A scratch dinner, but he gave us some good mutton and excellent potatoes. I wish I was living in a house. Balaklava is worse than ever, mud of the most filthy kind is everywhere in the streets. There are plenty of shops, but all very dear, and lots of dead and dying Turks. I never go in without seeing one brought out. A fine day—mild.

30 December. In England they are making great exertions for us. Here they do nothing. Bought a case of sherry, 48/- a dozen. Far too dear. It is a great shame to take advantage of our necessities in the way they do.

31 December [*Letter*]. A medal is to be given I see for the Crimea and for Inkerman, but nothing is said about Balaklava. This will not do. We are determined to have justice done to us in this point. The despatch of Lord Raglan designated our charge as one of the finest ever made and certainly the survivors of the Light Brigade deserve a medal. We were all exposed to the cross fire of three redoubts or batteries and although Lord Raglan may not like Lord Lucan, they have no right to deprive us of our hard earned honours.

I am so much obliged for the newspaper with the Queen's Speech. It was the only one that came. I long to write to the Duke of Newcastle [Secretary of State for War] about the way that things are done here.

I want to get a wooden house as a hospital for my men, and though there are plenty in Balaklava, they will not give us one.

31 December. The last Sunday of the year, and how have I passed it? Not in prayer and contemplation, but in writing what are really requisite and official letters, also some private to my dearest mother. God preserve her in health. Also in manual labour, in cutting wood for fencing in my horses to keep them from the wind and cold.

If two years ago I had been told that at the end of 1854 I should be warring in the Crimea I could not have believed them. It is however a stern reality. Here we are. The weather, though not cold, is still sharp for a tent. Last night the snow fell fast, and all was white this morning, but the day was tolerably mild. I have many parcels of warm and waterproof things that have been sent from England, but the arrangements here are so bad we can get nothing. Certainly our prospects and position are not enviable. Many [of the men] are in the hospital suffering from scurvy, the effects of constantly eating salt provisions.

We are as far from taking Sebastopol as we were 2 months ago, indeed I think further from it. Lord Raglan deserves no credit for the conduct of the campaign, and as to his staff they are abominable. Nothing can be worse. He abuses the cavalry, and blames us for the state they are in, when it is all his fault.

God grant that I may return home once more, and spend the rest of my days in peace. I have begun war too late in life. I prefer my comforts. As to honor & glory, they are empty bubbles.

Chapter 4

1 January – 23 May 1855

'In the event of my dying', wrote Colonel Hodge at the beginning of his diary for 1855, 'this book is to be sent to my mother, Mrs Hodge, Sydenham, Kent. My horses and saddlery to be sold. *Everything else* to be sent home to the above address. Likewise the boxes that are in the store at Scutari addressed to me.'

His entry for New Year's Day strikes a gloomy note:

> **1 January.** The cavalry encamped in a valley near Balaklava; our horses in a miserable state from exposure to weather, overwork and always having to stand upon the cold wet ground. It is really shocking to see them.

We now have horses left	171
N.C. Officers and men fit for duty	180
Sick in hospital	32
Sick at Scutari or elsewhere	43
	255

> Went to the Colonel of the 27th French Infantry and asked him to allow some of his men to come and sink my tent for me. He was most civil, and granted it forthwith. His sappers are to come tomorrow.
>
> Employed my afternoon in cutting brushwood to shelter my horses.

Webb dined with us, and we had quite a good dinner: roast turkey, roast mutton and roly poly pudding, and sherry. Quite a feast.

2 January. They now refuse to give the officers any clothing for their horses, consequently our really valuable horses must perish for want of shelter, whilst Troopers not worth £10 in their present state are to be clothed. The cavalry officers are indeed infamously treated.

Lieutenant Wombwell of the 17th Lancers, complaining of the same injustice, wrote in his journal: 'When the authorities are spoken to about it, they answer, "The officers can buy clothing for their horses themselves. They can afford it." Now clothing is not to be bought or had for love or money.'[1]

3 January. Rode into Balaklava to try to obtain a box that I heard was there for me, found it and carried it out upon my horse. On opening it I found a large fur coat, a beautiful one, but too big for me, also a fine fur cap, gloves, &c., &c. The coat is too good. It cost £15.15.

'Little Hodge', wrote Forrest to his wife, 'says that you have done a more sensible thing than Mrs Hodge in sending a sheep-skin, instead of an expensive fur.' When Hodge's arrived, Forrest wrote: 'Little Benjamin got his box with his fur coat, etc. It is very much too large for the little man.'[2]

4 January. We have had a fearful night, hail, wind and much snow. I thought much of my poor horses all standing without shelter.

5 January. This morning the thermometer was at 24 in my tent. Sold my fur coat to Webb for £16; bought a Greco coat which will do me quite as well, and cost £2 10s. If this frost continues it will stop our journeys to the front. The horses can never do it.

6 January. My stable has so far got on that tonight my three horses were put under a sort of cover, and already the poor brutes seem better.

7 January. Thermometer 4 below freezing in my tent at 8 a.m. I walked into Balaklava to try and obtain my men's pea coats, which are hid away under sundry bales of goods and

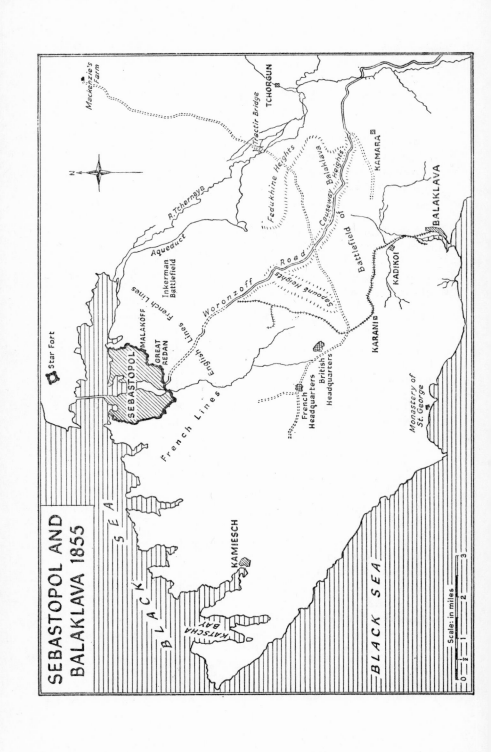

SEBASTOPOL AND BALAKLAVA 1855

Star Fort

Mackenzie's Farm

TCHORGUN

Tractir Bridge

R.Tchernaya

KAMARA

BALAKLAVA

Aqueduct

Fedukhine Heights

Causeway Balaklava

Battlefield of

Heights

KADIKOI

Inkerman Battlefield

MALAKOFF

Woronzoff Road

French Lines

Sapoune Heights

GREAT REDAN

SEBASTOPOL

English Lines

KARANI

French Headquarters

British Headquarters

French Lines

Monastery of St. George

B L A C K   S E A

KAMIESCH

KATSCHA BAY

B L A C K   S E A

Scale: in miles

0   ½   1   2   3

huts in the *Metropolitan* steamer. Tried all means, but could not get them.

The inadequacy of the wharves at Balaklava was chronic. They had a frontage of not more than 75 feet for the landing of everything needed by over 26,000 men. Later in the year further wharves and every sort of modern port facility were introduced.

There are hundreds of wooden huts, but we cannot get one.

Contracts for wooden huts had been entered into in England in the middle of November. They were real 'do-it-yourself pre-fabs'. The parts were 'so fitted that, with the aid of the printed directions and lithographed plans, which accompanied them, the whole might be put together, even by unskilled workmen.'[3] The first cargo of these arrived at Balaklava on Christmas Day. The trouble was that a single 25-man hut needed from 250 to 300 men to carry its parts up to the front, and, as Hodge wrote:

> The travelling is desperate. The whole country and the roads are nothing but frozen sludge.
>
> **8 January.** Lord Raglan for a wonder rode thro' our camp, and also into Balaklava. I hope he liked what he saw there. I suppose they have written to him from England to be more active, for this is the first time I have heard of his being out of his house. My stable all roofed in and finished and very comfortable I think it will be.
>
> **9 January.** Down to Balaklava and on board the *Sans Pareil* to dine and sleep. Lieutenant Anderson, who invited me, swung a cot outside his cabin door, but there were about 100 sailors sleeping all around me—not very pleasant companions. I found the heat and the smell of the ship most unpleasant, and wished myself back in my tent again.
>
> **10 January.** I got up unrefreshed from my frousty berth—a nasty cold rain was falling. Got the men's coats out of the *Metropolitan*. They are famous pea coats, really good and serviceable articles.
>
> **11 January.** Had to walk down to Lord Lucan's to answer a question about chopped straw. Really that man imagines that we have nothing to do! I lost my whole morning, and my temper, slipping and struggling through the mud and melted snow.

12 January. Sat in my tent writing all the morning with a
brazier of bad charcoal burning to keep my fingers warm.
They are dangerous things, though, in a small closed tent,
which however mine is not by day. 4 officers have died of them.

64 horses went to the front to get sick men. The frozen
ground has cut many of their legs. The sick men suffered
terribly. One man went quite mad from cold and pain, and
many nearly died from exhaustion.

14 January. Heard from my mother—God bless her. I hope
we may meet again. Oh, that this hard-hearted old Emperor
would die or make peace with us!

14 January [*Letter*]. *The Times* of the 23rd had an excellent
article about the state of things here, also a very good letter
from 'Our Own Correspondent' [W. H. Russell].* These
letters are not overdrawn and give a really true account of the
state of things here.

Russell's Crimean reports were frequently sensational, but they,
and his private letters to Delane, the editor, were sometimes used
by the latter to exaggerate the conditions in the army, as well as to
blacken, often unfairly, Raglan and his hard-pressed staff officers.
The Crimea was the first important war in which war correspon-
dents were active. They were despised by headquarters and no
sort of censorship was exercised. They could write, and their papers
publish, anything they liked. Delane and Russell, together, gave
out what would later have been considered highly secret information, gathered, often incorrectly, from junior officers in the course of
gossip. The paper itself once agreed that its articles had 'gone to the
verge of prudence' (7 Dec, 1854). Raglan, in May, 1855, wrote:
'The enemy at least need spend nothing under the head of Secret
Service.'[4]

My bed is very warm at night. I put my Regimental cloak,
a Greco coat, my sheepskin and two blankets to lie on, and then
I have two more blankets, a tweed wrapper, and a big blue

---

* (Sir) William Howard Russell (1820–1907); *The Times* correspondent in
Ireland, 1841 and 1843; special correspondent for *The Times* in the
Crimean campaign, 1854–5, in India during the Mutiny, 1858, and in
America during the Civil War, 1861–2; occasional correspondent for *The
Times* and *The Daily Telegraph*, from 1863 to the Zulu War, 1879.

coat over me. My head is supported by my valise, and by my clothes, laid so as to form a bolster. I have a small pillow and I really manage very well.

Our sufferings are nothing compared to the poor fellows at the front. What they are going through is dreadful. I hear that the men are quite reckless, and do not care whether they live or die.

Every man [in the cavalry] is well provided with warm drawers, socks and gloves, also jerseys and woollen comforters for the neck.

They refused to give me anything for my horse, who died from the effects of wet and cold and exposure. Rather hard this. How are we to keep up expensive studs of horses if we are not to be assisted when they die in the public service? I have managed to put my own remaining three horses into a shed that I have made, by scarping the side of the hill and putting some boards as a roof. How the poor brutes that are out in all this snow and cold can exist I know not. We generally find that some die every night.

So my Lord George Paget is coming back to command the Brigade. What a thing it is to be a Lord George! Colonels Smith or Jones would have been told to quit the service. I hear that Lady George is coming out with him. I pity her extremely if it is so.

15th. A large fur coat was given to each of us yesterday— the back, white sheepskin worked all over with gay flowers in worsted work. They are Asiatic coats.

'I was much amused', wrote Forrest, 'when the officers' coats arrived. Little Benjamin called to me saying, "Of course I shall take first choice, Major, and you will be entitled to second." I came out and saw the little man array himself in an immense great big long coat, the back of it being all embroidered. He has also got a pair of sailor's boots and a high fur cap. Altogether the little man was the funniest figure you can imagine. I thought of "Puss in Boots". He is very anxious that his mother should not know that he parted with [the fur coat which she had sent to him], so should you meet Mrs Hodge, you must be mum upon that subject.'[5] This was, in fact, quite untrue, for Hodge wrote to his mother telling her that he had sold it, and explaining why.

17 January. Ther. in my tent 22 at 8 a.m. Everything frozen, boots, water, ink, towels, everything. There was no dressing until I got a charcoal brazier lit to thaw my boots.

Saw a string of sick men coming from the front riding our horses—a really frightful sight. They were miserable looking objects, many frost-bitten, with no flesh on their legs.

I hear it takes 1100 a week off our strength does this sickness. About 5 days does for a regiment. The army is nearly done for. It was a noble army once. Now it is fearful to see the poor men.

18 January. Regimental Sergeant-Major Price obtained his cornet's commission. I hope now I may have an adjutant that will do me something.*

Dined with General Scarlett. He gave a very nice dinner, but still there was an air of much discomfort about his room. They all dined with their greatcoats and caps on. It was very hard work finding my way thro' the snow this evening. Really dining out here is beyond a joke.

19 January. A rapid thaw. The whole camp a sea of mud. Lord Lucan visited our lines for the first time since we have been in this camp.

20 January. Worked hard. My sappers came again. Had two men of my own cut a trench round my new tent hole. Got the tent up in it, and moved in my things, mackadamized it, and put in a stove. I find it much bigger than my tent not sunk, and I think it will be warmer.

One at least of Hodge's junior officers had managed by this date to house himself better than had his commanding officer. Cornet Fisher told his mother on 20 January that he had been much occupied during his leisure moments 'in fitting my little kennel. . . . The difficulties I had in getting it up were very great. The road was awful. I got it put on an araba, which very soon broke down, and then it appeared as if it might all be lost; however, with the kind assistance of the Commissariat, I got it carried up in mule carts. . . . I have now got it up, and am now employed in papering up the

---

* George Price's commission was backdated to 5 November. He was appointed Regimental Riding Master, 13 April, 1855.

cracks and covering the walls with matting, the floor with floor cloth.'[6]

I gave the sappers, 3 in number, 10 francs each, and by Jove they are well paid for what they have done for me. They were idle fellows, always talking and thinking of *mangé de la soupe.* However I think they have made me pretty comfortable. My stable must now be paved.

My servants have dug a hut for themselves, and I hope soon to get a place dug and roofed in, in which to put my pony and mule. Then, if the Russians will only leave us alone, I think we may exist thro' the winter.

21 January. I find my tent very cosy. I have put new corn sacks all round over the earth, which will I think make it drier. Lighted my stove for the first time. It is not a good one at all, but I think I can cure it. It smokes when the door is open, and when it is shut, it goes out for want of air. A very mild day indeed.

22 January. Examined the stables the men are building for their horses. Some will do well. The animals themselves are, however, in a miserable plight, and cannot ever be cleaned— the men are too busy.

In 1856, Lucan, in evidence before the Board of General Officers at Chelsea (see p. 98), described the duties of a trooper at this time who was not engaged upon commissariat duties: 'He has to clean his own horse, appointments, arms and clothing; he has to clean the horses and the horse appointments of the sick, and all men on dismounted duties, such as camp guards, hospital orderlies, cooks, prisoners, butchers, &c.; to attend three stable hours; to water the horses twice daily . . . sometimes at very great distances; he has to scrape and shovel away and remove to a distance all the dung, mud, &c. from the picket lines. . . . In bad weather he is constantly repitching tents and changing the ground for the picket lines. He has to attend his own or any spare horse when at the forge. He has to go upon divisional, brigade, regimental, and troop fatigues; to clean out the camp, draw provisions, fetch water and wood for the cooks. . . ; to bury dead horses . . . and to attend funerals. To do this, besides the stable hours, in the short days, he cannot be said to have more than three hours.'[7]

They make us pay income tax upon our Field Allowance. This is hardly fair, I think.

Many more troops arriving, both regiments and drafts, and quantities of stores.

24 January. Signed all the [men's] saving bank returns.

Rode to the Monastery of St George, a Greek Convent situated on a wild promontory on the sea shore, high above the sea. 17 monks are still there. They are watched by 14 Zouaves, and are fed by the French. There is an Englishman there, who was obliged to leave Sebastopol. When our army came he possessed houses in and around the town, but the war has ruined him, and now he and his family are dependent on Lord Raglan for their food. The day was lovely, fine, bright sun, and no wind. The cliffs very fine about the Monastery.

25 January. I have mice in the tent, which is a horrid bore.

26 January. At 11, all COs ordered to Lord Lucan's to report about their saddlery. I have reported that in the spring I do not consider that we shall have any fit for service. Lord Lucan wanted 10 more horses and 6 more men down to his stabling. I however got leave to keep them all. Two of our horses are glandered* down there. I am not surprised at it as they are put very crowded in a warm damp stable and clothed, and all these brutes have been out without clothing in this bad weather.

Hodge is here referring to the 'sick horse depôt' which had been established at Lucan's headquarters, the sole hutting for horses which had been erected before the end of the month. Hodge writing later in the year said that Lucan 'took all the carpenters and masons from the regiments and constructed stabling first for his own horses, then for those of his staff, and then he put ten horses a regiment into them as they were built. The situation and construction of these, however, was so bad that they were washed away, and some horses were drowned in them, and they were so close and damp that the glanders broke out amongst the horses he put in,

---

*The glanders is a contagious disease of horses, donkeys, mules, etc. Symptoms include discharge of mucous matter from the nostrils, and enlargement and induration of the glands beneath and within the lower jaw.

and the last evil was worse than the first. We lost, I think, every horse that was put into them.' (23 April, 1855).

Soon after the great storm of 14 November, Lieut-Col Griffiths of the Greys had suggested to Lucan that makeshift shelters ought at once to be erected. Lucan's typical reaction was to threaten to place the colonel 'under arrest for presuming such a thing'.[8] His only justification for such behaviour must be that there was at that date, and for some weeks to come, no certainty at headquarters of the army as to whether the cavalry camps would stay in the positions they then occupied.

Writing in 1856, Lieut-Col Forrest thought it 'just possible that Hodge may be ordered to England if there is any investigation held about the allegations made by Col Griffiths against Lord Lucan, as Hodge was present'. In fact, Hodge was not recalled, though the investigation was made (the Board of General Officers sitting at Chelsea, known as the 'whitewashing board'). Hodge does not state anywhere in his diary or letters that he was present, as Forrest asserts, at the interview between Lucan and Griffiths. Forrest goes on to say that he believed Lucan to have spoken 'with an un-necessary degree of sharpness to Griffiths. He is a very irritable man, and I daresay imagines that Griffiths meant to impute blame to him for the state of the cavalry, whilst he was himself urging Lord Raglan to allow them to move nearer to their supplies. Lord Lucan is a very obstinate man, and could not bear to have any suggestion made to him by anybody, and by his manner and address made many enemies. I do not think that Griffiths is the man to show him up. He is a bombastic fellow himself and is said oc-casionally to talk very wide of the mark and to imagine that he did a great deal more than was ever accomplished by him.'[9]

> Picked up large stones all the evening to make a road in front of my tent. Now is the time to do this during the fine weather. **28 January.** We have at last finished our hospital hut. They [the invalid men, of which there were 24 at this date, not counting 50 at Scutari] are very comfortable. I wish the men had been in them three months back.

Robert Cooper, the regiment's surgeon, answering a questionnaire of the Crimean Commissioners, later in the year, wrote: 'I shudder when I think over the shelter offered to the sick of my regiment until the first hospital hut was completed on 28 January. Blankets were issued to the hospital by the Quartermaster on 9th December. Some buffalo robes were obtained in January, rugs on 26 February, bedsteads on 14 March, mattresses on 29 April. I had made through a lengthened period, both by personal application and by means of requisitions, every effort to obtain the necessary articles for the comfort of the sick, long before they were available.' In his evidence before the Commissioners he stated that throughout November, December and January 'the sick men were in bell-tents, lying without mattresses on blankets, empty bags and matting, on the bare ground, which was continually damp. No hay or straw could be obtained, as there was not sufficient for the horses.'[10]

> **29 January.** I am put on as a member of a board to consider what is to be done with 5,000 revolver pistols. I particularly requested that the cavalry might not have them.

Hodge's second-in-command agreed with him about this. 'I strongly suspect', he wrote, 'in the event of a fight these weapons would be more dangerous to our officers, men and horses, than to the enemy. Besides, they would be constantly out of repair. Some good boots are much more requisite.'[11]

> One or two of the ships sent out with cheap things have arrived. I hope we shall benefit by them.

These were vessels sent out by the government with necessities and a few luxuries to be sold at cost price to the other ranks. On 22 December, Forrest, welcoming the news that these ships were to be sent, told his wife: 'At present the Maltese and others having shops in Balaklava rush on board ship directly one comes in, and generally succeed in buying everything up which they then retail to the soldiers at an immense profit.'[12] Now, on 29 January,

> the shops having all been put out of Balaklava, the town looks quite dull. They are removed to some rising ground near Kadekoi.
>
> **31 January** [*Letter*]. All the horses in my regiment are under cover in sort of sheds built by ourselves. I have 126, and if I save 100 out of them, I shall do more than any regiment out

16. *The Monastery of St. George.*
   From Sketches in the Crimea, *by H. J. Warre.*

17. *The Monastery of St. George.*
   From My Early Soldiering Days, *by Maj.-Gen. W. Allan, 1897*

18. *The hut of Captain Webb, 4th Dragoon Guards; photograph by Roger Fenton.*

19. *Colonel Hodge, Captain Webb and Captain Forster at the entrance to the marquee of Roger Fenton, the photographer.* (see page 107.)

here. Mine is still the strongest regiment out here,* and I think
in the spring, we shall be as good as any other, if we are
fortunate in our remounts.

The thermometer is now 49 in my tent. It is as mild and
balmy as May.

We hear that the Grand Dukes [Nicholas† and Michael]
have again arrived here, and they say 25,000 men also, from
which it is expected that some attack will again [be] made
upon our position. Let them come, however, where they will,
they will get preciously licked, for tho' the men have suffered
much, they are as ready to fight as ever. The dry weather and
the warm clothing they have received have gone far towards
ameliorating their health.

We hear that Lord Cardigan has been received in triumph
in England, and that all the shops are full of prints of him
jumping a gun, and sticking a Russian *en passant* in mid-air.
I do not think that he ever intends returning here, and better
that he should not. He does not get on with Lord Lucan, and
they are better parted. Whether my Lord George [Paget] will
answer better [as commander of the Light Brigade] I cannot
say.

Tell my aunt Jane I think the best use that she can make of

---

*This is quite correct. The following table shows the horse strengths and
deaths in the Heavy Brigade:—

	November 1854		December 1854		January 1855		February 1855		March 1855	
	str.	died	str.	died	str.	died	str.	died	str.	died
Royals	182	14	168	33	135	31	104	11	93	1
Greys	220	15	195	28	167	51	110	4	106	3
Inniskillings	189	28	161	29	131	23	108	3	105	1
4th Dgn Guards	220	22	198	35	163	38	125	8	117	3
5th Dgn Guards	196	19	177	56	113	28	85	14	70	3
	1007	98	899	181	709	171	532	40	491	11

Average strength: 727
Total deaths: 501   or 69% (*Chelsea Board*, p. 414.)

†Nikolai Nikolaevich (1831–1891); 3rd son of Nicholas I; commanded
army of the Danube in Russo-Turkish War (1877–78).

any money committed to her care for the use of the Army will be to give it to the Patriotic Fund, for the widows, children or wounded.* People need not send out anything more.

Some magnificent mules have come from Spain for the Commissariat Department. I hope they will take care of them. They are the finest animals of the kind I ever saw. They ought, however, to have sent an officer at the same time to France to have bought pack saddles, and mule chairs to carry the wounded in, and then we should have been at once provided with a Field Ambulance, but that conceited coxcomb, General Airey [the Quartermaster-General] thinks of nothing and it is quite enough to suggest anything to have it refused and yourself snubbed and called a meddler. They must remove him. He is a log round our necks, and quite undeserving of what has been done for him.

We have one or two excellent women here. One who washes for me is a hard-working good person. She cooks for the Captain of her Troop.

It was the women of the army who, as Forrest told his wife, were 'the worst off for comforts. Few people seem to have considered them. Little Ben has presented a pair of his flannels [flannel shirts or underclothes] to poor Mrs Rogers.'[13]

2 February. Roasted coffee first issued as a ration. Hitherto it has been given out green. [See p. 19].

3 February. Walked to Kadekoi to the shops, bought some sugar. It was so hard and slippery I could scarcely get along— and on such a day our horses are actually bringing poor miserable sick men from the front to be put upon shipboard! It is enough to kill them, poor half-naked men. This is by far the coldest and most bitter day that we have had. At $7\frac{1}{2}$ p.m. the thermometer was 28 in my tent, though a stove had been burning there all day. Wind very strong, and snow.

---

*A commission, headed by Prince Albert, had been appointed to raise and distribute a fund (called the Royal Patriotic Fund). The monies were to be used for the relief of the families of those that might fall in the war. A monster meeting was held in November, and by July, 1855, £1,171,270 had been raised at home and in the colonies. The 1856 figure was just short of £1,500,000. By 1874, £1,303,386 had been expended. In May, 1855, there was held a grand auction for the fund, to which the royal family and others contributed drawings and other items, which sold for high prices.

4 February. Lots of presents to the regiment are coming out; too late, however, to be much good; but it is kind of the senders.

5 February. The residue of our men and horses from Varna arrived [on board the *Simla*]. Balaklava cleaner and in better order. A magnificent fleet of steam transports in the harbour. The quantities of stores of clothing and all kinds of things in the town is quite incredible—and more coming. Our difficulty is transport.

Cornet Fisher was quite delighted with the change which was at long last taking place in the port. Gone, he wrote on 1 February, were 'the mud and filth, streets like sewers, through which the baggage animals could hardly drag themselves, the closely packed mass of people, fighting, swearing, crushing, through which it was hardly possible to force one's way until some heavy artillery wagon crashed through the throng, driving men and horses into the little holes of shops: the water-side with no piers to land goods.'

7 February. Went down early to Balaklava. Obtained a sheep, 12 chickens, 3 geese and 2 turkeys—rather good foraging for one day—sheep 15/-, a goose 4/-, turkey 6/-, fowls 1/6 each.

The navvies are laying down the rails.

As early as the end of November the Duke of Newcastle had been pushing ahead with the idea for a railway from the port to the front. On 2 December he wrote to Raglan to say that Mr Peto (later Sir Samuel Peto), and his partner Mr Edward Betts, 'have in the handsomest manner undertaken this important task, with no other condition than that they shall reap no pecuniary advantage from it. They will embark rails, engines, &c., with 300 skilled workmen, *in a very few days*, in steamers, and engage to have the railroad *at work in three weeks* after landing at Balaklava.'[14] In fact the materials for constructing the railway (which eventually, with its branch lines, extended to 39 miles) did not arrive till the beginning of February. The first part of the railway which was brought into use on 20 March, just reached as far as the cavalry camp.

Laid out the site of a row of huts I mean to try and get up for the men. Two are up now.

On this day, Forrest described in a letter home, what Hodge looked like. 'Little Ben's face', he told his wife, 'is all covered with hair. It is like a child's face looking out of a great furze bush.'

9 February. Rode with Webb over the hills at the back of our camp—a lovely ride—the scenery very fine, Balaklava harbour below us, full of fine steamers, beyond wooden huts and tents up to the top of the highest hills, with our High-landers in threes, a fine view to seaward. Numbers of vineyards, some with the vines uninjured, but all trees and houses gone. What must have been a rich fine country is now a desert. The French have done this. Saw a dead wolf. I had heard there were wolves here but I hardly believed in them.

10 February. Not out of camp. Round the men's dinners—all very beastly, mud and salt pork.

The regimental surgeon told the Crimean Commissioners that 'the arrangements for cooking were of the most rude and unsatisfactory description during the severe weather. It was lamentable to behold the men exposed to pelting rain, pitiless wind, and drifting snow, doing their utmost to ensure healthy meals for their comrades. The first kitchen was constructed at the beginning of February.'[15]

11 February. We had an excellent dinner of sheep's head broth and fried liver, &c., &c. put into a hash. In England we should discard this. Here we find it excellent.

12 February. Breakfasted with Col Griffiths, Scots Greys, a swell affair given to the Colonel of the 1st Zouaves. All sorts of good things there. I wish my dear mother could have seen the display of good things. She would not imagine that we were starving then!

13 February. About $5\frac{1}{2}$ p.m. Lord Lucan sent his son, Ld Bingham, to ask me to go down to him, when he informed me that he was recalled because he would not take upon himself the fault of the action at Balaklava. He seemed much cut up about his recall. Douglas [commanding officer of the 11th Hussars]* and myself were the only two he had sent for. I pity him. He has been uniformly kind and civil to me, and though I

---

*John Douglas, CB (1811–1871); ensign, 61st Foot, 1829; col., 1857; Major-General, 1868.

think he is not the man to command, being obstinate and headstrong, he will be better than Lord Cardigan, should he come out here.

After the battle of Balaklava, Raglan tried to make his inevitable and justified censure of Lucan as mild as possible. He suggested that there had been 'some misconception of the order to advance' and that Lucan 'fancied he had no discretion to exercise'.[16] With this Lucan was not satisfied. He wanted total exculpation, and wrote to the Duke of Newcastle, demanding it. This it was, of course, impossible for Raglan to grant. The Duke, therefore, rightly decided that the commander of the Cavalry Division must be recalled. 'It is quite a relief to get rid of Lord Lucan,' wrote Cornet Fisher. 'Poor old man [he was not yet 55!], he was a horrid old fellow.'[17] When Lucan returned home he applied for, and was refused, a court martial. He later abused his position as a peer, by airing his grievance in the House of Lords. He died at the age of 88, having risen, though he was never again employed, to the rank of Field-Marshal. Cardigan, whose head had been turned by the excessive public adulation which he received at home, did not, to the relief of everyone there, return to the Crimea. Instead, he became Inspector-General of Cavalry. He died in 1868, as the result of a fall from his horse, at the age of 71, having achieved the rank of Lieutenant-General.

14 February. Went down to call on General Scarlett, who has now the command of the cavalry. I wonder whether they will give me the temporary command of the [Heavy] Brigade. As soon as Scarlett is in orders, I shall certainly apply for it. I can but be refused.

Forrest considered that Scarlett, if he had permanent command of the cavalry division, 'would be a very efficient man, and in that case our little Colonel ought to succeed to the command of the Heavy Brigade. He is the senior "Heavy" out here.'[18]

Went into Balakava to obtain some of the good things that Fortnum and Mason are sending out. Lord Raglan in Balaklava for a wonder. This is the first time I have seen him since the Battle of Inkerman.

15 February. The ther. in my tent at 12 o'clock was 65. General Airey for the first time came thro' the camp. He

looked as sulky as usual—all importance—a ridiculous man—
a pompous ass.

16 February. Rode to Lord Raglan's to see General
Estcourt [the Adjutant-General]* to ask him to have me put
in orders to command the Heavy Brigade. I did not see him,
but I have hopes that it will be done.

Estcourt and Airey were the two major scapegoats for the sufferings
of the army. When, in January, Newcastle suggested that they might
be dismissed, Raglan wrote: 'It is with the deepest concern that I
observe that upon the authority of private letters, you condemn
Generals Airey and Estcourt. . . . Am I, or are the writers of private letters, in a better position to pronounce upon their merits?'[19]

16 February [*Letter*]. Lord Lucan vows that he will not sit
down quietly under such treatment. I pity him, and I think
they have dealt harshly with him. At the same time I am very
glad that he is going home. He is hasty and injudicious in his
ideas about cavalry, and he is no favourite with those under
his command. I have always been on the best terms with him.
He has always shown a partiality for me, and has more than
once praised the 4th Dragoon Guards in public orders.

They have not been working us to the front with provisions
lately, but we still have to bring down the sick.

You ask about General Scarlett, and say you never see his
name mentioned in the papers. Pray do not suppose that
those who are mentioned in the papers are the only people who
work. Scarlett is very active. He is constantly riding through
our lines, and looks well after his brigade. We have a regular
kitchen in which our food is cooked, and a soldier who cooks
for us. He makes us very good *scones* or Scotch cakes for
breakfast, very fair soup, boils things well, and can make a
rice pudding, when I can buy eggs for him. In fact we live
right well I assure you, and thank God I never had better
health. I only fear growing fat.

The Balaklava clasp is something, but I want the Inkerman

---

*James Bucknall Bucknall Estcourt, MP (1802–1855); ensign, 44th Foot,
1820; in 1834 he went on the Euphrates Valley Expedition to find a route to
India from the Persian Gulf; Brig-Gen. 1854; died of cholera, 24 June, 1855.

also, and I expect a CB. If they allow me the brigade, you shall yet, I hope, see your son *décoré*. The French soldiers are all wearing their Alma medals.

The story of Canrobert giving us *10,000 coats* is not true. The French now are envying our men their coats, their flannels and their high boots. Our men are better clad than they are, but too late, and they are not fed as well as the French. They [the French] have good bread three times a week and fresh meat the same.

I think *The Times* has done much good here, but I dislike the publication of the officers' letters. We can never get on as long as they allow this.

All are now complaining of *embarras de richesse*. A move would be a rare scene. But the army cannot move. The thing is quite impossible, we have too many encumbrances, and too little transport.

17 February. Rode with Forrest and Forster to the French Headquarters to call on Genl Rose,* who introduced me to General Canrobert. He was most polite, received me in a most flattering manner, talked for some time, said that the bravery and endurance of our men had made them rise much in the estimation of everyone. He said no army could be commanded as long as such a paper as *The Times* published such statements as they did, and he ended by inviting me to breakfast upon any day I liked to go there at 10 o'clock.

We then rode to the French attack, where we met a French officer whom I knew. He took us into the trenches. We had a good look at Sebastopol, were seen by the Russian riflemen, fired upon, escaped unhurt and rode home by the ravine, very much gratified by our day's work. I enjoyed it extremely.

---

*Sir Hugh Henry Rose (later 1st Baron Strathnairn), GCB, GCSI (1801–1885); ensign, 19th Foot, 1820; Lieut-Col, unattached, 1839; attached as D.A.G. to Omar Pasha, and twice wounded fighting the Egyptians, 1841; as secretary of embassy at Constantinople, 1851, played an important part in the diplomacy which led to the outbreak of the Turko-Russian war, 1853; appointed Queen's Commissioner at French HQ, 1854, where he acted as liaison officer; at Inkerman he exposed himself excessively. He made his name as one of the two great commanders (Sir Colin Campbell was the other) in the suppression of the Mutiny, 1857–61; Commander-in-Chief, India, 1860–5; General, 1867; Field-Marshal, 1877.

18 February. My sulky, stupid servant, Jones, wants to go to his duty. If I can find a sober, decent sort of man he shall go; but we are badly off for servants, and the trouble of teaching these fools is dreadful. How I do miss old Ryan.

19 February. In orders as Colonel Commanding the Heavy Brigade, dated 18 February. Rode into Balaklava. The railway is progressing, and the town somewhat better. On my road home I met Tom Tower [see p. 91] who has come out in charge of the Crimean Fund. I observed a crowd of horses about Sir Colin Campbell's house, and I found Lord Raglan, some French General and a large staff there. He received me very kindly. They were planning another attack upon the Russians.

At 12 o'clock [midnight] all the cavalry and artillery marched. It was pitch dark. We could see nothing. We remained some two hours on our horses. At $2\frac{1}{2}$ we started in a snow storm and tumbled over stones and thro' slush for some five miles, till daylight began to break.

20 February. At daylight we came upon a cossack outpost. They ran away leaving their arms behind them. It was so tremendous a day that the expedition against the Russians was abandoned, and we joyfully turned our steps homeward. The intention was for the French to attack the Russians in the village whilst we blocked the valley to prevent them from running away.

21 February. My eyes are so sore that I cannot bear the glare of the sun. This is caused by the intense cold yesterday. There are many men frost-bitten in the ears. The icicles hung from our moustaches and beards many inches down. The hair of my head behind was even frozen in masses of ice to my coat collar and worsted comforter.

'I am not going beyond the truth', wrote Sergeant-Major Cruse of the Royals, of this abortive and badly managed reconnaissance, 'when I say we were *solid masses of ice* from head to foot. I managed to get a bottle into the corner of my mouth, and took a good swig of grog (a thing I am never without) but I tried a long time to eat a bit of bread: my mustache [*sic*] and beard were so frozen together that it was an impossibility. . . . I had to hold my head over a charcoal fire before I could get my helmet thawed from my head. It was rather a painful operation to get the collar of my pea coat disentangled from my beard and whiskers.'[20]

I expect this Brigadier's command will give me: as pay as Colonel on the Staff, a day, £1.2.9d; field allowance, 10/- a day=£1.12.9d, less 4/6, my field allowance as Field Officer—makes £1.8.3d extra per day, a thing well worth having, as I have not much to do for it.

26 February [*Letter*]. Tom Tower is high busy, and horridly patriotic. I tried to get some candles out of him, but he would not heed at all. They are giving the things out to the different brigades in a very fair way.

This refers to the arrival on 13 February of the schooner *Erminia*. Aboard her were a son of her owner, the Earl of Ellesmere, and an energetic giant named Tom Tower. These two men were the 'honorary agents' of the 'Crimean Army Fund', of which Lord Ellesmere was President. Within a fortnight the *Erminia* was followed by two steamers chartered by the Fund's London Committee. They carried enormous quantities of 'comforts' supplied by private charity at home. These ranged from '37,000 flannel shirts and jerseys, . . . brushes and combs, . . . wine, ale and meat, down to pepper, mustard and salt',[21] and large quantities of oranges against scurvy. Though it came too late, this effort of private enterprise was massive, and excellently organised.

I am glad to hear that the Duke of Cambridge is better. I hope he will obtain some good command. He has behaved well out here. His speech of me was very flattering. I hope he did not say too much. We all like the change from Lucan to Scarlett. The latter is most active. He does his work like a gentleman and gives no unnecessary trouble.

It is rather hard that people should say that the officers and men exaggerate their hardships. I suppose they think that the men die to prove that their complaints are just. Where Mr Gladstone would find his 30,000 men here, I know not. The Grenadier Guards have not *100* men left for duty.

In the Commons debate of 29 January at the end of which the Government was defeated by 157 votes (see p. 94), Mr Gladstone, the Chancellor of the Exchequer, said, 'The number of those engaged in military duties before Sebastopol, according to the latest returns,

must somewhat exceed 30,000.' This was questioned in the House
on 8 February, but Gladstone stuck to it.[22]

These trenches have been the graves of thousands and will
be of thousands more, for we none of us expect to see the
inside of Sebastopol. It is far far stronger than it ever was. The
army are not a bit disorganized and what is left of them would
fight as well as ever, but I doubt our being able to march.
The men have had no rest for six months, and they are worn
out. Men cannot go on for ever.

27 February. Rode to the French headquarters and breakfasted with General Canrobert. He was most kind and civil,
and begged me often to return the visit. A number of French
officers there. I took with me a well turned-out orderly, who
created quite a sensation. He was very clean, his clothing quite
good and his horse in good condition. I was much compli-
mented on the fine appearance that my regiment must make.

28 February. The railroad has reached the village [of
Kadekoi] and they are building a station there. All this looks
as if they intended us to remain here for ever.

2 March. Walked about the hills in the neighbourhood. They
are full of crocuses, snowdrops, a small blue flower from a bulb.

3 March. Walked into Balaklava, now a very interesting place.
The railway with its workshops and landing stations, the quay
showing more order, the ships in tiers in good order, the
harbour cleaner, and the town also—and the great variety of
the dresses of the different nations, especially the Croats.

6 March. Rode into Balaklava to see my poor friend Pine, who
is ill, and I fear cannot recover. I never felt more shocked
than I did at seeing him. I should not have recognised him.

7 March. A report of the death of the Emperor of Russia [on
2 March] has reached us here, by special steamer from Varna,
sent by order of Lord John Russell from Vienna. [Russell had
just arrived there as plenipotentiary to the Congress which
was assembling in the hope of peace.]

My poor friend Pine died at 9.5 last night. I sincerely deplore
his loss both as a private friend and as a public officer. He was
one of the best and most active medical officers in the army.
Now comes to me the melancholy task of writing to his poor
wife.

Chilley Pine, after fourteen years as an Assistant Surgeon with two infantry regiments, had been appointed Surgeon to the 4th Dragoon Guards in 1847. On 6 October, 1854, he had been promoted Staff Surgeon of the 1st Class and attached to one of the infantry divisions.

Lieut-Col Forrest, writing home on 15 January, 1855, retailed a dialogue between Pine and Raglan, which sheds light on the surgeon's character.

'Lord Raglan (with the tone and manner of a man who quite expected to receive some smooth and pleasing answer, such as he is probably accustomed to): "How are you getting on with your sick in the Division, Mr Pine?" Answer: "Nothing can possibly be worse, my Lord." "What do you mean, sir?" Answer: "I mean, my Lord, that it is merely a question of time as to the existence of this Division. More men come into hospital than we can either accommodate or find medicines for. The sickness is occasioned principally through exposure without sufficient clothing. Many of the cases are such as should be either on board ship, or with a roof over them, and we have no means of transport for them." "Who do you mean to insinuate that blame rests with, sir, for these deficiencies?" Answer: "Everybody, my Lord—all the heads of departments. I have reported all these deficiencies and the injurious consequence arising from each, and have sometimes received no answer; in no case, any help." Lord Raglan, by this time considerably nettled: "How long have you been in medical charge of this Division, sir, and what regiment did you come from? I rather think that you are an old dragoon surgeon?" "I am lately appointed to this Division, my Lord, and I came from the 4th Dragoon Guards." "Well, sir, you have made most serious charges against the heads of departments, into the truth of which I shall cause enquiry to be made." Exit Lord Raglan. His Lordship paid Pine another visit upon the following day, and commenced questioning Pine, in a more affable mood, and ended by desiring him to send in a written report of all the deficiencies which he conceived to exist.'[23]

In essence this story is confirmed by Surgeon George Lawson, who wrote to his brother on 12 January: 'Lord Raglan has at last, and in inclement weather too, made his appearance in and about camp, brought out from his house, I expect, by a letter written by our Principal Medical Officer of the Division, Dr Pine, in which he stated to Sir R. England [commanding the 3rd Division] (for the information of Lord Raglan) that the immense amount of sickness in the Division depended on the men being half-starved, ill-clad, and over-worked, and that the Medical Officers were unable to bring up stores sufficient for the sick, or huts, or marquees to cover them, owing to no aid in the way of transport being given by either the Commissariat or Quartermaster-General's Department. Such being the subject of the letter his Lordship came down to camp to see Dr Pine, and was very indignant at such wholesome truths being told him, and left in rather a pet ordering the matter to be enquired into. . . . Suffice it to say . . . that his Lordship has since called at our tents to see Dr Pine, was most condescending in his manner, and hoped that he would ask for whatever he wanted for the sick, and that if it were possible he would have it immediately.'[24]

8 March. Wrote to poor Mrs Pine's brother. I hope that she will not hear of poor Pine's death too suddenly. At 2 p.m. we marched down to Balaklava and buried Pine with proper military honours. We laid him in the cemetery of the hospital in a nice spot facing the harbour.

9 March. The two Grand Dukes, we hear, went away from Sebastopol on Tuesday last. They doubtless heard of the Emperor's death, as it seems that by semaphore they obtain intelligence here in 60 hours.

10 March. We hear there is bad work in England. Very severe weather. The thermometer has been at 4 below zero. Thousands of people thrown out of employment. They cannot form a Ministry, and they talk of a General Election.

On 30 January the government of the Earl of Aberdeen had fallen. It had been defeated in the Commons, the day before, when the Radical MP, J. A. Roebuck, moved for a Select Committee to inquire into 'the conduct of those Departments of Government whose duty it had been to minister to the wants of our Army, before Sebastopol'. The motion was carried by a two-thirds majority. On 6 February, Lord Palmerston, over 70 years of age, formed his first Government.

February, 1855, was the coldest month on record in Britain. From 14 January till 24 February extremely cold weather continued without intermission. The lowest temperature officially recorded in February was 0·8°F. (i.e. not quite 1°). Deaths registered during the winter were some 20,000 in excess of the average. From 6 March till 26 June, the weather continued 'cold, nipping and miserable beyond record'.[25]

11 March. Left off flannel drawers. Mouse in my tent nibbled the biscuit.

12 March [*Letter*]. We are very busy cleansing our camp, burying dead horses, burning manure, &c., &c. My hospital huts are most comfortable and clean, and I have five huts up for the men. No army ever was so well provided as we are now.

I am very anxious to see what they will do about promotions by purchase. I have long feared it would be done away with. A nice mess I shall be in, for one. [The purchase system was to last for another sixteen years].

18 March. Sunday. As we are close to the Light Brigade, I took the 4th there, and did not attend the parade of the Heavies. Quite a grand parade, and a grand business Lord G. Paget made of it. I who went to say my prayers was astonished to find my brother Brigadier making quite a field day of it. He is a goose.

20 March. A very handsome present of two pairs of drawers, 2 Merino waistcoats and 2 pair socks was given us today by Government, all of beautiful manufacture.

21 March. Our big mortars frightened the people in Sebastopol yesterday. They threw a shell into a house at more than 4,000 yards' range. 14 lbs of powder was used. *On dit* it is to be war to the knife. No peace.

23 March. General parade of cavalry. Looking better.

25 March. Sunday, We had a Division parade for Divine Service. Rather a large square for one clergyman.

26 March [*Letter*]. On Thursday last there was a grand attack made upon our lines by the Russians. It took place about midnight, and they hustled the French out of their trenches. They (the French) ran towards the English trenches where they were received as enemies in the dark, and fired into. The Russians also got into our trenches, but were turned out and driven back. Our loss was more than fifty killed and wounded. The French lost some 200 men, and the Russians about 1,300.

Hodge is here referring to the so-called 'Great Night Sortie' of 22
March. Two minor sorties were made against the British, but the
main attacks, with 5,500 Russian troops, were against the French,
who lost some 600 [not 200 as Hodge states] killed and wounded in
repulsing them.

Yesterday [24 March, in fact] there was a truce of some
three hours to collect and bury the dead. I hear the scene was
most interesting. I regret very much that I did not hear about
it in time. I should so much have liked to see it. The inter-
mediate space between the lines was covered with English,
French and Russians, all fraternizing and chatting together.
The Russians had been led on by a Greek, very beautifully
dressed. He was killed in our trenches, and one of our men
stripped him, and besides his arms, which were very beautiful,
found 32 gold pieces in his pockets. The Russian officers chaffed
ours, and asked them why they did not take Sebastopol, and
whether they passed their time agreeably. Ours said very much
so, indeed so much so, they prolonged the siege in consequence.

I am very much annoyed with Col Beamish for publishing
my letter. It was a private letter of thanks and to a man that I
do not even know. He should have asked my leave ere he did
such a thing.

'Did you observe little Hodge's letter in *The Times* of the 9th?'
Forrest asked his wife on 23 March. 'He is terribly annoyed at its
having been published. He is very much afraid of its being supposed
at Headquarters that he is a correspondent of *The Times*, and of his
thereby getting into bad odour with Lord R. However he went up
to Headquarters yesterday and saw some of the staff, and abused
Col Beamish for publishing his letter. Fortunately there was nothing
in it which could cause offence to any of the authorities, but other
cavalry commanding officers are annoyed at his saying that the 4th
had managed to keep more horses alive than any other regiment.
'I am sure that neither the Greys nor Inniskillings need grumble at
his little puff, for they are actually having a picture painted of the
battle of Balaklava, in which those two regiments alone are represented, the officers having actually had their several individual
likenesses taken. This has been discovered here, and there has been

some chaff. It is simply ridiculous. The truthful pictures would in no way agree with this thing'.

30 March. Commenced getting up a hut between Forrest and myself.

Dined with Col Griffiths of the Greys. G gave us a good dinner—a *soufflé* made to perfection, and some good mutton. His cook, however, will not do after Scarlett's.

Cornet Fisher, who a few days before had also dined with Colonel Griffiths, wrote that he had 'brought the mess cook out with him as his private servant, and has lived in great style'.[26]

31 March. I regret to say that Genl Scarlett is going home today. Mrs Scarlett's health is so precarious that he is obliged to go. I consider him a very great loss to us at this moment. This will give Lord George Paget the command of the Division *pro tem.*—& Shewell the 1st [Light] Brigade. I hope that Scarlett will soon return.

1 April. The purple iris, also a yellow one, is in great beauty on our hill close to the camp.

5 April. Rode into Kadekoi and plundered an empty house of a window and a glass door. Got my hut finished, my window put in, and a good table, shelves, saddle pins & washing stands put in it. In fact I am exceedingly comfortable in it— too much so for service. All the place about it has been cleaned up. We have made a garden with flowers in it from the hills, and a rock work all round.

'Little Hodge and I', wrote Forrest to his mother, 'are living together. He occupies one end of the hut, and I the other. We have established a "garden", and we have poultry and a hen house—2 hens that lay eggs and more that we hope will do so.'[27]

7 April. At 11½ went down to Sir John McNeill, chairman of the investigating committee, who is on board the *Gottenburg* transport. I was there for two hours and a half answering their questions about rations, forage duties, &c., &c.[28]

In mid-February, the new government sent out a Commission of Inquiry into the supplies of the army. It consisted of two members, Sir John McNeill, a diplomatist, and Colonel Alexander Tulloch.

It reported first in June, 1855, and finally in January, 1856. The report included some 'animadversions' on, amongst others, Lucan and Cardigan. They were censured, chiefly for 'want of promptitude or ingenuity in devising . . . some means of temporary shelter, such as saved the baggage-horses of the Sappers and Miners at Balaklava'.[29] Both men objected to this and demanded a further inquiry. This was granted, and took the form of a Board of General Officers, sitting at Chelsea, in 1856. Both generals were exonerated by this Board, which came to be known as the 'whitewashing board'. (See p. 143).

9 April. A large flock of sheep strayed down our valley today without a guard or shepherd. Numbers of our men and the artillery carried them off on their shoulders. It was wrong I know, but I could not interfere. I was blind to the transaction.

10 April [*Letter*]. Everybody comes to see our camp, it is so pretty, clean and well arranged.

Lord Lucan in his speech [in the House of Lords][30] I see acknowledges that it was the charge in flank executed by the 4th Dragoon Guards that caused the Russian cavalry to turn and fly; but he takes upon himself the credit of having ordered it. This I declare he never did. It was quite my own idea. He also says that he ordered the 5th Dragoon Guards to charge the Russians in rear. He never ordered any such thing, nor was it ever done, nor could it ever have been done, the thing was impossible. The 5th found their way into action through the scattered ranks of the Greys, who were retiring as they best could do out of the mêlée. I think Lord L's speech a rambling tirade that has done his cause no good. He may now retire to his Irish estates as quick as he likes.

We are not overpleased at having Lord George in command of the Division. However it cannot last long, both Parlby of the 10th and Lawrenson of the 17th are his seniors.* I like those lined leather gloves that you sent amazingly. I presented our chaplain with one pair.

---

*William Parlby (1801–1881); cornet, 8th Light Dragoons, 1816; Lieut-Col. 10th Hussars, 1846–56; General, 1876.

John Lawrenson (1801–1883); cornet, 13th Light Dragoons, 1818; Lieut-Col. 17th Lancers, 1851–56; Inspector-General of Cavalry, 1860–65; General, 1875.

20. *Section of a stable hut erected on the slope of a hill by the 11th Hussars. From the Chelsea Board Report.*

21. Punch, *19 April, 1856.*

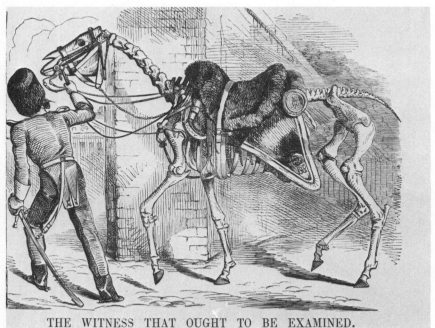

THE WITNESS THAT OUGHT TO BE EXAMINED.

22. *George Marshall, D Troop, 11th Hussars, 9 July 1855.
A page from William Simpson's sketchbook.*

11 April. Soft bread issued out to us as a ration today for the first time.

13 April. A distribution of one pair of overalls per man, free gift from the Government, was made today. Parade under arms to inspect them, and to present seven medals for distinguished service.*

14 April [*Letter*]. I have had a sketch of my camp taken, by a daguerrotype man out here. It is a very pretty spot. I have introduced my horse I rode at Balaklava† and myself, with a few more people into the picture. Has Henry‡ sent you one of the mounted likenesses of me? If so that is the horse I rode at Balaklava. Henry does those things very well. [This picture has not been traced.]

Tom Tower has nearly completed his labours, The Crimean Fund has given us many luxuries, and I for one feel much indebted to them. Their potted game affords me a good breakfast every morning.

14 April. The dead horses stink awfully. Some thousands of Omar Pasha's Turks have come, fine soldierlike fellows. The [British] artillerymen are so beat that they can hardly work the guns, and this rain will make the trenches in an awful state. Providence seems to favour the Russians. I hope our cause is not unjust.

15 April. Went to hear the Service read by Mr Hamilton at Headquarters, a most objectionable man, wears moustaches & beard and fixed spurs. The 10th Hussars have arrived from India.

This was the first of massive cavalry reinforcements which landed

---

* Eight other ranks of the regiment received Distinguished Conduct Medals. One of these, Hospital Sergeant-Major Joseph Drake, received a 'Medal for distinguished conduct in the field, and an annuity of £20.' The other seven were: Sergts Patrick Flemming, John Gilligan, William Percy and Frederick Wallace, Corporal Henry Preece, Privates Benjamin Courd and Thomas Marks. (Smith, H. S. *An Alphabetical List of the Officers of the 4th (R.I.) Dragoon Guards, from 1800 to 1856*, 1856, 30–31.)

† There is a note in Hodge's papers which gives the career of this horse: 'Foaled in 1845. Bought from Murray at Manchester in 1849. I took him out to Balaklava in July 1854, rode him at the Battles of Balaklava, Inkerman and the Tchernaya, took him to Scutari, and on 30 June, 1856, landed him at Portsmouth. Buried under Caesar's Camp at Aldershot, 17 July, 1863.'

‡ Captain Robert John Henry, joined the regiment in 1850.

H

at Balaklava between April and August. The 10th Hussars was at full Indian establishment: '670 strong,' exclaimed Lord George Paget, 'about double what our 10 regiments muster!'[31] Cornet Fisher's first reaction to the regiment's coming was: 'This will make the work much lighter than it was before.'[32]

The 12th Lancers, also at full Indian strength, followed a month later. On 10 May an order was given to reduce both the 10th and 12th to the Home Establishment. 'Now was ever such folly heard of,' exploded Hodge next day. 'Here we are in the field. We want every man and horse we can get, and then they give out one of *General Routine's* orders. Besides the gross injustice to the officers— the 2nd Lieut-Colonels, two Captains, and some subalterns will be reduced and put upon half-pay—they have been put to the expense of coming from India, fitting themselves out for a campaign. They had to sell their bungalows and furniture at a great sacrifice in India, and had the trouble of coming here, merely to be placed upon half-pay and sent home when they arrive.' (11 May, 1855).

From England, the Carabiniers (6th Dragoon Guards) disembarked between June and August, and the King's Dragoon Guards a little later. In July, the Cavalry Division was expanded to three brigades. These came to be known as the 'Heavies', the 'Bashis' (Light Brigade) and the 'Dirties' (Hussar Brigade).

> **16 April.** Rode down to see the 10th Hussars disembark. Their horses are beautiful, all entire Arabs, and in such condition. The *Etna* and the *Himalaya* are here with them. The latter has nearly 400 horses in her; Colonel Parlby in command, which shoves Lord George down to the Brigade. I hear Lord Raglan is very irate with the cavalry for complaining of being over-worked. We merely fowarded a statement made by the surgeons of the 1st and 17th, saying that if these heavy night duties, as 60 per night on out picket, were continued, we should have much sickness. I conceive I had no right to withhold such a statement from Lord Raglan, as he is not obliged to take any notice of it. If he chooses the men to die, we must die, but as the duty that is killing them is a farce, I see no harm in our trying to save the men. He has shown but little feeling for those under him, and that ignorant puppy Airey has much to answer for.

Some 200 Turkish cavalry arrived today. All these have to water their horses at the Karani troughs, which are now of very little use to us. This I have represented, for which I dare say Genl Airey will abuse me.

17 April. Met a Circassian today armed in Chain Armour, Bow and Arrows and Sword. The scene at the watering place was curious. There were these wild Indian horses of the 10th Hussars, our artillery, cavalry, and a lot of Turkish cavalry, all scrambling for water.

21 April. Breakfasted with Gen Canrobert. He is much changed since last I saw him. He does not look like the same man. They say he is likely to be recalled.

22 April. The Duke of Portland's things have been most acceptable. We got some beef done in some peculiar way that was excellent. In the trenches they gave him three cheers for his ale a few nights back.

The 5th Duke of Portland, a recluse, was immensely generous. He sent out to the Crimea at this time a whole ship-load of food and drink, including jars of the Welbeck home-brewed ale, which was very dark in colour, and extremely strong.[33]

24 April. Caught two men, one of the 10th and one of the Royals, breaking open and stealing therefrom a barrel of porter.

In the 4th Dragoon Guards there were 39 cases of punishments given for drunkenness, during the seven months, October to April. 'It is a remarkable fact,' declared the regimental surgeon before the Crimean Commissioners, 'that so little vice prevailed at a time when the men were in the most desponding state [November to January], so much so they had no desire to live in the majority of instances. A stranger to the scenes of camp life cannot estimate the misery and discomfort the poor fellows endured.'[34]

25 April. Bluebottle flies now swarm in our tents. Many ants are to be found running about.

28 April. Rode out with Forrest. In going over the hills we came upon a lot of camels grazing. One big beggar the moment he saw us, ran directly at us, and chased us. Luckily he selected Forrest and followed him. At times they are very savage.

Marsala wine of a very indifferent kind was given as a ration to us today. A pint to each. I prefer the rum.

28 April [*Letter*]. Lord Stratford de Redcliffe* and all his family are here on a kind of pleasure trip. Lady George Paget is with them. Lord George, of course, looks more after her than after his brigade. He has grown very old, and has a most defeated air always.

I have had a sketch made of my hut and camp by Mr Fenton, the photographer to the British Museum, who is out here. It is of course very correct, but it should be coloured to give you a good idea of the beauty of the rocks and hills. I must send a key to it to indicate the tents. (See plates 10, 11).

I think Lords Lucan and Cardigan had better not expose themselves before the public. Cardigan will get the worst of this if matters come to be looked into. There are some curious stories afloat about him here [including the totally unfounded one that he had never charged with the Light Brigade at all].

30 April. Sent to England, by Joseph Darker, carpenter in Mr Beattie's† employ, who is to go by *The Black Prince* steamer, a bayonet got at Inkerman, Russian sword knot and billet, and two photographic views of my camp, addressed to my mother.

2 May. A force is about to start upon a secret expedition. We are to send 46 horses for it from the Brigade, under Col Low [4th Light Dragoons] of the Light Brigade.‡ This is a decided insult to the Heavies. Rode down and saw the 14 horses of the 4th Dgn Gds put into the *St Hilda* transport. No order there seemed to be, no officer taking any notice of the embarkation.

4 May. Dined with old Griffiths of the Greys. He gave us an excellent dish of chickens, grilled and pulled, and as good an

---

* Stratford Canning, 1st Viscount Stratford de Redcliffe, KG (1786–1880), the great diplomatist. As early as 1810 he had been left in charge of the embassy at Constantinople; after other important posts, he returned to Constantinople as envoy, 1825–9, and again, as ambassador, 1842–6, and, finally, 1848–58. He twice visited the Crimea in 1855.

† James Beattie, (1820–1856), engineer-in-chief of the Crimean Railway.

‡ Alexander Low, (1817–1904); cornet, 1835; took command of 4th Light Dragoons when Paget took over the Light Brigade or was on leave; General, 1881.

omelette *soufflé* as I ever ate, but he will press bad sherry down one's throat, and insists upon your sitting there long after I wished to be off.

5 May. The Sanitary Commissioners, Mr Rawlinson and Dr Sutherland visited our camp. They recommend clearing away all the earth from around the huts, and from under the boards, and a layer of charcoal to be put under the floor.

At the end of February, the new government had sent out a Sanitary Commission to investigate the state of the hospital buildings and camps both at Scutari and in the Crimea. It was headed by Dr John Sutherland, a progressive official of the Board of Health. Another doctor and Mr (later Sir) Robert Rawlinson, a distinguished civil engineer, were the remaining members. Florence Nightingale was the true instigator of the Commission, though her friend Lord Shaftesbury actually suggested its formation. She believed that the labours of the Commission 'saved the British Army'.[35]

Visited Captn Biddulph, RA.* He has charge of the electric telegraph that communicates with Varna [a submarine cable between Varna and the Crimea had just been laid]. It was working when I was there. B told me that he had sent a long message from Gen Canrobert to the Minister of War in Paris, and had received back an answer within 24 hours.

7 May. Col Parlby had out the cavalry division. We performed a few things and then ranked past, and so home.

Of this, Cornet Fisher wrote: 'We had a magnificent field day—all the English Cavalry in the Crimea. I had a capital view of it all, as I was acting Aide-de-Camp to the Colonel [Hodge] who, as you know, has the command of the Heavy Brigade, in which I expect he will be confirmed soon. I hope he will, he is in every way fit for it,'[36]

8 May. Miss Nightingale and Monsr Soyer are both here. I wish I could be of any service to her. She is worthy of all honor.

Alexis Benoit Soyer was accompanying Florence Nightingale on

---

*Captain M. A. S. Biddulph, Adjutant, RA, 3rd Division in 1854, had recently been attached to the Electric Telegraph Department.

a tour of the Crimean camps. She had recently completed her Herculean task of putting the Scutari hospitals in order. He was the chef of the Reform Club, and a famous writer on cookery. With the government's authority, but at his own expense, he had come out to show the army how to make the best use of its rations. He was a curiously flamboyant character, who was followed everywhere he went by his mulatto secretary.

> **9 May.** The grass in the plain is beautiful. Mr & Mrs Duberly and Paulet Somerset out grazing. The publicity of all this is very disgusting.

Mrs 'Fanny' Duberly (nicknamed 'Jubilee' by the troops) had accompanied her husband, Paymaster Henry Duberly of the 8th Hussars, from the beginning of the expedition, and was to stay till the end of the war.

Recently she had been receiving considerable notice in the newspapers at home, as the 'Crimean heroine' and one of the few officers' wives who had remained with their husbands throughout the privations of winter.

Later in the year her *Journal Kept During the Russian War* appeared. It caused a considerable stir by its frankness, impudence and what was thought to be unladylike gusto.

Lieutenant-Colonel Forrest, whose own wife was about to come and live with him, found Mrs Duberly 'an odd woman. The French', he heard, 'have dedicated a Polka to her, as "The Amazone". I do not believe she is guilty of that which many say she is, but of course she has many "Followers" as the servant girls say, and her vanity causes her to encourage them.' One of her close friends in the Crimea was Lieutenant-Colonel Poulett George Henry Somerset who was Raglan's nephew and aide-de-camp.

In 1856, Lieutenant Heneage of the 8th wrote: 'We have not yet got Mrs Duberly's Journal—the price ought to pay her well, as it is pretty certain to have a large circulation, but I don't expect there is anything but nonsense in it, and probably a good deal about herself.'[37] This was not quite fair. The book is full of interesting details, and is not unreadable.[38]

> General Marmora and a part of the Sardinian contingent arrived. The plot begins to thicken.

Early in April, Cavour, with an eye to the eventual peace terms, arranged for Sardinia, of which he was Foreign Minister, to sign a convention with Britain and France. Under the terms of this, a contingent of 15,000 troops was to be supplied against Russia. Their commander was General (later Marchese di) La Marmora, who later became Prime Minister of Sardinia.

> **11 May** [*Letter*]. It is quite true that that foolish woman, Mrs Forrest, has left England, and I dare say is now at a filthy hotel at Pera. She might as well be at Pekin for all she is likely to see of her Major. He has applied for ten days' leave to go and see her. It has been refused, but I have made an effort in his favour to try and obtain it for him. I think she might have written to tell you [Mrs Hodge] of this move, but perhaps she did not wish me to know it, being well aware how strongly I disapprove of anything of the kind.

Forrest had told his mother a few days earlier that his wife, Annie, had written to say that 'she was very unhappy in England, and was sure that she should be less so if she were nearer to me, so I was induced to acquiesce in her coming out'. He added that she was 'very independent of servants, and generally makes friends wherever she goes'.[39]

> We are all much disgusted at the return of the expedition to Kertch. It seems they arrived off Kertch, and were just preparing to land under the most favourable circumstances, and there did not appear to be any preparations to resist them, when a steamer sent express from hence, recalled them—we hear by order of the Emperor of the French. Sir George Brown [commanding the Light Division],* Sir E. Lyons and Admiral Stewart† were furious I hear, and used very violent language. It will be quite impossible for us to carry on a war if we are to be controlled by orders from Paris or London. Lord Raglan should have full powers over the Army he has here. He should

---

*Sir George Brown, GCB (1790–1865); ensign, 43rd Foot, 1806; served with distinction, and was severely wounded in the Peninsular War; Lieutenant-Colonel, 1814; Adjutant-General, 1851; commanded the Light Division in the Crimea; wounded at Inkerman; General, 1855.

†Sir Houston Stewart, GCB (1791–1875); entered Navy, 1805; Rear-Admiral, 1851; 3rd-in-Command, Mediterranean, and Superintendent of Malta dockyard, 1853—Jan. 1855; 2nd-in-Command in the Black Sea under Sir E. Lyons, Jan. 1855–1856; Admiral of the Fleet, 1872.

promote the officers, decorate the men, send those home, or
retain those he pleases. He should not be obliged to write to
any Minister of War for instructions of any kind. England
should furnish him with the tools to work with, but leave the
labour and direction of them to him.

In late April, Raglan had obtained Canrobert's reluctant agreement
to an allied *coup de main* to destroy the defences at Kertch, so as to
open the Sea of Azov to allied shipping. At the very last moment,
long after the expedition had sailed, Canrobert, on peremptory
instructions from Paris, called the whole thing off. Sir George
Brown, in command of the British force (3,000; the French supplying
7,000), was told by Raglan that he would be supported should he
decide to go ahead alone. Brown wisely thought it better not to
proceed without the French.

I seldom go out of a night. I have no duties to do whatever.
We dine at $6\frac{1}{2}$, and I go to bed at $9\frac{1}{2}$ or 10, get up at 6, breakfast at 8, and I am out more or less all day. I ride often to the
front to look at the town [Sebastopol] and as little as I can
help into Balaklava, though the arrangements in that harbour
are worthy of much praise. I never visit the Diamond Wharf,
where they disembark the cavalry, without seeing Admiral
Boxer* there, and the landing piers and branch railways and
roads that have been constructed are very numerous.

I trust that Mrs Forrest will not come up here. He is not a
very active officer at any time, and should she come here, the
regiment may go to the dogs, for all that he will do for it.

I hope that you will receive the photographic views of my hut
and camp all safe. The man who did them has, I think,
returned to England. He has taken with him the original plates,

---

*Edward Boxer, CB (1784–1855); entered the Navy, 1798; Second-in-
Command, Mediterranean, December, 1854, and Superintendent at
Balaklava. He died of cholera in June.

He seems to have been inefficient. 'As regards Admiral Boxer', wrote
Raglan, 'I am powerless. No man can make him a man of arrangement.'
(Raglan to Newcastle, quoted in Hibbert, C. *Destruction of Lord Raglan*, 206.)
It was unfortunate that he should have been in charge at the worst time,
expecially as he did not even keep records of any kind. Nevertheless he
showed much activity, and worked extremely hard. On his death Raglan
gave him credit for improving the landing-places and for building wharves
on the west side of the harbour.

Pages from William Simpson's sketchbook.

23.   *Figures in the advanced trench of the left attack, 23 June 1855.*

24, 25. *11th Hussars.*

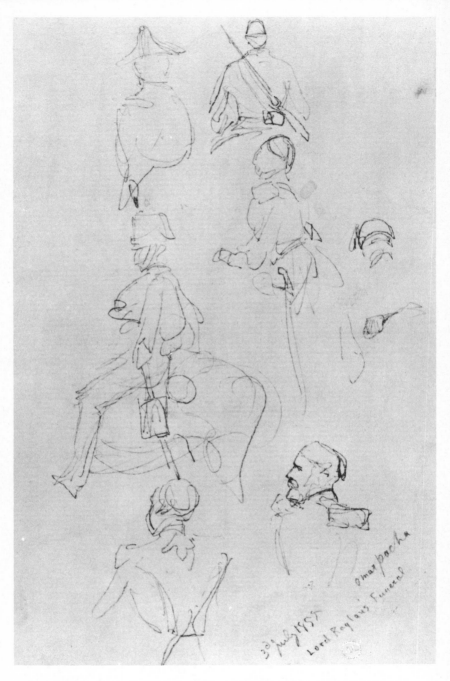

26. *Sketches at Lord Raglan's funeral, 3 July, 1855. Omar Pasha*
bottom right.

and he says that he will give copies of them at five shillings each to any of our friends who wish for them, and better done than those he did here. His address is as follows: Mr R. Fenton, Photographer to the British Museum, 2 Albert Terrace, Albert Road, Regent's Park. He did a very good thing of myself, Webb, Forster, sitting down at the door of his Marquee, and a white horse of Forster's being held by a servant. Then there is another of Webb, Forster and myself, with Mrs Rogers, and Webb's servant and pony. We are standing at the door of Webb's hut. He also did some others of the officers in groups, which are extremely good. I hope he will keep his work and carry the plates back with him to England. (See plate 19).

12 May. Rode to the French camp close by, and gave them some numbers of the *Illustrated London News*, containing accounts of the Emperor's visit to London.

Myriads of these ants. They get into my bed and I feel them creeping on me.

15 May. 50 horses with 31 men arrived from England in *The Crest of the Wave* transport. They left Kingstown on 19 April and arrived here yesterday—a fine passage.

Looked over all the Defaulters' Books, and extracted the sheets of the dead men and those gone to England.

17 May. Examined the young men and horses, and trooped them off. An ugly set of little dogs the men are as ever I saw. The calceolaria is now out in great beauty all round the camp. General Canrobert has given up the command of the French Army to General Pélissier*, and has returned to his Division. All the French praise him much for this act.

23 May. The Kertch expedition sailed.

Pélissier and Raglan had decided that a second attempt at a raid on Kertch should be made. It was again led by Sir George Brown. On

---

*Aimable Jean Jacques Pélissier (later Marshal, and Duc de Malakoff) (1794–1864); supported Louis Napoleon's *coup d'état*, December, 1851; commanded 1st army corps in the Crimea, 1854–5; succeeded Canrobert as Commander-in-Chief, 1855; Ambassador to London, 1858–59; Governor-General, Algeria, 1860–64.

It was he who is supposed constantly to have reiterated: *On ne peut pas faire des omelettes sans casser des oeufs*. Unlike the overcautious Canrobert, Pélissier was reckless both with his men's and his own safety. He was too fat to ride a horse with ease, and was often seen riding about in a pony trap.

26 May an unopposed landing was made, and the batteries destroyed. Within a short time an Anglo-French naval squadron was causing havoc in the Sea of Azov, sinking hundreds of Russian supply ships. (See p. 110).

Chapter 5

---

25 May – 31 August 1855

On 25 May the ground lost at the battle of Balaklava was regained, virtually without opposition, and largely by the considerable Sardinian contingent under General La Marmora, assisted by the French.

25 May [*Letter*]. I have just returned from a charming ride in company with a portion of the French Army, who started at 1 a.m. to surprise the Russians in our front. I started at four and rode to the Bridge over the Tchernaya, which was occupied by a French picket, but finding that the shot from the Russians' batteries over Inkerman came unpleasantly near, I turned to the right and went to Tchorgaum, a village hitherto occupied by the enemy. The French had just driven them out of it. I made for the best looking house, and I captured the musket and accoutrements of the Russian sentry, which I have brought home, and shall get Tom Tower to take to England for me. I have received two ships full of men and horses, which will bring us up to 210 horses, a more respectable force than most regiments have. It was a charming feel this morning to ride over the hills after being so long pent up as prisoner within these lines.

28 May. Rode along the ground where the Light Cavalry charged. I met Douglas and Paget and I heard the story of it from them on the ground where it occurred.

29 May. Many of these recruits are terrible. Their clothes are made so tight that they cannot mount their horses. If they were brought before an enemy they would stand no chance.

1 June. Forrest has brought his wife here, a proceeding that I by no means approve of. He cannot look after the regiment and after her also.

The rank grass in that plain stinks exceedingly.

The Guards, navvies, transport corps and Sardinians are all losing men by the cholera.

2 June [*Letter*]. Our weather is perfect. Such a beautiful country, such valleys with wild rocky hills, such growth of herbage, and such flowers everywhere! I wish I knew their names, or could send you some.

The Kertch expedition has been most successful. They have captured more than 100 guns and some 160 ships with corn &c. &c. The surprise was complete. In the town the ladies' work tables were left with their worsted and Berlin patterns lying about upon the tables. As soon as the Russians vacated, the Tartars commenced plundering the place, and the sailors completed what they left undone and gutted the place entirely. The ships have got into the Sea of Azov and are picking up no end of vessels. As the Russians draw a great portion of their supplies from thence, we expect that this will be productive of much trouble to them.

The centipedes and snakes are very numerous. I shall bottle one or two of the former and send them to you.

There are a great many ladies out here, and I fully expect to see some excursion steamers come out from England soon, with Manchester, Birmingham and Liverpool on board.

Lord Hardinge's statement that if the cavalry were without nosebags in the winter it was the fault of the Commanding Officers *is a falsehood*, and shows how ignorant his Lordship is of the state of matters here. The mud and wet was such that in one week a bag was rotten.

I have just been informed that a regular official application has been this day sent in by Mrs Duberly of the 8th, signed by Colonel Shewell, applying for the Crimean Medal and clasps for Balaklava and Inkerman. I rather think that Parlby refuses to forward it, but if she gets it, I will apply for one for Mrs Rogers who deserves it ten times more than half the men who will get it.

4 June. Forrest did not sleep here last night. I thought how it would be. How true it is we cannot serve two masters!

The water upon which we are dependent is now poisoned by buffaloes. We must move to the Tchernaya or we shall be done.

5 June. Dined with General Pennefather. After dinner went to have a look at the firing into Sebastopol. It shows very little. Vauxhall is far prettier as the *Gurls* say. We had a fine night to ride home.

6 June. At 3 p.m. our guns opened fire. I rode to the front to see the fire which was heavy enough, but as the wind came from the north, the smoke was too thick to see much. I stayed till 8 p.m. and then rode homewards. Met Lord Raglan and a large staff. He asked me to dinner, but I had dined, and in these cholera times I dare not tax my stomach with eating two dinners. I therefore bid goodnight to His Lordship and rode home. The firing was very heavy when I went to bed at 10 p.m.

7 June. Rode to the front after dinner and witnessed the French attack upon the Mamelon and the English upon the quarries in front of the Redan. At 7 p.m. a rocket was fired as the signal and we saw a heavy column of French scaling the Mamelon and driving out the Russians; the F then went at the Malakoff tower, but having no ladders returned to the Mamelon, and the Russians with them, who drove the F out.

They, however, rallied and took it. At the same time our
Light Division took the quarries. Shot, shell and rockets were
going all this time. The sight was awful, particularly where I
knew that friends were in the midst. It was grand, however,
as a spectacle. The firing continued very heavy all night. I
got home about 10, and I found letters from home. How great
a change from witnessing this scene, to reading the words of
those I love, but whom perhaps I may never see again. Much
thunder today, mixed with the firing, the effect was very grand.
8 June. Up at 3¾ and rode to the front; shot and shell still
going. I saw a number of Russian prisoners, ill-clothed scare-
crows they were. After dinner rode up again, saw Lord
Raglan going round the hospitals. We had nearly 40 officers
and 300 men k & w and the French, they say about 3000.
Had they stopped when they had secured the Mamelon, their
loss would have been about 300. The Russians were not returning our fire much. The situation of the men in the quarries
is very much exposed.

In capturing the Mamelon and the Quarries on 6 and 7 June, the
French took 73 guns, but suffered nearly 5,500 casualties. Napoleon
III told Pélissier 'that a pitched battle disposing of the fate of the
Crimea, would not have cost more men.'[1] The British losses
amounted to 670, of which 47 were officers. The Russian casualties
did not much exceed 5,000. The captured works were speedily
converted, so that they could form spring-boards for a further, and
it was hoped final, attack upon Sebastopol.

9 June. After dinner rode up to the front, found there was
a flag of truce to enable them to bury their dead. Went off to
the Mamelon, and leaving my horse at the entrance of the
trenches, had just time to go to the end, saw many dead bodies
of Zouaves and *indigènes*, fine looking fellows, bloated out with
the sun, and stiff in the attitudes in which they had died. The
wreck of guns and clothing was frightful. I had barely time to
get away ere the firing began again, and shot and shell fell
thickly around us. One passed just over my horse.
10 June. Forrest had his wife to sleep with him, in his half of
our hut. In my mind a very disgusting *exposé* to put any lady
to. However it only confirms my opinion of the two.

Transplanted some lettuces.

11 June. Mrs F here again. I wish I had not been so civil as to divide a hut with him—live and learn.

14 June. Rode out to see the Light Brigade at drill under Lord G Paget. I go to learn, having had so little opportunity. He had them in six regiments rank entire: 18 squadrons. The 10th work very well, the 12th very indifferently.

16 June [*Letter*]. Major Baring of the Coldstream [see p.32] who lost his arm at Alma and was so long with me in the *Sans Pareil* [has arrived from home]. He is a good soldier. He need not have come out but he preferred doing so to being put upon the Viceregal Staff in Dublin, to which he had been appointed.

17 June. The cannonade commenced at $3\frac{1}{2}$ a.m., and was most furious. This is by far the hottest day we have had. The thermometer in my hut was 90 at midday. In the afternoon rode to the front, where preparations are being made for the assault tomorrow. God be merciful to us. Shook hands with Warre of the 57th. I hope he will escape; but he leads the assault.* How dreadful is this war. By this time tomorrow, how many fine fellows will be struck down.

18 June. Left my camp at 3 and rode to the front. I found the French hard at work attacking Malakoff, and our men at the Redan. The smoke was so thick that we could not see anything, but it was soon evident that we were repulsed.

I remained behind a heap of stones watching the cannonade from the hill above Chapman's Battery till 8 a.m. when I saw that our men were being withdrawn from the works, so I went to Straubenzee's† hut and got some breakfast.

Our loss is frightful. Quantities of officers killed.

Returned to camp, dined and then to the front again. All much down. This repulse will do us much harm, and dispirit the men. The French put down their loss at 5,000, a whole regiment of Zouaves, and 2 generals killed. I know not when

---

* (Sir) Henry James Warre, KCB, FRGS, FRHS, (1819–1898); ensign, 1837; Major-General, 1870; Commander-in-Chief, Bombay, 1878–81. He wrote *Sketches in the Crimea*, 1855. (See illustrations facing pp. 82, 115).
† (Sir) Charles Thomas van Straubenzee, KCB (1812–1892); ensign, Ceylon Rifles, 1828; Brig-Gen, May, 1855; commanded brigade which captured the Quarries on 7th June; commanded 1st Brigade of the Light Division in both attacks on the Great Redan, being wounded in that of 8th September; General, 1875.

I have felt so melancholy. This horrid war will I think continue for ever.

This was the feeling of everyone in the allied camps, for extreme optimism had preceded the attack. On 17 June, 600 siege-guns and the guns of the fleet had opened on Sebastopol. Their fire was kept up all day, and caused massive casualties in the Russian lines. Originally the allied plan had been to re-open the bombardment at dawn next day, the anniversary of Waterloo, and to continue it for a good two hours before the assaults went in. Late that night, however, Pélissier altered his mind. He informed Raglan that the French, dispensing altogether with the bombardment, would go in at dawn. Since it was a clear night, the Russians, not being under the fire of the guns, observed the French infantry being marched into position. They were entirely prepared, therefore, when the assaults were made just after 3 a.m.

Due to a muddle, the three French attacks were not co-ordinated, and consequently failed miserably. Raglan, seeing this, felt bound to throw his own waiting troops in at this moment, so as to encourage their retreating and wavering allies. It proved a great mistake, and it ended in heavy casualties and no gains.

The Russians lost about 1,500 men on the 18th, the French not less than 3,500 and the British about 1,500.

19 June. A flag of truce to bury the dead. No officers allowed to go up to it. Osten Sacken [commandant of Sebastopol] vows he will not have it. Too many officers use their glasses when near their works.

22 June. After dinner rode across the Tchernaya thro' Tchergoum, and into some beautiful country beyond it. Every valley shows where the cossacks have been bivouacking during the winter—small hovels or else bowers made with three sticks and boughs of trees. Some of them are cut into the ground and covered over with boughs. Tchergoum must have been a pretty thriving village; now it is a heap of ruins done by the cossacks, not by us. The plain is now brown and bare of herbage, and cracked with the drought. Flowers are now very scarce.

That woman [Mrs Forrest] here again. I fear she intends taking up her residence here.

Bersaglieri,
Sardinian

officer, Bersaglieri,

27.   *Sardinian Bersaglieri. From William Simpson's sketchbook.*

28. *Balaklava Harbour, 1855.*
   From My Early Soldiering Days, *by Maj.-Gen. W. Allan, 1897.*

29. *The Baidar Valley.*
         From Sketches in the Crimea, *by H. J. Warre.*

23 June. Had the Brigade out in marching order on the plain. After dinner rode thro' Tchergoum. When near the out-posts we met a Russian soldier who gave himself up as a de-serter to us. A well-dressed fine-looking man with '10' on his shoulder straps. We brought him in, and I met Genl Canrobert to whom I gave him up. 4 more had come in today. I think this argues an attack is likely to be made upon us.

Rode home by the French cavalry camp and reached my hut just as a thunderstorm reached us. In a few minutes it came down in torrents, bringing down large rocks and stones and carrying away tents and everything. Our mess tent and mess kitchen is destroyed, buried beneath 3 foot of stones and rocks, all our cooking pots and cooking apparatus gone. My horses have escaped but are in a sad plight. My hut stood, but let in the wet rather. The men's huts flooded, and horses and saddles all adrift. I never saw so much water fall in so short a time.

24 June. Went thro' our lines at 4 p.m. Found all the men asleep, and all the saddlery dirty, Some of the horses even not removed out of the mud. Of course, as no one looks after them, all will soon go to the dogs. [This, of course, is a dig at Forrest.]

26 June. Dined on board a ship with Lord Ward.* He has a steamer here that he has brought out from England. I do not like these board-a-ship dinners.

Lord Raglan is very ill. I can well imagine the worry he has undergone has at last affected him.

28 June. Rode to enquire for Lord Raglan, who is worse to-night. Even should he recover, he will, I think, have to go home. What a scatter together for all his nephews! I will bet something, however, that the greater part of them go home on some excuse or other.

The Forrests have put up a marquee tonight.

28 June [*Letter*]. The siege is no siege as long as we leave open the whole north of the Crimea. We cannot, however, move for want of transport. This Land Transport Corps is a failure.

---

* William, 11th Baron Ward (later 1st Earl of Dudley of the 2nd creation) (1817–1885). He came out to the Crimea in a private capacity as a tourist, in a hired ship.

I

The men are drunk and mutinous, and the proportion of men to animals is so small that the latter are wandering loose all over the country.

Then it seems to me that we have no information about our enemy, whilst in my opinion the Russians are kept well informed of all we do and are going to do. Our camp is full of Greeks, Tartars and all kinds of people. Indeed anyone who likes it perambulates where he pleases. All this is wrong. Everybody who is not a soldier should carry a passport, which he should be obliged to show if asked for by any officer. [This did not in fact happen until 22 November. See p.137].

That horrid Mrs Forrest is still here. She has no maid, nothing but a great he-dragoon to do all she wants. I have not spoken to her for the last ten days. I always avoid her. I think her coming to live here so disgusting. I believe that she expected that we should ask her to breakfast and dine with us, but that I will not stand, so they get the things after we have done with them, and they send an old jam pot down to us to have their rum put into it, for this, I know, is the only liquor there is in his tent. Considering that there are no rations drawn for her, all this is to me a wonderful proceeding, and not quite what a lady ought to do.

Her husband, not surprisingly, was writing home to his mother on this very day, complaining that his wife had 'grown thinner since she arrived, which she attributes to not getting enough to eat—not porter nor food enough—she says that she never was so hungry as she is here'.[2]

29 June [*Letter*]. Lord Raglan died last night at 9 p.m. of exhaustion from dysentry, added to, I hear, by worry of mind, poor fellow. Peace to his soul. General Simpson* has assumed the command of the army until a successor is named, Sir George Brown having gone on board a ship.

In February, Major-General Simpson had been appointed 'Chief of Staff' to Raglan, to report, in reality, on him and his staff. To

---

* (Sir) James Simpson, GCB (1792–1868); ensign & lieut, 1st (Grenadier) Guards, 1811; severely wounded at Quatre Bras, 1815; Lieut-Gen, 1855.

the consternation of the government he reported soon after his
arrival, that he considered 'Lord Raglan the most abused man' he
had ever heard of. 'The Staff here at headquarters', he added,
'have, I am convinced, been very much vilified. . . . I must say I
never served with an Army where a higher feeling and sense of
duty exists than I remark in the General Staff Officers of this Army.
It pervades all ranks, except among the low and grovelling cor-
respondents of *The Times*.'
On Raglan's death, as senior officer present, Simpson succeeded
him in chief command, in which, much to his unhappiness, he was
soon confirmed. 'I sincerely trust', he wrote, 'that a General of
distinction will be sent immediately.'[3] He had to wait, in fact, till
9 November before he was relieved. (See p. 135).

Scarlett arrived last night; also Colonel Lawrenson. This
puts Lord George Paget out of the command of the Light
Brigade, also Parlby, for I understand that for the present at
any rate I am not to be displaced. Parlby told me this
this morning. I can scarcely however expect to retain my
command with so many senior officers to me out here.

29 June. Mrs F here again, screaming in her vulgar way for
our cook to bring things to her. I was quite driven out of my
hut by her. I can hear the two washing and dressing and
talking to each other—disgusting!

1 July. Attended Service with the Brigade at 10½. Mr
Hamilton gave us a long sermon 'How long halt ye between
two opinions'.* This is the third time he has preached the
same.

2 July. Mrs F here again, sponging upon us for her food, living
out of our rations. How any man can demean himself to such
an extent as to permit his wife to be thus the common gossip
of the camp, I cannot understand. At night heavy rain. How
this suits the loving couple in their tent on the ground I
wonder.

3 July. Funeral Procession of Lord Raglan. Two squadrons
of the 4th Dgn Gds formed part of the escort. They left here at

---

* 1 Kings 18:21: 'And Elijah came unto all the people, and said, How long
halt ye between two opinions? If the Lord God be God, follow him: but if
Baal, then follow him. And the people answered him not a word.'

2 p.m., and did not get home till 11 p.m. I remained in camp, to which all the troops not employed were strictly confined. All the 4 A.D.C.s are to go home with the body. Captn Calthorpe of the 8th [Hussars], whose regiment is in the field, ought to be ashamed of himself for so doing. He has lived on the fat of the land all the winter, and now runs away just when something is likely to be done.*

He was the youngest of Raglan's four aides-de-camp, all of whom were his nephews. He wrote, and published anonymously, in 1857, a controversial book, called *Letters from Head-Quarters; or the Realities of the War in The Crimea, by an Officer on the Staff.*

5 July. It is now decided that three brigades of cavalry shall be formed, and Lawrenson of the 17th is to have the Heavy Brigade. I am glad that it has fallen to him, and not to George Paget.

6 July. My functions cease as Brigadier. As far as pocket goes, it makes a considerable difference.

7 July. The Forrests have withdrawn from our mess, in doing which he has done quite right. It is more respectable; but still she has no female attendant about her. The dragoon still 'empties the leather bucket'.

Finished reading *Lady Lee's Widowhood*, a book that has been highly recommended to me, but in which I see no recommendations.

Lady Lee's Widowhood was the first novel of that versatile General, Sir Edward Bruce Hamley, KCB, KCMG.
It first appeared in 1853 and was republished in two volumes with his own drawings as illustrations in the following year. Hamley was in the Crimea at this time as a Captain of artillery.
His single volume history of *The War in the Crimea,* an excellent work, was published in 1891.

9 July [*Letter*]. No shelter is provided for the men [in the trenches] either from the sun or from the shot. The casualties

---

*Hon (Sir) Somerset John (Gough) (later 7th Baron) Calthorpe, KCB (1831–1912); cornet, 8th Hussars, 1848; later Lieut-Gen.

are frightful every night. The soldiers lie in a trench with a low parapet of earth thro' which the cannon shot penetrates, over which the shells and grape shot burst, and the least movement brings a shower of Minié balls.* With all this no attempt is made to shelter the men.

The Russians build bomb-proof shell traps into which the men can get when the shells are seen coming. Captain Peel [R.N., who was with the Naval Brigade] offered to break up his ship [H.M.S. *Diamond*, a 27-gun frigate] to afford timber for this purpose, but the Admiral would not listen to such a proposition, though leave could be obtained from England; or easier still some of these prizes could be brought here and broken up. The want of timber should be no excuse. Frames ready to put up should be sent from England. No expense should be spared to save the lives of the men. I really look upon our infantry and siege artillery as heroes *all*. For 24 out of every 72 hours these men's nerves are at the full stretch, watching the moment when the enemy may jump upon them, or when a shell bursting in the midst of them may kill or wound half their numbers. Then the heat in the trenches is frightful, and a heavy storm fills them with water, but there the men must remain. I really think that no rewards are too great for the men who have borne this since the beginning of the siege, as many have done. As to *our* services they are nothing compared with these men. We have had discomforts but very few hardships and dangers.

I am once more in command of my regiment, and barring the loss of the extra pay, I am quite as happy as when I had the brigade.

The recruits we have got are wretched boys; half of them

---

* In 1849, Claude Etienne Minié (1814–1879), who had entered the French army as a private soldier (and left it as colonel in 1858), invented the revolutionary Minié rifle. The bullet had a hollow base and an iron cup in it, which was self-expanding. In Britain, about 1852, with the introduction of the Minié rifle, it was decided to do away with all smooth-bores and replace them with rifles. Most countries did the same before long. By 1854, all French regiments were equipped with rifles. Several of the British regiments started the war with the old-fashioned smooth-bore musket, but were soon re-equipped. Muskets were also standard in the Russian army at the beginning of the war; but by July, 1855, many regiments already possessed the rifle.

are in hospital; two have died, and five were sent away last week, and six more today. England cannot expect to fight battles with these weeds in an unwholesome climate. In India the men are not exposed to the sun and obliged to do the work that these boys are. They are fed on salt pork. This makes them thirsty, and they drink lots of cold water, which brings on fever and dysentry to a certainty. We get fresh beef every other day; mutton we seldom obtain.

11 July. Our sick list is very great. 49 today. Neeson of F Troop died of cholera.

Went to the Monastery of St George, heard the monks at vespers, but was not struck with the solemnity of it. All was truly Greek to me.

14 July. Rode out towards Baidar with Garratt, Wombwell, Thesiger, Blakeney, Captn Earle, 2 Webbs,* and others. We carried our luncheon with us, and sat down near a fountain and ate it, as jolly as possible. We found the Turks encamped there, which added much to the scene, their camps being well arranged and prettily situated amongst the rocks and trees. We returned home by Kamara, and I enjoyed my ride extremely. It is singular that so many old friends from Dublin should be picknicking merrily upon Russian ground surrounded by Turks.

20 July [*Letter*]. I really think that in England you are all more affected by Lord Raglan's death than we are. It is with us so common an occurrence to hear that such a man is dead, or that so and so is wounded, that we are but little affected by it, and though we have lost our Commander-in-Chief, matters go on in the same way; the guns fired in the batteries just as hard as ever and no change was apparent. As to General Simpson, I know nothing about him. He is a quiet looking old gentleman, cleanly shaved, and looks healthy; but what capacity he has for the command of an army I know not. I do not think that we trouble our heads very much about it.

I had a very interesting trip yesterday with Lord Ward, who is out here in a steamer that he has hired. He gave us a *déjeuner*,

---

*There were two officers named Webb at this time in the 4th Dragoon Guards. The other officers were not in the regiment.

and then we went round to look at the sea front of Sebastopol. I had not seen it since the 22nd of October last, and much changed I found it. Large works have been thrown up, which have greatly added to the strength of the place, and we could see a vast multitude of men employed in throwing up a new work in rear of the Malakoff. In fact the place looks to me more unapproachable than ever, and if they can keep supplying the town with fresh armies, and with provisions and munitions of war, I see no reason why the present style of warfare should not last for many years.

21 July. I am amongst the CBs—one of a batch! I should like to see my name solus in the Gazette, for some really good service performed.

23 July. Lawrenson and myself went to the trenches of our left attack, to Sir Colin Campbell who took us into the rifle pits under the Redan, and all thro' the left attack. The heat was intolerable and the men were lying in the sun with no shelter, and rifle balls and shells pinging and bursting around us. I never had such a walk. Today is the hottest that we have had. Ther. in the sun at 9 a.m., 110 in hut; at 2 p.m., 96; at 9 p.m., 84; a hot wind was blowing; we all felt roasted.

25 July. To the new Sanatorium [recently erected near the Monastery of St George] to see my men, whom I found most comfortable: sheets, blankets and most excellent bedsteads. The men said they were well found in everything, and that already they were getting better.

28 July. The wild hollyhocks grow to a great height here. I rode through some on the plain here last night which reached higher than the top of my cap as I sat on horseback.

30 July [*Letter*]. I had intended taking my regiment out today for a kind of picnic to a beautiful spot full of cypresses, pines and a great variety of other sorts of trees surrounded by mountains of rocks clothed with trees to the edge of the sea. I went yesterday to reconnoitre the ground well, and there I found a large camp of Turks cutting down all these beautiful trees, and utterly destroying one of the loveliest scenes you ever looked upon. I did not like, as the Turks were there, to take our men there, so I must look out for some other spot for them. I wish to give them a little change, and let them see the country beyond the hills.

In his diary, Hodge gives another reason: 'I found that getting to [the spot] was out of the question with our old Troop horses.' Perhaps he did not like to confess the state of the regiment's mounts to his mother!

> In three month's time the winter will be upon us, and I see no preparations being made. The roads are not being mended or repaired. The railway is merely laid down upon sleepers, no stone or ballast even between them, so that when the wet weather comes, the horses will soon cut it up and render it useless. We are not told to prepare to hut our men or horses, or even make roads through our camps, all of which must be done if we want to avert the miseries of last year.

> My Soyer's cookery book was buried in my kitchen in the thunder storm. Send me another with the shirts.

> Lord George Paget has been given £100 a year *good service* pension. [See pp. 123 and 124].

> The Duke of Newcastle is here. I hope he likes the pudding he has helped make. [He had resigned from the War Office on 1 February, and came out to the Crimea in a private capacity.]

> **30 July.** Saw a cricket match being played between the infantry and the cavalry. The latter won easy.

> **1 August.** How I should enjoy a piece of really good English roast beef, and some good cream and butter. I wonder whether I shall ever again enjoy my ease and my book in England.

> **7 August.** Inspected very carefully the horses that have come from England from the Bays [the 2nd The Queen's Dragoon Guards]. Such a set of old screws or weedy cripples! Campbell [Colonel William Campbell, commanding the Bays] shall be made to be ashamed of himself.

> **10 August.** Received my Cross of CB. A very handsome jewel, but one I must send home lest it be lost here. I hope to get another or two ere the war is over. My mother will be much pleased at my having them. I wish I could get the Legion of Honor, and a high caste Turkish order. [Both of these he did, in fact, receive before the end of the war. He was made an *Officier du Légion d'Honneur* and a Knight of the Order of Medjidie.]

11 August. A sale in the camp of Brigstocke's things. He has deserted and has sent in his papers, and has gone home today. I yesterday forwarded Webb's papers. He also wants to sell out. I do not approve of officers doing this.

13 August [*Letter*]. I do not think that we need care about the letters in *The Times*. I come very well out of the correspondence and I have not in any way provoked it. George Paget must feel small.

This refers to letters from 'Fair Play' and 'A Civilian', which appeared in *The Times* on 21 and 24 July referring to the £100 Good Service pension given to Paget (see p. 122). That from 'A Civilian' stated that 'good and able men' would be deterred from entering the army 'if they have reason to believe that services performed at the cost of their health and their lives will be set aside whenever they may chance to clash with the interests of . . . the "Upper Ten Thousand" of society'. It then contrasts the services of Colonels Hodge and Shewell of the 8th Hussars, with those of Lord George Paget, and goes on to deplore the award of a good service pension to an officer whose total length of service was less than either Hodge's or Shewell's, to say nothing of their continuity of service in the Crimea. Whatever the reason for Lord George receiving the pension rather than the other two, 'it had better be speedily explained', threatened the writer. 'It must be explained', he added, 'before the Commander-in-Chief who recommends officers for this distinction to the Crown can stand acquitted of gross favouritism.'

17 August. Lt-Col Beamish has sent me his book upon cavalry, in which he makes favourable mention of the 4th at Balaklava.

Lieut-Col N. L. Beamish was the author of the *History of the King's German Legion*. He also translated two German books on the duties of cavalry, published in 1855, one of which was called *On the Uses and Application of Cavalry in War, from the Text of Count F. A. von Bismarck, with Practical Examples selected from Ancient and Modern History*. In this he writes of the Charge of the Heavy Brigade: 'The Scots Greys and Inniskilling Dragoons, led on by the gallant Major-General Scarlett, and supported by a flank attack of the 4th and 5th Dragoon Guards, in which the former regiment, under

Colonel Hodge, was much distinguished, defeated and dispersed a body of the enemy's cavalry, estimated at *three times* their number.'[4] Beamish had joined the 4th Dragoon Guards in 1816, and remained in the regiment till 1823. In 1829, he retired from the army. He was appointed Lieut-Col in the Hanoverian army in 1852.

20 August [*Letter*]. [On the 16th there took place] the battle of the passage of the Tchernaya, where we were merely spectators of the victory that was gained by the French and Sardinians over the Russians. The latter have, I believe, lost quite 5,000 men, the allies about as many hundreds. A Russian General Reid or Wrede* was killed, and upon him was found the whole plan of attack. They were about 60,000 strong. They were to have driven back the French, then have occupied the hills on our right, have cut off the Turkish army, taken Balaklava, eaten up the English cavalry and some sixty guns, have burned all our shipping and then to have attacked and taken Kamiesh. Poor misguided people, they never got beyond the first of our line of defences, and then they left some thousands dead, wounded or prisoners. I hear that some of the officers who were taken are furious at their defeat.

I quite agree with you that I have lost a friend in Lord Raglan. He knew me, and old Simpson does not know me. I must bide my time, and hope for the best.

Thanks for *The Times* of the 3rd. Lord Palmerston speaks well out for Paget. On the whole I do not think he has lost by the motion.

On 2 August Mr Lewis Dillwyn, the Member for Swansea, had initiated a debate in the Commons. He said that the country wanted to be assured that the Good Service Pension awarded to Lord George Paget had not been given on account of his 'high birth or connexions'. Mr Frederick Peel, the Secretary-at-War, a son of Sir Robert, replied that as Paget was the senior cavalry Commanding Officer in the Crimea, there was no choice. Palmerston, intervening, defended the award on rather different grounds, namely that the Commander-in-Chief should know best and that it

---

* General N. A. Read, 'a dashing cavalryman'. (Curtis, J. H. *The Russian Army under Nicholas I 1825-1855*, 1965, 319.)

would undermine discipline if his discretion were interfered with.

Mr Byass and the beer have not yet arrived. It will be soon bought up at the prices named in his advertisement. [See p. 132].

I find my inverted mess tin, resting on a little bit of stick to which a wire and bait is attached, makes an excellent mouse trap. I catch two or three a day. An impudent mouse is now running on the table where I am writing. I must have him tonight.

21 August. The new Army Works Corps have arrived, fine strong navvies. They are camped near us.

22 August. Saw very many of our Army Works Corps extremely drunk, lying on the roadside. I blushed for my country. There were Turks, Greeks, Croats and men from all parts of the East, French, Sardinians and Tartars passing by, and spurning almost these giants of men lying helpless.

26 August. Saw Pélissier in his carriage drawn by 4 artillery horses, a seedy Spahi in front, and a poor looking picquet of cavalry in rear. I suppose he cannot ride.

27 August. Attended a grand parade for the installation of Sir Colin Campbell and other GCBs &c &c. Gen Pélissier, Gen La Marmora and others there. Lord Stratford held a Court, the guns fired and drums beat, but the cannonade of Sebastopol was louder than all.

The Russians have finished their bridge over the harbour and are removing many things from the South to the North side. Our batteries are firing at it heavily all day.

30 August. Parade at $5\frac{1}{2}$ to read Articles of War, and Court Martial: punished one of the recruits, 6 times drunk since May. I hope this will be a warning to the others. We have more than 700 sick in our hospitals here, in the Cavalry Division.

31 August. I think of building a small hut for the winter. I shall never be able to remain in this thin leaky brown paper business. I have been searching about for bricks today, and I have found some, which I shall immediately appropriate. I have lots of work to do. My stable must be paved and enlarged, roads made, drains cut, and a good deal of broken stone put down by my hut.

31 August [*Letter*]. The French and Sardinians are laying down a railway towards the Tchernaya. They are likewise fortifying their position very strongly. All this looks as if they anticipated remaining where they are during the winter.

This early work is telling upon our young men. They never get a night's rest. They rise at $2\frac{1}{2}$ every morning, and we are then saddled, and remain ready for the Ruskie till it is ascertained that all is right. This breaking every night's sleep sends many of these weak boys into hospital.

Chapter 6

---

10 September – 31 December 1855

10 September [*Letter*]. The newspapers and telegraph will have informed you that the Russians have vacated and burnt the south side of Sebastopol, at least so much of it as the bombardment had spared. Their defence of it is, I conceive, one of the noblest things on record. The town was a mass of ruins, and their batteries were not the formidable works that I had imagined them to be.

As you will read the account written by Mr Russell in *The Times*, I shall only tell you of my share, and what I saw and did. On Saturday morning I received orders to take 4 squadrons of cavalry; 1 of the 4th; 1 of the 5th; 1 of the 8th Hussars; 1 of 4th Light Dragoons, and march to the hills overlooking the town, to prevent people approaching it during the assault.

At 12 the French took the Malakoff. They ran onto it without firing a shot, quite taking the Russians by surprise. It had been previously arranged that when the French were established in the Malakoff, the English should attack the Redan. The order was accordingly given and the attack began. Amidst a storm of grape and musketry our fellows advanced and got into the Redan (about 1,500 strong). There they were met by, they say, 10,000 Russians against whom they could do nothing. The attack of the French had given notice to the Russians and they had strengthened the usual guard. Our men were not supported, not a soldier was sent from the trenches to their assistance. They were mowed down by scores, and finally obliged to retire leaving their dead and wounded.

I consider that General Codrington* who commanded was much in fault for not sending in the reserve. He should have poured them in by thousands and we should have carried the Redan with a loss of a tenth of the numbers that have now been slaughtered. I have carefully examined the ground, and in my opinion the Malakoff being in our possession, there was no occasion for attacking the Redan, the Malakoff so completely commands the town.

This was very true. The loss of the Malakoff was the sole reason for the Russian evacuation of the south side of the town.

The fight raged till after dark, and during the whole night we could see bright flames rising from Sebastopol, and many tremendous explosions took place during the night.

On Sunday morning very early I heard that the Russ had vacated. I accordingly ordered my horse and orderly, and rode direct to the town. Orders had been given to the troops on duty not to allow anyone in. My rank carried me thro', and I was about the first English officer in the town. I found many soldiers in it plundering, but no guards, fears being entertained of mines. I went all thro' the Great Dockyard buildings and stores, all in ruins and nearly empty. I could see the Russians still in the houses below me, and saw them fire Fort Paul, which soon after blew up. I brought away a few mementoes, but not much. I then crossed over to the town side which was all in flames, and rode through the burning houses, some of them very handsome.

I afterwards visited the Redan, and was much disgusted at seeing them throwing the bodies of our brave men into the ditch of it, higgledy piggledy with the dead Russians, anyhow all of a heap. There was not any occasion for this, and the brave men deserved a more decent grave.

I was also much disgusted at seeing our cavalry posted to prevent men from carrying away things from the town. With

---

*Sir William John Codrington, GCB (1804–1884); ensign, Coldstream Guards, 1821; commanded 1st Brigade of the Light Division, never having before seen action, at the Alma and at Inkerman; assumed command of the Division, when Sir G. Brown was wounded at Inkerman; in November, 1855, succeeded Simpson as Commander-in-Chief and remained as such till final evacuation of the Crimea in July, 1856.

my own eyes I had seen that nothing but useless rubbish was to be got there, and I am sure the poor men have borne hardships and gone through enough to entitle them to a share of any of the things that were there. The French in particular were much disgusted at being stopped, and well they might be. I met the Adjnt-General (a stupid sump of a man) [Estcourt], and I told him about it, but he gave no order to the contrary. I had a most interesting day and I was most pleased at being one of the first into the town.

The Russians are, I suppose, on the opposite side of the town, but we know nothing of their movements. Some of their ships are burned but many still remain. The loss of our officers is again very great, especially the seniors as the list will show you. I hear that the young officers behaved most nobly, but the recruits on the contrary *badly*. I have told you before we cannot win battles with such stuff as they are.

The British part in this final act of the war was indeed a shameful failure. When the men, mostly new recruits, reached the parapet of the Redan, they panicked and retired. The British losses were some 2,500 men, the French about three times that number.

10 September. Rode to Sebastopol, through the Redan and thro' the Admiralty. Numbers of soldiers still carrying away helmets, coats, linen, cloth, all kinds of things. Looked at the docks which are magnificent—such gates, such granite blocks; then to the store houses near Fort Paul where we found a Russian steamer coming to the shore under a flag of truce, to carry away the wounded. We found the stores full of dead and wounded—a horrid sight. There being no English officer of rank superior to my own, I endeavoured to be of use. I got into conversation with the Russian Captain, R.N. [*sic*], who admired my orderly extremely. We shook hands and parted great friends. Rode home by the end of the town. All the Russian sailing men of war are destroyed, their steamers remain.

The Russians' retreat was so well conducted that nothing was known of it till 5 a.m. yesterday.

12 September. Found large parties of our men bringing these putrid dead Russians out of the stores. The stench was horrible. I would have made the steamer carry them all away on Monday, if I had had any authority. Rode through the whole town. Many of the houses must have been very handsome. There is not one standing. All are burnt. Visited Fort Nicholas. The Russ was firing, and an officer's horse was killed close to us. Two French bands were playing.

I cannot help thinking that the war is over. We have no object to gain now our work is done.

13 September. 200 dead Russians were found in the cellar of a store near Fort Paul. They seemed to have been wounded, and have died in this place.

14 September. The 200 dead Russians found yesterday are all supposed to be officers, as they were in coffins.

18 September. The French are gone to Bakshiserai to see what the Russians are doing there.

19 September. Commenced papering my hut and stuffing it with tow and paper to keep out the wind, but the roof leaks terribly, and the dripping of the rain into the vessels that I put to catch it is a melancholy sound.

Received all the Crimean Medals—a vulgar looking thing, with clasps like gin labels. How odd it is, we cannot do things like people of taste. This is a heavy vulgar thing.

20 September. At 2½ p.m. had a full dress parade and gave away the Crimean medals, 185 in number. I made the men a speech, and tried to instil into them the necessity of care of their horses and their appointments.

Blankets for the horses were delivered to us today. Brown blankets, value about 12/6. The men are to be charged 17s if they lose them—rather high methinks. No surcingle or means of putting them on are given.

21 September [*Letter*]. I wish they would make a *small* Maltese Cross out of the gun metal taken in Sebastopol, and give it to those who were *under fire* in the trenches and *to none other*. These medals given to all the world are of no value. They are *too* common.

I have sent you some roots of a kind of flag [iris] that bears a handsome purple flower. I took them from the public gardens at Sebastopol—literally dug them out from amongst the shot and pieces of shell.

21 September. The sixpence a day field allowance has been granted to the men since the 1st of July.

30.   *Sketches by Général Vanson, Varna, 1854; Six studies of officers
and men of the Scots Greys.*

31. *The Earl of Lucan.*

32. *General Sir Edward Cooper Hodge,*
KCB, c. 1877.

33. *General Scarlett.*
From William Simpson's sketchbook.

34. *General Sir William Codrington.*

24 September. Rode into Sebastopol. We saw the French busily engaged in taking down the bas reliefs from the Museum. Two marble sphinxes are covered up, ready to be carried off. They are also removing some of the ornaments from the Armenian Church on the hill, a beautiful building like a Grecian temple.

30 September. The plain is full of a sweet-scented lilac, and yellow crocus, a very pretty flower. Got up many of the bulbs to try and keep them to send to England.

2 October. Sent a party to assist the Electric Telegraph in conveying messages. It is found out to be done quicker by heavy dragoons.

3 October. Had the graveyard where our men are buried put into decent order, a wall raised round it, and the graves more covered over.

4 October [*Letter*]. I saw Mrs Straubenzee [wife of Brig-Gen Straubenzee, (see p. 113)] yesterday. She is living in camp, and to my idea (although *they* have a hut to themselves) not very comfortable. She was engaged in pasting newspaper over the boards. This we all do. I have various scenes from *Punch* and the *Illustrated London News* depicted on the walls of my domicile.

5 October [*Letter*]. I wish you would buy for me at Colnagi's two lithographs from drawings by Lieut Coles of the Royal Navy, representing the naval fight off Sebastopol on the 17th of October. One drawing represents the position of the *Agamemnon* and the *Sans Pareil* in four different points. Buy it for me, and keep it as a memento of that day's work.

Should this war come to an end, I shall endeavour to obtain money to go on half-pay; but if the officers do not make me up a sufficient sum, I shall remain where I am, shelved as a Major-General [See p. 65]. I do not expect that Forrest will do much for me, and if he does not pay me what I think right, I shall stick to the Regiment, though my interest in it is much decreased. *All* my old friends are gone, and the men are quite a new lot to me.

My hospital sergeant, Sergeant-Major Joseph Drake, is going home to England today. He has been 28 years in the Regiment with me, and is a truly excellent man. He will, I hope, call and see you. I have given him your direction.

K

Mr Byass's agent was not very long in clearing his ship. I bought some very nice sherry from him at 25/- a dozen. I wish more public-spirited individuals would come and sell things at a fair price. It would pay them.*

6 October. The officers commenced putting newspapers into our marquee in order that all may see them. It will not answer I know. Some have already disappeared. The British officer is of such a careless genus that he has no idea of having things kept in order.

One of the wild dogs of the country has a litter of pups in a hole in the hill above our camp, and all night she keeps up a most wearing bark. I shall have her shot as a nuisance.

8 October. President of a board to investigate a charge against de Salis† of the 8th [Hussars], for flogging a man after he had fainted.

We have much drunkenness owing to this sixpence a day they have given to the men. How sad it is that the only use that a soldier can find for money is to get drunk.

9 October. I have had to try my orderly room clerk by Court Martial and break him; also had to flog a man today.

11 October. The Forrests have caused me much annoyance by turning their half of our hut into a cooking kitchen, and today the stench of some greasy concoction has turned me quite sick. I therefore spoke to F about it. I told him that he had *three* places to live in, whilst I have but one, and I hoped he would not cook in the hut as it was offensive to me. He said he could not of course cook in the tent or marquee as that would offend him, so he expects that I am to quietly submit to be annoyed by his beastly cooking. If it goes on I shall request that he may be restricted to his camp accommodation. He is a vulgar selfish man, and I ever thought so since we were in Glasgow, where he brought his kept woman to reside in the same passage with myself, much to my disgust.

---

* Mr Byass was presumably the founder of the firm of Gonzalez Byass. The firm's records were destroyed in World War II. The fact that this shipment also included beer (see p. 125) is of interest, since the firm has always been engaged in shipping wine and never has had a direct connection with brewing. It was probably acting as an agent for some brewer.

† Rodolph de Salis, CB (1811–1880); cornet, 1830; Major commanding, 28 Nov, 1855, and Lieut-Col commanding, 8th Hussars, 1856; Lieut-Gen, 1877.

12 October [*Letter*]. I'm glad that my account of the action on the 8th interested you. Mr Russell, *The Times* correspondent, is wrong in stating that the cavalry sentries were posted within sight of Sebastopol. I carefully avoided so doing, and the shells thrown at Mr Russell and other lookers-on were not directed on them because the cavalry were seen. Had such people as Mr R not been present with the army, there would not be the same occasion for sentries.

The mouse traps are very useful, especially the one that catches them alive.

14 October. *The batman* was seen yesterday picking the fleas out of Mrs F's drawers, after which he hung them out to air. The latter part I saw. Her infernal cackle nearly drove me out of my hut today. Her laugh is quite like that of an idiot.

17 October. Some cavalry races. Poor, dull, uninteresting things, and the ground like iron. Old Simpson was there, looking like an old woman—one scrubby A.D.C., no orderlies. Had Pélissier been there he would have had a proper staff, and been attended by a picquet of hussars. I fear all we do tends to lower us as a military nation in the eyes of the Allies.

22 October. Some of the cavalry are to embark almost immediately for Scutari [where it had, at last, been decided they should winter.]

22 October [*Letter*]. The *Himalaya* arrived here today, and is to take away 340 horses of the Heavy Brigade. The sick and dismounted men will, of course, go the first. I declare I am quite sorry to go, but I cannot find many to agree with me.

I must say that I can only look back upon the days spent here as amongst some of the most interesting and enjoyable of my life.

23 October. Breakfasted with Scarlett, and discussed the Battle of Balaklava. His account and mine do not quite agree. I am sure that in an affair of that sort, we only know what is taking place immediately about us.

25 October. Anniversary of my first cavalry action: *Balaklava*. General Scarlett had out the cavalry and horse artillery, and a very good show we made. The 4th mounted 201 horses. The marching past was good, also the trotting past. The rest I thought very indifferent. I fear that Scarlett cannot handle a large body of troops, and I think he is very wrong for not

having his division out oftener. This is the second time only
that we have been out.

Much singing in the men's huts and of course much drunkenness.

26 October. Driscoll and Chapman returned from captivity
in Russia. On the whole they have been well treated.

These two men, together with a third (who probably died in
captivity), had been taken prisoner by cossacks whilst on patrol on
17 October, 1854. They were released as part of an exchange of
prisoners effected at Odessa a year later. Lieut-Col Forrest questioned one of the men on his return. He had been wounded in five
places, 'but says that he was taken to hospital and well treated
there, and that a Russian lady came to see him, and gave him "5
silver roubles", which however the Russian soldiers stole from him
whilst he was on the march. They are great thieves; but small
blame to them (says the man) for they get "no pay" '.
'If any of our men got bad treatment,' the ex-prisoner told Forrest,
'it was their own fault, for (says he) some of them were obliged to
try them ourselves by court martial, and flog them.'[1]

28 October. My cook, Clipsham, having taken himself off
altogether, I am obliged to try a youth named Munro, a clean
sort of lad, but utterly ignorant of cooking. Still by teaching
him I hope we shall make something of him.

29 October. Our new cook managed very well today. We
had two chickens very well roasted, and a boiled ham. The lad
is much cleverer than our late beast, who has this day been
tried by a court martial for breaking his confinement to camp.
This is the effect of drink. A disgraceful punishment: loss of a
penny a day good conduct pay, and a quiet comfortable berth
in which he had little to do. Now he will get worked.

Private Elijah Clipsham seems to have been the typical old soldier.
He had served in India, for he held the Punjab Campaign Medal,
1848–9. He was probably in the 3rd Light Dragoons, the 9th
Lancers or the 14th Light Dragoons in that campaign.

1 November. Received an order to send in the name of the
individual whom I conceived best entitled to distinction. I
sent in that of Sergt William Percy. It is I believe to receive a
French Order [in fact, the Cross of the Legion of Honour].

3 November. The abusive articles in *The Times* against Simpson are scandalous.

Typical of the sort of invective employed by *The Times* leader writer is the following, which appeared on 23 October: 'Lord Raglan was not young, but was well able to ride, so we replaced him by a General of the same age, whom physical infirmity forbade from getting on horseback.'

5 November. Sir Colin [Campbell] has gone home in consequence of his having lost his temper, and used violent language at a Council of War.

This was not in fact the case. Sir Colin was the next senior officer after Simpson, who had now sent in his resignation; but he was 63, whereas Codrington, who was only 51, was preferred by the government for the command-in-chief. Campbell, who was not aware of Codrington's succession till he arrived in England, had earlier been offered the Governorship of Malta: 'to go from duty with a division in the field', as he contemptuously put it, 'to become schoolmaster to the recruits in Malta'. This he had seen as a devious means of removing him from the Crimea and was the chief reason for his return home. On arrival in England, however, he was persuaded, chiefly by the Queen in person, to whom he said that he was prepared 'to serve under a corporal if she wished it',[2] to return to the Crimea as a divisional commander under his junior, Codrington. There he remained till the end of the war.

I have just had a present of quarter of a fine goat. We shall let it hang for a day and then eat it.

I do not think Eleanor would relish dining with us, though faith the food is not bad. We get plenty of fine beef now (skinny stuff it would be thought in England). Sometimes we roast it very well. I have converted a tin case that the coffee comes in into a Dutch oven and we manage to roast our meat very well.

7 November. I called at the French Headquarters. Their *salon* with a chimney made out of the altar piece of a Russian Church is very nice.

9 November. Sir William Codrington is to be our new Commander-in-Chief. He is a gentleman, and has a cool good head, and though he has not been a very dashing Division leader, he may not make a bad no. 1. I hope he will be respected by our Allies, which I fear poor Simkins [Simpson] was not. This will be a triumph to *The Times*, which I hate.

10 November. The English army in the Crimea yesterday amounted to 40,500 men.

11 November. At 12 went to see General La Marmora review the Sardinian Army, about 12,000 of them, cavalry, guns and infantry. A fine lot of men; gun horses very bad; cavalry not equal to many of our Yeomanry; the Bersaglieri, or Riflemen, a very smart active lot of men. There was first a kind of High Mass, opera music playing the whole time, the Colours and Standards being brought up to be blessed. Then the infantry in three lines were inspected, and the guns and cavalry in rear of them. Afterwards the whole marched past in quick time, the officers making a family [*sic*] salute in passing. A large number of officers of the English and the French Army were present, and for the first time our officers looked smart and well dressed.

13 November. Took the regiment out to the Highland Camp at Kamara to let the men see that and the Piedmontese Camp, which is very complete, with their huts made of mud and wattles. Rode into Balaklava to Captn Gordon's stores, where I chose a sealskin coat £3.10, also some warm gloves. The quantities of excellent clothing accumulated there for the Army is very cheery to look at: blankets, coats, socks, drawers, jerseys, gloves, boots, spades, pickaxes, saws in great abundance. How different from last year.

14 November. At this same hour last year, I was lying half frozen and without a bit to eat or drink, underneath a wet tent which had fallen on me, a tempest raging, and the camp a sea of mud.

18 November. All round the lines and men's huts. What an uncomfortable creature is the British soldier!

Cooper [the regimental surgeon] tells me he has examined a man of the 11th Hussars who received thirty-one lance and sword wounds at Balaklava, where he was taken prisoner, and sent into Russia. He was at Tchorgoum two days without having his wounds dressed, and afterwards three months in hospital at Simpheropol, after which he went 800 versts to Veronitz, and has just returned.

Of the 295 soldiers who came on service, 62 are dead;

deserted, 2; commissioned, 2; invalided to England, 43; sick, absent, 12; in hospital here, 8; present at their duty, 166.

19 November [*Letter*]. Young Wilkinson, when he went to the Horse Guards for another month's leave, was told that he could have two if he liked, and some friend of his, a Member of Parliament, told him that if he wished to join the depot without going to the Crimea, he had plenty of interest to get this done. He, however, refused both offers and rejoined here.

I hope Sir Colin Campbell will be given something. He is a fine brave energetic soldier, and being senior to Codrington, and having been fighting for many years when C was dancing about in London, he naturally feels extremely hurt at being superseded. Still I am of opinion that Sir Colin would never have got on as Commander-in-Chief. His temper was very violent, he has no manners and would inevitably have been in hot water with all his superior officers in no time. General C is very gentlemanly and I believe accomplished; and he has good looks and good manners, all of which tell with the mass. Windham,* as Chief of Staff, has issued an order desiring that all reports and correspondence shall go through him. He will not allow any other channel of communication between the army and the General but himself. He is right and I hope he will carry out his plans.

22 November. The camps are so changed I hardly could recognise them: such roads, such stacks of wood, corn and stores of all sorts, railways, stone cottages, huts, &c. &c.— quite a different aspect to what it was—and how different from last year. The absence of the vultures strikes me. Last year there were hundreds.

Orders have been issued that all persons not in the service of H.M. are to have passports. This is a very proper order. [See p. 116].

23 November. Rode through the Kadekoi bazaar, full of costume and Eastern manners: Turkish barbers shaving the heads of the faithful, Turks sitting in rows on benches smoking, Kabab shops, French restaurants, porter shops, stores of every-

---

* (Sir) Charles Ash Windham, KCB (1810–1870); ensign and lieutenant, Coldstream Guards, 1826; QMG 4th Division in Crimea, 1854; commanded 2nd Brigade of 2nd Division, 1855; Maj-Gen, 1855; commanded 4th Division, 1855.

thing, English or French; vendors of oranges, fish, plenty of good mutton. In fact by paying well for it, almost everything can be bought. A fine broad hard road now runs past Kadekoi to Balaklava, and locomotive engines are running on the railway. [Until now horses had been the chief motive agents on the railway.] The Tartars must stare at all these changes.

25 November. I get a good deal of rain in from my charming neighbour. They have not taken the trouble to do anything to their half. Last evening I was forced to read out aloud to drown the chatter she made.

28 November. Went to Henry's hut and played a rubber of whist. I would have them over to my hut to play, but they will smoke, and they bring such a quantity of mud with them into my hut, which I manage to keep pretty clean.

29 November. Scarlett went away today in the *Earl of Aberdeen*—some of the Inniskillings gone with him. It is very unfair his sending them & the 5th away before us. He has always been jealous of us, since Lord Lucan said in his speech that by our charge in flank, the Russian column was defeated—also the 5th being put under my command at Varna.

30 November. Went after dinner to Henry's hut and played whist, tizzy [sixpenny] points; won my money.

5 December [*Letter*]. My regiment commences embarking tomorrow.

I hear wonderful packing and arrangement going on next door. Mrs F and her lady's maid, Private Denis Shine, are stowing the goods away in various boxes.

6 December. The road from the camp to the quay is a sea of mud, and near the quay the jostling of carts, wagons, railway carriages and men carrying away huts was beyond anything I ever saw.

Mrs Forrest arrived seated on the top of a baggage cart drawn in triumph by two mules. Forrest was absent from his duties all day, waiting on his wife. Not a thing did he do. He had three wagon loads of baggage, 2 goats, a lot of cocks and hens, and his wife.

8 December. Early in the morning we began to warp out, and after breakfast at 9½ we got clear of Balaklava, took a last look at the bold cliffs and curious old Genoese towers, marking the entrance to the harbour.

The *Oneida* is a fine iron screw ship. We have 200 horses on board, all well put up, and 185 men, many of them as sick as dogs, all dirty and miserable, also a poor wretched native Egyptian, who it is supposed was left behind by the 10th Hussars. Nobody can understand him, so we are taking him down with us to turn him loose at Constantinople.

10 December. We came to anchor at Scutari.

11 December. Our men were much amused by the Muezzin calling the hour of prayer from a neighbouring minaret. They first imitated him, and then called out 'What's up, old fellow?' Times are indeed changed in Constantinople when this can be done.

14 December. [*Letter*]. Scutari. We are here, and in a miserable plight; such mud, such rain, such snow and sludge. We are under cover certainly, but crowded into buildings hastily erected, the mud all round, which is quite 18 inches and 2 feet deep.

16 December. Made an arrangement with a man named Joseph Zitelli, to come and mess us. We are to give him 5/6 and our rations daily, and he is to find everthing and four meals a day.

17 December. Rode down to Scutari to see General Scarlett who goes on leave today. He leaves a flourishing order behind him about Commanding Officers getting their regiments in order for next year's campaign. No thanks to him if we do so. He is regularly deserting us, when really there is much to do.

18 December. How curious it is our living here in a Palace of the Sultans, and riding rough-shod all over the place. Ten years ago who would have thought this.

21 December. Cooper and myself took a Kayik [caique] to Pera. Many insinuating boys wished to show us the road, but we found it without their aid. The scene was most charming— the costumes, the Kayiks, the dirty old ships, some carved all all over with flowers and fruit, and the ugly women with their faces all covered up, their yellow boots and skinny legs—all new, all interesting.

24 December. Anything but a merry Christmas for our men, I am thinking. Still it is better than last year.

25 December. Dined with the Carabineers. We had soup, fish, turkey, goose, roe deer, cutlets, mackerel, salad, woodcocks, wild ducks, rice pudding, and a very bad attempt at a plum pudding. We shall not starve at this rate.

29 December. Went to the opera. We had a box—a good one—17/6: the piece, *Il Trovatore*,* the singing and acting very respectable. The house without ornament, but a handsome glass chandelier. Otherwise scarcely any light in the house.

30 December. The Europeans go where they like now. The dogs no longer bark at them, and the Turks 'Johnnie' us, and are as civil as possible.

31 December. Our Mess is now established and is very good. We had a large bustard for dinner today, a most excellent bird. The weather fine, bright sunshine but rather cold wind. And thus ends 1855. How thankful I feel to have seen the end of it. It has been a most eventful year. I have been a participator in the most extraordinary siege on record, and have passed twelve months encamped in the midst of an immense army, and surrounded by natives of the greater part of the Eastern World. Certainly the Bazaar at Kadikoi produced more costume, and in it were seen a greater variety of people almost than the Bazaar of Stamboul. I have witnessed great battles and many awful scenes of suffering and death. I am now writing in a room of one of the Sultan's Palaces, where English songs resound on every side, and I am able to view at leisure the beautiful Constantinople, the City that for years I have longed to visit.

I rejoice that all I love and care for in this world are well and comfortably settled in their own house. May God preserve them and may we be all once again united in this world.

---

*Verdi's opera received its first performance in Rome in 1853. It was not performed in London until 10 May, 1855.

Chapter 7

1 January – 30 June 1856

1 January [*Letter*]. Scutari. I have arranged to go to a great Ball at the Embassy. The idea of going to Balls out here! The worst of going out at Pera is that there is no possible way of getting about except on foot, and the streets are perfectly dark and ankle deep in filth. Ladies get Sedan chairs, but gentlemen walk in large boots and carry paper lanterns, the affect of which in the street is very curious.

On Saturday I went to the opera—splash, splash through the mud, paper lantern in hand. The gallery contained the noisiest set of fellows I ever heard. They beat Dublin or any place I ever was in. The noise was quite enough to prevent ladies attending.

21 January [*Letter*]. Nothing is talked of here but peace. We shall see. Should such be the case, what a joyful meeting will ours be, and how pleased you will be to know that I remained here, and did not desert my post when *all* others went away [a pardonable exaggeration!].

I have been over the great Mosque of St Sophia. We arrived during Prayer. We took off our boots and went into a kind of outer passage, which was full of women kneeling. As soon as the prayer was over we went down into the body of the Mosque, and there, where a few years back, a Christian would have been murdered, we walked about. Many of the Turks crowded round and stared at us and asked who we were; but they offered no opposition to our going where we liked. The prayer being over, the women were allowed into the Mosque, and they sat on the ground round a Priest who was reading and expounding the Koran. We stood close to them for some time and were objects of much curiosity to them.

In St Sophia we saw many well dressed Turks, but turbans are now uncommon. All wear the red fez, and all the troops and everyone in the service of the Government wear a frock coat and trowsers.

I am growing horribly fat: this change of life and getting good nourishing food. I must take to the field again to regain my shape.

I dined with Paget a few nights back. They have a tolerably comfortable house, and live like gentlefolks. She is a nice quiet person and very handsome. [Fenton, the photographer, called her 'the belle of the Crimea'. She was a cousin of her husband's, and died in 1858.] He is in great glee about these rumours of peace. He makes no secret of his wishes upon that score.

30 January [*Letter*]. I am most obliged to you for thinking about Sergt-Major Drake. He is a thoroughly honest man, never drinks, and is most methodical and regular in his habits. He would make an excellent overlooker.

I am going tomorrow to a fancy dress ball at the Embassy. I intend going in uniform. I hear that Lady Stratford talked about not allowing uniforms, as if any of us could go to the expense of fancy dresses!

18 February [*Letter*]. In Stamboul I met many women in their bright yellow or orange or blue stuff garments, and a boy escorted by a tall nigger, the boy dressed in jacket, waist-coat and trowsers of pale pink stamped velvet. He was the child of some noted Turk. On Saturday I met one of the Sultan's children in the Bazaar, escorted by two blacks. The boy was dressed in violet-coloured velvet, and his jacket and trowsers were covered with embroidered silver stars. He was a pale look-ing lad, very like Sultan Abdul Medjid. Poor wretch! His probable fate is strangling.*

---

*The Sultan Abdul Medjid I (1823–1861) was succeeded by his brother Abdul Aziz (1830–1876) who either killed himself or was murdered. He, in turn, was succeeded by his nephew, Mjrad V (1840–1904), the eldest son of Abdul Medjid I, who, after reigning for less than a year, was declared insane (being suspected of Liberalism). He was replaced on the throne by his

Peace certainly begins to look more promising. I shall be in my barrack yard again I do believe. I expect that by the time I return, people will have ceased to care about those who return from the wars. I hear of all sorts of men having swords presented to them, and one officer who belongs to the Inniskillings got drunk and lost the sword on returning from the dinner where they had given it to him. Certainly we who have stayed away from home all this time ought to be remembered for it.

12 March [*Letter*]. I see they have appointed a Commission of some marvellous old gentlemen to stir up the mud and make more stink.

This was the so-called 'whitewashing board': *the Board of General Officers appointed to inquire into the Statements contained in the Reports of Sir John McNeill and Colonel Tulloch, animadverting upon the Conduct of Certain Officers on the General Staff, and Others in the Army.* The board sat at the Royal Hospital, Chelsea, and its voluminous report appeared in late July, 1856.

I am glad that I am not at home, and I am still more glad that I said nothing in my evidence [to the Crimean Commissioners, McNeill and Tulloch] that could throw blame on any one.

I went over to Pera on Monday, where I saw Mr Russell of *The Times* on his way to the Crimea. I gave him a most flourishing account of the state of the cavalry, and painted all as *couleur de rose*.

I called yesterday on Mrs Forrest. They have got a dirty house, and the Dragoon as their only servant. Thank heaven they are not near me.

I see that Sir de Lacy Evans [commander of the 2nd Division in the Crimea, giving evidence before the Board]* talks

---

brother, Abdul Hamid II (1842–1918). His rule lasted till he was deposed in 1909. He died while confined in the Beylerby Palace.

Abdul Medjid I had at least six other sons. What happened to them is not recorded. Hodge may well have encountered either Murad, who was 15, or Abdul Hamid, who was 13 in 1856.

*Sir George de Lacy Evans, GCB (1787–1870); ensign, 22nd Foot, 1807; attached to Picton's Division as DQMG at Waterloo; elected M.P. first, 1830, for Rye, as an advanced radical, and later, 1833, for Westminster; General, 1861.

about the men's knapsacks being left on shore. Even when we arrived at Balaklava our men's valises were ordered to be left on board a ship. Some few days afterwards the Captain of the ship put the valises all on shore without sending any notice to the officer in command of the regiment. The valises therefore remained lying on the beach without any guard for some considerable time. They were plundered of many things and numbers were stolen altogether. As we marched into a standing camp from which the army could not move except to retreat on board a ship, I never could see the use of leaving our valises. The men literally had nothing but the clothes on their backs, and many remained the winter thro' in this state.

19 March [*Letter*]. I went yesterday to see the howling dervishes, a very extaordinary exhibition. For nearly two hours they kept up a wild chaunt and chorus accompanied by the most violent rocking and swaying of the body. It was a curious but scarcely a pleasing sight. At the end of the performance babies and children were laid at the feet of the Chief Dervish, who put his foot on their stomachs. Men afterwards laid down and were treated in the same manner. They made no opposition to our witnessing it. On the contrary, they invited us to take coffee and smoke, which we did in a very small, not over-clean room full of men sitting round. The chapel where they danced was very clean, and the whole operation was gone through with the greatest decorum.

I hear from the Crimea that at the signing of the armistice, the squadron of the 11th Hussars that attended General Codrington, looked as superior to the squadron of Chasseurs d'Afrique that attended Pélissier, as these latter did to the regiment of cossacks that attended the Russian General, and who were the crack cossacks of the army.

The Congress of Paris, which was to agree the peace terms, began work on 25 February. Its first act was to order an armistice which was to last until the end of March. In the treaty, which was signed on 30 March, no mention was made of the Holy Places, which were the war's ostensible cause, nor was there anything to show who was the victor and who the vanquished.

The Black Sea was declared neutral, and the Danube free. The integrity of Turkey was guaranteed by the Great Powers, and so were the Danubian principalities. The Russians were to cede a small part of Bessarabia, and the Sultan declared his readiness to improve the condition of all Christians within the Ottoman Empire.

What luck the Emperor of the French has! He is the happy father of a strapping boy. I hope the boy will thrive.

Napoleon III's only son, Eugène, was born on 16 March. 'The Prince Imperial', as he was called, was killed in an ambush at the age of 23, serving with the British army during the Zulu War.

3 April [*Letter*]. So peace is indeed all signed and settled, and in the course of a few months I hope to have the unspeakable joy of once more seeing you.

We had an excellent run with the hounds yesterday: 45 minutes and a kill in the open. It is very fine galloping over these hills, with Constantinople and its minarets rising in front of you, or the Sea of Marmora with the mountains of Asia and Mount Olympus covered with snow. The panorama on every side is splendid, and when this is combined with a fine gallop after a pack of hounds, it is indeed very fine.

15 April [*Letter*]. I see in the *Illustrated London News* a drawing of a Crimean snowdrop. I think you can produce some originals. There were thousands of them close to my hut, and I sent many of the bulbs home.

I see that Lord Lucan is the first that is to be tried. I shall be surprised if he does not make out a case for himself. He is a clever man, and he has with him all the necessary documents to prove that the cavalry were employed every day during the months of December and January, and could not therefore carry up the means of hutting themselves.

23 April [*Letter*]. I got back here on Monday evening, having left Athens [where he had been on a short sightseeing trip] on Saturday night. Our passage back was pretty good. We had on board fifteen of the *Soeurs de Charité* going out to the French hospitals to replace 15 who had died of typhus fever. Poor things. They seemed very cheerful, and took no notice of the scenery. I remarked its beauty to one of them, and she quite gaily said, 'Oh, we have nothing to do with that', and pointing to her knitting, she said 'This is pleasure enough for us.'

28 May. [*Letter*]. I am happy to say that my depôt [in Ireland]

is ordered to England, where the regiment is to be stationed
on its arrival, but whereabouts I know not. I hope not in the
manufacturing districts. I have had enough of them. If I were
allowed to choose I would take Exeter, Dorchester, Brighton,
and those stations.

14 June [*Letter*]. We embark today for England in the *Simla*
steamship, a fine vessel, and the same that conveyed us from
Varna to the Crimea.

29 June [*Letter*]. Portsmouth. We have arrived here this day,
after a very prosperous voyage.

30 June [*Letter*]. Spithead. We have lost three horses on the
voyage, but I have brought 54 of my old campaigners with me,
and I shall take care to show them to everybody as a proof
that we were not so bad as they represented us to be.

I am sorry to say that we are ordered to go to Aldershot. I
really think they might have spared the regiments coming
home this farce, and have allowed us to go at once to our
destinations by the shortest and most convenient routes. We
are of course quite unprepared with the various little
requisites required for a camp life in England. Some old uniform and three flannel shirts constitute the kit of the majority
of the officers, and as they did not anticipate campaigning in
England, they gave away all the articles that were very useful
in a camp, but useless in barracks. Many of the officers have
but one horse, so how they are to march up to Leeds I know
not, except at great expense.

Then I cannot show my regiment to advantage, not having
had my clothing this year, and the coats the men are now
wearing will offend the eyes of the authorities, being large
and roomy, and made so that the men could wear plenty of
warm clothing under them, which though very useful, do
not look smart. However I suppose we shall do as well as our
neighbours, but I think our authorities crazy.

I shall take the earliest opportunity of running up to see
you, so if your servants see a ragged looking ruffian in a red
jacket trying to get into No 19, beg them not to call the police.

Epilogue

Of the remaining thirty-eight years of Hodge's life little, except the bare bones, is known.

Soon after its arrival at Aldershot his regiment was inspected by the Queen. Orders were then received for it 'to march into the interior of the country. Sheffield was honoured', as the local paper declared on 30 July, 1856, 'by the headquarters being stationed here, an honour which was much looked for and coveted by the people of Leeds.' A dinner was given to the officers by 'the chief men of Sheffield'. It was 'of a most *recherché* description, supplied by Mr Bishop of the Royal Hotel. The wines also were choice and abundant.'[1] The chief guest was Lord Cardigan, and the numerous speeches and toasts were exactly what would be expected on such an occasion.

In the following year, 1857, the regiment was stationed at Manchester. The inspection reports for each year are laudatory, except for that of 1858, in which it is written: 'The Duke of Cambridge [who had become Commander-in-Chief in 1856] relies upon every attention being paid to the riding of all ranks, which the Earl of Cardigan [who was Inspector-General of Cavalry] states is not as perfect as it should be.'

A desultory correspondence over the years between both Cardigan and Lucan with Hodge has been preserved. The only one of any interest is very typical of its writer:

'Portman Square,

Novr 19th, 1857.

'My dear Col Hodge,

A friend of mine, Hubert de Burgh, is interested about Miss Reynolds, one of the principal actresses at the Haymarket Theatre, and who is going to act immediately at the Manchester Theatre, and he has requested me to ask you and your officers to patronize her.

> 'Believe me yours very truly,
> 'Cardigan.'

There also survives a letter from the Duke of Cambridge, from which it is clear that Hodge refused some sort of semi-military appointment in 1858. 'The only reason I offered it to you', wrote the Duke, 'was that I thought you would do the work remarkably well, and that it would be agreeable to you to have something to do, should you go on half-pay. I would, myself,' he added, 'greatly prefer your continuing at the head of your very fine regiment.'[2] The following year, Hodge was in fact placed on half-pay.

*   *   *

Having observed him from his writings during the war, the reader might well suppose that Hodge was likely to remain an established bachelor. In fact, he married at the age of fifty, four years after his return from the east. His bride, who was 31, was the daughter of a Yorkshire squire.*

There were three sons and one daughter of the marriage. The daughter, who was the youngest of the family, was born when Hodge was sixty-one years of age and his wife forty-two. She died of scarlet fever when she was seven. The eldest son, Edward Francis was born in 1861. He, like his youngest brother, Ferdinand Harper, born in 1867, was an army officer. Both entered by way of 'Honorary Queen's Cadetships', secured for them by their father's influence with the Duke of Cambridge.

Edward, a Captain in the 4th Battalion, the Rifle Brigade, died of fever aged 28 in Upper Burma. Surprisingly enough, he was six feet tall. His father, in memory of him, gave £640 to the Soldiers' Daughters' Home at Hampstead, in payment of a 'Perpetual Presentation' or scholarship. 'The child, Eliza Barry, now in the Home', the Secretary told Hodge, 'will be the first Scholar, and I will intimate this to the officer commanding the 4th Dragoon

---

* Lucy Anne (1829–1885), 2nd daughter of James Rimington of Broomhead Hall, Bolsterstone, Yorkshire. One of her two sisters married the 3rd Earl of Ranfurly, Governor-General of New Zealand.

Guards.'³ She was no doubt the daughter of an ex-trooper of the regiment.

Ferdinand, the third son, only passed his preliminary examination for the army at the fourth try. He was then gazetted to the 1st Battalion of the Yorkshire Regiment, and served in Cyprus, Alexandria and at home. He died in 1941.

The second son, Frederick Arthur, born in 1866, joined the training ship H.M.S. *Britannia* at the age of twelve. Another cadet who joined at the same time was Prince George, later King George V. He served all over the world as a Lieutenant, R.N. until his resignation from active service in 1895, the year after his father's death. Returning to the active list in 1914, he reached the rank of Commander before again resigning at the end of the First World War. Like his father he was very short in height, but he was also exceptionally powerful. In the Navy he was known as 'the pocket Hercules'. He married twice, and died, leaving issue (including the present owner of his father's papers), in 1936.

* * *

After a little over three years on half-pay, Hodge resumed his military career. He was promoted to the rank of Brigadier-General and offered command of the cavalry brigade at Aldershot in succession to Lord George Paget. In December, 1862, he accepted this, his last post and took up residence in Anglesey House, where he lived with his family for five years. In 1863, he became a Major-General, and in 1870 was appointed Regimental Colonel of the 18th Hussars. This honorary position he relinquished when the Colonelcy of his own regiment became vacant in 1874, and this he held till his death.

In 1871 he had been promoted to Lieutenant-General and in 1873 became Sir Edward Hodge, KCB. Four years after that elevation, he was made full General and, on the occasion of the Queen's Golden Jubilee, in 1887, GCB. Two years before this final honour his wife died, predeceasing him by nine years. His beloved mother, to whom his Crimean letters had been addressed, had died, just short of eighty, in 1864.

In the course of the years which followed his Aldershot command, Hodge's energies seem to have been directed, in part, to organisations concerned with the welfare of ex-soldiers and their families.

He was closely connected, for example, with the Corps of Com-
missionaires, which provided jobs for old soldiers. In 1878, he was
made a member of the executive and finance committees of the
Royal Patriotic Fund (see p. 84).

There survives a letter written to him in the last year of his life from
'J. W. O'Brien, late Band, 4th Dragoon Guards'. 'I am not unknown
to you,' it reads, 'having served in the 4th D.G. while under your
command, as did my father for 25 years, including the whole of the
Crimean campaign, as did my mother who accompanied the
regiment there. My mother is dead now some years, but my father
is alive, and, I am sorry to say, married again, and in his 74th year
of age has three young children, all now dependent on a private's
pension. If you could kindly interest yourself with the Patriotic
Fund to obtain him some increase of pension for the little remaining
time he has to live, it would be a mercy for which I shall be ever
grateful.' What the outcome of this application was is not known.

Hodge was also an active member of a committee formed to provide
a monument to those who fell at Balaklava in St Paul's Cathedral.

As one would expect, he attended the Balaklava Dinner held each
year in London on 25 October, and was often in the Chair. Amongst
his papers are a number of letters from Lord Lucan concerning the
arrangements for this famous function.

Nearly every year Hodge, until he got too old, took his family abroad
to Europe for a few weeks in the summer. Once or twice a year the
whole family, when the children were of sufficient age, would stay
at Lady Hodge's Yorkshire home or in the country houses of friends
and relations. Over the years, the family occupied a number of
different houses. One was at Ryde, another at Sydenham and there
was generally a house in London proper as well.

For twenty years from 1867, when 'Ferdi', his youngest son, was
born, Hodge kept an occasional journal to record his boy's progress.
From this touching document we learn that he was christened on
13 July, and that a week later he was 'vaccinated by Surgeon
Fleming of the 4th Dragoon Guards'. In the following year Ferdi
was 'very ill, in consequence of the cook supplying skimmed milk
for the nursery'. When he was five, he went to church for the first
time 'and yawned a good deal', and then in the following week was
photographed 'in a helmet, which he insisted on wearing'. At the
age of ten, he was 'dressed up (at a child's party given at home)',
in the costume worn by his father as Page of Honour at George IV's

coronation fifty-six years before, and which is still preserved by the family. In 1878 Hodge took his son 'to the Temple, and to see Cleopatra's Needle, which is being put up on the Thames Embankment'.

In 1883, Ferdi 'first came out in a tail coat' and his father proudly recorded that, at sixteen, he was five feet, four-and-a-half inches in height—an improvement of three-and-a-half inches upon his own height at the same age. At nineteen, Ferdi had reached five feet, eight-and-a-half inches: obviously a great relief to the one time cox of the *Victory* longboat at Eton, whose second-in-command in the Crimea, all those years back, used to refer to him as 'little Hodge'. He breathed his last in his London house, 26, Cornwall Gardens, South Kensington, on 10 December, 1894, five months short of his eighty-fifth birthday. He was buried in the Brompton cemetery, in the same grave as his wife and daughter.

NOTE ON THE 4th (ROYAL IRISH) DRAGOON GUARDS

Beyond Richard Cannon's ninety-four page *Historical Record*, published in 1839, and the Rev Harold Gibb's even shorter *Record* of the regiment in World War I, published in 1925, no regimental history has ever been written. This gap, which is not unique among British heavy cavalry regiments, is easily explained. Until the 20th century very few regiments had seen less active service than the 4th. It started its career as part of the earliest augmentation of Britain's first permanent standing army. James II, in 1685, the year of his accession, used Monmouth's insurrection as an excuse to add a further twelve infantry and eight cavalry regiments to the four of foot and three of horse raised by Charles II soon after the Restoration of 1660. Thus was born what eventually became the 1st to 6th Dragoon Guards, and the two senior hussar regiments, the 3rd and 4th.

The 4th Dragoon Guards was first known, as were all regiments at that date, by the name of its Colonel: The Earl of Arran's Regiment of Horse, or Arran's Cuirassiers. Later it was usually called the 5th Horse. It first saw action at Steenkirk in 1692, under William III at the head of the Grand Alliance against Louis XIV. At Landen the following year, the regiment was one of six with which the King, near the end of that hard-contested battle, tried unsuccessfully to save his beaten infantry.

In 1698 the 4th was posted to the Irish establishment, and there it stayed, keeping the peace, for 95 unbroken years, generally split up into widely separated troops and sub-troops. In 1746, the regiment was re-named the 1st Irish Horse, though it was commonly referred to as The Blue Horse, from the colour of its uniform facings. In 1762 directions were given that all recruiting, which till then had been carried on chiefly in England, was to be done in Ireland. 'In a few years afterwards', as Cannon relates, 'the ranks of the First Irish Horse were composed almost exclusively of Irishmen.'[1] In 1854 there was still a very considerable element of Irish troopers in the regiment.

The conversion to Dragoon Guards took place in 1788, when all four regiments of horse on the Irish establishment were thus designated. At that date the regiment gained the title which it was to hold for the next 134 years. At the same time the words 'Royal Irish' were added 'in consideration of its long and faithful services in Ireland'.[2]

In 1793, on the outbreak of the Revolutionary War with France, the regiment crossed over to England in readiness for service on the Continent. The call, however, never came, and two years later the 4th was back in Ireland. There it took a prominent part in suppressing the rebellion of 1798.

For the next twelve years the regiment was stationed chiefly in England and Scotland, until, in 1811, it went on foreign service for the first time in 113 years, joining Wellington in Portugal. First in Le Marchant's brigade and later in Slade's, the 4th advanced and retreated with the army all through the campaigns of 1812, but it never came properly into action. In 1813 it was one of four regiments which were ordered to transfer their horses to make up deficiencies in other regiments. The officers and men returned, dismounted and disconsolate, to England. In the following year, with new mounts, the 4th returned once more to Ireland.

Between that country and Scotland and England, the regiment spent the next forty years of what came to be known as the 'Long Peace'. It was much employed in maintaining law and order. In one month of 1832, for instance, it furnished fifty-one parties to assist the civil power in Ireland in making tithe collections, dispersing illegal meetings, suppressing election riots and quelling riots at fairs. In 1838 approval was given for the regimental standards and appointments to bear the Harp and Crown, as well as the Star of the Order of St Patrick, with the motto 'Quis separabit?'

In 1839, during the Chartist riots the regiment was in Birmingham, when one of its squadrons dispersed a violent mob in the Bull Ring. Nine years later the presence of the regiment in Nottingham ensured a peaceful ending to a 'seditious' meeting of Chartists. Its establishment during the years Hodge was with it varied little from what had been laid down five years before he joined. There were 28 officers and 335 N.C.O.s and men, divided into six troops.

*   *   *

The regiment's first active service after the Crimean War was with Wolseley's expedition to Egypt in 1882. Its first tour of duty in India started in 1894 and lasted till 1903, thereby preventing it from taking part in the Boer War. In 1922, it was amalgamated with the 7th Dragoon Guards (Princess Royal's). The regiment is now known as 4th/7th Royal Dragoon Guards.

Source Notes

(pages x–18)

EDITOR'S NOTE

1 Fisher-Rowe, Major L.R. (ed.) *Extracts from Letters of E. R. Fisher-Rowe (late Captain, 4th Dragoon Guards), during the Crimean War, 1854–55,* privately printed, Godalming, 1907.

PROLOGUE

1 *Keate's Entrance Book*; *Etoniana*, no. 34 (1923), 529–30; information kindly supplied by P. Strong Esq., Eton College Librarian.

2 Kinglake to Hodge, 29 Oct, 1866, *Hodge Papers*.

3 MS family book, *Hodge Papers*.

CHAPTER I

1 For details of Forrest's troubles with Cardigan, see Woodham-Smith, Cecil, *The Reason Why*, 1953, 55, 65, 95.

2 Hansard, H. of C., 16 Feb, 1852, CXIX, 552.

3 Churchill, W. S., *A History of the English-speaking Peoples*, IV 'The Great Democracies', 1958, 57–8.

4 Shirley, Lieut-Col Arthur, late of the 7th Queen's Own Hussars, *Remarks on the Transport of Cavalry and Artillery: With Hints for the Management of Horses, Before, During, and After a Long Sea Voyage*, 1854.

5 Capt Cresswell's letters to a friend from Bulgaria are quoted in Williams, G. T., *Historical Records of XI Hussars*, 180–83.

6 Mrs Duberly to Mrs Marx, 23 July, 1854, Tisdall, E.E.P. (ed.) *Mrs Duberly's Campaigns*, 1963, 49.

7 Rogers, Col H. C. B., *Troopships and Their History*, 1963, 105–6.

CHAPTER II

1 Raglan to Cardigan, 3 July, 1854, P.R.O., K.B. 1/265, 26–7.

2 16 July, 1854. MS letters of Troop Sergeant-Major George Cruse, 1st Royal Dragoons (property of Marquess of Anglesey).

3   27 Aug, 1854, Forrest, Gen W. C., MS letters home, 1854–1855, National Army Museum.

4   Fisher, 12.

5   Cruse, 7 Aug, 1854.

6   Fisher, 21 Sep, 1854.

7   Fisher, 25 Sep, 1854.

8   [McNeil, Sir John and Tulloch, Col Alexander] *Report of the Commission of Inquiry into the Supplies of the British Army in the Crimea*, 1855, 76.

9   Fisher, 12 Oct, 1854.

10 Bonner-Smith, D. (ed.) *The Russian War, 1854: Baltic and Black Sea Official Correspondence*, 1943, 227.

11 Kinglake, A. W. *The Invasion of the Crimea: its origin and . . . progress down to the death of Lord Raglan*, 1868, III, 424.

12 7 Oct, 1854, MS letters of Capt C. M. J. D. Shakespear, Royal Horse Artillery (property of Mrs L. S. Bickford).

13 [Cardigan, Earl of] *Eight Months on Active Service; or, A Diary of a General Officer of Cavalry in 1854*, 1855, 86.

14 Fisher, 12 Oct, 1854.

CHAPTER III

1   Kinglake, V, (6 ed.), 89.

2   Maj. F. R. Forster to Hodge, 7 Feb, [1864], *Hodge Papers*.

3   Gen. (Sir) Richard Dacres to Mrs Hodge, 8 Dec, 1854, *Hodge Papers*.

4   27 Oct, 1854.

5   Forrest, 7 Dec, 1854.

6   Kinglake, V, 145–6, 158.

7   Forster to Hodge, 7 Feb, [1864], *Hodge Papers*.

8   Kinglake, V, 160.

9   5 Dec, 1854, MS letters of Lieut-Col John Yorke, 1st The Royal Dragoons (property of Marquess of Anglesey).

10 Maj Thornhill, quoted in May, E. S. *Changes & Chances of a Soldier's Life*, 1925, 184.

11 Lt-Col Griffiths, 1854, P.R.O. (W.O. 44/701).

12 Wood, Gen Sir Evelyn, *The Crimea in 1854, and 1894*, 1896, 114.

13 Lucan's Explanatory Statement to Kinglake, Kinglake, V, 404.

14 Kinglake, (1868 ed.), IV, 382.

15 Divisional Order, signed W. Paulet, Col, A.A.G., 30 Oct, 1854, *Report of the Board of General Officers appointed to inquire into the Statements contained in the Reports of Sir John M'Neill . . . Chelsea*, 1856.

16 Raglan Crimean Papers (Royal United Service Institution) (M.M. 184 Raglan to Newcastle, Private, 28 Nov, 1854.)

17 R.C.P. (M.M. 190 Filder to Trevelyan, 13 Nov, 1854).

18 19 Jan, 1855, MS letters of Lieut Clement W. Heneage (property of Mrs B. Walker-Heneage-Vivian).

19 Forrest, 2 Dec, 1854.

20 Cardigan's affidavit, P.R.O. K.B. 1/265, 22.

21 Forrest, 22 Dec, 1854.

22 Shakespear, letters, 22 Dec, 1854.

23 Lucan to Adjt-Gen, 17 Jan, 1855, *Chelsea Board*, 15–16.

24 Lucan's evidence, *Chelsea Board*, 26, 116.

25 Cruse, 14 Jan, 1855.

26 Forrest, 22 Dec, 1854.

27 Forrest, 17 Dec, 1854.

28 Forrest, 25 Dec, 1854.

29 Forrest, 15 Jan, 18 Jan, 1855.

CHAPTER IV

1 5 Jan, 1855, MS diary of Lieut George Orby Wombwell, 17th Lancers (the property of Capt V. M. Wombwell).

2 Forrest, 1 Jan, 5 Jan, 1855.

3 McNeill and Tulloch, 33.

4 R.C.P. (M.M. 184 Raglan to Newcastle, Private, 1 May, 1855).

5 Forrest, 16 Jan, 1855.

6   Fisher, 20 Jan, 1855.

7   *Chelsea Board*, 187.

8   Col D. Griffiths, in examination, McNeill and Tulloch, 10.

9   Forrest, 28 Mar, 1856.

10 McNeill and Tulloch, 21, 387.

11 Forrest, 28 Jan, 1855.

12 Forrest, 22 Dec, 1854.

13 Forrest, 5 Feb, 1855.

14 Newcastle to Raglan, 2 Dec, 1854, quoted in Kinglake (1868 ed.), VI, 385.

15 Cooper, in reply to questionnaire, McNeill and Tulloch, 375.

16 Newcastle Papers, quoted in Hibbert, C. *The Destruction of Lord Raglan*, 1961, 151.

17 Fisher, 5 Mar, 1855.

18 Forrest, 15 Feb, 1855.

19 R.C.P. (M.M. 184, Raglan to Newcastle, Private, 15 Jan, 1855).

20 Cruse, 22 Feb, 1855.

21 Kinglake, VI, 393–4.

22 Hansard: H. of C., 29 Jan, 1855, 1187; 8 Feb, 1855, 1374–5.

23 Forrest, 15 Jan, 1855.

24 Bonham-Carter, Victor (ed.) *Surgeon in the Crimea*, 1968, 141.

25 *Annual Register*, 1855, 122.

26 Fisher, 24 Mar, 1855.

27 Forrest, 9 Apr, 1855.

28 Hodge's evidence appears on p. 75 of McNeill and Tulloch.

29 McNeill and Tulloch, 36.

30 Hansard: H. of L., 19 March, 1855.

31 Paget, Gen Lord George, *The Light Cavalry Brigade in the Crimea*, 1881, 91.

32 Fisher, 19 Apr, 1855.

33 Portland, Duke of, *Men, Women and Things*, 1937, 173.

34 Cooper, before Crimean Commission, McNeill and Tulloch, 401.

35 Woodham-Smith, Cecil, *Florence Nightingale, 1820–1910*, 1950, 204.

36 Fisher, 9 May, 1855.

37 Heneage, 18 Jan, 1856.

38 Duberly, Mrs H. *Journal kept during the Russian War; from the departure of the Army from England on Apr 7, 1854, to the Fall of Sebastopol*, 1855. See also Tisdall, E. E. P. (ed.) *Mrs Duberly's Campaigns*, 1963.

39 Forrest, 8 May, 1855.

CHAPTER V

1 Derrécagaix, G. *Le Maréchal Pélissier*, 1911, 431.

2 Forrest, 28 June, 1855.

3 Simpson to Panmure, 16 Apr, 1855, *Panmure Papers*.

4 p. 180.

CHAPTER VI

1 Forrest, 3 Nov, 1855.

2 Shadwell, L., *The Life of Colin Campbell, Lord Clyde*, 1881, I, 393, 394.

[*No Source Notes for Chapter VII*]

EPILOGUE

1 *Sheffield Daily Telegraph*.

2 Duke of Cambridge to Hodge, 11 July, 1858, *Hodge Papers*.

3 24 Jan, 1890, *Hodge Papers*.

NOTE ON 4TH (R.I.) DRAGOON GUARDS

1 Cannon, R. *Historical Record of the Fourth, or Royal Irish, Regiment of Dragoon Guards . . . 1685 . . . to 1838*, 1839, 25.

2 Cannon, 33.

Index

DANS LE LIT DES ROIS

JULIETTE BENZONI

DANS LE LIT DES ROIS

Nuits de noces

FRANCE LOISIRS
123, Boulevard de Grenelle, Paris

Edition du Club France Loisirs, Paris
avec l'autorisation de la Librairie Plon

Tous droits de publication, adaptation et reproductions
réservés pour tous pays.

© Librairie Plon, 1983.
ISBN : 2-7242-1675-X

A mes enfants,
Anne et Jean-François.

AU COMMENCEMENT
ÉTAIENT LES DIEUX...

LA NUIT DE BABYLONE

Les rayons brûlants de Shamash, le dieu-soleil, s'apaisaient peu à peu sur Babylone, emportant avec eux la trop grande chaleur du jour. Mais la capitale de Nabuchodonosor restait folle, depuis douze jours, et sa folie allait atteindre, cette nuit, son paroxysme car on était au dernier jour des grandes fêtes de l'année nouvelle que l'on célébrait chaque printemps au mois de Nisan.

Les héros de ces fêtes, les plus importantes de l'année étaient Marduk, dieu de la prospérité, de la fertilité et maître des dieux, et Ishtar, déesse de l'Amour, fille de Sin, le dieu-lune et sœur de Shamash. Et tout à l'heure, quand la nuit serait close, Marduk posséderait Ishtar dans la chambre-chapelle dorée qui couronnait les sept étages multicolores de l'Entemenanki, la plus grande ziqqourat de Babylone, celle du temple de Marduk, l'Esagil.

Sous les rayons déclinants du soleil, les couleurs qui teignaient chacun des étages de la tour s'exaltaient et se mettaient mutuellement en valeur. Le blanc d'Ishtar supportait le noir ébène d'Adar qui portait lui-même le pourpre profond de Marduk. Puis, se rétrécissant toujours sur l'étage inférieur, venaient le bleu céleste de Nebu, le flamboiement orangé de Nergal, la douceur argentée de Sin pour aboutir à l'or fulgurant de Shamash.

Rien n'était plus beau, pour un cœur babylonien que l'Entemenanki dont la splendeur se dressait entre l'immense quadrilatère du temple et le palais du roi paré de la masse verdoyante de ses Jardins Suspendus, merveille du monde antique. La voie des Processions et l'Euphrate bordaient, de part et d'autre, les trois édifices qui tenaient toute la largeur de la ville, de la porte d'Urash à celle d'Ishtar, et qui depuis douze jours étaient le théâtre d'incessantes et fastueuses cérémonies car tous les dieux particuliers des villes et des villages de l'empire d'Entre les Fleuves venaient rendre hommage à Marduk « créateur, destructeur, plein de compassion et de pitié et, dans ses ordres, plein de bienveillance à l'égard des dieux... »

Ils venaient parfois de fort loin, de trop loin même pour ceux dont les épaules charriaient les pesantes statues sous l'implacable soleil quand le transport par voie fluviale ou par canaux était impossible. Mais le sort de ces esclaves-là n'attirait pas plus la pitié que celui des captifs qui, enfouis sous les trois étages des fabuleux Jardins Suspendus, dans une obscurité gluante et boueuse, actionnaient incessamment les immenses norias chargées de hisser les eaux du fleuve jusqu'aux luxuriantes merveilles dues au caprice d'une reine légendaire...

Tant que durait la fête, les tympanons et les flûtes, les tambours et les cithares, les cymbales et les sistres escortaient les cortèges sacrés depuis le fleuve ou depuis les portes de la ville, rythmant les danses des prêtres et des courtisanes sacrées qui se succédaient au parvis de l'Esagil comme autant d'entrées de ballets. La marée des robes blanches, jaunes ou rouges, enrichies des fameuses broderies babyloniennes dont le secret s'est perdu envahissait les rues, les cours et la grande voie des Processions. Les bijoux d'or et d'argent brillaient, moins toutefois que les cuirasses astiquées des soldats aux robes pourpres, aux barbes noires bouclées plus serrées que de l'astrakan. La cité enfiévrée regorgeait de couleurs, étouffait sous les parfums et les odeurs des cuisines de plein vent. Cette dernière nuit, elle se saoulerait d'amour... et de vin de dattes.

A mesure que la lumière déclinait, les regards se

tournaient irrésistiblement vers le sommet de l'Entemenanki. Là-haut, dans l'ultime chapelle accrochée sur le ciel
comme un joyau d'or, une vierge attendait entre un grand
lit d'ivoire garni de coussins de soie et une table d'or pur
qui étaient les seuls meubles de la chambre divine.

Elle était arrivée quand le soleil avait commencé sa
descente vers l'horizon, portée comme la statue même
d'Ishtar sur les épaules d'un groupe chatoyant de prêtresses de l'Amour mais personne n'avait pu contempler sa
beauté réservée au dieu car un amoncellement de voiles
l'enveloppaient de telle manière qu'il était impossible de
rien distinguer d'elle.

La chaise à porteuses l'avait déposée au pied de la
ziqqurat, devant l'escalier qui escaladait le premier étage,
celui qui était blanc. Elle l'avait monté seule, lentement et,
sur la dernière marche, elle avait abandonné son premier
voile, blanc lui aussi. Puis, elle avait gagné l'escalier noir
d'Adar et, sur la dernière marche, elle avait abandonné son
voile noir pour apparaître drapée de pourpre. La pourpre
était tombée de ses épaules en atteignant la base du
quatrième étage, celui qui était bleu comme le ciel d'été et
le voile bleu avait couvert l'entrée de la terrasse où s'élevait
Nergal l'orangé. Puis était venu le tour de ce cinquième
voile. La fiancée du dieu était déjà haut, dans le ciel, mince
silhouette argentée puis dorée quand, enfin, elle avait mis
le pied sur la dernière terrasse où l'attendaient les prêtres
pour la conduire à la chambre nuptiale au seuil de laquelle
elle avait laissé tomber son dernier voile pour entrer nue et
attendre, déjà offerte, celui qui allait venir.

Cette femme – cette jeune fille plutôt – avait été choisie
parmi des centaines de postulantes pour sa beauté et rien
que pour sa beauté qui devait être sans défaut. Elle pouvait
être aussi bien fille de noble lignage qu'une captive ou
même une esclave. L'étreinte du dieu l'arracherait à jamais
à sa condition mais ce serait l'unique possession qu'elle
connaîtrait jamais car, la nuit achevée, l'élue ne rejoindrait
pas les servantes d'Ishtar vouées à la prostitution sacrée,

mais la cohorte des prêtresses de Marduk, vouées à cet
unique maître, donc à la chasteté perpétuelle. Du moins
officiellement.

En effet, le dieu n'ayant que fort peu de chances de se
manifester en personne, c'était son grand-prêtre qui
l'incarnait à moins qu'il ne soit trop âgé ou hors de forme,
ce qui eût été une catastrophe pour les récoltes à venir.
C'était alors le roi lui-même qui se dévouait avec certainement une grande bonne volonté.

Si sa compagne d'une nuit savait le captiver, il n'avait
guère de peine à la faire passer du temple aux appartements féminins de son palais et si le grand-prêtre ayant
officié lui-même tombait amoureux, il pouvait facilement
retrouver, dans l'énorme dédale de l'Esagil, celle qui lui
avait fait si forte impression. Quand l'enfant paraissait, ce
qui était fréquent et considéré comme le signe indubitable
de la bienveillance de Marduk, il se trouvait tout naturellement destiné au service du dieu son père...

Quoi qu'il en soit, lorsque celui-ci pénétrait dans la
chambre d'or, la vierge devait se prosterner devant lui en
récitant le poème d'amour rituel venu de l'antique
Sumer

Tu m'as captivée, laisse-moi demeurer tremblante
[devant toi
Époux, je veux être conduite par toi vers la couche
Époux, laisse-moi te caresser
Ma caresse amoureuse
Ma caresse amoureuse est plus suave que le miel...

Ce qui devait s'accomplir s'accomplissait. Il aurait fallu
être de bois ou de granit pour résister à pareille invite
prononcée par une fille ravissante et uniquement vêtue de
sa chevelure. En cette matière les prêtres de Marduk
jugeaient sage de ne prendre aucun risque et le résultat
était certain. D'autant que la belle, bien éduquée, joignait
le geste à la parole et s'empressait de démontrer que ses

caresses étaient, en effet, beaucoup plus douces et surtout plus savantes que le miel.

Néanmoins, avant de succomber au vertige, le dieu devait épier le ciel où bleuissait la nuit car, selon la tradition, Marduk ne pouvait posséder sa compagne qu'à l'instant précis où paraissait l'étoile d'Ishtar. Alors seulement le grand lit d'ivoire devenait autel et le corps intact s'ouvrait pour l'amant divin.

Mais le couple n'était pas seul. Quelqu'un d'autre était là. Un prêtre de Marduk – le Veilleur Sacré – se tenait debout au bord de la terrasse près de l'entrée de la chambre. Son devoir était d'annoncer au peuple que tout s'accomplissait pour la réalisation de ses vœux et de son plus grand espoir.

En bas, des milliers de regards étaient braqués sur sa silhouette blanche, érigée sur le ciel, si petite à cette hauteur, et ne la quittaient pas jusqu'à ce que par sept fois le veilleur eût dressé ses deux bras vers les étoiles. Une immense clameur éclatait alors et Babylone, assurée d'avoir obtenu des dieux la fertilité de ses terres et de ses ventres pour une nouvelle année, s'engloutissait tout entière dans une frénétique orgie d'amour qui durait jusqu'à la première lueur grise de l'aube... pour ceux, tout au moins, qui possédaient assez d'énergie pour ne pas s'endormir avant.

Ainsi Babylone considérait la femme et, singulièrement, la vierge comme la compagne désignée du dieu. Il semblerait, d'ailleurs, que la notion de virginité n'ait pas été très précisément délimitée avant l'époque sumérienne où les connaissances anatomiques étaient encore dans l'enfance. Était réputée vierge celle qu'aucun homme n'avait encore approchée, celle qui était neuve et, tout naturellement, l'idée de virginité se confondait avec celle de puberté. Était réputée neuve celle dont les seins commençaient à pousser et le corps à prendre ses courbes féminines...

De là vint la coutume, longtemps conservée même en

Occident et surtout dans les familles royales, de marier les filles à peine pubères. Une manière comme une autre de prendre ses précautions contre d'éventuelles et désagréables surprises qui ne troublaient guère les hommes des antiques civilisations car il était fréquent parmi les peuples qui entouraient la Méditerranée d'offrir aux dieux la virginité des filles que l'on menait au temple pour y être déflorées rituellement par les prêtres, revêtus de la puissance du dieu. Hommage, sans doute, mais aussi précaution car le mystère du corps féminin encore scellé n'était pas sans inspirer quelque inquiétude. Nul ne pouvait dire quel danger, quel maléfice, quel démon pouvait se cacher dans l'obscurité moite des flancs d'une vierge. En s'en remettant à un dieu, il n'y avait plus rien à craindre : le hiérodule prenait le danger pour lui, traçait le chemin dans lequel, ensuite, l'époux éventuel pouvait s'engager en toute tranquillité.

On retrouve, chez les Hébreux, dans les Proverbes, la trace de cette vieille crainte de l'homme en face du mystère féminin :

Il y a trois choses qui me dépassent
Quatre que je ne connais pas :
Le chemin que suit l'aigle dans le ciel
Le chemin que suit le serpent sur le rocher
Le chemin que suit le navire au cœur de la mer
Le chemin que suit l'homme dans la jeune femme...

Depuis Ève par qui toute joie et toute souffrance étaient venues à l'homme, cet innocent qui s'était laissé conduire si joyeusement au péché, la femme avait acquit des droits imprescriptibles à la suspicion et à la méfiance masculines. De là l'enthousiasme avec lequel les Anciens menaient leurs filles à la couche d'un dieu ou de son représentant. De là aussi le plus ancien principe du fameux « droit du seigneur » mis en pratique lorsque le christianisme ayant fait son apparition, les vieux dieux avaient déclaré forfait.

Le seigneur devenu tel parce que brave entre les braves (ou malin entre les malins) avait pris la place de la divinité défaillante. Les choses, bien sûr, avaient quelque peu changé dans la suite des jours et des nuits; la corvée sacrée des premiers temps s'était muée très rapidement en fort agréable privilège appliqué exclusivement aux seules jolies filles et les épouseurs avaient depuis longtemps cessé de souhaiter voir plus courageux qu'eux leur ouvrir la mystérieuse porte derrière laquelle attendait le temple de la fécondation.

Mais revenons vers les dieux au temps où leur puissance s'étendait sur les quatre horizons. Splendide était donc la nuit que Babylone amoureuse offrait à son dieu. Beaucoup plus austère était celle que la sévère Assyrie offrait, à Kalah puis à Ninive, à son dieu Nabn, le troisième jour du mois d'Igyar. Là, pas d'orgie générale, pas de vierge divine offerte nue au désir de Nabn. Il n'en aurait eu que faire car aucun humain n'étant digne de l'incarner, fût-il roi, c'était sa statue d'or et d'émail qui pénétrait dans la chambre à mi-chemin du ciel où attendait une prêtresse.

« Ce jour-là, on consacrait son lit dans la cité et le dieu pénétrait dans sa chambre; il retournait à sa place le jour suivant... » mais, entre-temps, il n'avait vraiment pas fait grand-chose.

Après la consécration du lit et la présentation des offrandes rituelles, la prêtresse prenait un brin de roseau, le trempait dans l'huile parfumée et en purifiait les pieds de l'image divine. Puis, par trois fois, elle s'approchait du lit qu'elle parfumait et saluait avant de revenir baiser les pieds de la statue. Cela fait, elle allait tout bêtement s'asseoir à côté pour un petit moment.

Au bout de ce laps de temps, les prêtres revenaient. Ils consacraient des bois aromatiques, les faisaient brûler et, avec les cendres, offraient des libations. Ensuite, venait le banquet nuptial : on préparait de longues tables somptueusement servies pour tous les dieux farouches du panthéon assyrien mais seules les effigies d'or ou d'argent y prenaient place, que l'on servait avec respect et révérence. Enfin, cette nuit « échevelée » s'achevait par une prière générale pour le roi afin que les dieux acceptent de bénir ses armes toujours plus ou moins prêtes à servir.

Au lever du soleil, on ramenait le pauvre Nabn chez lui en procession. On l'installait dans un chariot, à côté du conducteur et on l'emmenait faire un petit tour jusqu'à certain bois sacré où il recevait l'hommage d'autres prêtres barbus, accueillait des sacrifices mais ne rencontrait pas la moindre bacchante aux appas tentateurs disposée à batifoler un moment avec lui. Après quoi on le réintégrait pour un an dans son temple obscur où il n'avait d'autres distractions que les psalmodies des prêtres, les fumées de l'encens, des sacrifices et du sang des bêtes égorgées alternant avec quelques bains de pieds huileux. Avec aussi, dans les jours fastes, le massacre rituel de quelques prisonniers de guerre ou de quelques esclaves lorsque l'ennemi manquait de bonne volonté...

On a les dieux que l'on mérite. Nabn n'était pas un dieu gai. En 612 avant Jésus-Christ l'Empire assyrien, rapace et essentiellement guerrier s'effondrait sous les coups des Mèdes et des Babyloniens laissant pour traces principales les gigantesques taureaux androcéphales ailés et les bas-reliefs au style officiel du palais de Sargon à Khorsabad... et aussi le bûcher hautement fantaisiste de Sardanapale dû au pinceau romantique et génial mais assez peu documenté d'Eugène Delacroix. Cependant que s'éternisait, de siècle en siècle, dans la mémoire des hommes le souvenir des Jardins de Babylone, du rêve de Sémiramis et de cette étonnante « culture aux ailes de briques » née à l'aurore du monde avec Sumer et qui avait ébloui les siècles, asservi des peuples et enfanté les nombres et la science du Ciel avant de se perdre, sous la main même de Dieu, dans les sables du désert...

LE HAREM MÉRIDIONAL D'AMON...

Ainsi Ipet-ressout-Imen, Thèbes aux Cent Portes, appelait-elle le nouveau temple de Louqsor que le pharaon Aménophis III venait d'élever sur la rive orientale du Nil, à la prière de Teje, sa Grande Épouse royale et sa bien-aimée, pour y célébrer chaque année les noces d'Amon-Râ avec la terre d'Égypte que sa semence divine devait féconder pour la plus grande richesse et le plus grand bonheur de tout un peuple.

Grand bâtisseur, Aménophis III n'en était pas à un temple près. Sur l'autre rive du fleuve, celle des morts car elle était celle où le soleil se couche, il avait construit un palais gigantesque. dont il ne reste malheureusement que les fameux Colosses de Memnon, pour y vivre et y régner sous la protection de l'Éternité. De même, sur la berge de la vie et du soleil levant, il avait agrandi, embelli, magnifié le grand temple de Karnak, temple principal d'Amon dont le nouveau sanctuaire ne pouvait être qu'une dépendance.

Comme Karnak, l'Ipet-ressout-Imen était dédié non seulement à Amon mais aussi à son épouse, Mout, et à leur fils Khonsou. Le maître des dieux y était représenté sous forme humaine, coiffé de deux grandes plumes et pourvu des avantages du dieu Min, c'est-à-dire le sexe érigé symbolisant sa puissance de fécondation. Mout, corps de femme à tête de vautour, y portait la double couronne de la Haute et de la Basse-Égypte. Quant à Khonsou, il y était révéré sous sa forme habituelle : gainé dans un suaire et coiffé du disque lunaire.

Au jour prescrit qui était toujours fixé à la même date dans le mois de Paochi, la statue d'Amon quittait, sur les épaules d'une centaine de porteurs, le naos du grand temple et descendait jusqu'au Nil pour y prendre place dans la nef sacrée peinte de vives couleurs et dorée. Derrière lui venaient Mout, puis Khonsou, puis Pharaon lui-même. Chacun des membres de la famille sacrée était déposé dans une barque presque aussi magnifique que celle d'Amon. Le trône d'or de Pharaon occupait la poupe de la dernière.

Les quatre barques divines remontaient alors le Nil jusqu'au nouveau temple dont le sol surélevé était à l'abri des plus grandes crues. Là les dieux abandonnaient leurs véritables embarcations pour des navires symboliques, faits de bois doré et munis de brancards auxquels s'attelaient les plus vigoureux des prêtres.

Dans cet équipage, au son des tambours sacrés et des chants religieux, Amon, Mout, Khonsou et Pharaon étaient conduits jusqu'au plus secret du temple dont les portes de cèdre incrustées d'or se refermaient sur eux pour dix jours tandis que les barques-chaises à porteurs étaient garées chacune dans une chapelle particulière.

Comme dans la chambre dorée de l'Entemenanki, une femme attendait là. Elle avait dormi dans le temple la nuit précédente et devait accueillir, dans son corps, Pharaon, fils préféré d'Amon-Râ et son remplaçant pour ces noces divines. Une femme dont on disait qu'elle n'avait eu et n'aurait de commerce avec aucun autre homme. Et le peuple rêvait sur le sort de cette créature, qui ne pouvait être qu'idéalement belle et qui, après dix nuits d'amour avec le dieu, ne vivrait plus que de ses souvenirs.

En fait, le rôle de l'épouse divine était tenu la plupart du temps par la reine d'Égypte elle-même ou par l'une des nombreuses épouses qui peuplaient l'imposant harem du Pharaon car il arrivait que la Grande Épouse royale fût enceinte au moment de la fête ou que Pharaon souhaitât une autre compagne. On évalue à environ trois cent vingt femmes les effectifs du harem d'un pharaon normalement constitué. Ainsi, il arrivait que la « vierge » du temple fût l'une de ces princesses étrangères que leurs pères, les rois vaincus, envoyaient en Égypte pour y devenir les épouses du Pharaon, telle cette princesse Tadukhipa, fille du roi Tushratta de Mittani qui fut offerte à Aménophis IV (et connut les dix nuits d'amour de Louqsor) et que certains historiens ont assimilée à Néfertiti « la Belle que voilà... [1] »

Une fois refermées les portes du temple sur le couple divin, un cérémonial secret commençait, infiniment plus compliqué et plus étrange que celui, simple et naturel somme toute, qui était pratiqué sur les ziqqourats méso-potamiennes. Pharaon et son épouse ne tombaient pas dans les bras l'un de l'autre pour dix nuits et dix jours sans autre forme de procès. Le rituel voulait que l'assimilation des rois aux dieux fût complète. Amon déposait sa divinité pour devenir chair en s'emparant du corps du Pharaon et celui-ci, dès l'instant qu'il devenait Amon, devait revêtir le costume et les attributs du dieu : la coiffure à longues plumes, la croix ansée, symbole de la vie, et le sceptre à tête de chacal. Autour de lui prêtres et prêtresses couvraient leurs visages de masques représentant les diverses divinités animales qui devaient escorter Amon jusqu'à la couche royale et bientôt une étrange procession d'hommes à têtes de chacal, de crocodile, de faucon, d'ibis, de femmes à têtes de vaches ou de grenouilles se formait autour du dieu et l'escortait jusqu'à la chambre de la reine pour la consom-mation du mariage mystique et charnel selon le texte de la loi sacrée.

« Ainsi parla Amon-Râ, roi des dieux, seigneur de Karnak, souverain maître de Thèbes, quand il prit la forme de ce mâle (ici le nom du pharaon en exercice) roi de

---

1. Qui était l'épouse d'Aménophis IV (Akhenaton).

la Haute et de la Basse-Égypte, dispensateur de la vie. Il vint trouver la reine pendant qu'elle reposait dans la splendeur de son palais. Le parfum suave du dieu l'éveilla et la ravit. Aussitôt Sa Majesté s'approcha d'elle, s'empara d'elle, fit entrer son cœur en elle et lui révéla sa forme divine. La beauté du dieu à son approche jeta la reine dans le ravissement. Son amour se répandit dans tous ses membres, l'odeur et l'haleine du dieu étaient chargées des parfums de Pount... »

La reine, ainsi honorée, se devait de se montrer convenablement reconnaissante : « Que ta puissance soit deux fois grande! Sublime à contempler est ton visage lorsque tu me fais la grâce de t'unir à moi. Ta rosée imprègne tous mes membres... »

Et, généralement, la fête de la fertilité et les noces divines débouchaient sur la naissance d'un enfant royal, fils ou fille de dieu sans qu'il vînt à l'idée de personne de mettre en doute une si auguste paternité...

Pendant dix jours, les prêtres faisaient des affaires d'or car les Égyptiens du haut ou du bas pays accouraient en foule, chargés de présents comme il convient d'offrir lorsque l'on est invité à des noces. Les pauvres apportaient des fruits, des fleurs, des animaux. Les riches de l'or, de l'ivoire, de l'ébène du pays de Kush, des parfums et de l'encens du pays de Pount et, venus de la plus lointaine Asie, des épices, des bois précieux et des pierres rares.

Le temps de la lune de miel royale achevé, Amon-Râ abandonnait la forme terrestre de son hôte et repartait vers sa mystérieuse demeure céleste. Pharaon rentrait chez lui en compagnie des trois statues qu'il ramenait à Karnak mais, cette fois, par voie de terre. Seules les barques de procession étaient utilisées et, tanguant sur les épaules d'une foule de prêtres et d'esclaves nubiens gigantesques, Amon, Mout et Khonsou regagnaient le grand temple de Karnak en empruntant une large voie triomphale bordée de sphinxs à visages humains.

Ainsi se déroulait, en Égypte, la grande fête d'Opet (ou

Ipet) qui marquait à la fois le Nouvel An et le renouveau du cycle agraire car, ensuite, venait la grande crue du Nil qui, noyant les terres brûlées de soleil, faisait revivre et reverdir la glèbe noire des deux pays. Pharaon qui, durant cette longue nuit de noces, avait vaillamment œuvré pour la plus grande gloire d'Amon et la plus grande richesse de l'Égypte, s'accordait une petite retraite de deux ou trois jours dans le temple du Dieu pour y rendre grâces et reprendre haleine avant de retourner vers son harem personnel...

L'INTERMINABLE NUIT
DE NOCES DE ZEUS

Il appartenait à Zeus, qui fut assurément le dieu le plus polisson et le plus inventif de tous les temps, d'établir le record absolu de la durée en matière de nuit de noces, un record qui n'est pas près d'être battu car sa nuit de noces avec Héra (plus connue sous son nom romain de Junon comme Zeus lui-même sous celui de Jupiter) ne dura pas moins de trois cents ans...

L'île de Samos – qui s'appelait alors Stéphane à cause de la luxuriante végétation de fleurs et de plantes qui la couvraient – a, de tout temps, revendiqué l'honneur d'avoir abrité la « nuit la plus longue ». Elle s'est vouée à Héra et les ruines de son superbe temple, l'Héraeion, y sont encore visibles. Mais elle n'est pas la seule car l'Argolide, vouée elle aussi à l'épouse de Zeus, émet exactement les mêmes prétentions mais en sens contraire si l'on peut dire car, pour les départager, il faut aussi départager les légendes qui racontent l'événement et, selon le lieu, le raconter de façon opposée. Selon Samos, c'est Héra qui aurait décidé de séduire son jeune frère et, selon Argos, l'initiative appartiendrait entièrement au jeune dieu tombé inopinément très amoureux de sa grande sœur.

Car Héra et Zeus, comme Déméter et Hestia, Hadès et Poséidon, avaient eu les mêmes géniteurs : Cronos (le Temps) et Rhéa (la Terre) qui constituaient un couple assez mal assorti. Leurs grands-parents étaient Ouranos (le Ciel) et Gaïa (la Mère primordiale) avec lesquels avaient commencé le conflit des générations.

En effet, chaque fois que Gaïa mettait un enfant au monde – et elle en avait fabriqué tout un assortiment qui allait des Titans à la Justice en passant par l'Océan et quelques autres personnages tout aussi hauts en couleur – Ouranos qui les détestait les renfonçait automatiquement dans le ventre de leur mère où ils ne tardaient pas à se trouver légèrement à l'étroit. Gaïa, ne se sentant pas non plus au mieux de sa forme appela les captifs à son secours, inventa l'acier, et en fabriqua une sorte de serpe, ou de faux qu'elle remit à Cronos avec mission de dissuader Ouranos la première fois qu'il entreprendrait de lui faire l'amour. Elle fut scrupuleusement obéie : caché dans le ventre maternel, Cronos guetta l'envahisseur et le mutila d'un coup de faux bien appliqué.

Douloureusement surpris, Ouranos se retira et laissa tomber dans la mer féconde un peu de sa semence dont allait naître un jour la divine Aphrodite. Mais il n'en maudit pas moins son rejeton auquel il annonça, en manière de représailles, qu'il serait lui aussi vaincu par l'un de ses enfants. Malheureusement il ne précisa pas lequel.

Aussi, chaque fois que la pauvre Rhéa donnait le jour à un fils, Cronos l'inscrivait à son menu et l'avalait tout rond au repas suivant. La malheureuse mère souffrait affreusement de cet état de choses et, quand apparut au jour le petit Zeus, elle le trouva si beau qu'elle décida de « se le garder ». Pour le sauver de la voracité de son père, elle se mit à la recherche d'une grosse pierre ayant à peu près les dimensions de l'enfant nouveau-né, l'emmaillota selon les règles et, avec la mine de circonstance qui convenait, alla présenter le tout à son époux qui se contenta d'ouvrir un large four et d'engloutir le faux nourrisson avec l'espèce d'indifférence qu'il y mettait habituellement. Outre que ses goûts gastronomiques devaient être assez nuls, Cronos ne prenait pas un plaisir particulier à absorber ses propres enfants. Simplement ils lui semblaient mieux à l'abri des tentations malsaines dans son estomac qu'à la lumière du soleil.

Pendant qu'il digérait, Rhéa mettait Zeus en sûreté dans l'île de Crète où elle était chez elle et où sévissait une tribu particulièrement bruyante et agitée de prêtres guerriers, les Courètes, gens primitifs et volontiers agressifs qui passaient leur temps en interminables danses guerrières avec éclats de cymbales, fracas d'armes entrechoquées et hurlements de circonstance. Cela entretenait dans l'île un assez joli vacarme d'un agrément incertain mais tout à fait propre à couvrir les vagissements d'un nouveau-né divin et à les empêcher de rejoindre les oreilles susceptibles de Cronos.

Doué du bienheureux sommeil de l'enfance, Zeus se trouvait bien dans l'île de Crète. Il y grandit, nourri d'abord du lait de la bonne chèvre Amalthée puis, plus tard, de ses fromages et de toutes les succulences échappées chaque jour de sa corne coupée, bien connue sous le nom de corne d'abondance. De leur côté, les Courètes, entre deux ballets-tintamarres, lui enseignèrent l'art de la guerre et l'endurance au combat. Tant et si bien que, devenu Zeus-Couros, le jeune dieu se trouva bientôt apte à régler ses comptes avec son père.

Il s'arma de la foudre et, en guise de cuirasse revêtit l'Égide (ou peau de chèvre) que sa nourrice lui avait laissée avant de prendre sa retraite dans le ciel sous forme d'une constellation : le Capricorne. Puis il se mit à la recherche de Cronos. Mais, se trouvant un peu seul pour attaquer le vieux sacripant, il usa de ruse et lui fit avaler un vomitif.

Affreusement malade, ce qui n'alla pas sans quelques convulsions sur terre et sur mer, Cronos restitua intacts tous les enfants qu'il avait si goulûment avalés depuis leur naissance et qui, dans son vaste estomac avaient assez bien profité. Cette réapparition dota Zeus de deux compagnons de combat non négligeables : ses deux frères Hadès (ou Pluton) et Poséidon (ou Neptune).

Mais il vit aussi Héra et la trouva belle...

Mais Héra vit Zeus et le trouva beau...

Lequel vit l'autre le premier, lequel s'extasia le premier sur la beauté de l'autre, c'est là que les thèses diffèrent et que nous retrouvons face à face les gens de Samos et ceux d'Argos. Sans compter d'ailleurs les Crétois qui pensaient avoir, eux aussi, leur mot à dire sur la question...

Ils prétendaient, en effet, qu'Héra, soustraite elle aussi par sa mère à l'appétit de Cronos, avait été élevée dans l'île d'Eubée au milieu des vaches — dont elle avait gardé par mimétisme ce beau « regard de génisse » qui séduisait tant Homère — comme Zeus au milieu de ses Courètes, et qu'ayant ouï vanter la beauté de son jeune frère, elle serait allée le retrouver secrètement dans sa bergerie où elle lui aurait inculqué, à sa grande satisfaction, les charmants principes de l'amour.

Les gens de Samos défendaient une version à peu près similaire : Héra décidée à séduire Zeus et doutant peut-être de ses charmes, aurait emprunté à Aphrodite sa ceinture qui était le premier aphrodisiaque connu et, ainsi parée se serait mise à la recherche du jeune dieu et l'aurait entraîné à sa suite parmi les fleurs de l'île où, dans une grotte tapissée de jasmins, sur une couche de lys embaumés ils se seraient aimés passionnément, interminablement.

Pour Argos, c'est tout le contraire. A peine sortie des entrailles paternelles, Héra qui était alors une vierge au doux visage aurait choisi l'Argolide pour y vivre chastement sous la protection d'une vieille femme, Macris, qualifiée de « nourrice » mais dont le rôle nourricier devait s'apparenter davantage à celui de cuisinière gouvernante-porte-respect. La céleste créature et son mentor se seraient installées sur une montagne à laquelle on a donné le nom de Montagne du Coucou. Voici pourquoi :

Par un jour d'hiver particulièrement froid, Héra était allée prendre un peu d'exercice dans la campagne quand, grelottant et transi, un petit coucou vint se percher sur son épaule. Apitoyée, la jeune fille le prit dans ses mains et le mit sous sa robe pour le réchauffer. C'était tout juste ce qu'il voulait car le coucou n'était autre que Zeus qui inaugurait là son goût bien connu pour les métamorphoses amoureuses. Parvenu dans ce doux nid qui lui parut un lieu de délices à explorer longuement, il reprit sa forme habituelle – Coucou! Le voilà! – et prétendit rester où il était en tant que Zeus – et même pousser un peu plus loin. Indignée, la jeune vierge invoqua sa mère Rhéa et fit savoir qu'elle n'entendait s'abandonner que contre une promesse de mariage en bonne et due forme.

Zeus s'exécuta aussitôt :

« Oh! Héra! lui dit-il. Je veux que tu sois ma légitime épouse. Suis-moi, déesse aux larges yeux et je ferai que tu règnes à ma droite, assise dans l'Olympe sur un trône éclatant... »

Héra n'en demandait pas davantage et Zeus, pour célébrer leur union la transporta sur le sommet boisé de la montagne. La terre leur offrit un lit d'herbes moelleuses, les fleurs s'ouvrirent devant eux, principalement les lys qui étaient l'emblème de la jeune fille, les arbres inclinèrent leurs ramures pour les protéger et les sources répandirent une odeur d'ambroisie quand elles ne changeaient pas leurs eaux en un nectar de la meilleure année.

Durant une nuit qui, pour eux, dura trois cents ans, les jeunes dieux se prouvèrent leur amour. Après quoi, Zeus prit Héra par la main, l'emmena dans l'Olympe, la présenta aux autres dieux comme son unique et légitime épouse, l'installa sur le trône resplendissant qu'il lui avait promis... et ne s'en occupa plus guère. Une nuit de noces aussi « performante » lui paraissant un hommage suffisant, même pour les charmes d'une déesse, il s'en alla voir ailleurs si l'herbe était plus verte.

Il avait cru s'apercevoir d'une certaine mélancolie chez les déesses de sa famille et, déjà soucieux, en bon chef de tribu, du moral de tous et surtout de toutes, il s'occupa de celles qui lui semblaient par trop solitaires en leur procurant les joies de la maternité. A sa tante Thémis, il fit les Heures, à son autre tante Mnémosyne, il fit les Muses nées chacune d'une nuit d'amour. Puis il s'occupa de sa sœur Déméter, qui bientôt accoucha de Proserpine.

Tant qu'il ne s'occupa que de la famille, Héra qui de son côté avait donné le jour à deux fils d'un commerce peu agréable, Arès (ou Mars) un va-t-en-guerre prétentieux, et Héphaïstos (ou Vulcain) qui était travailleur mais handicapé et très laid, ne dit trop rien. On était entre soi. Mais quand son époux se mêla de procurer aux mortelles quelques nuits de noces originales en se présentant sous forme de cygne, de taureau, d'ours, de pluie d'or ou plus simplement d'un aimable jouvenceau ou encore d'un général thébain, les choses se gâtèrent. Héra venait d'inventer la jalousie et la scène de ménage et l'Olympe retentit de ses criailleries et des bagarres du ménage, Zeus refusant farouchement de se laisser embourgeoiser.

« Ta colère me laisse indifférent, grondait-il de sa voix de tonnerre. Quand bien même tu courrais jusqu'aux bornes extrêmes de la terre et de la mer ou dans l'insondable Tartare, je ne me préoccuperais ni de toi ni de ta colère... »

Il avait beau jeu de le prendre avec désinvolture. Lui seul était à blâmer dans cette affaire. Quand on commet l'imprudence de s'attarder à ce point auprès d'une femme, elle n'en peut tirer que des conclusions extrêmement flatteuses pour son charme et elle éprouve alors de grandes difficultés lorsqu'elle s'aperçoit que l'époux si attentif et si câlin manifeste soudain l'intention d'aller se dégourdir les jambes loin de ses regards. Zeus aurait dû savoir qu'il n'est jamais bon d'épuiser toutes les joies en une seule fois. Héra n'aurait pas dû le laisser s'empiffrer ainsi à satiété de sa charmante personne. Mais allez donc faire comprendre cela à une déesse qui s'était crue unique!

Héra ayant donc instauré les scènes conjugales, il ne restait plus à Zeus lequel, d'ailleurs, se préoccupait des états d'âme de sa compagne beaucoup plus qu'il ne voulait bien le dire, d'inaugurer, à grand renfort de nuages complices et de séances d'invisibilité, ces retours clandestins sur les chaussettes du petit matin qui allaient connaître, chez les hommes, une si longue carrière.

ALEXANDRE ET LES NOCES DE SUSE

Apparemment, à la fin du mois de novembre de l'an 357 avant Jésus-Christ, Zeus était encore très vert et n'avait pas renoncé à ses galantes expéditions auprès des belles mortelles. Cette nuit-là au palais de Pella, en Macédoine, le roi Philippe II qui avait épousé, dans la journée, la belle Olympias, fille du roi d'Épire Neoptolème, avait entrepris de faire de sa fiancée son épouse. Malheureusement il avait beaucoup bu. On buvait toujours beaucoup chez les Macédoniens où il fallait tenir la barrique pour avoir droit à la considération de ses pairs mais ce n'était pas pour déplaire à la timide fiancée qui était adonnée à la magie, au culte orgiaque de Dionysos et était initiée aux mystères orphiques, et aussi ophites car elle avait un curieux talent de charmeuse de serpents.

Quoi qu'il en soit, Philippe ne devait garder de sa nuit de noces qu'un souvenir très vague. Il ne prêta même pas attention à certain coup de tonnerre qui éclata au-dessus de la couche nuptiale et qui était la façon qu'avait Zeus de s'annoncer. C'est du moins ce qu'Olympias prétendit par la suite quand elle se retrouva enceinte : Zeus l'avait visitée durant la nuit de ses noces tandis que son époux ronflait grossièrement à ses côtés. Et quand, neuf mois plus tard elle donna le jour à un fils que l'on nomma Alexandre, elle ne cacha pas qu'elle le tenait pour le fils du maître des dieux et non de ce lamentable Philippe.

Autant dire que le ménage ne marcha guère et que Philippe regretta plus d'une fois le voyage à Samothrace où il s'était rendu pour s'initier aux mystères des Cabires, ces fils d'Héphaïstos le forgeron, qui maîtrisaient les forces telluriques, et où il avait rencontré Olympias. Il ne marcha même plus du tout le soir où, rejoignant sa femme dans le lit conjugal, Philippe la trouva en compagnie d'un serpent qu'elle présenta comme un dieu qu'il convenait de révérer.

Ce compagnon de lit ayant déplu au roi, celui-ci répudia sa dangereuse épouse, la renvoya en Épire chez son cousin Arruba qui avait succédé à Neoptolème. Elle emmena avec elle son jeune fils, que Philippe avait pourtant pris bien soin de faire instruire par Aristote, et l'y fit initier aux cultes dionysiaques. Pendant ce temps Philippe épousait une jeune Cléopâtre de quinze ans, fille d'un de ses généraux : Attale.

Cela ne lui réussit pas : Olympias le fit poignarder, se réinstalla au palais de Pella et n'eut rien de plus pressé que faire assassiner dans les bras de sa mère la petite fille que Cléopâtre venait de donner à son époux, avant de la faire elle-même étrangler.

Alexandre, lui, avait vingt ans. Il était beau comme le dieu qu'il croyait être. Ne descendait-il pas d'Achille (et de Zeus) par sa mère et d'Héraklès (et donc de Zeus!) par son père. Superbement bâti il avait de grands yeux bleu-clair, des cheveux châtains, abondants et ondulés et son élégance était sans pareille, même si un rétrécissement des muscles du cou l'obligeait à porter la tête légèrement penchée de côté.

Se croyant fils de Zeus foudroyant, il entreprit de donner le monde comme champ de course à son cheval Bucéphale, ne ménageant ni le glaive, ni la torche, ni la sueur de ses hommes. N'était-il pas né le jour même où Érostrate faisait flamber le temple de Diane à Éphèse?

« J'ai choisi, dira l'incendiaire pour se faire valoir, le jour où la déesse était absente, se trouvant au chevet d'Olympias... » Les femmes, décidément, s'apprêtent à jouer un grand rôle dans la vie du jeune conquérant mais on ne peut pas dire qu'il les traite toujours avec beaucoup d'aménité. La première à s'en apercevoir est la Pythie de Delphes qu'Alexandre, désireux de connaître son avenir et ce que pensent de lui les dieux, ses parents, traîne littéralement à son trépied sulfureux.

« Mon fils, soupire la prophétesse quelque peu chiffonnée et malmenée en remettant de l'ordre dans les plis de sa tunique, nul ne saurait te résister!...

— C'est tout ce que je voulais savoir, riposte Alexandre. Pas besoin de consulter l'oracle! »

Et il plante là Dame Pythie, un peu interloquée sur son trépied, saute à cheval et disparaît dans un nuage de poussière.

Le monde civilisé de l'époque le verra chevaucher ainsi, dans la lumière irradiée de sa cuirasse ornée d'or qui étincelle au soleil. Qui voit, un jour, passer Alexandre ne l'oubliera plus... Et les femmes moins encore que les hommes : il a tellement l'air d'un dieu!...

La Grèce ne lui suffisant pas, le voilà en Asie Mineure avec 35 000 hommes, un maigre trésor et des vivres pour un mois. Cela ne l'empêche pas, à Issos de battre à plate couture Darius, le puissant Roi des Rois dont les soldats sont innombrables et la richesse fabuleuse. Alexandre lui prend tout ce qu'il a amené avec lui, y compris sa mère et sa femme qu'il traite d'ailleurs avec révérence. Encouragé par cette urbanité, Darius lui offre l'Asie Mineure tout entière et sa fille Statira assortie d'une dot fabuleuse.

« J'accepterais si j'étais Alexandre, suggère le vieux Parménion, l'ancien lieutenant de Philippe.

— Moi aussi, répond le jeune homme... si j'étais Parménion! »

Et il continue son chemin. Statira attendra. Alexandre, pour sa part, vient de succomber au charme de Barsine, aux yeux sans pareils. Barsine est la veuve du général perse Memmon. Alexandre l'épouse de la main gauche, se gorge d'elle puis poursuit sa course vers les confins de l'univers, la laissant enceinte...

Sans désemparer il soumet la Syrie, la Phénicie et la Judée. De Gaza, qui lui a résisté sept mois, il traîne le corps du gouverneur sept fois autour des murailles. Il passe en Égypte, y fonde Alexandrie puis s'enfonce de six cents kilomètres dans le désert pour consulter l'oracle d'Amon. Terrifiés, les prêtres lui promettent tout ce qu'il veut et jurent même qu'Amon lui-même l'a adopté. Fils de Zeus en même temps que son petit-fils, le voilà à présent fils d'Amon. On n'a jamais trop de dieux dans sa famille...

Ainsi réconforté il rentre à Tyr d'où il repart, au printemps pour continuer à pourchasser Darius, le retrouve à Arbelles et le bat une fois de plus. Le voilà à Babylone où la végétation des Jardins Suspendus est devenue fabuleuse mais où l'Esagil et l'Entemenanki ne sont plus que ruines grandioses où l'on vient chercher des pierres, comme dans une vulgaire carrière. Il promet de restaurer l'ancienne splendeur et continue son chemin. L'Asie profonde l'attire et il veut conquérir le monde jusqu'à sa limite ultime, la mer Extérieure. Le voilà dans ce qui sera le Turkestan puis l'Afghanistan. C'est au bord du Syr-Daria qu'on lui amène une fille d'une grande beauté, presque une enfant. Elle se nomme Roxane et elle est la fille d'un chef.

Mais elle pourrait être n'importe quoi d'autre : elle est si belle qu'Alexandre décide d'en faire sa déesse et l'épouse. Cette nuit de noces-là se teinte aux couleurs sombres d'une orgie dionysiaque où le sang des bacchantes se mêle au vin, et le vin à celui de Roxane brutalement déflorée. Le dieu semble possédé à présent par l'esprit du mal. La folie le guette, la folie homicide si le génie du stratège est toujours présent. Il exige les marques de respect dues à un dieu et frappe quand on les lui refuse, même ses meilleurs amis, même Clitos, même Parménion. Quiconque refuse de voir en lui un dieu est condamné...

Pourtant, ces hommes qu'il traîne avec lui depuis la

Grèce ont assez de courage pour exiger que l'on arrête cette continuelle fuite en avant quand on atteint la ligne de partage des eaux de l'Indus et du Gange. Furieux, Alexandre devra se contenter d'ériger une colonne proclamant : « Ici s'est arrêté Alexandre... » Et l'on prend le chemin du retour.

Revenu à Suse à laquelle il veut restituer la splendeur des anciens Rois des Rois (il est un peu trop tard pour Persépolis qu'il a incendiée à son précédent passage), il décide que lui-même et ses hommes vont épouser la Perse afin de se l'assimiler totalement. Il a ordonné qu'on lui amène cette Statira qu'il avait si dédaigneusement refusée naguère. Miracle! Elle est encore plus belle que Barsine et Roxane réunies.

« Je l'épouse! » déclare-t-il.

Certains esprits timides essaient bien de lui expliquer qu'il est déjà marié et que la polygamie n'est guère de mise en Grèce ni d'ailleurs en Macédoine, mais il balaye l'objection. Pourquoi ne serait-elle pas désormais légale puisqu'il le veut? Il va donc épouser Statira et, afin de mieux impressionner les peuples, il décide que dix mille de ses hommes – et les chefs en premier – épouseront des filles perses en même temps. Que tous ces hommes aient déjà des épouses en Grèce est de peu d'importance. Les filles du pays sont belles, ses généraux auraient tort de se plaindre.

Et il ordonne les noces les plus folles que l'on ait jamais vues. D'ailleurs, pour faire bonne mesure il épousera lui-même non seulement Statira mais aussi sa cousine, une fille d'Artaxerxès III, le prédécesseur de Darius.

Au signal des trompettes, chacune des dix mille vierges se dirige vers l'époux qui lui est assigné. Statira, vêtue d'une robe dorée, va vers Alexandre et la plus jeune fille de Darius va vers Héphestion, l'ami de cœur d'Alexandre. Selon le rite perse Alexandre embrasse Statira et dix mille baisers claquent en même temps. Puis, après les sacrifices aux dieux – Zeus côtoyant, que cela lui convînt ou non, Ahura Mazda – c'est le gigantesque banquet.

Pour la centaine de ses proches qui convolent en même temps que lui, Alexandre a fait dresser une tente de sept cents mètres de long, une tente somptueuse, toute de soie, d'or et de tissus précieux. On y festoie puis, quand le moment est venu de consommer le mariage chaque couple se retire dans une alcôve prévue pour la circonstance avec coussins et fumées de parfums.

On veut espérer qu'à partir de cet instant la suite des opérations fut laissée à l'initiative privée et qu'Alexandre ne poussa pas le souci de la discipline jusqu'à charger quelque stentor de beugler l'ordre d'attaquer tous ensemble, et au commandement, les tendres forteresses...

On dit qu'au cours de cette nuit mémorable Alexandre envoya ses deux épouses rejoindre Héphestion après les avoir faites femmes et accueillit dans sa couche la compagne du jeune homme. On dit aussi qu'il acheva sa nuit nuptiale avec Héphestion lui-même qu'il aimait plus ardemment que les femmes honorées de ses attentions, fussent-elles belles entre toutes les belles...

La dernière nuit de noces d'Alexandre, c'est avec lui d'ailleurs qu'il la vivra.

Quelques mois après les noces de Suse, Héphestion meurt des excès de toutes sortes auxquels il s'est livré en compagnie d'Alexandre. La douleur du conquérant est aux dimensions de sa divinité.

Alexandre est alors à Babylone où il fait exécuter de gigantesques travaux, retraçant les canaux, asséchant les marais, ressuscitant le port. Il se passionne tellement pour cette résurrection qu'il contracte la malaria et il est malade quand on lui apprend que son ami vient de mourir. Alors il se déchaîne.

Le médecin qui n'a pu sauver le jeune homme est exécuté. Puis Alexandre rase sa superbe chevelure, fait couper les crinières de tous ses chevaux et les fait jeter au pied de la couche d'Héphestion où il s'étend lui-même, étreignant le cadavre de son ami en criant un terrifiant désespoir.

Dans les derniers jours du mois de mai 323, le corps du disparu est hissé sur un bûcher tellement gigantesque qu'il a fallu abattre un coin des terrasses des Jardins Suspendus et que les flammes montent plus haut que n'atteignait jadis le dernier étage de l'Entemenanki. Alexandre tremblant de fièvre et les yeux brûlants le regardera brûler jusqu'au bout avant de se jeter dans la folie d'une suite de banquets funéraires qui achèveront de le détruire. Le 13 juin à la tombée du jour Alexandre s'en va rejoindre Héphestion avec le dernier éclat du soleil...

Le dernier dieu à face humaine venait de quitter la terre.

Ceux qui, après lui, prétendraient à l'essence divine n'arriveraient jamais à dépasser le stade du simulacre...

NUIT DE NOCES AU RABAIS
POUR LE DIVIN AUGUSTE

En admettant qu'il l'eût voulu, Auguste aurait eu bien du mal à faire croire qu'il était le fils d'un dieu aussi « bien de sa personne » que Jupiter, l'avatar romain de Zeus. C'était un petit homme malingre, au teint pâle et tavelé, aux cheveux mal plantés et aux vilaines dents. Craignant le soleil autant que le froid il enfonçait toujours un chapeau à larges bords sur les épis de ses cheveux et s'habillait comme un oignon, empilant sous sa toge une incroyable quantité de vêtements variés qui ôtaient toute noblesse au célèbre « drapé à l'antique ». Affligé, en outre, d'un coryza chronique il avait perpétuellement le nez rouge et humide... Non, en vérité, aucun dieu ne se fût trouvé flatté d'un rejeton pourvu d'un extérieur à ce point minable. Mais ce n'était que l'extérieur car le génie habitait cette triste enveloppe, un génie dont les éclairs se laissaient voir, parfois, dans les yeux, très grands, très brillants et d'une curieuse couleur d'acier...

Tel qu'il était et bien que, d'après les mauvaises langues, il eût vu le jour dans la famille d'un changeur (ou d'un épicier..., les mauvaises langues s'agitant toujours sur des relations fort vagues) le jeune Octave, neveu de César en réalité et adopté par lui, n'allait pas moins franchir tous les degrés d'une fabuleuse ascension : il fut consul, tribun, pontife, prince, empereur et finalement dieu et il devint tellement auguste que le nom lui était resté. Dûment divinisé par le peuple romain – il s'est d'ailleurs laissé faire une douce violence – Auguste se retrouve fils de Jupiter et il faudra bien que le maître des dieux s'en accommode.

Mais il n'en est pas encore là, s'il est déjà Auguste, quand en 39 avant Jésus-Christ il rencontre celle qui va être le grand amour de sa vie et sa seconde passion si l'on tient compte du fait que la première est la haine féroce que lui inspire son beau-frère Marc-Antoine, le guerrier, le héros, l'homme à femmes qui a su remplacer César dans les bras de Cléopâtre. Il a alors vingt-quatre ans et Livie en a dix-neuf.

Ce n'est pas n'importe qui, Livie. Sa famille, la gens Claudia est peut-être la plus noble de Rome mais comme son père s'est toujours opposé à César, Livie a vécu toute son enfance au milieu des dernières convulsions de la République. Son père, d'ailleurs, est mort dans les rangs des derniers partisans de Brutus et elle est à peine sortie de l'enfance quand on la marie à un autre Claude, Tiberius Claudius Nero, nettement plus âgé qu'elle, mais qui ne fait pas exception au reste de la famille : il est déjà l'ennemi d'Octave, ce « petit jeune homme qui doit tout à son nom ».

Cette attitude l'oblige bientôt à fuir, en compagnie de Livie qui lui a déjà donné un fils, le futur Tibère. On gagne d'abord la Campanie puis la Sicile et enfin la Grèce et Sparte.

Quand ils reviennent la trêve s'est instaurée entre Octave et Antoine qui a épousé Octavie, la sœur de son ennemi. Octave pour sa part a épousé Scribonia fille d'un chef du parti de Pompée avec qui les deux autres se sont aussi réconciliés. Qu'importe que Scribonia en soit à son troisième mari et qu'elle ait déjà deux filles, c'est une alliance intéressante et, pour le moment, Rome et ses leaders baignent dans les bons sentiments.

Cela ne dure guère. Lorsque paraît Livie avec sa blondeur et ses yeux clairs, si transparents qu'ils approchent le vide et que l'on ne sait trop sur quel abîme ils ouvrent, Auguste s'aperçoit qu'il est mal marié, que Scribonia a cessé de lui plaire. D'ailleurs il découvre tout à coup qu'elle est de mœurs douteuses, facilement adonnée à la débauche. Et la voilà répudiée avant même d'avoir eu le temps de s'apercevoir de ce qui lui arrive... et tout juste le jour où cette innocente met au monde Julie, l'unique enfant qu'elle aura de son époux momentané.

Reste à présent à épouser Livie. Livie qui est mariée, elle aussi, mère de famille et enceinte par-dessus le marché... On ne sait trop comment Auguste réussit cette espèce de miracle, ou même si c'est lui qui le réussit car les avis diffèrent sur celui qui prit l'initiative. Pour certains, Livie aurait été offerte en holocauste au maître de l'heure en dépit de la différence de naissance : la plus belle fleur de la plus grande famille patricienne livrée au monstre de naissance inférieure. Pour d'autres, dont l'empereur Claude son petit-fils, Livie aurait, d'elle-même, décidé d'épouser Auguste, héritier de César en dépit de sa naissance et de son peu d'aspect. Elle aurait, elle-même, accusé Scribonia d'adultère et aurait même poussé l'impudence jusqu'à aller trouver son époux et lui déclarer :

« Répudie-moi. Je suis enceinte de cinq mois déjà mais ce n'est pas toi le père car j'avais fait vœu de ne plus donner d'enfants à un lâche. Je tiens parole... »

Forte parole! Essentiellement romaine et, surtout, mensonge évident mais que Tiberius Claudius Nero parut avaler sans broncher. Il demanda à rencontrer le responsable et, au cours de l'entretien qu'il eut avec Auguste, il aurait déclaré :

« Si tu aimes cette femme, prends-la mais que les convenances soient respectées... »

On ne sait trop comment il l'entendait et, bien certainement, ce que les Romains appelaient « convenances » échappe en partie à notre entendement. Les choses, en tout cas, se passèrent de la façon suivante : Tibère l'Ancien répudia conformément à la loi sa belle Livie et poussa la bonté jusqu'à assister au mariage, quelques semaines plus tard et même à conduire lui-même, comme un père, devant le pontife, une rougissante fiancée dont la robe n'arrivait pas à cacher un ventre gros de six mois.

Il serait intéressant de savoir quel fut, en la circonstance, le cérémonial suivi. La coutume voulait que la fiancée, vêtue d'une tunique sans coutures serrée par une ceinture de laine et recouverte d'un manteau jaune safran, portant sur la tête un voile couleur de feu sous une couronne de fleurs champêtres, attendît dans sa maison tendue de tapisseries et abondamment ornée de verdure, le fiancé et sa famille. Un sacrifice était alors offert en présence de dix témoins le plus souvent dans l'atrium magnifiquement décoré et éclairé. Ensuite venait l'échange des consentements : « *Ubi tu Gaius, ego Gaïa...* », après quoi le nouveau couple recevait les félicitations des parents et des amis avant de passer à table pour l'un de ces banquets monstres dans lesquels les Romains étaient passés maîtres et dont, d'ailleurs, Auguste tenta de modérer le luxe.

Enfin, le moment venu, l'épousée était conduite à la maison de son époux au milieu d'un joyeux cortège avec joueurs de flûte et porte-flambeaux dont l'un, le « pronubus » brandissait la torche nuptiale à la lumière de laquelle deux autres garçons devaient soulever la mariée pour lui faire franchir le seuil de sa nouvelle demeure où sa première fille d'honneur la menait enfin à la chambre nuptiale...

Tout cela, bien sûr, était charmant lorsqu'il s'agissait d'une jeune et timide vierge mais ne devait pas manquer d'un certain sel comique en se déroulant autour d'une femme enceinte.

Il est bien certain que le collège des pontifes aurait pu émettre quelques objections mais l'ex-époux de Livie était lui-même pontife, Auguste l'était également. Quant au *Pontifex Maximus,* il n'était autre que Lépide qui se serait bien gardé de contrarier Auguste en quoi que ce fût... D'une façon ou d'une autre, le mariage eut lieu et, trois mois plus tard, Livie mettait au monde Drusus. Ce qui fit dire aux méchantes langues qu'Auguste était véritablement divin puisqu'il était capable de faire un enfant en trois mois...

C'est là que se place un mystère : Livie ayant déjà mis deux enfants au monde n'avait plus à faire la preuve de sa fécondité. Auguste non plus car, sans parler de sa fille Julie, il passait pour avoir au moins quatre enfants naturels. Or, ce mariage-là demeura stérile : jamais Auguste et Livie n'eurent d'enfants ensemble.

Certains ont avancé, discrètement, une explication de ce curieux état de fait : jamais le mariage n'aurait été consommé, même après que Livie se fut délivrée d'un fardeau qui avait dû inciter les nouveaux époux à une parfaite sagesse durant la nuit de leurs noces. Et cela pour une raison que nos psychanalystes actuels expliqueraient sans doute aisément par une inhibition. Très pieux, craignant ces dieux dont on tenait tellement à ce qu'il descende, Auguste, pontife par-dessus le marché et se trouvant donc mieux placé que quiconque pour savoir que son mariage constituait une grave impiété, aurait été totalement incapable de le consommer en dépit de l'amour ardent que lui inspirait Livie.

Évidemment il semble difficile de croire à une inhibition résistant à cinquante années de vie commune, même en tenant compte du relais pris par l'âge et les déficiences de la santé mais à l'appui de cette thèse s'inscrivent les prédictions de la Sibylle de Cumes qu'Auguste lui-même avait recueillies et consignées par écrit. Voici le texte qui le concernait :

« Le second César sera le fils de celui-là (entendez Jules César) sans l'être. Il a des cheveux en toison. Il donne à Rome du marbre au lieu d'argile, des fers étroits et invisibles. Il mourra de la main de sa femme qui n'est pas sa femme pour le profit de son fils qui n'est pas son fils. » C'est en effet, Tibère, fils de Livie qui lui succédera.

Livie, d'ailleurs, n'aima jamais Auguste et il est possible

que son impuissance envers elle, si impuissance il y avait, l'eût arrangée. Elle ne cessa, sans trop prendre la peine de s'en cacher, de regretter le temps heureux de son premier mariage mais s'en consola aisément avec l'usage du pouvoir illimité qu'elle possédait sur l'Empereur.

Pour sa part, Auguste aima Livie jusqu'au dernier jour, au point d'exiger pour elle les honneurs de la divinisation et si – la chose est certaine – il ne lui fut pas fidèle selon la chair, son cœur toujours lui demeura attaché peut-être comme l'homme s'attache à certaines choses désirées qu'il ne peut atteindre réellement.

Quant à l'Empire romain, ignorant les misères psychologiques ou physiques de son maître, il connut, avec le Siècle d'Auguste, le plus grand éclat, la plus grande puissance et surtout une paix profonde que rien ne vint troubler de l'instant où, après le double suicide d'Antoine et de Cléopâtre, leur vainqueur, au jour de son triomphe, referma solennellement les portes de bronze du temple de Janus, les portes redoutées de la guerre. Elles n'allaient plus s'ouvrir avant deux cents ans...

LA NUIT D'UN CHRIST SUR LA TERRE :
LE BASILEUS SE MARIE

Entre le règne de Constantin le Grand et le drame de 1453 qui vit s'écrouler l'Empire byzantin et le Croissant remplacer la Croix, le voyageur qui arrivait à Byzance soit par mer, en débarquant aux quais de marbre de la Corne d'Or, soit par terre en franchissant la double et formidable enceinte aux cent douze tours carrées était censé avoir quitté la terre pour pénétrer dans quelque cité céleste, la Cité de Dieu, chère à saint Augustin, la Jérusalem divine annoncée par l'Apocalypse.

« Et il mesura la ville avec une mesure en or et toute la ville était d'or pur, semblable à du cristal pur... »

Les édiles de la ville s'étaient donnés, au cours des siècles, beaucoup de mal pour confirmer cette impression et jamais cité n'avait fait, pour ses bâtiments une telle consommation d'or. Les cinq cents églises voient leurs coupoles revêtues d'une épaisse couche d'or et il en va de même pour les dômes des palais. Les mosaïques d'or éclatent un peu partout. Dans la rue, la principale industrie est la joaillerie, le ciselage de l'or, la coulée des monnaies, le tissage des vêtements parfilés d'or. Quant à l'empereur, à l'impératrice et à leur Cour, ils vivent au milieu d'une nuée dorée et, en fait, Byzance est le plus grand entrepôt mondial du métal jaune. Et il faut qu'il en soit ainsi car les Byzantins mettent leur orgueil à imiter le Paradis en toutes choses et entendent créer leur société à l'image de la société céleste, peuplée d'anges, d'archanges, de trônes et de dominations avec, au sommet de la pyramide, le Christ-Roi dont l'empereur, le Basileus, se doit d'incarner constamment le personnage.

S'il parvient à éviter la crasse des ruelles sordides avoisinant le port et où grouille la multitude haillonneuse de la puissante et dangereuse confrérie des Mendiants, le voyageur, l'œil encore enchanté par sa découverte de la ville couchée au bord du croissant bleu du Bosphore dans le doux vallonnement de ses sept collines et le foisonnement de ses jardins, ira de surprise en surprise. Il rencontrera des personnages vêtus, comme les saints qui décorent les églises et les icônes, de longues robes raides de broderies; il verra surgir tout à coup, au coin d'une rue, une immense croix d'or, portée au milieu du chant des cantiques et des fumées de l'encens, par une troupe armée et devra revenir de sa surprise avant de s'apercevoir qu'il a rencontré, non une procession mais un officier et ses soldats. S'il est un personnage de quelque importance et s'il est admis, au palais de la Magnaures, au Palais Sacré ou aux Blachernes en présence de l'empereur, il verra que la plupart des salles de ces palais ressemblent à des chapelles ornées, sur fond d'or, de gigantesques images du Christ Pantocrator ou de la Théotokos, la Mère de Dieu. Il verra enfin qu'auprès du trône (d'or naturellement!) érigé dans une abside où se tient assis le souverain, vêtu exactement comme les images qui éclatent au-dessus de sa tête, il y en a un autre, encore plus riche mais vide, à l'exception d'un lourd évangéliaire ouvert à la date du jour. Et s'il s'étonne, quelqu'un lui fera comprendre que le Basileus n'est que l'image du Sauveur et que le véritable maître de Byzance, c'est le Christ.

La vie religieuse d'un basileus, pourtant, aurait de quoi excéder le pape le mieux trempé. Chaque jour, accompagné du patriarche, il assiste à quelque cérémonie religieuse dans l'une des églises de Byzance. Il vit au milieu des nuages d'encens. A la fin de chaque repas, après le dessert, il renouvelle les gestes de la Cène, rompt le pain et trempe

ses lèvres dans une coupe de vin et, le jour de Pâques pour
symboliser la Résurrection, il apparaît entouré des Douze
Apôtres, enveloppé de bandelettes comme une momie et le
visage peint en blanc. Enfin ses palais fourmillent d'eunuques, formule élégante apportée en réponse à la fameuse
– et combien byzantine! – querelle sur le sexe des anges.
C'est cela que représentent les eunuques à la cour du
Basileus : les Anges serviteurs du Christ et non les gardiens
d'un gynécée qui n'en avait pas besoin, la Basilissa, dûment
couronnée avant même la cérémonie de son mariage,
possédant presque les mêmes pouvoirs que son époux...

Car, à Byzance, le Christ se marie. Cette effigie divine
que l'on ne peut approcher qu'à genoux, ce symbole du
Seigneur-Dieu dont les audiences portent le nom de
Révélations et au cours desquelles il exprime sa volonté par
de simples battements de paupières, ce dieu vivant dont le
sceptre est une croix, qui porte une autre croix sur sa
couronne constellée de pierreries, il faut bien qu'à défaut
de l'intervention toujours problématique du Saint-Esprit,
il prenne femme et accomplisse, comme tout un chacun, les
gestes de l'amour s'il prétend avoir des enfants et constituer
sa dynastie.

Mais la recherche de l'élue ne lui appartient pas.
Lorsque semble venu pour lui le temps de convoler, les
conseillers de la Cour se réunissent en assemblée plénière
afin de déterminer les canons minutieux auxquels devra
répondre la future Basilissa. Tout est réglé au gramme ou
au centimètre près : la taille, le poids, les mensurations
exactes, le grain de la peau, la qualité des cheveux et leur
couleur, la teinte des yeux. Plus, bien entendu, une
indiscutable virginité.

Une fois établis, ces canons sont recopiés à plusieurs
dizaines d'exemplaires par les scribes du Palais Sacré et
remis aux nombreux messagers que l'on envoie ensuite,
deux par deux, dans toutes les provinces de l'empire afin de
les fouiller et d'y découvrir les jeunes filles correspondant à
ce que l'on demande, qui d'ailleurs varie suivant les goûts

du Basileus ou du futur Basileus à marier. Ces messagers doivent passer au peigne fin les villes, les villages et jusqu'aux plus misérables bourgades sans s'occuper le moins du monde du rang social ou de la fortune des candidates.

Suivant cette coutume essentiellement démocratique, n'importe quelle jeune fille, si elle était très belle, pouvait espérer devenir, non une quelconque et éphémère Miss Byzance mais l'épouse du Christ sur la terre et la toute-puissante Basilissa, future mère de souverains et bel et bien couronnée. Telle fut l'aventure miraculeuse mais néanmoins désastreuse de Marie l'Arménienne.

Quand mourut, en 780, son époux Léon le Khazare, l'impératrice Irène s'empara du pouvoir avec une avidité qui en disait long sur les dimensions exactes de son ambition. En fait, depuis qu'on l'avait amenée à Byzance, petite Athénienne sans naissance, pour participer au concours de beauté rituel, Irène, à peine élue, se fixa un but, un seul mais immense et enivrant : posséder un jour le pouvoir. Pas celui, intéressant, certes, mais tout de même limité d'une épouse de basileus : le pouvoir absolu, le pouvoir suprême, celui que l'on exerce en régnant seule.

Ce pouvoir, elle l'avait attendu des années, tremblant seulement que la mort d'un époux peu aimé ne le lui apportât trop tard, lorsque son fils, majeur serait en âge de régner. Mais le dieu de colère et d'impitoyable justice qu'elle priait et qui ressemblait bien davantage au Jupiter tonnant qu'au miséricordieux Galiléen, avait apparemment écouté les prières ardentes de cette fanatique aux yeux d'émeraude : Léon avait quitté ce monde, lui laissant l'empire en régence, pour quelques années tout au moins car son fils, le jeune empereur Constantin VI, n'avait alors que dix ans.

Sans laisser à quiconque le temps de se retourner, Irène entreprit de faire place nette : les cinq beaux-frères qui auraient dû participer à la régence furent, soit exilés sous de vagues prétextes, soit nantis de charges où ils se retrouvaient pieds et poings liés tandis que les anciens serviteurs de leur père, Constantin V, et de leur frère Léon IV se voyaient limogés quand ils n'étaient pas discrètement supprimés s'il leur prenait fantaisie de protester. Politique brutale? Sans doute. Dangereuse? Peut-être mais Irène avait compris qu'elle ne pourrait se permettre de louvoyer. Bientôt, nul n'ignora plus dans l'empire que la Basilissa entendait régner, non en simple régente, mais bel et bien en « souverain » absolu. Et il est probable que si la nature lui eût permis de se laisser pousser la barbe, elle l'aurait fait sans hésiter.

Cette attitude ne manquait pas de courage ni d'audace car depuis des années Byzance vivait la fameuse querelle des Images et les derniers empereurs avaient tous été des iconoclastes acharnés. Or, Irène adorait les Images. Elle aimait la majesté terrible, presque sauvage, des grands Christs Pantocrators des anciennes basiliques, les Vierges hiératiques, raidies dans leurs robes-joyaux, les Saints aux longues figures ravagées par la flamme intérieure de la Foi et les macérations de la pénitence...

En sept années de règne, cette femme virile parvint à rétablir le culte des Images. En même temps, connaissant à fond l'orgueil et l'amour des richesses de son peuple, elle faisait fructifier le commerce, favorisait les arts et les échanges avec les peuples les plus éloignés, et même, sur la réputation du puissant monarque d'Occident, un roi franc nommé Charles, qui régnait sur la plus grande partie de l'Europe de l'Ouest, elle se laissait gagner par l'idée d'un mariage entre son fils Constantin et l'une des filles de ce « Charlemagne », la petite Rothrude.

Ce mariage, elle l'envisageait d'ailleurs à sa manière dédaigneuse, comme une faveur accordée par une souveraine hautement civilisée à un monarque à peu près barbare mais elle n'en avait pas moins fait ce qu'il fallait : des eunuques de haut rang – les fameux anges! – étaient partis pour le pays des Francs afin d'enseigner à l'enfant les rites compliqués d'une étiquette effroyablement tatillonne, ainsi que l'usage de la langue locale.

Les choses n'avaient pas marché. Le « Barbare » n'avait pas aimé les eunuques en robes brodées ni leur politesse oblique. En outre, il aimait sa fille. Il fit traîner les choses avec tant de virtuosité que la jeune Rothrude eut tout le temps de s'éprendre d'un jeune seigneur de la suite paternelle et, avec beaucoup de regrets apparents mais en se frottant discrètement les mains, Charles fit reconduire les seigneurs byzantins aux frontières de son empire avec beaucoup de politesses.

Contrairement à ce que l'on pourrait penser, Irène les vit revenir aussi avec une sorte de soulagement. Elle n'en était pas à son premier regret de s'être embarquée dans cette affaire, tout à fait inhabituelle pour le mariage d'un basileus et qui, en outre pouvait devenir dangereuse pour elle. Soutenu par un beau-père dont la puissance se développait de jour en jour, Constantin n'aurait eu aucune peine, l'âge venu, à se débarrasser d'une mère devenue encombrante. Or, justement, elle n'entendait pas se faire évincer par son fils.

Elle se contenta donc d'informer le jeune souverain de ce qui venait de se passer : il ne devait plus songer à la fille du roi des Francs. Or, le jeune Constantin s'était peu à peu, épris de la princesse lointaine qu'on lui destinait. Il refusa de la chasser de ses rêves ou de ses pensées et Irène se trouva devant un nouveau problème. Elle pensa le résoudre de la manière la plus simple : une épouse de chair, si elle correspondait à l'idéal féminin du jeune garçon, parviendrait sans peine à chasser l'image de la barbare inconnue et, comme Constantin venait d'avoir dix-huit ans, les messagers cuirassés d'argent furent envoyés à la recherche de l'oiseau rare. Mais à la liste des perfections physiques exigées par le Conseil, Irène avait joint un codicille bien dans sa manière : les candidates devaient être d'une grande douceur de caractère, pleines d'humilité et de timidité comme il convenait à de vraies jeunes filles. Il ne s'agissait pas, pour elle, de se retrouver un jour encombrée d'une belle-fille aussi ambitieuse qu'elle-même et qui pousserait doucement son époux à envoyer sa mère dans quelque riche couvent, méditer le reste de sa vie sur son salut éternel et y continuer, mais sur le plan métaphysique cette fois, son rôle d'épouse du Christ.

La quête des messagers dura longtemps. Il y avait toujours quelque chose qui clochait.

Un soir, deux de ces hommes qui ont parcouru longuement l'Arménie parviennent dans un village reculé du thème de Paphlagonie. Il est tard. Les messagers impériaux sont las, recrus de soleil et de poussière, affamés, assoiffés et avec un moral des plus bas : il y a des semaines qu'ils sont partis et, sur la longue route qui leur a été assignée, ils n'ont rien rencontré dont ils puissent espérer la victoire. En outre, dans cette véritable cambrousse il n'y a même pas une auberge : rien que des maisonnettes misérables, presque des huttes, où vit une humanité couleur de terre...

Un paysan qui rentre des champs leur indique, à l'écart du village, une maison moins misérable que les autres et cachée par un bouquet d'arbres. Il y a là un saint homme nommé Philarète, un prêtre du Seigneur Dieu qui a sans doute en lui le plus zélé de ses serviteurs. Bien qu'il soit loin d'être riche, il fait l'aumône régulièrement. Il accueillera sans doute des voyageurs attardés...

Philarète les accueille, en effet, non sans s'excuser d'une si misérable hospitalité. Il n'oublie pas non plus de se plaindre de la dureté des temps et des difficultés de subsister dans ce pays oublié de Dieu pour un homme qui a charge d'âmes. Car il est grand-père. Il a trois petites-filles en âge de se marier et qui sont, sans doute, condamnées à se faner dans la solitude.

Des filles en âge de se marier? Voilà qui intéresse les quêteurs découragés. Et comment sont-elles, ces jeunes personnes? Philarète ne se fait pas prier pour les montrer. Il frappe dans ses mains et l'on va chercher les jeunes filles.

En vérité, elles sont charmantes toutes les trois mais l'aînée, Marie, est une vraie beauté et, du coup, les messagers un peu endormis par le vin résiné se réveillent, consultent fébrilement leurs instructions. Quel âge a-t-elle? Quinze ans. C'est tout juste l'âge désiré. Les cheveux? le teint? la taille? tout correspond point par point aux exigences du fameux parchemin qu'ils traînent avec eux depuis des mois.

Immensément soulagés et au comble du ravissement, les messagers dévoilent alors au vieillard le but exact de leur quête et le supplient de consentir à entreprendre, avec eux, le long voyage vers Byzance. Un voyage bien fatigant certes mais qui risque de se terminer glorieusement.

L'idée de voir sa petite-fille élevée à la pourpre impériale a de quoi séduire Philarète. D'autant qu'au cas où elle ne serait pas choisie, un royal dédommagement lui serait offert, à titre de consolation comme à toutes les autres candidates éliminées. Il n'hésite donc même pas et à l'aube, toute la famille prend le chemin de la cité impériale tandis que tout le village bâille d'admiration à la nouvelle : Marie d'Amnia va concourir pour devenir Basilissa!

Marie, qui est une fille douce et simple, est éblouie par la splendeur de Byzance et plus encore par celle du palais de la Magnaure où elle est conduite dès son arrivée. Là, tout n'est qu'ors, marbres, mosaïques précieuses, étoffes rares, parfums, fleurs et joyaux, mais elle ne perd pas la tête pour autant, se réjouissant simplement de sa chance d'être admise à contempler tant de merveilles. Et comme elle n'imagine pas un seul instant qu'elle possède la moindre chance d'être élue, elle se fabrique des souvenirs à raconter lorsqu'elle retournera dans son pauvre village de Paphlagonie.

Au jour fixé, après l'avoir baignée, parfumée, habillée et dûment instruite de la façon dont elle doit se comporter, on la conduit dans une salle immense au plafond de laquelle un Christ gigantesque règne sur les Quatre Évangélistes. Une douzaine de jeunes filles s'y trouvent déjà. Toutes sont belles et superbement parées mais toutes sont nobles et riches : Marie est la seule paysanne du lot et ces filles de hauts fonctionnaires ou de généraux regardent avec dédain cette inconnue dont on ne sait d'où elle sort. Aussi se hâte-t-on de le lui faire sentir car si ces demoiselles sont prêtes à s'entredéchirer, toutes griffes dehors, pour la possession de l'empereur et de la couronne, elles se retrouvent singulièrement d'accord pour se moquer de « la paysanne ».

« Pourquoi donc ne pourrions-nous être d'accord? s'étonne Marie sans montrer la moindre amertume. Ne ferions-nous pas mieux de nous entendre? Ainsi, celle d'entre nous qui sera élue pourrait s'occuper de l'avenir des autres? »

Cette naïveté déchaîne l'hilarité générale.

« Ce serait évidemment ton avantage, lui répond la plus hautaine des jeunes concurrentes, car tu n'as aucune chance n'ayant ni naissance, ni fortune... ni véritable beauté d'ailleurs. Tu sens par trop ta campagne, ma fille! Mais moi qui suis fille de stratège, j'ai toutes les chances d'être choisie et donc aucune raison de " m'entendre " avec toi. Cesse donc de nous importuner... »

Malheureusement pour elle, la fière concurrente ne se départit pas de cette attitude superbe lorsqu'on la présenta devant ce que l'on pourrait appeler le jury. Il est composé de l'impératrice Irène, de son conseiller préféré, l'eunuque Staurakios, de quelques conseillers de moindre importance et, bien entendu tout de même, du jeune empereur. Cela ne lui réussit pas. Irène l'interroge puis, fronçant soudain les sourcils, lui montre la porte :

« Tu es belle et de bonne maison, lui dit-elle, mais le trône n'est pas pour toi... »

Les autres jeunes filles lui inspirent une méfiance analogue. Elles sont trop nobles, trop riches donc trop ambitieuses. Elles pourraient constituer, plus tard, un danger contre son pouvoir. En revanche, Marie d'Amnia suscite son intérêt car elle est visiblement timide, douce et déjà soumise. Elle pourrait faire une belle-fille idéale car, sans doute, elle passerait sa vie prosternée devant celle qui la tirerait de sa misérable condition pour la hisser au trône...

Et, comme c'est, en fait, Irène qui choisit, la petite Marie se retrouve élue. Pour marquer ce choix, Constantin descend de son trône pour lui offrir une pomme d'or. Et, tandis qu'elle pleure de joie, elle peut entendre, le soir venu, les hérauts proclamer son nom aux quatre horizons de Byzance tandis que s'élèvent les acclamations de la foule.

On pourrait s'étonner évidemment de ce que le jeune souverain n'ait pas pris une part plus active au choix de sa future épouse, ainsi que le veut la coutume. Mais c'est que Constantin se marie uniquement pour faire plaisir à sa mère. Au fond de lui-même, il n'est pas parvenu à oublier la princesse franque à laquelle il a été si longtemps fiancé et dont on lui avait tracé une merveilleuse image. Aussi, quand Irène l'a invité à venir se choisir une épouse parmi les candidates réunies pour lui (mais en se promettant bien d'aiguiller discrètement son choix) a-t-il coupé court à tous ses préparatifs oratoires en déclarant simplement :

« Choisis toi-même, Mère. Je prendrai celle qui te conviendra... »

Il ne restait plus à Irène qu'à remercier le Ciel et sa bonne étoile... et à activer les préparatifs du mariage. En novembre 788, après avoir reçu la couronne impériale, Marie l'Arménienne épousait le Basileus Constantin.

Elle avait pleuré de joie au soir de son élection. Au soir de son mariage elle pleure encore, mais c'est de déception et de chagrin, car elle a aimé Constantin au premier regard qu'elle a osé lever sur lui. Et voilà que, sans la moindre nuance, il lui laisse entendre qu'il ne l'a épousée que pour complaire à sa mère, qu'il n'éprouve aucune sorte d'amour pour elle, que son cœur appartient toujours à la fille de

Charles le Grand... et qu'elle n'a rien à attendre de lui, pas même l'ombre d'un désir pour sa beauté.

Mais Marie n'est que douceur. Elle pleurera tout à l'heure, quand elle sera seule car il va la laisser seule, elle en est persuadée. Pour le moment, elle s'incline simplement :

« Seigneur, je serai ce que tu voudras. Épouse ou amie. Sache seulement que tu n'auras pas de servante plus fidèle que moi... et que je saurai attendre. Un jour peut-être, si Dieu m'exauce, j'aurai une petite part de ton affection... »

Elle ne l'eut jamais. Bien sûr, au bout de quelque temps Constantin fit de Marie sa femme selon la chair mais il ne s'y décida que sur l'ordre d'Irène. C'est dire qu'il ne se mit guère en frais pour plaire à sa jeune épouse. Néanmoins, comme Marie était extrêmement belle et qu'il n'était pas complètement aveugle (pas encore tout au moins!), il éprouva quelque plaisir à posséder cette ravissante créature qui, en échange, lui donna deux filles : Euphrosyne et Irène.

Peut-être qu'avec le temps ce ménage-là eût pu devenir valable s'il n'y avait eu l'autre Irène, la grande. Elle allait se charger de tout gâcher irrémédiablement car, toujours aussi avide de puissance, elle tenait son fils à l'écart des affaires. Celui qui gouvernait, devant qui l'on s'inclinait, c'était son favori Staurakios, l'eunuque... ou soi-disant tel!

Un beau jour Constantin s'insurge, complote avec quelques téméraires contre le tout-puissant ministre. Mal lui en prend. Le complot est découvert. Les conjurés sont arrêtés, torturés, exécutés. Le jeune empereur lui-même est battu de verges comme un gamin, puis Irène exige que l'on reconnaisse son pouvoir supérieur à celui du Basileus.

Cette fois elle est allée trop loin. Les armées d'Asie se soulèvent, exigent la mise en liberté du « Christ Incarné ». Irène, ulcérée voit à son tour ses serviteurs emprisonnés.

Staurakios, tondu, est enfermé dans un monastère. Irène enfin se voit écartée du pouvoir, enfermée dans son palais d'Eleuthérion.

La pénitence est assez douce. Eleuthérion est sa résidence préférée, une merveille de luxe, de fleurs et d'eaux jaillissantes mais cela ne suffit pas à l'ambitieuse. Elle connaît bien son fils et règle sa conduite en conséquence. Constantin est faible, elle le sait bien. Il aura bientôt besoin d'elle et, de fait, le jeune empereur se laisse aller à la rappeler auprès de lui et ne devine pas que sous le masque de cette mère qui le couvre de tendresse se cache sa plus mortelle ennemie. Car désormais Irène n'a plus qu'un but : abattre son fils et reprendre le pouvoir.

Pour cela, elle emploie la ruse la plus perfide, le brouille avec ses partisans et ses meilleurs amis, manœuvre de façon à lui aliéner l'armée, donne en son nom des ordres iniques. Enfin elle entreprend de le perdre dans l'esprit de la toute-puissante Église et, pour cela, sacrifie impitoyablement Marie qui ne lui a jamais rien fait.

Celle-ci pourtant souffre bien suffisamment. Constantin ne l'aime toujours pas. Le Christ fait homme a des maîtresses. Sa tendre mère va lui en procurer une de plus, une affolante beauté, dûment endoctrinée par elle et qui se nomme Théodote.

Elle a bien choisi. Victime d'un violent coup de foudre Constantin ne songe plus qu'à répudier Marie. Mais pour chasser une basilissa couronnée et ayant déjà donné des enfants il faut une raison bien forte... Prête à tout pour le bonheur de son cher fils, c'est encore Irène qui ourdit le misérable complot : grassement payées par elle, des servantes accusent la Basilissa de tenter, par jalousie, d'empoisonner son époux. Immédiatement, et sans l'entendre, on décide d'envoyer Marie dans un couvent...

Personne n'est dupe de ce coup monté et le Patriarche moins encore que tout autre. Il connaît la jeune femme et, sans désemparer il fait entendre à l'empereur sa défense formelle de répudier son épouse...

C'est tout juste ce que souhaitait Irène. Excitant sournoisement le ressentiment de son fils et, en même temps, son désir pour Théodote, elle le pousse à passer outre l'interdiction. Et Constantin tombe dans le piège : officiellement répudiée, sous l'inculpation de lèse-majesté, Marie, la tête rasée est conduite de nuit dans un couvent éloigné où elle mourra quelques années plus tard, désespérée de n'avoir jamais pu revoir ses enfants.

Au tour de Constantin, à présent! En septembre 795 il épouse Théodote sous les huées de l'empire tout entier et consomme sa nuit de noces avec un enthousiasme qui en dit long sur ses sentiments. Cette fois le Christ incarné est complètement tombé de son piédestal, mais Irène lui accorde une année de plaisirs défendus, une année qu'elle saura bien employer au mieux de ses propres intérêts en travaillant artistement toutes les couches de la société. C'est facile : quelques condamnations stupides ici ou là que l'empereur signe distraitement sans même sortir du lit de sa bien-aimée qui s'entend comme personne à l'y retenir.

Il ne reste plus, au bout de ce laps de temps qu'à cueillir les fruits de l'intrigue. Se posant tout à coup en libératrice et se déclarant « indignée par les excès auxquels s'est livré le jeune empereur » cette mère parfaite fait, une belle nuit, arrêter Constantin dans les bras de Théodote et le livre au bourreau pour qu'il lui crève les yeux : une pratique assez courante à Byzance lorsque l'on voulait rendre quelqu'un inutilisable.

Cela fait, le malheureux reçut permission maternelle d'aller finir doucement ses jours dans une superbe villa insulaire en compagnie de sa chère Théodote dont cet exil doucha sérieusement la grande passion. On peut la comprendre : elle était impératrice et se retrouvait garde-malade. Mais de cela Irène n'avait cure : elle était à présent « seul maître à bord » et entendait bien le rester jusqu'à son dernier jour.

Le Destin, lui, ne l'entendait pas de la même oreille et

l'ambitieuse trouva son maître sous les aspects singulièrement dissonants d'un vulgaire général, un certain Nicé-
phore sans grande naissance mais encore plus malin
qu'elle et qui, après lui avoir soufflé le trône, l'envoya
mourir sous bonne garde dans l'île de Lesbos où la vie,
depuis la disparition de l'illustre Sapho, avait perdu tout
son charme. Dégoûtée, Irène choisit de quitter ce monde au
mois d'août 803 tandis que, dans le Palais Sacré, Nicé-
phore entreprenait d'offrir à ses sujets sa version personnelle d'un Christ sur la terre.

Au cours des siècles qui suivirent, d'ailleurs, le doux
Galiléen allait se voir introduit, bon gré mal gré, dans une
incroyable collection de défroques humaines aussi peu
saintes que possible et qui devaient l'incommoder beaucoup. Les Comnènes ne valurent guère mieux que les
Anges qui ne l'étaient guère et la révolution de palais,
quand ce n'était pas la révolution tout court, finit par
devenir le mode normal de transmission du pouvoir à
Byzance.

Veut-on quelques chiffres? Sur les cent neuf souverains
qui se succédèrent sur le trône depuis Constantin jusqu'à
l'entrée en scène des Turcs en 1453, vingt-trois ont été
assassinés, douze moururent au couvent ou en prison, trois
moururent de faim, dix-huit furent castrés, essorillés,
privés de leur nez ou de leurs mains, huit périrent à la
guerre ou par accident, trente-quatre seulement eurent le
privilège de s'éteindre dans leur lit tandis que les autres
étaient étouffés, empoisonnés, étranglés, poignardés, jetés
du haut d'une muraille ou simplement chassés. Et le pire
c'est qu'à peu près tous le méritaient amplement...

SOUS LES BALDAQUINS COURONNÉS

Après les dieux, demi-dieux, presque-dieux ou copies plus ou moins conformes du seul vrai Dieu, voici les rois, oints du Seigneur, investis par lui de pouvoirs et d'obligations qui les placent si fort au-dessus du commun que le moindre de leurs gestes ne se peut accomplir que sous la surveillance plus ou moins bienveillante et plus ou moins sincère de quelques centaines de regards. Voici aussi les princes, leurs corollaires et quelques grands qui les tiennent de si près que leurs existences procèdent de la même indiscrétion publique.

La vie d'un roi est publique, en effet. L'intimité lui est le plus souvent refusée et si l'on ne voit alors aucun appareil photo en batterie dans les appartements royaux — ce qui, à tout prendre est une bonne chose car les phototèques s'orneraient certainement de précieux documents touchant la manière royale qu'avait Louis XIV d'aborder sa chaise percée — du moins se trouve-t-il toujours un ou plusieurs témoins, ambassadeur étranger (les Vénitiens sont les plus habiles à ce jeu), courtisan ou simple serviteur capable de restituer, par le truchement d'une correspondance ou de mémoires, les instants les plus intimes d'une existence royale. Naturellement, outre la mort, les scènes les plus recherchées sont celles des mariages, en général, et des nuits de noces en particulier auxquelles préside un cérémonial que d'aucuns, et surtout d'aucunes, jugeront sinon barbare du moins extrêmement gênant...

Grâce à ces indiscrets, les alcôves princières sont ouvertes à tout vent. On peut, à la manière du démon Asmodée, prince des Curieux, soulever tel ou tel ciel de lit couronné et constater qu'il s'y passe souvent d'étranges choses... En effet, le choix du ou de la partenaire n'est pas un droit royal ce qui vaut, à toutes ces nuits de noces, des couleurs différentes suivant l'état d'âme de leurs acteurs. Certains abordent l'épreuve avec résignation si d'autres s'y montrent franchement récalcitrants. Et si, de-ci de-là, on rencontre parfois un enthousiaste réel ou simulé, il se trouve malheureusement bien des nuits dramatiques débouchant sur une catastrophe.

La reine Marie-Caroline de Naples, sœur de Marie-Antoinette, soupirait avec quelque raison : « Nous autres filles du Trône, on nous jette à la mer... » Elle aurait pu ajouter « que l'on sache nager ou pas... ». Vers quoi portait le flot au péril duquel étaient livrées ces innocentes? Ile heureuse ou bande de grève désolée susceptible d'être recouverte par la première grosse vague? Paisible et hospitalière baleine restituant la contrepartie féminine de Jonas intacte après une navigation sans histoire ou requin vorace qui n'en laissera que l'or de la couronne trop difficile à digérer?

Mieux valait parfois un époux rétif qu'un époux résigné qui s'entendait trop bien à faire payer très cher le sacrifice exigé par la raison d'État. Deux résignés pouvaient s'entendre mais moins bien parfois que deux révoltés. Le drame naissait souvent d'un paroxysme ou d'un désespoir.

En soulevant les rideaux de brocart que l'on refermait solennellement sur un jeune couple, on s'expose à bien des surprises, comiques, désolantes, dramatiques ou franchement burlesques car « les perles seules brillent sur la Couronne. On n'y voit pas les blessures... ».

LES NUITS RÉSIGNÉES

LA NUIT DE CATHERINE DE MÉDICIS

Le 8 octobre 1533, un petit cortège de cavaliers arrive à Marseille venant d'Aubagne. L'équipage est somptueux mais le train réduit; une cinquantaine de personnes tout au plus. En tête, dépassant tout le monde du toquet et des épaules, une sorte de géant barbu dont les yeux vifs rient encore plus que la bouche qui cependant ne s'en prive pas sous le long nez gourmand. Et tout de suite on l'acclame car, même sans considérer le velours pourpre et les joyaux qui le parent, personne ne doute d'avoir en face de lui le roi. C'est en effet François Iᵉʳ qui pénètre ainsi en trombe dans sa bonne ville de Marseille, escorté de ses fils, de ses filles et d'une poignée de gentilshommes (il a laissé à Aubagne la reine Éléonore). Personne ne l'attend mais c'est tout juste ce qu'il souhaitait car il vient voir où en sont les grands préparatifs dont il a chargé Montmorency promu pour la circonstance architecte décorateur.

C'est qu'en effet un grand événement se prépare, un événement inouï même : Sa Sainteté, le pape Clément VII doit arriver trois jours plus tard pour rencontrer François. On va causer politique bien sûr mais, surtout, le Saint-Père doit célébrer en personne le mariage de sa nièce, la jeune duchesse de Florence, Catherine de Médicis avec le duc d'Orléans, Henri, second fils du Roi-Chevalier. Et le roi qui a toujours eu le souci du faste et de sa renommée, amplement méritée, de magnificence, tient à ce que tout soit plus que parfait.

Il se rassure rapidement. Montmorency a bien travaillé. Avec l'aide d'un peuple d'ouvriers, il a complètement transformé tout un quartier de Marseille entre la place Neuve et le port. Sur la place, d'abord, il a fait construire un véritable palais de bois qu'une galerie, de bois elle aussi, relie à la maison qu'occupera le roi, sur cette même place et qui est l'ancien logis des comtes de Provence remis au goût du jour. La palais de bois, réduction à peine moins éblouissante du Camp du Drap d'Or d'illustre mémoire, est destiné au pape et le grand maître Montmorency (il ne sera connétable que quatre ans plus tard) n'y a pas été de main morte pour faire riche : il a pratiquement déménagé le Louvre, Amboise et Blois pour meubler son pape. Il est vrai que celui-ci est un Médicis et que, dans la famille, on s'y connaît en meubles, tentures, sculptures, tapis, joyaux et autres raretés hors de prix sans lesquelles ne saurait vivre un grand seigneur de l'époque.

En outre, Montmorency a fait percer la muraille de la ville et celles des maisons qui y sont accolées pour établir des passages faciles entre la place et le port. L'un de ces passages est prolongé d'une longue passerelle recouverte de tapisseries et de brocarts (heureusement il ne pleut pas souvent à Marseille en octobre!) et s'avance jusqu'au milieu du Vieux-Port afin que le pape, quand il fera son entrée dans la ville puisse prendre place sur la *sedia* au beau milieu des eaux...

Satisfait, François Ier, à la manière de n'importe quel touriste emmène les enfants visiter le château d'If (malheureusement il n'aura pas le plaisir de leur montrer le cachot de Monte-Cristo ni celui de l'abbé Faria!) puis il ramène tout son monde à Aubagne! Le pape peut venir. Il ne sera pas déçu.

Justement, le voilà! Le samedi 11 octobre, la flotte papale apparaît aux premiers rayons du soleil. Et quelle flotte! Dix-huit grandes galères tendues de damas rouge, de damas violet, de damas jaune, de satin cramoisi et de soie pourpre avec, brochant sur le tout, de l'or et de l'argent à profusion. Sur l'eau unie et lisse qui les reflète, elles offrent un merveilleux spectacle que le peuple massé sur les berges acclame frénétiquement.

En tête vient la *Duchesse*. Elle porte le Saint Sacrement. Le pape ne vient qu'après sur la *Capitanesse* mais toutes deux ne sont qu'or et pourpre. Le *Bucentaure* du Doge en pâlirait de jalousie...

La flotte est aux ordres de l'amiral du Levant, Claude de Tende, mais le duc d'Albany commande l'une de ces galères en face desquelles les Marseillais, après avoir braillé d'enthousiasme, s'agenouillent...

A bord d'une frégate toute tendue de damas à crépines d'or, voici Montmorency, qui vient, au nom du roi, accueillir le Saint-Père et met genoux en terre pour baiser sa main. Clément VII n'a que cinquante-six ans mais c'est un homme usé. Son pontificat a été l'un des plus dramatiques de l'Histoire : il a subi le sac de Rome sous les lansquenets de Frundsberg et les miquelets espagnols; il a vu l'Angleterre d'Henri VIII se séparer de l'Église pour les beaux yeux d'Anne Boleyn, enfin il a dû, à Bologne, couronner empereur Charles Quint qu'il déteste autant qu'il s'en méfie. Néanmoins, il fait encore bonne contenance et, sous le trirègne étincelant, c'est toujours l'élégant, le superbe Jules de Médicis que contemple Montmorency intimidé.

Le pape prend place dans la frégate du grand maître. Elle le conduit jusqu'au Jardin du Roi, voisin de l'abbaye Saint-Victor dont il est d'ailleurs l'abbé commendataire et où il passera la nuit. Dans le Jardin le couvert est mis et le pape va dîner en compagnie des quatorze cardinaux et des soixante archevêques, évêques et abbés qui l'accompagnent. Le lendemain seulement il effectue son entrée solennelle dans Marseille au moyen de la fameuse passerelle où l'attend la *sedia*. Cette fois, encadré du jeune duc d'Orléans et du duc d'Angoulême, et bénissant à tour de bras à droite et à gauche, il va prendre possession de son éphémère palais tandis qu'Orléans et Angoulême regalopent jusqu'à Aubagne afin d'être aux côtés du roi quand il arrivera officiellement le lendemain.

Volontairement assourdie, l'entrée de François avec la reine et toute la Cour qu'il promène depuis deux ans sur toutes les routes de France est néanmoins fabuleuse car aucune cour européenne ne peut rivaliser avec celle de France. Cela n'a rien de surprenant : elle a reçu jadis les leçons d'un étonnant génie nommé Léonard de Vinci venu mourir sur les rives de Loire après avoir illuminé de ses merveilles les châteaux milanais de Ludovic le More. Et le roi François a parfaitement assimilé ses leçons.

Tout ce monde, souverains en tête vient, comme une vague scintillante, se prosterner devant le pontife romain et baiser sa main où brille l'Anneau du Pêcheur. Clément VII regarde avec curiosité la nouvelle reine de France, cette Éléonore d'Autriche qui est la sœur de l'encombrant Charles Quint. Elle est grande et assez belle avec un visage long, très blanc de teint, un vrai teint de lait qui s'accorde à sa chevelure rousse, une fabuleuse chevelure que les poètes déclarent d'un blond « ardent » et qui lui tombe jusqu'aux pieds quand ses femmes la dénouent. Il y a bien cette signature des Habsbourg, cette lèvre inférieure un peu épaisse mais d'autres qu'elle s'en accommoderont dans la suite des temps et n'en seront pas moins charmantes, témoin Marie-Antoinette.

François lui montre beaucoup de déférence. Il l'aimerait peut-être si son cœur et ses sens n'appartenaient à cette petite blonde pétulante, dorée comme un missel, que l'on a faite duchesse d'Étampes et qui tient insolemment ce rôle de favorite royale que l'on n'avait pas vu en France depuis Agnès Sorel...

Mais le pape n'est pas là pour faire la morale au roi de France. Il a bien d'autres chats à fouetter. Il s'agit de discuter – et âprement même – la dot de la fiancée qui attend à Nice qu'on l'autorise à venir. Car, pour un fils de France, la descendante des banquiers florentins est à la limite de la mésalliance bien que sa mère, Madeleine de La

Tour d'Auvergne, ait cousiné avec François Ier, et son meilleur titre est celui de nièce du pape, ce qui fait d'elle une excellence affaire (une affaire que l'Empereur a ratée bien stupidement). La naissance moindre a d'ailleurs peu d'importance : le duc d'Orléans n'est que le second fils et, grâce à Dieu, le dauphin est bien vivant.

Au fait, le voilà qui tombe malade, le dauphin François! Une sorte de fièvre maligne qui, heureusement, n'est pas la peste, toujours à craindre dans un port méridional. Inquiet, Clément VII lui envoie son propre médecin : si celui-là allait mourir, le mariage de Catherine tomberait sans doute à l'eau... ou alors les exigences du Français deviendraient astronomiques!

Le médecin papal fait merveilles et les discussions aboutissent. La dot est de cent mille écus d'or plus – en traité secret pour éviter que cela n'aille battre les grandes oreilles de Charles Quint – Milan, Gênes et Naples. L'Italie, décidément, a toujours été le péché mignon de François Ier qui aimerait bien venger Pavie. A présent, la fiancée peut venir.

Elle arrive, par la route, le 23 octobre et Marseille peut admirer son cortège dans le milieu de l'après-midi. Catherine monte une haquenée rousse, toute caparaçonnée de toile d'or. La duchesse de Camerino et Maria Salviati qui a veillé sur sa jeunesse orpheline la suivent avec douze autres dames.

La duchesse a quatorze ans (l'âge même de son fiancé). Sous d'épais cheveux noirs, elle a un visage blanc, assez plein avec un nez un peu fort, des yeux bruns légèrement globuleux mais abrités sous des cils et des sourcils bien fournis. Comme celle de la reine sa lèvre inférieure est un peu épaisse. Elle n'est pas vraiment belle mais elle a beaucoup de grâce, des mains admirables et des jambes ravissantes, ce que personne ne saurait voir pour l'instant mais n'ignorera plus quand, plus tard, elle inventera la monte en amazone pour les mettre en valeur.

Au moral, elle porte beaucoup plus que son âge et son

intelligence est bien supérieure à celle de la plupart des gens qui l'entourent mais elle a celle de n'en point faire étalage. C'est que la vie ne lui a pas ménagé les rudes leçons. Sa mère est morte en la mettant au monde, précocement ravagée par la vérole que lui avait si généreusement transmise son époux, Laurent de Médicis abattu d'ailleurs par le mal presque en même temps qu'elle; Madeleine n'avait pas seize ans et elle était mariée depuis quelques mois...

Les premières années de sa fille se sont écoulées à Rome, sous la tutelle du pape et en compagnie de son demi-frère Alexandre (la future victime de Lorenzaccio) né des amours de son père avec une belle paysanne de Collavechio. Mais elle est duchesse de Florence et doit résider dans sa ville où elle est ramenée à huit ans, toujours en compagnie d'Alexandre, pour y vivre au Palais Médicis et, l'été, dans la belle villa de Poggio a Cajano, le tout sous la surveillance des Strozzi. Mais, à Florence, des troubles éclatent bientôt, un « tumulte » comme on s'entend si bien à en fomenter dans la cité du Lys Rouge quand apparaît la moindre possibilité de devenir une république. L'Empereur, alors, envoie du secours à la ville déchirée par la guerre civile et la fait assiéger par le prince d'Orange qui s'arrangerait bien d'un mariage avec la petite duchesse...

Celle-ci, réfugiée au couvent des Murate, est en grand danger et le sait. Les meneurs, Bartolini, Cei et Castiglione hésitent sur le sort qu'on lui réserve : ou bien on la met dans une maison close pour la livrer à la prostitution, ou bien on l'attache nue sur les remparts de la ville jusqu'à ce que les assiégeants s'en aillent, ou bien on la livre tout bonnement à la soldatesque. Et de ces agréables perspectives, l'enfant n'ignore rien. Elle y pare avec une présence d'esprit incroyable à cet âge : elle se fait raser la tête, prend l'habit de moniale et proteste de sa décision irrévocable d'entrer en religion dans ce couvent de cloîtrées.

Naturellement quand la ville capitule, il n'en est plus question et la fillette repart pour Rome où le pape entend désormais la garder : il a eu trop peur. C'est Alexandre, confié à l'Empereur qui régnera sur Florence dont Catherine ne portera plus que le titre. Pour elle, ce sera un grand mariage mais on ne sait pas encore très bien avec qui. Le plus intéressant bien sûr!...

Mais, pour l'heure présente, la politique n'intéresse plus Catherine. Elle a rencontré l'Amour. Et quel amour! Le beau, le superbe, le charmant Hippolyte de Médicis, son cousin dont d'ailleurs jadis le pape Léon X (frère de Clément VII) souhaitait qu'elle devînt l'épouse et il suffit de regarder le portrait qu'en a fait le Titien, pour comprendre l'élan de ce jeune cœur. Hippolyte, lui aussi aime Catherine : elle a tant de vivacité, de charme et d'esprit! Il est cardinal mais jetterait volontiers, pour elle, la simarre aux orties. Ce sont de ces choses qui se font aisément à Rome au XVIe siècle...

Dans le cas particulier, pourtant, cela ne se fera pas. L'idylle inquiète le pape. Il a d'autres projets pour sa nièce et, prenant prétexte du mauvais air de Rome où la malaria sévit à l'état endémique, principalement l'été, il la renvoie à Florence en avril 1532. Elle n'a plus rien à redouter. La ville est définitivement matée. Quant à Hippolyte, s'il veut continuer à mener l'existence somptueuse qu'il affectionne, il faudra qu'il se contente de son chapeau de cardinal. Un jour, peut-être, il sera pape...

Catherine n'a pas protesté. Elle sait que la politique et l'amour ne vont guère ensemble et si elle souffre de renoncer à son amour elle ne le montre pas. Machiavel qu'elle sait par cœur a déjà en elle une excellente élève. Telle est l'enfant étrange qui, en ce jour d'octobre va s'agenouiller devant François Ier aussi respectueusement que s'il était le pape. Il la relève aussitôt, l'embrasse, puis lui présente son fiancé, le duc d'Orléans avec lequel on échange des baisers protocolaires...

Au fait, comment est-il ce prince de quatorze ans qui

sera un jour un roi à idées courtes? On sait qu'il est assez grand et vigoureux pour son âge, plus que le dauphin. Le grand voyage lui a fait du bien et, s'il gardera toujours quelques stigmates de la prison sans air et sans lumière de Pedrazza où Charles Quint l'avait contraint de remplacer son père, il a tout de même repris quelques couleurs. Mais c'est un enfant mélancolique et sombre nourri à satiété de romans de chevalerie et qui s'efforcera de vivre son existence comme un héros desdits romans. En outre, il est déjà amoureux, lui aussi. Et de qui? D'une femme qui a vingt ans de plus que lui mais qui, au dramatique jour de mars 1526 où, sur la rive de la Bidassoa, il attendait d'être échangé contre le roi, son père, l'a embrassé tendrement. Il n'oubliera plus jamais ce baiser, ni cette femme : Diane de Saint-Vallier de Poitiers, comtesse de Brézé, Grande Sénéchale de Normandie. Chose curieuse, c'est chez elle, ou tout au moins chez son mari, au château d'Anet qu'a été signé le contrat décidant du mariage d'Henri avec Catherine de Médicis...

Quatre jours après l'entrée de la fiancée, le 27, on dresse le traité de mariage puis, le lendemain, ce sont enfin les noces.

Elles ont lieu dans la chapelle du logis pontifical. François Iᵉʳ tout satin blanc et drap d'or conduit à l'autel Catherine en robe de brocart avec corsage de velours violet couvert de joyaux et doublures d'hermine. Elle porte les fabuleuses perles que son oncle lui a offertes comme cadeau de mariage et qui, bien plus tard, feront rêver Sacha Guitry. Mais il y en a un peu plus que sept : en fait il s'agit de gigantesques sautoirs de perles rondes, superbes, admirablement assorties et que l'on peut encore admirer sur certain portrait de la Reine-Vierge, Elisabeth Iʳᵉ. Sur sa tête une couronne d'or et de pierreries, présent du roi.

Le pape célèbre le mariage puis le cardinal Sabriena chante la messe. Ensuite on échange des présents tous plus beaux les uns que les autres. C'est ainsi que le cardinal

Hippolyte, qui refusait farouchement d'accepter quelque chose, se voit gratifié du grand lion apprivoisé, naguère offert à François par Khayr el-Din Barberousse, le corsaire barbaresque...

Puis, naturellement, c'est le repas de noces et, enfin, vers minuit, le pape s'étant retiré, la reine Éléonore conduit Catherine dans la chambre nuptiale entièrement tapissée de brocart d'or. Elle préside au déshabillage, au coucher de la mariée dans le grand lit qui est lui aussi tout cousu d'or (on évalue sa décoration à 60 000 écus d'or). Puis, quand le roi amène le jeune époux, elle se retire. Mais François reste. Il n'est pas très sûr des dispositions amoureuses de son fils, ni d'ailleurs de ses capacités, et il préfère être là pour lui donner quelques conseils...

Si l'on en croit certains témoignages, il aurait été très vite rassuré : « chacun des deux jeunes époux se montrait vaillant dans la joute ». Et c'est l'âme en paix qu'il s'en va rejoindre la duchesse d'Étampes.

De son côté, le pape Clément choisit de venir aux aurores voir comment les choses se passent. Il « vint les surprendre au lit et constata avec joie le contentement qu'ils affichaient... » Peut-être l'affichaient-ils justement un peu trop. Qu'avait pu être cette nuit de noces entre ces deux adolescents déjà marqués par la vie? Un jeu nouveau? La satisfaction purement animale d'instincts sexuels déjà développés? L'un et l'autre aimaient ailleurs, mais l'un comme l'autre étaient certainement doués d'un tempérament amoureux incontestable. Catherine est italienne et c'est une Médicis, une famille dans laquelle personne, jamais, n'a boudé le lit. La révélation de l'amour physique va déboucher, pour elle, sur un amour total, une passion douloureuse, déchirante car, peu de mois après le mariage, le pape Clément meurt et la dot ne sera jamais payée.

Pour garder sa place et l'époux qu'elle s'est mise à aimer, Catherine devra tout accepter, tout subir, même que ce soit la maîtresse en titre, l'odieuse Diane de Poitiers, qui

traîne presque de force Henri jusque dans sa couche pour
lui faire les enfants qu'exige la dynastie. Elle apprendra le
silence, la dissimulation, la diplomatie à la plus cruelle
école. Il en sortira la Florentine en son deuil éternel, froide
et calculatrice parce que son cœur s'est définitivement figé
dans sa poitrine, mais grande reine et qui saura maintenir
l'Espagnol hors des frontières du royaume. Sans la tache de
la Saint-Barthélemy elle eût mérité, cent fois plus qu'une
autre, qui d'ailleurs avait aussi ses taches, d'être nommée
Catherine la Grande. La princesse de la Renaissance,
cultivée, lettrée, gracieuse, pleine de cette gaieté italienne à
fleur de peau, douée d'un charme certain n'en déplaise à
ses détracteurs – sans cela comment expliquer l'espèce de
tendresse que lui portait François Iᵉʳ, ce connaisseur si
averti – finit par accoucher d'une sorte de Louis XI
femelle : c'est dire sa qualité politique...

Quant au futur Henri II, en dehors de ses amours
chevaleresques et quelque peu retardataires avec la Dame
de Brézé – amours qui cessèrent assez vite de rester
platoniques – on sait les exigences et les brutalités de son
tempérament. La sauvagerie qui caractérisera son fils
Charles IX lui est due tout entière et la belle Philippa
Duco qu'Henri violera sans autre préambule à Milan sera
là pour en témoigner. Il n'aura certainement eu aucune
peine à faire preuve de virilité au cours de sa nuit de noces.
Ne fût-ce d'ailleurs que pour prouver à un père qu'il
n'aimait guère et qu'il enviait secrètement, qu'il pouvait
faire aussi bien que lui. La nuit de noces de Catherine de
Médicis ne fut pour lui qu'un exercice d'école où le cœur
n'eut aucune part. Henri ne se préoccupa guère de
l'effet ressenti par sa jeune épouse et, quand il se sut
aimé d'elle, il eut plutôt tendance à en montrer de
l'ennui...

Trois jours après son mariage, il quittait Marseille en
compagnie du dauphin et du duc d'Angoulême pour
gagner Aix, laissant Catherine derrière lui avec une
parfaite désinvolture. Pour celle-ci un long calvaire se

profilait déjà à l'horizon. Supporté avec une résignation qui devait tout à la politique et à la raison d'État, il la conduirait plus tard à ordonner froidement d'autres mariages, d'autres résignations...

LA NUIT « SCIENTIFIQUE » DU GRAND-DUC

Politique et raison d'État constituant généralement la base des mariages royaux ou princiers et l'amour n'y jouant qu'un rôle accessoire, la résignation se voulait de rigueur chez les parties contractantes. Mais résignation ne signifiait pas toujours aveuglement et il est arrivé à certains fiancés de faire preuve d'une véritable méfiance. C'est ce sentiment, poussé peut-être un peu loin, qui valut à Christine de Lorraine une nuit de noces aussi rabelaisienne que baroque lorsqu'elle devint l'épouse de Ferdinand Iᵉʳ de Médicis, grand-duc de Toscane.

Mais d'abord quelques mots sur ce Médicis qui, à l'exception de Cosme l'Ancien, de Laurent le Magnifique et de la reine Catherine fut sans doute le plus intelligent, le plus sage et le plus artiste de toute la famille.

Quatrième fils de Cosme Iᵉʳ et d'Éléonore de Tolède, il reçoit le chapeau de cardinal à quatorze ans et prend la chose au sérieux. Il se crée, au sein du Sacré Collège une forte position personnelle qui lui permet de tenir tête au pouvoir pontifical et même à Sixte Quint ce qui représente une manière d'exploit. Fondateur de l'œuvre de la Propagation de la Foi, il n'en est pas moins, comme presque tous les Médicis d'ailleurs, un enragé collectionneur. C'est ainsi que la Ville Éternelle et les futurs Prix de Rome lui doivent la construction et la décoration de la célèbre Villa Médicis qu'il peuple d'une prestigieuse collection de statues grecques et latines.

Quand meurent son frère, Francesco, et son épouse, la superbe et détestable Bianca Capello, il se retrouve grand-duc à trente-huit ans et n'en éprouve nulle tristesse. Il n'a jamais aimé son frère. En revanche, il aime Florence qu'il veut prospère, puissante et surtout paisible. Aussi ne perd-il pas une seconde pour se mettre au travail et, disons-le tout de suite, le résultat sera à la hauteur de ses ambitions. En créant le port de Livourne et une puissante marine assez forte pour délivrer, le temps de son règne tout au moins, la Méditerranée des corsaires barbaresques, il assure à son pays le droit de travailler en paix. Et cette paix, même, il l'organise : fini les tournois, les fêtes guerrières, les prises d'armes, tout ce qui pourrait ranimer, si peu que ce soit, l'humeur si volontiers batailleuse des Florentins! Place au théâtre, aux marionnettes, à la musique et à la danse! Sans le savoir, Ferdinand Iᵉʳ vient de créer le premier festival d'art...

Mais comme il entend asseoir sa dynastie, il lui faut une épouse. Justement sa cousine, la reine mère de France, Catherine de Médicis lui en propose une qu'elle assure parfaite : c'est sa petite-fille Christine de Lorraine, fille de sa fille Claude et du duc Charles II de Lorraine. La fille est charmante, du moins on le prétend, la dot sera belle. Ferdinand n'hésite plus : il jette définitivement sa simarre cardinalice (cela n'a aucune importance car en recevant le chapeau il n'avait pas pour autant reçu les ordres) et le mariage a lieu...

Quant à ce qui se passe au soir de ce grand mariage, mieux vaut laisser à Brantôme le soin de le raconter :

« Le soir, quand le duc l'épousa et qu'il voulut aller coucher avec elle pour la dépuceler, il la fit avant pisser dans un beau urinal de cristal, le plus beau et le plus clair qu'il put et, ayant vu l'urine, il la consulta avec son médecin. Le médecin l'ayant bien fixement et doctement inspicée (du latin *inspicere*) il trouva qu'elle était telle comme quand elle sortait du ventre de sa mère et qu'il y

allât hardiment et qu'il n'y trouverait point de chemin
nullement ouvert, frayé ni battu : ce qu'il fit et en trouva la
vérité telle; et puis, le lendemain, en admiration dit :
" Voilà un grand miracle que cette fille soit ainsi sortie
pucelle de cette cour de France "... »

La naïveté de l'exclamation lui enlève beaucoup de son
insolence, mais il est certain que la cour des Valois où
s'ébattaient des femmes de réputations certaines comme la
reine Margot, son amie Henriette de Nevers ou les belles
de l'Escadron Volant n'avait que très peu de ressemblance
avec une institution pieuse. Il est vrai qu'à vingt-quatre
ans, Christine de Lorraine était déjà, pour l'époque, une
sorte de vieille fille et qu'il pouvait y avoir des doutes sur la
réalité de sa virginité à un âge aussi avancé. Comme elle
n'était pas laide, il est probable qu'elle fut sauvée du péché
par la religion car c'était une effroyable bigote qui, devenue
veuve, dilapida la plus grosse part du trésor de son époux
en fondations pieuses et entretien d'une foule de prêtres et
religieux de toute sorte. Elle ne s'en montra pas moins
excellente épouse et, en dépit de son « âge avancé » elle
donna tout de même huit enfants à Ferdinand.

C'est à celui-ci qu'Henri IV, dont il fut toujours le fidèle
soutien et ami, dut d'épouser la désastreuse Marie de
Médicis qui était la nièce du grand-duc et qui, si elle
apporta une dot intéressante, n'en fut pas moins mêlée à
une trop grande série de catastrophes – à commencer par le
coup de couteau de Ravaillac – pour que l'on se réjouisse
de l'avoir vue sur le trône de France...

LA NUIT DES REGRETS : LOUIS XIV

Le plus célèbre des résignés est sans doute Louis XIV et celle qui eut le plus à se plaindre d'un tel mariage, l'infante Marie-Thérèse, reine méconnue, bafouée à la fois par son mari et par la postérité qui trouva commode de la faire passer pour une idiote, relayant ainsi les courtisans du Roi-Soleil qui, sachant bien de quel côté leur pain était beurré, s'efforcèrent à l'envi de fournir le plus d'excuses possible à une conduite qui n'en avait aucune et qui, chez quelqu'un de moins puissant, eût été jugée parfaitement inqualifiable. Il semble que, dès le lendemain de son mariage, le délicieux mari ait pris à tâche de faire payer à son innocente épouse l'extrême déplaisir qu'il s'était imposé en renonçant à l'amour d'une ambitieuse qui se voyait déjà reine de France.

Prise au piège d'une nuit de noces incontestablement réussie, la pauvre infante, après en avoir tiré des conclusions aimables et apparemment logiques, allait pouvoir constater rapidement ce qu'en valait l'aune en se retrouvant prisonnière à la fois d'une langue qu'elle eut quelque peine à assimiler et de grossesses réitérées, tandis que son époux s'en allait gambader, au propre dans les nombreux ballets que lui tricotait Benserade et, au figuré, dans les aimables plates-bandes que composaient, sur fond de Fontainebleau, Saint-Germain ou Versailles, les nombreuses jolies femmes de sa Cour. Mais revenons un peu en arrière pour examiner les faits qui conduisirent à cette nuit de noces, cause de tout le mal subi par Marie-Thérèse...

Ce jour de 1659 où le jeune roi vint lui dire qu'il souhaitait épouser sa nièce Marie Mancini, le cardinal Mazarin eut un éblouissement. Il fut à la fois abasourdi, stupéfait et un peu tenté. Voir sa propre nièce à lui, petit Italien sans naissance, escalader le trône de France pour y coiffer une couronne qu'il avait su redorer savamment, quel rêve! Mais c'était un homme qui savait mesurer ses rêves et, en fin de compte, il se retrouva épouvanté. Le négociateur espagnol, don Antonio Pimentel, ministre du roi Philippe IV, l'avait suivi à Paris après l'avoir rejoint à Lyon où il se donnait un mal affreux pour faire croire à un possible mariage du roi avec sa cousine de Savoie dans le seul but d'appâter l'Espagne. Le piège avait joué à plein; Pimentel était accouru, secrètement mais il était tout de même venu (Mazarin avait pleuré de joie en apprenant son arrivée) et si, à présent, il fallait rompre des négociations si délicates, si difficilement engagées, il n'y avait aucun doute à garder : ce serait la guerre car Philippe IV, même à peu près ruiné, ne passerait pas l'éponge sur un pareil affront : sa fille dédaignée au profit d'une petite Italienne de rien du tout...

Toutes ces pensées lui avaient traversé l'esprit à la vitesse de l'éclair mais il n'en avait pas moins gardé le silence pendant quelques instants. Et comme Louis s'inquiète de ce silence, qu'il espère peut-être joyeux, il lui répond :

« Sire, ayant été choisi par le roi votre père et, depuis, par la reine votre mère pour vous assister de mes conseils, et vous ayant servi avec une fidélité inviolable, je n'ai garde d'abuser de la confidence que vous me faites de votre faiblesse, ni de l'autorité que vous me donnez dans vos états pour souffrir que vous fassiez une chose si contraire à votre gloire. Je suis le maître de ma nièce et je la poignarderais plutôt que de la voir s'élever par une si grande trahison... »

Grandes paroles, dignes d'un grand ministre mais qui ne pénètrent guère l'entendement du jeune fou. Louis tourne les talons, file chez sa mère et va lui demander, à elle qui est femme et qui doit être sensible à ce genre de romance, de consentir à ce qu'il considère comme le bonheur de sa vie. Et même de l'aider à l'obtenir en faisant entendre raison au cardinal. Mais là aussi il se heurte à un refus.

Certes, Anne d'Autriche a de la sympathie pour cette jeune Marie et le souvenir de ses amours passées avec Buckingham, plus récentes avec Mazarin, lui permet de comprendre un tourment d'amour et un si grand désir de le vivre jusqu'au bout. Mais avec les années écoulées, elle s'est retrouvée reine avant tout, c'est-à-dire esclave de la raison d'État et elle refuse de se laisser fléchir. Louis a beau prier, supplier, se jeter à genoux en pleurant et en couvrant ses mains de larmes, elle demeure ferme sur ses positions. Et son langage rejoint beaucoup celui du ministre.

« Entre l'amour de cette fille et l'Infante, un roi de France ne saurait balancer. Songez que, si vous rompez l'alliance espagnole, c'est la guerre. Vos peuples ne vous seront guère reconnaissants d'avoir préféré votre bonheur à leur tranquillité. »

Au fond, elle ne croit guère à cette grande passion. Elle a déjà vu son fils tomber amoureux deux ou trois fois. Il oubliera cet amour-là comme les autres. C'est une question de patience...

Seulement Louis ne veut pas oublier. Marie, qui a attendu son heure dans l'ombre quand il courtisait sa sœur Olympe ou la petite de La Motte Argencourt, le tient et le tient bien. Elle se croit déjà victorieuse, surtout depuis qu'il lui a offert le magnifique collier de perles racheté à la reine Henriette, veuve de Charles Iᵉʳ d'Angleterre. Elle sait qu'elle pourrait demander à Louis de renoncer pour elle à la Couronne mais il se trouve que ladite Couronne l'intéresse un peu elle aussi...

Et Mazarin s'en aperçoit bien quand il fait venir sa nièce pour l'engager dans la voie austère du devoir et lui faire renoncer à cet amour impossible. Hautaine, narquoise, sûre d'elle, Marie se moque ouvertement de son oncle. Il n'est que ministre tandis qu'elle va être reine. Alors, à quoi rime sa mercuriale? Ne ferait-il pas mieux d'accepter une fortune aussi glorieuse pour sa famille? Puisque aussi bien elle est la plus forte. Quant à la France, elle s'y fera, elle aussi...

Mais elle a été trop loin et ne va pas tarder à le regretter car, cette fois, Mazarin, toujours si aimable, si conciliant, se fâche. Il est un peu tôt pour jouer à la reine. Pour l'heure présente elle n'est qu'une insolente sur laquelle il a tout pouvoir. Qu'elle sache bien qu'il aimerait mieux la tuer de sa propre main que lui permettre de se jeter au travers de sa politique. Et comme la Cour doit prochainement partir pour Saint-Jean-de-Luz afin d'y rencontrer l'Infante, elle-même partira, dès le lendemain, pour Brouage en compagnie de ses sœurs et de sa gouvernante, Mme de Venel.

Alors Marie pleure, Marie supplie. Qu'il ne la renvoie pas, elle ne pourra pas le supporter!...

« Il a bien fallu que moi je vous supporte, vous et votre impudence, lance Mazarin. Vous partirez demain!... »

Il n'y a pas à y revenir. Le cardinal, en effet, possède pouvoir paternel sur sa nièce et Marie a beau pleurer dans les bras de Louis, celui-ci sait bien qu'il est battu. Le lendemain, 22 juin, il escorte son amie jusqu'au carrosse qui l'attend dans la cour du Louvre et, comme il ne peut cacher ses larmes, elle lui jette avec rancune, par la portière et au moment où le carrosse s'ébranle :

« Ah, Sire! Vous êtes roi, vous pleurez et je pars!... »

Là-dessus elle pique une crise de nerfs tandis que la voiture prend la route de Fontainebleau et que Louis, incapable de rester au Louvre, s'en va chasser... et entamer la première d'une longue suite de lettres d'amour.

Car Mazarin n'en a pas fini avec ces deux-là. Marie tente d'interrompre son voyage en se disant malade. Du coup Louis part pour Fontainebleau pour être plus près d'elle. Mazarin ordonne alors que malade ou non elle continue : l'air marin de Brouage la remettra. C'est souverain dans ces cas-là... Outre cela, des volumes de lettres s'échangent entre les amoureux. Courriers et mousquetaires sont sur les genoux. Mazarin, qui est parti pour la frontière, n'y peut pas grand-chose, sinon écrire :

« On dit, et cela est confirmé par des lettres de la Cour à des personnes qui sont de ma suite, que vous êtes toujours enfermé à écrire à la personne que vous aimez. Cela n'est point d'un roi... »

Ledit roi s'en moque et continue de plus belle et s'il accepte de partir enfin pour le pays où coule la Bidassoa c'est surtout parce que la route suivie est celle de Marie. D'ailleurs, faible pour une fois, la reine consent à ce que Louis et Marie se revoient à La Rochelle. Dans son esprit il ne peut s'agir que d'un adieu définitif mais elle est bien la seule à penser cela car les deux autres ont chacun sa petite idée sur cette entrevue. Louis, qui a vu naguère Olympe Mancini lui tomber dans les bras aussitôt après son mariage avec le comte de Soissons, en est venu à penser qu'il n'y aurait aucune raison pour que Marie n'agisse pas de la même façon.

Il pourrait ainsi conjuguer les exigences de la Couronne et celles de sa passion. Si elle l'aime autant qu'elle le dit, Marie trouvera certainement la solution parfaite... Il ignore que, dans l'esprit de la jeune fille, Louis et le roi ne font qu'un et elle le lui dit sans ambages :

« Si vous pensez qu'il vous sera possible d'en user avec moi comme avec ma sœur Olympe qui fut vôtre après son mariage, vous vous trompez, Sire! Je ne serai à vous qu'en mariage et jamais autrement... »

L'entrevue dure trois heures, vainement. Marie ne veut rien comprendre. Tant pis pour elle : c'est Brouage qui l'attend cependant que le roi, mécontent, à nouveau hésitant peut-être, rejoint Mazarin à Saint-Jean-de-Luz. Mazarin qui lui porte l'estocade finale en lui faisant entendre qu'il ne transigera pas avec ce qu'il considère comme son devoir.

« Au cas où je devrais rompre la négociation avec les envoyés espagnols, j'aurais l'honneur de remettre à Votre Majesté la démission de toutes mes charges. Après quoi je me retirerai sur l'heure en Italie... avec mes nièces bien entendu. »

Cette fois il a gagné. Louis XIV épousera l'Infante et, déjà le duc de Gramont chargé de demander officiellement la main de l'Infante galope vers l'Espagne avec l'escorte qui convient à un ambassadeur extraordinaire.

Étant donné les liens de famille qui existent entre les deux royautés (la reine Anne d'Autriche est la sœur de Philippe IV), il s'attend à une réception chaleureuse, familiale, pas tout à fait à la bonne franquette mais pas loin. C'est un Béarnais chaleureux fort ami des fêtes et, quand il pénètre dans Madrid en liesse, entouré d'une armée de gentilshommes en casaques roses avec plumes et rubans assortis, il pense que toute cette gaieté va l'accompagner jusqu'au trône du roi.

Or tout change quand il franchit les portes du palais royal. Pour un peu on se croirait à Byzance! Un peu abasourdi, sa troupe à falbalas sur les talons, Gramont parcourt des salles immenses et sombres au long desquelles toute une noblesse glacée qu'on dirait peinte par Le Greco, vêtue de sombre la plupart du temps mais portant des joyaux fabuleux qui ont dû, jadis, appartenir aux Aztèques, le regarde passer et tracer son chemin muet vers une sorte d'abside tendue de drap d'or où le roi, tout vêtu de noir, chapeauté de noir mais la Toison d'Or au cou le regarde venir sans un mot, sans un geste. Et le Roi Catholique ne dira pas un mot, ne fera pas un geste, n'aura même pas un battement de paupières tandis que Gramont s'agenouille et débite son discours auquel on ne répondra pas. C'est cela l'étiquette espagnole et Louis XIV y puisera certaines idées quand il se déifiera lui-même.

Après cette chaude réception on emmène les Français

qui se sentent bizarrement gênés et font un peu figure de parvenus avec leurs rubans roses, chez la reine qui les attend avec l'Infante. Les toiles de Vélasquez nous ont familiarisés avec cette mode espagnole aux immenses vertugadins qui faisait d'une femme une idole et n'était pas sans grandeur. Gramont se trouve en face d'un double Vélasquez somptueux... et tout aussi immobile qu'une toile du maître sévillan, tout aussi silencieux. Il a tout juste le droit de baiser l'ourlet des robes de brocart et de se retirer sur la pointe des pieds sans avoir osé, cette fois, délivrer sa harangue. Mais on lui permet d'assister au souper des deux princesses que des dames vêtues de blanc servent « à genoux »! Et c'est une reine élevée de cette incroyable façon que Louis XIV, plus tard, contraindra à partager son carrosse avec une La Vallière, avec une Montespan...

Heureusement pour l'ambassadeur quelque peu déphasé, le duc d'Ossuna se charge de le recevoir avec sa suite et, cette fois, la réception (et le banquet donc! six cents plats!...) est à la hauteur de sa mission.

Quant à l'infante il l'a trouvée charmante bien qu'il n'ait pas entendu le son de sa voix. Elle est petite mais fort bien faite, un visage un peu long au teint très frais, des yeux bleus légèrement globuleux et une superbe, une luxuriante chevelure blonde. De son caractère il ne peut rien deviner. Pourtant il en vaut la peine car ses éléments dominants sont la foi, la soumission, la timidité, la pureté, la dignité et une passion magistralement contenue. Il ne saura pas que cette somptueuse poupée possède de l'esprit, de la finesse et du discernement, mais les Français ne le sauront pas davantage car, à la veille du mariage, Philippe IV « met un cachet sur les lèvres » de sa fille. Elle est un otage et elle doit s'engager à n'être que le reflet d'un époux dont le sort de l'Espagne va dépendre pour longtemps, un époux qu'il faudra surtout ne jamais indisposer. Tout ce que sauront d'elle ses sujets c'est que sa charité est inépuisable et qu'elle ne craindra pas de soigner elle-même, dans les hôpitaux, les malades dangereux ou les blessés les plus rebutants.

Encore est-ce le peuple qui découvrira cela. Les courtisans, eux, jugeront plus commode de la déclarer stupide...

Bientôt c'est le départ pour Saint-Sébastien où a lieu le mariage par procuration le 3 juin 1660. Philippe IV conduit lui-même sa fille, vêtue d'une simple robe de laine blanche brodée d'argent jusqu'à l'autel où l'attend don Luis de Haro qui représente Louis XIV. Pour une fois le Roi Catholique est vêtu de gris et d'argent, assez simplement mais un énorme diamant « le Miroir du Portugal » étincelle à son chapeau auprès de la « Peregrina » qui doit être la plus grosse perle connue. Le moment venu l'Infante tend le bras vers Don Luis qui en fait autant, puis offre sa main à son père qui baise en pleurant – mais oui! – cette main qui est désormais celle de la reine de France.

Le lendemain, dans l'île des Faisans où se sont déroulées les conférences avec Mazarin, c'est la rencontre avec Anne d'Autriche de part et autre d'une ligne frontière au-dessus de laquelle la reine tend le cou pour embrasser un frère qu'elle n'a pas vu depuis quarante-cinq ans. Mais Philippe IV n'aime pas les embrassades qui compromettent la dignité et évite le baiser de sa sœur en rejetant la tête en arrière. On commence à causer un peu froidement quand un gentilhomme vient annoncer un « étranger » qui demande à entrer. C'est naturellement Louis XIV qui n'a pas encore le droit de voir sa fiancée mais qui souhaite quand même se renseigner. La mise en scène est d'ailleurs bien montée. Comme si de rien n'était, Mazarin et Don Luis de Haro vont en bavardant jusqu'à la porte mais en laissant entre eux assez d'espace pour que l'on puisse apercevoir le jeune roi.

« Voilà un beau gendre, consent enfin à déclarer Philippe IV. Nous aurons des petits-enfants! »

L'Infante, elle, a pâli. Anne d'Autriche qui s'en est aperçue lui demande doucement :

« Que vous semble cet étranger? »

Elle n'a pas le temps de répondre. Son père s'interpose :

« Il n'est pas temps de le dire! »

Encore un froid. Décidément ces Espagnols sont impossibles! C'est du moins ce que pense le jeune Philippe d'Orléans, le frère de Louis XIV, le ravissant Monsieur qui jette plaisamment :

« Ma sœur, que vous semble de cette porte?... »

Marie-Thérèse qui a rougi, bien sûr, ne peut s'empêcher de sourire :

« La porte me paraît fort belle et fort bonne! » dit-elle.

Quatre jours plus tard, c'est pour elle la séparation d'avec les siens au milieu d'un déluge de larmes. Tout le monde pleure, y compris Louis XIV. On se demande bien pourquoi à moins que ce ne soit sur lui-même. Puis Marie-Thérèse va quitter ses vêtements espagnols pour une robe française tandis que Mazarin, au comble du soulagement, remercie humblement Philippe IV d'avoir accompagné lui-même sa fille.

« Je serais plutôt venu à pied, riposte l'autre qui jouit visiblement de la stupeur du cardinal qui s'est donné tant de mal pour obtenir une princesse qu'on ne demandait qu'à lui donner... »

Le 9 juin le véritable mariage est célébré à Saint-Jean-de-Luz. Le roi est vêtu de drap d'or voilé de noir. Marie-Thérèse traîne derrière elle un grand manteau de velours pourpre semé de lys d'or, long de cinq mètres et que soutiennent à mi-distance les princesses d'Orléans et, à l'extrémité la princesse de Carignan. Une couronne de diamants est posée sur ses beaux cheveux et elle porte au corsage une rose de diamants et de perles. Elle est émue, mais il est visible qu'une joie l'habite. Derrière elle, les couleurs des costumes rappellent un peu l'Espagne : la reine mère est drapée dans des voiles noirs givrés d'argent et la Grande Mademoiselle ferme la marche avec la majesté d'une frégate entrant au port. Elle aussi est tout de noir vêtue (elle porte le deuil de son père) mais les vingt rangs de perles qui lui pendent sur la poitrine enlèvent beaucoup de sévérité à l'ensemble.

Après la cérémonie, le jeune couple, la reine mère et Monsieur dînent ensemble chez le roi mais auparavant Louis et Marie-Thérèse sont apparus au balcon pour répondre aux acclamations de façon substantielle en jetant à poignées des pièces de monnaie. A peine la dernière bouchée avalée, le roi déclare qu'il veut aller se coucher. Mais mieux vaut peut-être laisser la parole à un témoin de la scène, Mme de Motteville :

« La reine dit à la reine sa tante avec les larmes aux yeux : *Es muy temptano...* [C'est trop tôt] qui fut depuis qu'elle était arrivée le seul moment de chagrin qu'on lui vit et que sa modestie la força de sentir. Mais enfin, comme on lui eut dit que le roi était déshabillé, elle s'assit à la ruelle de son lit sur deux carreaux pour en faire autant sans se mettre à sa toilette. Elle voulut complaire au roi en ce qui même pouvait choquer en quelque façon sa pudeur et comme on lui eut dit que le roi l'attendait, elle pressa ses femmes : *Presto! Presto! Que el Rey me espera...* [Vite, vite! Le roi m'attend!]. Après une obéissance si ponctuelle qu'on pouvait déjà soupçonner être mêlée de passion tous deux se couchèrent... »

Anne d'Autriche, témoin de l'extrême confusion de la jeune reine a pitié d'elle. Visiblement, depuis que Louis l'a rejointe, Marie-Thérèse ne sait plus où se mettre. Alors, saisissant elle-même les rideaux du grand lit, la reine mère les tire avec décision après avoir béni le jeune couple puis invite tout le monde à sortir. Personne, contrairement à ce qui se faisait jusqu'alors, ne surveillera les premiers épanchements des jeunes gens :

« On ne doute point, écrit un spectateur du mariage, qu'un prince si vigoureux que le nôtre n'ait consommé le mariage... »

Confiance amplement justifiée. Dès le lendemain chacun peut constater la véritable adoration que la jeune reine porte à son époux. Elle lui voue, dès à présent, un amour total. Henriette d'Angleterre qui sera bientôt Madame et qui ne cessera d'envier à Marie-Thérèse un époux qu'elle

confisquera un temps à son seul usage, écrira plus tard :
« Sa passion est telle qu'elle cherche à lire dans ses yeux
tout ce qui peut lui faire plaisir; pourvu qu'il la regarde
avec amitié, elle est gaie toute la journée. Elle est bien aise
que le roi couche avec elle... et si joyeuse lorsque cela est
arrivé, qu'on le voit tout de suite. Elle aime à ce qu'on la
plaisante là-dessus, rit, cligne les yeux et frotte ses petites
mains... »

« Quant à Louis, toujours d'après Mme de Motteville
citant la reine mère : ... "aussitôt après les noces, [Anne
d'Autriche] parlant de la satisfaction et du contentement
du roi [dit] qu'il l'avait remerciée de lui avoir ôté du cœur
Mlle de Mancini pour lui donner l'Infante qui vraisemblablement allait le rendre heureux tant par sa beauté que
par sa vertu, sa complaisance et l'affection qu'elle lui
témoignait..." »

Belle déclaration maternelle destinée surtout à masquer
la vérité. Louis est tellement heureux, il a si bien oublié
Marie Mancini que lorsque le 27 juin, au cours du voyage
de retour vers Paris, on atteint Saintes, il décide d'aller
visiter La Rochelle tandis que la Cour continuera sur
Saint-Jean-d'Angély...

Cela sent terriblement le coup fourré. Bien sûr Marie
n'est plus à Brouage. Elle est rentrée à Paris où elle attend
d'épouser un grand seigneur romain, le connétable
Colonna – ces Colonna chez qui l'oncle Mazarin était jadis
camérier! – mais la route de La Rochelle n'en est pas moins
celle de Brouage et Mazarin ne peut s'empêcher d'être
inquiet. Heureusement, il est lui-même gouverneur
d'Aunis et de Saintonge : il accompagnera donc le roi, il lui
montrera La Rochelle... Ce beau projet essuie un refus fort
net : le roi entend voyager tout seul, ou presque. Rien que
deux gentilshommes... et Philippe Mancini!

Naturellement, à La Rochelle, Louis ne jette qu'un coup
d'œil distrait au grand port protestant... et file à Brouage
où il va s'offrir une nuit lamartinienne : durant une partie
de la nuit, le plus « grand roi du monde » va errer sur la

plage comme un enfant perdu en pleurant à creuser les
galets. Puis, quand il consentira à aller se coucher ce sera
dans le lit même où a dormi Marie. Et là il continuera à
pleurer.

Ces larmes-là, Marie-Thérèse les paiera de beaucoup
d'autres larmes. Il y aura d'abord, à peine rentré à Paris,
Olympe Mancini qui reprendra un temps quelque
influence, puis Madame, puis La Vallière, ce « chandelier » devenu grand amour, puis l'éblouissante Montespan
et les accrocs accessoires comme la princesse de Monaco ou
la belle d'Artigny.

Ce sera l'honneur... et aussi la mort de Monsieur de dire
un jour son fait, touchant Marie-Thérèse, à son auguste
frère. La scène se passe en 1701 et le roi est à présent
l'époux de la veuve Scarron et, comme Louis XIV
reproche à Monsieur la vie déréglée de son fils, le futur
Régent, Monsieur explose, déclare à son frère que « les
pères qui ont mené de certaines vies ont peu de grâce et
d'autorité à reprendre leurs enfants » et qu'il serait bon
pour lui de se souvenir « des façons qu'il a eues pour la
reine avec ses maîtresses jusqu'à leur faire faire des
voyages dans son carrosse avec elle ».

La dispute qui suit est tellement violente que le pauvre
prince, étouffant d'indignation, en meurt peu après d'apo-
plexie mais avec l'immense satisfaction d'avoir enfin fait
entendre à son frère ce qu'il pensait de lui depuis tant
d'années...

UNE NUIT AVEC MONSIEUR...

Pauvre Monsieur! Lui qui n'aimait guère les dames autrement que dans leurs ajustements, leurs plaisirs et leurs façons d'être, devait se trouver par deux fois obligé de se marier à seule fin de servir la politique de son potentat de frère! Il avait épousé la charmante et cruelle Henriette d'Angleterre quand le rétablissement du trône des Stuarts avait rendu cette alliance souhaitable mais il avait fait, avec elle, le plus mauvais ménage qui fut. Et il ne goûtait les douceurs du veuvage que depuis un peu plus d'un an quand le roi lui fit entendre qu'il lui fallait se remarier.

Avec qui, mon Dieu? Avec une Allemande, cette fois; Élisabeth-Charlotte, dite Liselotte, fille de l'Électeur palatin Charles-Louis et cousine issue de germains de feu la première Madame et dont, du point de vue de la naissance, c'est à peu près le seul titre de gloire. En dehors de cela, elle est pauvre, laide à faire rougir un miroir, aussi large que haute avec un visage épais, sans la moindre grâce mais troué de petits yeux vifs et malin. Car ce laideron a de l'esprit. Elle prend d'ailleurs fort joyeusement parti de son physique : « On n'a jamais été laide avec plus de verve, écrit-elle, ni plus à cœur joie! » Et, bien plus tard, elle fera d'elle-même cette flatteuse description :

« Ma taille est monstrueuse de grosseur, je suis aussi carrée qu'un cube : ma peau est d'un rouge tacheté de jaune; mes cheveux deviennent tout gris; mon nez a été bariolé par la petite vérole ainsi que mes deux joues; j'ai la bouche grande, des dents gâtées... »

Sur ce point elle n'est pas la seule. Les belles dents ne sont guère l'apanage du XVIIe siècle. Le roi, le premier, n'est pas très bien « meublé », la reine pas davantage. Il faut être un raffiné comme Monsieur pour exhiber de jolies quenottes...

Quoi qu'il en soit et quoi qu'il puisse en penser Monsieur épousera Liselotte. Pourquoi ce mariage en apparence désastreux avec une fille qui arrivera avec six chemises en tout et pour tout? Mais parce que Louis XIV guigne le Palatinat et que, l'Électeur n'ayant sans doute pas la moindre envie de payer la dot convenue, la petite clause de renonciation de la princesse à la succession de ses parents qui occupe modestement un bout du contrat de mariage tombera d'elle-même. Alors?...

Alors, en août 1671 le mariage est conclu, et le 16 novembre de la même année, à Metz, la maréchal du Plessis-Praslin épouse par procuration Élisabeth-Charlotte au nom de Monsieur. Pour la sécurité de son départ des terres paternelles, la princesse ne se convertit au catholicisme (du bout des lèvres d'ailleurs!) qu'une fois en France. Cette formalité remplie elle s'achemine vers son destin et vers Monsieur qui, justement s'en vient à sa rencontre en fastueux équipage. Et c'est, sur la route entre Bellay et Châlons la rencontre que l'on peut sans peine qualifier d'historique. La nouvelle Madame voit descendre de carrosse un fabuleux étalage de joaillerie scintillant sur un homme « qui, sans avoir l'air ignoble, était petit et rondouillet avec des cheveux et des sourcils très noirs, des grands yeux de couleur foncée, le visage long, mince, un grand nez et une bouche trop petite garnie de vilaines dents... » (lui aussi!...)

Quant à Monsieur, laissé d'abord sans voix par l'aspect « rustre » de cette grosse fille blonde, il ne sait que murmurer, assez haut pour qu'elle l'entende :

« Oh!... Comment pourrai-je coucher avec elle?... »

« Je vis bien, écrit Madame, que je déplaisais à
Monsieur mon époux, ce que je ne dois pas trouver
merveilleux, laide autant que je le suis mais je pris dès ce
moment la ferme résolution de vivre avec lui de telle sorte
qu'il s'accoutumât à ma laideur. Ce à quoi j'ai réussi... »

En effet, le côté grenadier de sa nouvelle épouse finit par
convenir assez bien au duc d'Orléans : « Le premier choc
subi, écrit Philippe Erlanger, Monsieur éprouva une
surprise heureuse. Quel repos d'avoir une femme qui ne
serait pas une rivale, une femme étrangère à la coquetterie,
ignorante des intrigues, indifférente aux jolis garçons, une
femme qui ne prétendait être ni une égérie ni Machiavel,
une femme enfin si gaillarde, si crue que la pudeur envers
elle semblait ridicule et qu'il était loisible de la traiter en
camarade, voire en confidente!... »

Et il réussit parfaitement à lui faire trois enfants...

Reste le problème de la nuit de noces sur laquelle
Madame n'a pas laissé de témoignage direct mais dont on
peut déduire ce qu'elle fut grâce à un autre passage de ses
Lettres dans lequel elle raconte comment Monsieur se
comportait au lit et par quel étrange artifice il réussit à
tenir une place fort honorable dans l'échelle comparative
des géniteurs royaux.

« Monsieur, écrit la jeune épouse, a toujours paru dévot.
Il m'a fait rire, une fois, de bon cœur. Il apportait toujours
au lit un chapelet d'où pendait une quantité de médailles et
qui lui servait à faire ses prières avant de s'endormir.
Quand cela était fini j'entendais un gros fracas causé par
les médailles, comme s'il les promenait sous les couvertu-
res. Je lui dis :

« – Dieu me pardonne, mais je soupçonne que vous
faites promener vos reliques dans un pays qui leur est
inconnu!

« Monsieur répondit :

« – Taisez-vous! Dormez! Vous ne savez pas ce que
vous dites...

« Une nuit, je me levai tout doucement. Je plaçai la lumière de manière à éclairer le lit et, au moment où il promenait ses médailles sous la couverture, je le saisis par le bras et lui dis en riant :

« – Pour le coup, vous ne sauriez plus le nier.

« Monsieur se mit aussitôt à rire et dit :

« – Vous qui avez été huguenote vous ne savez pas le pouvoir des reliques et des images de la Sainte Vierge. Elles garantissent de tout mal les parties qu'on en frotte.

« Je lui répondis :

« – Je vous demande pardon, Monsieur, mais vous ne me persuaderez point que c'est honorer la Vierge que de promener son image sur les parties destinées à ôter la virginité.

« Monsieur ne put s'empêcher de rire et dit :

« – Je vous en prie, ne le dites à personne... »

Quoi qu'il en soit il semble bien que la croyance absolue de Philippe dans le pouvoir de ses médailles ait constitué pour lui la mise en condition nécessaire à l'accomplissement de ses devoirs conjugaux avec ses femmes, mais le miracle fut sans doute plus évident avec Henriette d'Angleterre, femme jusqu'au bout des ongles, qu'avec la Palatine qui devait regretter toute sa vie de n'être point homme, qui jurait comme un reître, montait à cheval comme un hussard, adorait les histoires scabreuses et se goinfrait de bière et de choucroute. Faire l'amour avec elle devait apparaître à Monsieur comme une expérience somme toute divertissante.

Néanmoins, cinq ans plus tard, quand Madame eut donné le jour à son troisième enfant, Élisabeth-Charlotte dite Mlle de Chartres qui, en épousant Léopold, duc de Lorraine, deviendrait l'ancêtre de tous les Habsbourg à venir, de François-Joseph, jusqu'à l'assassiné de Sarajevo et jusqu'à nos jours, Monsieur pensa qu'il était temps de laisser reposer ses reliques. L'accouchement, en effet, avait été plus que pénible et avait failli devenir dramatique.

Toujours est-il qu'il s'en alla proposer à sa femme de faire désormais chambre à part. Liselotte accueillit la proposition avec enthousiasme.

« J'ai été bien aise, soupire-t-elle, car je n'ai jamais aimé le métier de faire des enfants. Lorsque Son Altesse me fit cette proposition, je lui répondis : " Oui, de bon cœur, Monsieur! J'en serai très contente pourvu que vous ne me haïssiez pas et que vous continuiez à avoir un peu de bonté pour moi. " Il me le promit et nous fûmes tous deux très contents l'un de l'autre. C'était aussi fort ennuyeux que de dormir près de Monsieur. Il ne pouvait souffrir qu'on le troublât pendant son sommeil; il fallait donc que je me tinsse sur le bord du lit au point que, parfois, je suis tombée comme un sac. Je fus donc fort contente lorsque Monsieur, de bonne amitié et sans aigreur, me proposa de coucher chacun dans un appartement séparé. »

Disons les choses telles qu'elles furent : Liselotte n'aima jamais son époux. Celui qui l'avait séduite, dès le premier coup d'œil, c'était le roi, ce prince rayonnant, fabuleux qui avait fait des cérémonies de son mariage une sorte de conte oriental et qui lui montrait une amitié réelle, prenant plaisir à son esprit acéré autant qu'à partager avec elle sa passion pour la chasse. Madame ne devait jamais guérir de cette « maladie-là » et souffrit mille morts quand il épousa secrètement l'ancienne gouvernante de ses bâtards, cette Maintenon pour laquelle la Palatine n'eut pas d'injure assez féroce... Traitée successivement de guenille, de guenipe, de loque, de casserole, de truie, de sorcière, de voleuse, d'accapareuse de blé, d'empoisonneuse et d'incendiaire [1], la « vieille ordure du grand homme » retourna à Madame une haine féroce et d'autant plus dangereuse qu'elle était plus sournoise. La Maintenon réussit à détacher Louis XIV de sa bonne amitié avec sa belle-sœur et brouilla plus ou moins le ménage Orléans bien que

---

1. On se prend à regretter que Madame eût ignoré le terme d' « emmerdeuse ». Elle en eût certainement fait un usage admirable...

Monsieur l'exécrât presque autant que sa femme.

Après la mort de Monsieur, Liselotte se réconcilia avec le roi et, en cette occasion, laissa pour une seule et unique fois parler son cœur :

« Si je ne vous avais pas tant aimé, aurais-je tant détesté Mme de Maintenon?... »

LA NUIT SURVEILLÉE DE ‹ CARLIN ›

La seconde fille de Monsieur et d'Henriette d'Angleterre, Mlle de Valois, avait épousé le roi de Sardaigne, Victor-Amédée II. Elle en eut quatre enfants. Deux filles d'abord : la première, Marie-Adélaïde, devint, avec son jeune époux, le duc de Bourgogne, les délices de Versailles et la mère de Louis XV; la seconde, Marie-Louise, épousa le roi d'Espagne, Philippe V, petit-fils de Louis XIV. Vinrent ensuite deux garçons : Victor-Amédée, prince de Piémont, et Charles-Emmanuel. Mais, autant le roi de Sardaigne adorait son premier fils, autant il vouait au second une espèce d'aversion teintée de méfiance tout à fait désagréable.

Or, voici qu'en 1715 ce prince tant chéri s'avisa de mourir d'une chute de cheval. Ce fut abominable et, à la cour de Turin, chacun se persuada qu'aucun des deux époux ne résisterait au choc. La reine s'alita et, durant de longs jours, elle condamna son appartement aux courtisans aussi bien qu'au soleil et au grand ciel bleu d'Italie. Quant à Victor-Amédée, après avoir menacé tour à tour de passer au fil de l'épée tous les chevaux de ses écuries, de se retirer dans un couvent, puis de faire un pèlerinage en Terre sainte, il choisit de cesser de s'occuper des affaires de son royaume qui, naturellement, ne tardèrent pas à s'en aller à vau-l'eau.

Ce fut au point que la reine Anne-Marie jugea prudent de mettre un terme aux manifestations de sa propre douleur afin de remettre un peu d'ordre dans la maison.

« Nous n'avons pas le droit de nous laisser aller ainsi au désespoir, dit-elle à son époux. Il nous reste un fils et il nous faut dès à présent le préparer à vous succéder.

— Lui? grogna Victor-Amédée II. Il en est bien incapable : c'est un idiot... »

La reine savait bien que son époux détestait son cadet mais elle ignorait que celui-ci le lui rendait bien. Un peu bossu, un peu goitreux, laid, méfiant et profondément dissimulé, Charles-Emmanuel à quatorze ans n'avait évidemment que fort peu d'attraits mais l'aversion que lui montrait son père en toutes occasions n'arrangeait rien. Le jeune prince reprochait surtout à son royal géniteur le surnom de « Carlin » qu'il lui avait accroché, jouant à la fois sur le diminutif de son prénom à l'italienne [1] et sur son aspect général en s'obstinant à employer une traduction française nettement injurieuse.

Néanmoins, Anne-Marie entreprit de défendre son rejeton.

« Il n'est pas idiot, loin de là. Mais jusqu'à ce jour vous avez ordonné que l'on négligeât, à dessein, son éducation afin que l'âge venu il ne pût porter ombrage à la royauté de son aîné. Il faut réparer cela. Grâce au ciel il est encore jeune et il a encore le temps d'apprendre son métier de roi... »

Victor-Amédée renifla de façon peu gracieuse mais avec le maximum de mépris.

« Lui? Je l'en crois incapable. D'abord, il est si laid! Comment croire raisonnablement qu'il soit le frère de nos autres enfants? »

La reine dédaigna l'intention blessante. Ses filles étaient ravissantes, tout le monde le savait et le défunt prince était beau, lui aussi. Mais si Charles-Emmanuel n'était pas un prix de beauté, Victor-Amédée lui-même ne constituait pas

---

1. Carlino.

une réussite exceptionnelle. Sa figure étroite, grêlée de petite vérole offrait un fond peu aimable à un nez fort long qui s'ornait, au bout, d'une manière de boule. En outre, il était rouquin avec, sous ledit nez, deux virgules de même nuance qui prétendaient au rôle de moustaches. Au moral : entêté comme un âne rouge du Poitou et presque aussi malin. Sa diplomatie souterraine mais efficace était passée à l'état de proverbe comme d'ailleurs son avarice qui était sordide.

Été comme hiver, Sa Majesté sarde portait le même habit marron sans garnitures, les mêmes gros souliers de cuir solide, les mêmes chemises de toile rude et, pour ne pas user les basques de cet éternel habit, il avait fait garnir de cuir la poignée de son épée. Brochant le tout venait une vaste houppelande bleue assez minable grâce à laquelle on aurait pu le prendre pour un simple meunier si le roi n'avait réfugié dans ses perruques et ses chapeaux tous ses éclats de magnificence. Personne n'avait de perruques comme les siennes! On les lui envoyait d'ailleurs de Paris et ses chapeaux, parisiens eux aussi, compensaient par l'exubérance du plumage la regrettable absence de dentelles des jabots.

Néanmoins, pour son fils aîné, le roi n'avait pas lésiné et lui avait offert une éducation soignée en se rattrappant sur celle du cadet. Et voilà que tout était à recommencer! Mais comment faire autrement?

Alors, bien vite, on essaie de rattraper le temps perdu. L'infortuné Carlin se voit accablé de professeurs. On l'assomme d'économie politique, de balistique, de stratégie, de littérature, de mathématiques, de diplomatie. Puis, pour l'égayer, on le fait danser, ferrailler, tirer au pistolet, monter à cheval, sauter des obtacles avant de le replonger dans ses livres. Tant et si bien que le malheureux se voit à deux doigts de parvenir à l'état prédit depuis toujours par son père : un ahuri complet.

Pour couronner le tout, à vingt et un ans, on le marie. En 1722, il épouse Christine-Louise de Neubourg, fille du comte palatin de Sulzbach. Dès lors, destinée à porter couronne, la pauvre fille se voit soumise au même régime coupé, il est vrai, durant les loisirs de neuvaines nombreuses pour assurer la descendance royale...

Mais, dix-huit mois plus tard, Christine-Louise meurt, à peu près épuisée, sans avoir éprouvé la plus petite nausée, annonçant la plus faible intention de donner un héritier à son mari. Qui, d'ailleurs, n'est pas tout à fait son mari car si Carlin est laid, il n'est pas aveugle et il a pu constater sans la moindre peine que son épouse princière était encore plus laide que lui. Il s'est bien gardé d'y toucher.

Ce qui n'empêche Victor-Amédée, retour des funérailles, de laver copieusement la tête du veuf.

« Apparemment vous n'êtes bon à rien, Carlin? Voilà votre épouse partie pour un monde meilleur sans nous avoir donné d'héritier? Savez-vous qu'il va falloir vous remarier et que cela coûte très cher, un mariage!...

Carlin accepte la mercuriale sans broncher. S'il n'avait tant espéré régner un jour, il eût volontiers envoyé promener Monsieur son père et ses projets matrimoniaux avec tous les honneurs dus à leur majesté. D'ailleurs, les femmes ne l'intéressent pas. Les filles d'honneur de sa mère se moquent de lui et il n'est jusqu'aux chambrières qui ne se permissent, sur son passage, des rires étouffés aussi désobligeants que possible.

Cet état de choses n'a pas échappé à l'une des dames d'honneur de la reine qui a les meilleures raisons de se vouloir dans les bonnes grâces de la famille royale. A quarante-cinq ans Anne-Thérèse de Cumiane, marquise de Spigno Monferrato, est une belle créature aux cheveux noirs, aux dents superbes et à l'esprit avisé. Son teint de lait, ses beaux yeux sombres et sa gorge florissante lui ont toujours valu, de la part de Victor-Amédée, un accueil flatteur tandis que sa piété et son apparente absence d'ambition en font l'une des conseillères les plus écoutées de la reine.

Et un beau jour, Mme de Spigno s'en va faire connaître à Anne-Marie le fond de sa pensée. Trouver·une nouvelle épouse au prince est la chose du monde la plus aisée mais ne servira rigoureusement à rien... si l'on ne surveille pas étroitement ce qui se passe dans sa chambre.

Et comme la reine s'étonne, elle développe son propos. Le prince qui n'a jamais approché une femme en a peur et celle qu'on lui avait donnée n'avait vraiment rien pour le mettre en appétit. Il faudrait des conseils avisés, pertinents, éclairés... Des conseils que la mère est bien incapable de donner. Que la chère marquise aille donc en toucher un mot au roi! Ce genre d'affaire est davantage de son ressort...

Victor-Amédée écoute sa visiteuse avec d'autant plus d'intérêt qu'il la trouve charmante. Et c'est, entre eux, le début d'une intimité fort agréable où le bonheur de Carlin sert de prétexte à toutes sortes de marivaudages. La marquise est chargée de trouver matière à déniaiser Carlin et à le mettre en condition de faire bonne figure lors de son prochain mariage. Elle devra même le surveiller de près dès que le mariage aura eu lieu.

« Il n'est pas question, déclare Victor-Amédée, de laisser mon fils faire ce qu'il voudra quand sa nouvelle épouse sera auprès de lui.

— Puis-je tout de même, suggère Mme de Spigno, adjurer Votre Majesté de faire en sorte qu'elle ne soit point trop laide? »

Elle ne l'est pas. Elle est même ravissante. C'est une petite Allemande fraîche comme une rose, douce comme un ange et blonde comme le soleil, mais affublée d'un nom impossible : Polyxène de Hesse-Rheinfeld. C'est sans importance pour Carlin qui, dès le premier coup d'œil se montre enchanté. Il l'est même tellement qu'on craint, en haut lieu, les méfaits d'une trop grande timidité.

Pourtant, Mme de Spigno s'est arrangée pour que Carlin se débarrasse de son encombrant pucelage avec l'aide d'une jolie fille dont l'Histoire n'a malheureusement pas retenu le nom. Mais il paraît tellement extasié, tellement heureux tout d'un coup!... Il y a là de quoi lui faire perdre ses moyens tout neufs.

« Ma chère, dit alors le roi à la marquise, il n'y a qu'une solution à ce problème : il faut que nous soyions là!

— Qui? Vous, Sire?...

— Non : nous! Vous et moi!... »

C'est ainsi qu'au soir du mariage, après que, sur les dernières révérences, la Cour se fut retirée et que les rideaux du lit eurent été tirés, le roi alla se jeter dans un fauteuil pour y attendre la suite des événements tandis que Mme de Spigno s'installait discrètement derrière les rideaux qu'elle écartait de temps à autre d'un doigt prudent pour chuchoter tel conseil qui lui semblait judicieux. Ils devaient l'être car, se retirant sur la pointe des pieds aux petites heures du matin, elle alla réveiller Victor-Amédée qui avait fini par s'endormir dans son fauteuil, bercé sans doute par l'écho des soupirs, et lui glissa des informations tellement encourageantes que celui-ci, enchanté, décida que l'on continuerait à « aider » Carlin. Mais pas lui. Les veillées étaient trop fatigantes pour un homme de son âge et puis Mme de Spigno se tirait tellement bien de sa délicate mission qu'il n'y avait aucune raison pour qu'elle ne continuât pas.

Et cela donne le résultat suivant : chaque soir, la marquise se rend chez le roi pour y prendre ses ordres et les communiquer au prince qu'elle doit discrètement conseiller. Et le lendemain matin, elle y retourne pour rendre compte de sa mission et de la façon dont les conseils ont été suivis.

Cela vaut, aux deux complices une infinité de conciliabules chuchotés dans le silence du cabinet royal et sur un sujet suffisamment brûlant pour que Victor-Amédée s'enflamme à son tour. Et l'une des nuits de surveillance s'achève le plus naturellement du monde dans le lit du roi où la belle marquise fait merveille.

Dès lors, Carlin, enfin laissé à lui-même, put s'offrir le

luxe d'aimer sa jeune femme comme il l'entendait et ne réussit point si mal...

Mme de Spigno non plus car, en 1728, la reine Anne-Marie ayant quitté ce monde, elle se vit offrir par son amant un mariage morganatique béni à minuit dans la chapelle du palais de Turin. Enfin, elle atteignait son rêve : devenir une sorte de Maintenon savoyarde, régner par l'entremise de son époux, tout régenter, être reine sans couronne mais reine tout de même...

Hélas! il y a loin de la coupe aux lèvres. A peine marié, est-ce que Victor-Amédée ne décide pas d'abdiquer « afin de vivre désormais à l'abri des soucis du pouvoir, en simple gentilhomme campagnard entre sa bonne épouse et ses chiens... »? La malheureuse crut en mourir de dépit car elle n'avait aucun moyen de dissuasion : c'eût été avouer que son amour si désintéressé s'adressait bien plus à la Couronne qu'à son porteur. Et il fallut, la rage au cœur, partir pour le glacial château de Chambéry après avoir assisté, le 7 septembre 1730, à l'abdication solennelle de Victor-Amédée...

L'hiver fut affreux. La vieille forteresse médiévale était pleine de courants d'air. Victor-Amédée eut des rhumatismes et Madame un coryza chronique. En outre il n'y avait pas le moindre confort.

Après tant d'épreuves, la Maintenon savoyarde crut que tout allait changer : son époux en eut assez de Chambéry et décida soudain de rentrer à Turin et d'annuler son abdication...

Mal lui en prit. Carlin était devenu Charles-Emmanuel III et entendait le rester. Il lança ses troupes aux trousses de Monsieur son Père et le fit arrêter une nuit dans le lit de la marquise. L'ex-roi devait mourir de rage, au château de Moncalieri, quelques mois plus tard. Quant à son épouse, arrachée à demi nue du lit conjugal, elle fut conduite au couvent de la Visitation à Pignerol où elle vécut encore quarante interminables années, inconsolable du marché de dupe qu'elle avait eu l'imprudence d'accepter.

UNE NUIT « À VUE DE NEZ »
POUR LE GRAND DAUPHIN

Un jour de l'automne 1678, Louis XIV convoque, à Saint-Germain, un homme dans les capacités duquel il place une grande confiance car il le sait diplomate, avisé, et homme d'expérience. En un mot le président Colbert de Croissy, frère cadet du ministre qui est âgé de cinquante-trois ans, qui est fin, habile et qui sait la Cour comme personne. Il est l'un des négociateurs de la paix de Nimègue signée depuis peu et c'est avec un secret espoir qu'il se rend à l'invitation du souverain. Va-t-on lui octroyer une récompense en rapport avec ses mérites?

Certes, on le remercie mais, surtout, on le charge d'une nouvelle mission tout aussi délicate : cette fois il s'agit de marier l'unique fils (légitime et encore vivant à ce jour) de Sa Majesté.

A cet énoncé, Colbert de Croissy marque une surprise flatteuse pour le roi mais qui masque sa déception : a-t-on besoin d'un diplomate de sa force pour marier le Dauphin, l'héritier du plus beau trône du monde? C'est à la portée de n'importe quel grand seigneur, même légèrement obtus...

« Si mon fils me ressemblait, admet enfin le grand roi avec plus de sincérité que de modestie, j'en demeurerais d'accord. Mais tel n'est pas le cas. Lorsqu'il ne chasse pas le loup, Monseigneur demeure des heures entières assis dans un fauteuil à contempler le bout de ses souliers ou le pommeau de sa canne...

— Le Prince est un silencieux, Sire. Il réfléchit beaucoup sans doute. On ne saurait l'en blâmer.

— Un silencieux? Hum!... Un peu trop peut-être. Il ne dit pas trois paroles dans une année.

— C'est qu'il pense en conséquence...

— Vous croyez? Croissy, Croissy! Je commence à craindre que vous ne soyez trop bon diplomate! Vous n'osez pas me dire que mon fils ne parle pas parce qu'il n'a rien à dire et que, s'il montre un goût si vif pour la musique c'est qu'elle lui permet de rester assis à ne rien faire en s'accordant même, de temps à autre, un petit somme... »

Au supplice, Croissy choisit de ne pas répondre. Il est de mode, à la Cour, d'accorder au Grand Dauphin « un certain génie » mais c'est uniquement parce que l'on ne sait trop quel autre talent lui octroyer. A dix-sept ans, déjà grassouillet, lourd et endormi, son seul véritable passe-temps est la chasse au loup, mais il s'est donné tant de mal pour détruire les rares spécimens assez las du monde pour s'aventurer encore autour de Saint-Germain ou de Fontainebleau que, depuis quelque temps, sa louveterie en est réduite à chasser le lapin. Réduit à l'inaction, Monseigneur s'est résigné à s'ennuyer dans un fauteuil ou bien à s'endormir en écoutant un concert.

Dieu sait pourtant qu'il a été élevé soigneusement! Son premier gouverneur, le duc de Montausier, partisan convaincu de la manière forte, l'a roué de coups presque quotidiennement tout en partageant avec lui un savoir certain. Quant au second, Bossuet, le grand Bossuet, son enseignement, moins énergique, ne péchait ni par manque de science ni par défaut d'élévation. Seulement, s'adressant à Monseigneur le Dauphin, ses hautes leçons entraient par une oreille et ressortaient par l'autre. En fait, fils d'un tel père, le jeune Louis aurait eu quelque peu tendance au complexe d'infériorité, bien qu'il s'en accommodât parfaitement...

Laissant au roi le soin d'estimer lui-même les capacités de son héritier, Croissy se contente d'attendre que l'on veuille bien lui confier le nom de la princesse à laquelle on pense. On le renseigne rapidement : il s'agit de la jeune sœur de l'Électeur de Bavière, la princesse Marie-Christine. Une alliance avec la Bavière conviendrait assez à Louis XIV car, dix ans plus tôt, il a passé, avec l'Électeur, un traité d'alliance stipulant qu'en cas de décès de l'Empereur le Bavarois soutiendrait sa candidature au trône impérial. En outre on dit la princesse pleine d'esprit, de cœur et ornée d'une haute culture...

A merveille! En ce cas il n'y a guère d'obstacle... Eh bien si, il y en a un : le roi craint que sa candidate ne soit laide. Il sait bien que, lorsque dans une cour étrangère on s'étend sur les qualités morales d'une fille à marier, cela cache généralement de sérieux défauts physiques. Et c'est en cela que réside la mission de Colbert de Croissy : découvrir la vérité sur l'aspect de Marie-Christine de Bavière. La famille royale compte déjà un monument de laideur avec la seconde Madame qui est d'ailleurs une « Bavière » elle aussi, il ne s'agit pas de hisser au trône de France un autre épouvantail. Et le roi d'insister :

« Je veux la vérité!... »

Et voilà l'ambassadeur extraordinaire parti pour Munich!

Il n'a pas encore quitté le territoire français que, là-bas, on sait déjà ce qu'il vient faire. Il y a cette grande écrivassière de Palatine qui n'arrête pas de noircir du papier à destination de l'Allemagne et puis les « observateurs politiques » et les espions ne manquent pas dans les entours du Roi Très-Chrétien. Aussi, à Munich règne une certaine fièvre mêlée d'une certaine anxiété. Principalement chez la princesse Marie-Christine-Anne-Victoire.

Comme une bonne partie des princesses d'Europe, elle tourne depuis longtemps ses regards vers ce pays de France où un roi fastueux est en train de construire un palais où travaille un peuple d'artistes et dont on dit qu'il sera le plus beau du monde. Or, quand elle apprend qu'un ambassadeur vient tout exprès pour elle, la jeune fille éprouve une véritable angoisse. Elle a trop d'intelligence pour ignorer qu'elle a peu de beauté et, justement, elle désire passionnément plaire et être épousée. Que faire dans ce cas?...

Eh bien, d'abord essayer de se mettre en valeur et quand elle apprend que le Français est entré dans Munich, Marie-Christine décide de le recevoir vêtue de sa plus belle toilette – une robe toute brodée d'or – et debout sur une estrade abritée par un dais de velours rouge dont les crépines d'or retomberont gracieusement autour de sa tête et mettront une ombre douce sur son visage. Car c'est là qu'il y a un problème...

Quand vient l'heure de la réception, Colbert de Croissy entre, fait ses révérences, débite un compliment bien tourné auquel la princesse répond en excellent français et avec beaucoup de bonne grâce. Puis, pour se donner le temps de l'examiner sans trop avoir l'air d'y toucher, l'ambassadeur se lance dans une harangue tellement longue et tellement filandreuse que la pauvre enfant (elle n'a que dix-huit ans) doit lutter contre une somnolence dont la sauve heureusement la station debout.

Rentré chez lui, Croissy après avoir tourné en rond pendant un moment dans sa chambre, s'installe à une table, prend une plume neuve, du papier et se met en devoir d'écrire à son maître :

« Quoique je l'aie regardée fort fixement et que je me sois attaché à considérer sa taille et tous les traits de son visage, loin d'y trouver quelque chose de choquant, il m'a paru, quoiqu'elle n'ait aucun trait de beauté qu'il résulte de ce composé quelque chose qu'on peut bien dire agréable. La taille m'a paru d'une moyenne grandeur, parfaitement bien proportionnée, la gorge assez belle, les épaules bien tournées, le tour du visage plutôt rond que long, la bouche ne peut être dite ni petite ni fort grande, les dents sont blanches assez bien rangées, les lèvres rebordées assez régulièrement; elles ne sont pas véritablement fort rouges mais on ne peut dire qu'elles soient pâles; le nez est un peu gros par le bout, mais on ne peut pas dire qu'il soit choquant et qu'il fasse une grande difformité; les joues sont assez pleines, les yeux ni petits, ni grands, ni bien vifs, ni trop languissants. Je n'ai vu sa main et son bras qu'un instant et n'en puis faire la peinture; j'avoue seulement que je n'y ai pas vu la même blancheur qu'à la gorge; son teint m'a paru un peu brun et de la manière que l'on voit la plupart des filles qui ne savent pas ce que c'est que polir un peu la Nature. Enfin, Sire, ce sera une princesse très parfaite et, à mon sens, plus capable de plaire que de plus belles personnes... »

Cette belle page achevée que n'eût pas désavouée un Normand, Croissy la relit, pousse deux ou trois soupirs et s'en va se coucher, remettant au lendemain l'envoi du courrier pour la France. Il lui est, en effet, revenu en esprit qu'il doit, le lendemain également, déjeuner au palais et il espère pouvoir, ayant contemplé la princesse en pleine lumière, parfaire ainsi sa description dont il n'est pas pleinement satisfait. La chose qui le tourmente le plus est le nez de la princesse. Même dans l'ombre des tentures il lui est apparu plus important qu'il n'a osé le dire et il se demande honnêtement s'il n'a pas été victime d'un jeu de lumière ou des ombres de ces maudites tentures.

Le lendemain venu, Croissy rentrant du palais, reprend sa lettre et ajoute, très vite et en *post-scriptum* :

« Je viens d'assister au repas de la princesse et, l'ayant examinée en plein jour et longtemps, je me vois forcé d'avouer qu'elle a le tour de la bouche et le bas des joues très rouges et quelques taches jaunes sur le haut du visage. D'ailleurs, toutes les vertus morales et les grâces de l'esprit... »

Et, cette fois, il expédie le tout.

Au reçu, ce morceau de littérature issu d'une plume aussi éminemment diplomate, laisse le roi perplexe. Il en conclut sans peine que Marie-Christine est loin d'être une beauté mais, d'autre part, il est attaché à ce mariage qu'il juge souhaitable sur bien des points. Ne serait-il pas possible que cette jeune fille, sans être belle, eût tout de même quelque charme?

Il va poser la question à Mme de Maintenon qui n'est pas encore marquise mais dont il prend déjà volontiers le conseil.

« Le roi ne possède-t-il pas déjà un portrait de la princesse de Bavière? dit la dame.

— Si fait! mais vous savez ce que sont ces portraits de cour : un tissu de flatteries, de rubans et d'affiquets qui s'entendent à déguiser la vérité. C'est pourquoi j'ai dépêché M. de Croissy.

— Alors, Sire, il faut lui envoyer ce portrait et lui demander d'en écrire sur ce qu'il en pense. »

L'idée paraît excellente à Louis XIV qui envoie incontinent le tableau en Bavière porté par un chevaucheur de sa Grande Écurie. Colbert de Croissy le reçoit sans aucun plaisir car, entre-temps, il s'est pris d'une amitié pour une jeune princesse à la fois sage, bonne et intelligente et il aimerait bien qu'elle épouse le Dauphin. Mais, esclave du devoir, il n'en répond pas moins que le portrait est flatté puis il se perd, pour noyer le poisson, dans des considérations vagues :

« La princesse a le bas du visage plus agréable, surtout quand elle ne rit pas mais le peintre lui a fait le visage un peu plus long qu'il n'est et, surtout, le nez un peu moins gros... »

Ah! Ce nez! Il en pleurerait, le malheureux ambassadeur! Pourtant c'est impossible de le passer sous silence. Il est tellement évident, tellement... Non, jamais embarras plus cruel n'a été infligé à un diplomate doublé d'un homme de cœur.

A Saint-Germain, Louis XIV commence à s'inquiéter lui aussi de ce nez qui paraît traumatiser son ambassadeur. Aussi, pour en avoir le cœur net, décide-t-il d'envoyer en renfort l'un de ses portraitistes favoris : le jeune De Troy.

« Et surtout, recommande-t-il, pas de flatteries, pas de

complaisance! Je veux la vérité... quelle qu'elle soit. »

De Troy jure tout ce que veut le roi et gagne Munich où, sous l'œil mi-inquiet, mi-sévère de Croissy il se met à l'ouvrage. Un ouvrage qui d'abord, n'avance guère : Marie-Chritine est atteinte, dès le début des séances de pose, d'une fluxion qui lui fait une joue deux fois plus grosse que l'autre. On doit attendre que les choses rentrent dans l'ordre. Après quoi le peintre met les bouchées doubles, usant sans jamais réussir à la lasser la patience de la jeune fille.

Enfin, le portrait est achevé, emballé, envoyé en France tandis que, soupirant de plus belle, Colbert de Croissy reprend sa plume : ce malheureux De Troy, séduit sans doute par le charmant caractère de son modèle, l'a enjolivé. Il a diminué le fameux nez et, cela, il faut que le roi le sache.

En possession de la lettre et du tableau, Louis XIV est bien près de se mettre en colère. De qui se moque-t-on ? De Troy a juré de faire ressemblant et cependant Colbert de Croissy dit qu'il a flatté, que son nez n'est pas assez gros du bout. Mais qu'est-ce qu'il peut bien avoir, ce nez ?...

Mme de Maintenon hasarde que la princesse a peut-être du charme et que le charme n'a rien à voir avec la beauté. Sinon comment expliquer les circonlocutions de Croissy et l'aberration d'un peintre qui prend le risque de déplaire au roi en déguisant une vérité qu'on lui demande ?

« Des regards différents peuvent voir une même femme différemment », dit-elle.

C'est une grande vérité mais à double tranchant. Colbert de Croissy a vu la princesse d'une façon, De Troy d'une autre, comment la verront les courtisans d'abord, ces impitoyables dénigreurs, puis, surtout, le Grand Dauphin ? Après tout, c'est lui qui doit épouser... Et si quelqu'un s'avisait de faire sentir sa laideur à la pauvre princesse ? Quel scandale ! Un scandale toujours possible avec les fauves policés qui peuplent les palais royaux...

Louis XIV connaît bien sa Cour et il décide que le mariage aura lieu et qu'il n'y aura pas de scandale car il entend prendre ses précautions. Et, un beau soir, au souper de la reine on voit soudain apparaître le roi dans un appareil fort inhabituel : Sa Majesté, sans perdre un pouce de son habituelle dignité, fait son entrée, portant sous le bras un tableau. Un valet armé d'un marteau et de clous marche gravement derrière elle.

Arrivé près du fauteuil de Marie-Thérèse, Louis la salue, laisse peser sur l'assemblée inclinée un regard olympien puis désigne au valet l'un des murs tendus de soie :

« Mettez le crochet ici. »

Quand l'homme a fini, le roi accroche lui-même le portrait de Marie-Christine, recule de quelques pas pour juger de l'effet puis déclare :

« Voici la princesse de Bavière qui va, sous peu, devenir notre fille très chère. Quoiqu'elle ne soit pas belle, elle ne déplaît pas et elle a beaucoup de mérite. »

C'est sans appel. Personne ne s'y trompe et, avec un petit silence, il reste à venir contempler le portrait et à faire entendre tout ce que l'on peut trouver de flatteur. Évidemment, dès que le roi a tourné les talons, on se précipite, on échange des commentaires consternés. Dieu qu'elle est laide! Moins que Madame bien sûr, mais très laide tout de même. Et la marquise de Sévigné d'écrire, peu après :

« Il y a quelque chose à son nez. Cela fait mauvais effet tout d'abord... »

Il y a bien quelqu'un qui pourrait se permettre de protester et c'est naturellement le premier intéressé : le Grand Dauphin. Et l'on est à l'affût de sa réaction, on attend son avis qu'il ne se presse d'ailleurs pas de donner. Entre une chasse, un concert et un somme, il vient tout de même donner un coup d'œil distrait au portrait en compagnie de son ancien gouverneur Montausier devenu Premier Gentilhomme de sa chambre. On retient son souffle... Que va-t-il dire?

« Pourvu que ma femme ait de l'esprit et soit vertueuse, déclare-t-il paisiblement, je serai content quelque laide qu'elle puisse être... »

Et voilà. Et il s'en retourne écouter ses violons laissant les potineurs à leur déception. Monseigneur est très content comme cela et si quelqu'un se tourmente, ce n'est certes pas lui. Au fait c'est le roi. Louis XIV finit par rêver de ce fameux nez et quand il apprend que la princesse est entrée en Lorraine, il n'y tient plus : il expédie à sa rencontre son maître d'hôtel, Sanguin, avec ordre de rapporter son impression première dans toute sa fraîche nouveauté. Sanguin, le roi le sait, est « un homme vrai et qui ne sait point flatter... »

Et Sanguin part, suivi de près par la Cour qui doit rejoindre la princesse à Vitry-le-François. C'est là que, deux jours avant l'arrivée officielle, le messager secret rejoint son maître.

« Alors?...

– Eh bien, Sire, sauvez le premier coup d'œil et vous serez fort content... »

Le premier coup d'œil? Diable! Il doit tout de même y avoir quelque chose. Le surlendemain, à deux lieues en amont de Vitry, c'est la minute de vérité... Des carrosses poudreux qui s'approchent, s'arrêtent... Une portière qui s'ouvre... Une forme féminine, pleine de juvénilité saute de la première voiture et court s'agenouiller devant le roi qui, tout à coup, aimerait fermer les yeux mais se force à regarder en face l'arrivante. Et, aussitôt il sourit : quoi? Tant de bruit pour si peu? Certes, Marie-Christine n'est pas belle : il y a ce teint trop foncé et puis ce nez trop gros du bout mais quel charmant sourire et quels yeux pleins de douceur...

Tout heureux, il la relève, l'embrasse puis, faisant avancer le Dauphin :

« Voilà de quoi il est question, Madame : c'est mon fils que je vous donne... »

Et un nouveau miracle se produit. L'indifférent, l'apathique Dauphin se trouve si content qu'il tombe amoureux de sa petite femme au nez trop gros qui d'ailleurs le lui rend. Et la nuit de noces de ces résignés-là sera une vraie nuit d'amour, une nuit de gens heureux d'être ensemble qui aura lieu à Châlons au milieu de l'allégresse générale. Le roi était si content de sa belle-fille qu'il la couvrit littéralement de joyaux, déchaînant même la jalousie de la reine. Mais il avait eu tellement peur que ce mariage-là ne fût un échec...

Cette première nuit châlonnaise allait ouvrir sur une existence quasi bourgeoise. Quand le roi s'installa à Versailles, le jeune couple se fit construire à Meudon une petite maison, trop modeste au goût de Louis XIV mais où il se trouvait bien : Louis chassait, écoutait de la musique, Marie-Christine lisait, jardinait et faisait des enfants. Elle en fit trois... et beaucoup trop de fausses couches qui la menèrent au tombeau à trente ans.

Son mari la pleura beaucoup mais, par la suite, il lui trouva une remplaçante en la personne d'une certaine Emilie Joly de Choin qu'il épousa morganatiquement et qui était bien la créature la plus affreuse que l'on eût jamais vue. La Cour, accablée, ne l'appela jamais autrement que « La Choin »... Mais Monseigneur se moquait de la Cour : il l'aimait comme ça!

LA NUIT DES LARMES :
MAURICE DE SAXE MARIE SA NIÈCE

La scène qui se déroule à Nangis, soixante-sept ans plus tard, le 6 février 1747, pourrait n'être que la réédition de celle qui s'est déroulée près de Vitry-le-François en 1680. Là encore, un roi, sa cour s'en viennent au-devant d'une princesse étrangère qui va devenir dauphine. Là encore, c'est la raison d'État qui commande le mariage, mais choses et gens sont bien différents et c'est fort heureux sinon nous ne serions pas là.

Le roi, c'est Louis XV. Le Dauphin... eh bien, il est absent. Il traîne quelque part derrière et on ne le retrouvera que le lendemain à Brie-Comte-Robert. La princesse vient encore d'au-delà du Rhin mais n'est qu'à peine allemande. Fille de l'Électeur de Saxe et roi de Pologne Auguste III, Marie-Josèphe est polonaise de cœur et d'éducation ayant été élevée au couvent des Dames du Saint Sacrement de Varsovie et aimant de tout son cœur ce pays sur lequel règne son père. Enfin, il y a là un personnage de tout premier plan : le héros de Fontenoy et de Raucoux, le fameux, l'immense, le gigantesque maréchal de Saxe qui est le *deus ex machina* du mariage.

Marie-Josèphe est sa nièce – ou sa demi-nièce car si Auguste III et Maurice de Saxe sont tous deux fils d'Auguste II, le premier a eu pour mère une très régulière princesse royale et l'autre la très belle comtesse Aurore de Kœnigsmark. Et ce mariage, le grand homme l'a voulu comme une récompense supplémentaire couronnant toutes celles que sa valeur lui a méritées : le bâton de maréchal de France, le château de Chambord avec le droit d'y faire stationner son régiment et d'y garder les canons pris à Raucoux, le rang de prince souverain sur ses terres où le curé n'arrête pas de baptiser des bébés diversement colorés dus aux cavaliers, diversement colorés eux aussi, qui composent le superbe régiment de Saxe-Volontaires. A présent, il s'est mis en tête de donner une reine à la France et il est en train d'y parvenir, ayant fait tout ce qu'il fallait pour cela.

Il s'est occupé de tout, même des détails les plus inattendus chez un maréchal de France. C'est ainsi que la mère de Marie-Josèphe a reçu de lui cette lettre qui fait sourire venant d'un guerrier aussi fameux.

« Je suis informé du trousseau. En général tout ce qui est garde-robe appartient à la dame d'atours qui est Mme la duchesse de Lauraguais; elle fournit toutes les parures, linge, dentelles et reprend ce qui ne sert plus. C'est le plus grand bénéfice de sa charge. Quant aux bijoux, diamants et pierreries, il y en a une quantité considérable pour le service de Mme la Dauphine mais dont elle ne peut disposer, qui sont pierreries de la Couronne; quant à celles qu'on lui apporte et qu'elle acquiert, elle peut en disposer comme bon lui semble et cet article ne va pas à la dame d'atours.

« Votre Majesté ferait bien de donner à la princesse quelques pièces d'étoffe de Hollande, s'il y en a de belles, fond satin ou or, dans le goût des étoffes des Indes ou de Perse parce qu'ici il n'y en a pas et que l'entrée de ces étoffes est défendue; s'il s'en trouvait de belles chez les Arméniens à Varsovie, il serait bon d'en faire acheter.

« Comme on ne trouve point de belles fourrures ici, il serait bon de donner aussi à la princesse une belle palatine doublée de martre zibeline, comme on les porte en Russie, qui sont longues et chaudes et font un bel ornement avec le manchon assortissant. L'on ne fait nulle part les tours de

robes et des corsets baleinés aussi bien qu'à Dresde, il
faudra en donner quelques-uns qui pourront servir de
modèles par la suite.

« Il faut seulement observer une chose qui est que le
tailleur ne fasse pas la taille trop longue. C'est un défaut
dans lequel nos tailleurs tombent souvent, ce qui donne un
air gêné et rend les jupes trop courtes, ce qui n'est pas dans
le goût du maître de ce pays-ci. Je ne sais si je me fais
entendre en parlant ajustements et ma façon de m'expri-
mer paraîtra peut-être ridicule à Votre Majesté mais je la
supplie de m'excuser de ma bonne volonté... »

La lettre du maréchal n'étonna guère la reine. Comme
toute l'Europe elle savait les retentissantes aventures
sentimentales de son beau-frère. Il connaissait trop bien les
femmes pour ne pas savoir les habiller aussi bien qu'il les
déshabillait...

Mais retournons sur la route de Nangis où Louis XV
attend toujours. Cette fois, aucune inquiétude ne l'habite
touchant le physique de sa future belle-fille : ses portraits
sont charmants et sa réputation aussi. Il se tourmenterait
plutôt sur la façon dont va se comporter son fils en face de
sa nouvelle épouse car, veuf depuis huit mois de l'infante
Marie-Thérèse, Louis n'a pas encore fini de pleurer son
épouse. Il n'a même pas voulu venir jusqu'ici alléguant
qu'il verrait sa fiancée bien assez tôt.

L'inquiétude, elle est tout entière du côté de Marie-
Josèphe et il faut avouer qu'il y a de quoi.

D'abord, si elle se sent polonaise de cœur, cela risque de
ne pas suffire à lui attirer les bonnes grâces de la reine.
Marie Leczinska certes est polonaise de sang mais il se
trouve justement que son père, le joyeux Stanislas Leczinsky a été détrôné par Auguste III et ce sont de ces choses
dont on n'aime guère à se souvenir.

En outre, la nouvelle venue n'ignore pas qu'elle épouse
un veuf et quel veuf! Un veuf de huit mois qui ne se console
pas d'avoir perdu sa jeune épouse morte en couches après
tout juste dix-sept mois de bonheur. Car, pour une fois, ce

mariage-là était un mariage d'amour... Quel accueil va-t-il lui faire? De temps en temps, Marie contemple la miniature du Dauphin qu'elle porte attachée par une chaîne d'or à son poignet droit depuis qu'en l'accueillant à la frontière française, sa première dame d'honneur, la duchesse de Brancas, la lui a offerte. Il est charmant, ce jeune prince et le duc de Richelieu qui l'escorte depuis le mariage par procuration à Dresde assure que le portrait est fidèle. S'il pouvait l'aimer un peu, elle pourrait, peut-être, être heureuse?...

Mais voici que le carrosse s'arrête. Une foule scintillante barre la route avec des voitures dorées, des chevaux empanachés. Mme de Brancas fait descendre la princesse et lui indique le roi devant lequel elle doit aller s'age-nouiller. Marie-Josèphe a si peur d'apercevoir le modèle de la miniature avec une mine sinistre qu'elle se précipite avec toute l'ardeur de ses quinze ans, s'affale aux pieds de Louis XV et supplie :

« Sire!... Je vous demande votre amitié... »

Louis XV sourit comme il sait sourire quand il veut, relève cette jolie blondinette qu'il trouve charmante, l'embrasse et l'assure que, cette amitié demandée, elle vient de se l'acquérir et pour toujours... Il est très heureux de la voir arrivée à si bon port et elle peut être certaine de trouver en lui un véritable père. Quant au Dauphin... eh bien, mais on le rencontrera demain. Il était souffrant la veille au soir mais il a écrit une lettre... Et on donne la lettre à la princesse.

Or elle n'est pas adressée à la fiancée, cette maudite lettre mais bien à Mme de Brancas. On ne s'en aperçoit que trop tard quand Marie-Josèphe éclate en sanglots : le Dauphin y confie à la dame d'honneur que personne au monde ne réussira à lui faire oublier sa première femme... C'est la catastrophe! On s'indigne. Le roi est très mécontent. L'oncle Maurice aussi qui a embrassé et réembrassé sa nièce et qui s'efforce de la consoler. Il tordrait volontiers le cou de ce galopin stupide comme il sait si bien **le faire**

avec un fer à cheval qu'il transforme en tire-bouchon d'une
seule main. Mais enfin on ne peut pas rester indéfiniment
sur cette route glaciale et l'on repart. Marie-Josèphe cette
fois prend place avec le roi.

Le lendemain, à Brie, le premier contact avec le dauphin
Louis n'a rien d'encourageant. Le Prince a les yeux rouges
et il est tout juste poli. Pendant tout le temps que durera le
voyage de retour à Versailles, c'est Louis XV qui fera tous
les frais de la conversation. Le Roi est gai, enjoué, il montre
à la jeune fille tout ce qui, sur le chemin peut l'intéresser et
celle-ci lui en est reconnaissante car cette gentillesse rend
un peu moins pénible le silence obstiné de Louis qui
regarde par la portière et s'occupe bien plus des foules que
l'on rencontre que de sa fiancée.

Le 9 février c'est la grande cérémonie. Les dames de la
dauphine l'ont revêtue d'une robe tissée d'or et rebrodée
d'or dont le poids est de soixante livres. Le maréchal de
Saxe qui l'a soupesée, a hoché la tête en contemplant la
silhouette blonde, si juvénile encore de sa nièce :

« Elle pèse plus lourd qu'une cuirasse! » déclare-t-il.

Et c'est en fait ce qu'elle est pour la fiancée du désespéré.
Elle lui permet de se tenir bien droite en tenant bien haut sa
tête couronnée de diamants durant l'interminable cérémonie, le banquet et le bal qui suivent. Le Dauphin a ouvert la
danse avec sa femme puis il a disparu dans un coin.

Pour amuser sa belle-fille, le roi a commandé un bal
masqué. Des dominos de toutes couleurs s'y croisent mais
l'on remarque bientôt certain domino jaune qui n'arrête
pas de visiter les buffets dressés dans les premiers salons
des grands appartements. Il s'empiffre, repart, revient,
recommence à manger et à boire comme s'il n'avait encore
rien pris, repart encore, revient de nouveau...

Son manège intrigue le roi qui le fait surveiller. Qui
peut bien être ce glouton? Quand on découvre le pot aux
roses c'est un éclat de rire général : le domino sert d'abri à
tous les Suisses de la Maison du Roi qui viennent à tour de
rôle manger et boire à la santé des mariés.

Seul le Dauphin n'a pas ri. L'heure tragique est arrivée pour lui. Il est temps d'aller au lit et d'y aller en présence d'une foule considérable : la famille royale et les principaux de la Cour, marquise de Pompadour en tête.

C'est la seconde fois que Louis subit cette cérémonie mais la première fois il était joyeux et n'avait qu'une hâte : voir disparaître tout ce monde afin de rester seul avec sa petite infante rousse. Aujourd'hui, il donnerait n'importe quoi pour qu'elle refuse de s'en aller, cette foule, afin qu'il puisse y demeurer isolé comme il l'était à la chapelle et durant le festin... ou alors qu'un cataclysme se produise! La foudre sur le toit de Versailles, un tremblement de terre, n'importe quoi! Mais qu'il puisse échapper à ce supplice : donner à une inconnue, à une étrangère la place de la bien-aimée disparue...

Marie-Josèphe n'est guère en meilleure forme mais elle ne le montre pas ainsi qu'en témoigne la lettre que le maréchal de Saxe enverra le lendemain à son frère, le roi de Saxe :

« A quinze ans, il n'y a plus d'enfants dans ce monde-ci et, en vérité, elle m'a étonné. Votre Majesté ne saurait croire avec quelle présence d'esprit Madame la Dauphine s'est conduite et Monsieur le Dauphin paraissait un écolier auprès d'elle. Une fermeté noble et tranquille accompagnait toutes ses actions et, certes, il y a des moments où il faut toute l'assurance d'une personne formée pour soutenir avec dignité ce rôle. Il y en a un, entre autres, qui est celui du lit où l'on ouvre les rideaux lorsque l'époux et l'épouse ont été mis au lit nuptial, ce qui est terrible car toute la Cour est dans la chambre. Et le roi me dit pour rassurer Madame la Dauphine de me tenir auprès d'elle.

« Elle soutint tout cela avec une tranquillité qui m'étonna. Monsieur le Dauphin se mit la couverture sur le visage; mais la princesse ne cessa de parler avec une liberté d'esprit charmante, ne faisant pas plus attention à ce peuple de Cour que s'il n'y avait eu personne dans la chambre. Je ne l'ai quittée et ne lui ai souhaité la bonne

nuit que lorsque les femmes eurent refermé les rideaux.
Tout le monde sortit avec une espèce de douleur car cela
avait l'air d'un sacrifice et elle a trouvé le moyen
d'intéresser tout le monde pour elle.

« Votre Majesté rira peut-être de ce que je lui dis là,
mais la bénédiction du lit, les prêtres, les bougies, cette
troupe brillante, la beauté, la jeunesse de cette princesse,
enfin le désir que l'on a qu'elle soit heureuse, toutes ces
choses ensemble inspirent plus de pensées que de rires. Il y
avait dans la chambre tous les princes et toutes les
princesses qui composent cette Cour, le roi, la reine, plus
de cent femmes couvertes de pierreries et d'habits brillants.
C'est un coup d'œil unique... »

Tandis que son carrosse l'emporte vers son château du
Piple où l'attend la jolie Marie de Verrières [1], Maurice de
Saxe est loin d'être tranquille. Il donnerait beaucoup pour
savoir ce qui se passe, à la même heure, derrière ces sacrés
rideaux. Il sait bien, lui, qu'à la place de ce benêt de
Dauphin, il n'irait pas se cacher sous ses draps alors
qu'une si charmante enfant attend son bon plaisir.

Ce qui s'y passe? Il vaut mieux que le bouillant
maréchal ne le voie pas. A peine la chambre s'est-elle vidée
que le prince s'est mis à sangloter comme un enfant perdu
et ne semble pas décidé à s'arrêter. D'abord interdite par ce
bruyant chagrin, la Dauphine s'est laissée gagner peu à
peu par l'ambiance. Bientôt les larmes lui viennent, à elle
aussi, et la voilà qui pleure, puis qui sanglote. Et voilà les
deux jeunes époux, chacun le nez dans son oreiller, qui
pleurent à qui mieux mieux...

La Dauphine pleurait-elle en contrepoint de son époux,
ou bien le prince eut-il conscience des légères secousses que
leur double chagrin imprimait au lit, toujours est-il
qu'entre deux hoquets il parvint à articuler :

« Par... pardonnez-moi... Madame... de... de vous donner une telle... image! »

---

1. Qui sera l'aïeule de George Sand.

Seigneur! Il a parlé!... Du coup, les larmes de la Dauphine tarissent comme par enchantement. Elle essuie ce qu'il en reste puis, avec beaucoup de gentillesse, elle se penche vers son larmoyant époux :

« Laissez couler vos larmes, Monsieur, et ne croyez pas que je sois offensée. Elles me prouvent, au contraire, ce qu'il m'est permis d'espérer si je sais, un jour, mériter votre estime. C'est le propre d'un noble cœur que la fidélité au souvenir et je sais trop ce qu'il a dû vous en coûter d'accepter notre mariage... »

Cette voix douce, compatissante, agit comme un baume. A son tour, Louis cesse de pleurer. Pour la première fois, il regarde vraiment sa jeune femme. Elle est bien mignonne avec ses beaux cheveux blonds, ses yeux bleus pleins de compréhension et son petit nez rougi par les larmes... Alors il tente un sourire, le réussit presque et murmure :

« Merci, mon petit cœur... »

Bientôt, Marie-Josèphe sera « mon petit cœur » pour toute la famille royale conquise par sa bonté, sa patience et sa gentillesse. Pour l'heure présente, les deux époux finissent par s'endormir chacun dans son coin et quand, au matin, les dames de la Dauphine viendront examiner les draps, elles n'y trouveront pas ce qu'elles étaient venues chercher. Mais les oreillers eux, sont encore humides...

Le roi fronça les sourcils mais jugea préférable de ne rien dire et de laisser faire la nature. C'était la sagesse car cette nuit si bien trempée marqua le début d'une affection, fraternelle d'abord mais qui, peu à peu, devint plus tendre. Le Dauphin découvrit rapidement qu'entre sa jeune femme et lui il y avait bien des goûts communs : la lecture, l'étude, la piété, la musique, les fleurs et une certaine simplicité dans la vie quotidienne. Leur appartement devint une sorte d'îlot paisible au milieu de l'agitation d'une cour frivole et brillante...

On ne sait pas exactement au bout de combien de temps le Dauphin se décida enfin à considérer Marie-Josèphe comme une épouse et non plus comme une sœur. Il semble que ce fut tout de même assez rapide car lorsque, le 26 août 1750, la Dauphine donna le jour à une petite fille, Marie-Séphirine qui ne devait vivre que cinq années – elle avait déjà eu trois enfants mort-nés. Mais à partir de cette naissance, le Dauphin ne s'arrêta plus. Vinrent ensuite le duc de Bourgogne qui mourut à dix ans, ce dont ses parents pensèrent périr de chagrin, puis le duc d'Aquitaine qui ne vécut que quelques mois. Le suivant, Berry, allait être beaucoup plus solide. Il avait trente-neuf ans quand sa tête tomba sur l'échafaud de la place de la Révolution : on l'appelait Louis XVI. Les suivants aussi demeurèrent de ce monde : Louis XVIII, Charles X puis Marie-Adélaïde, reine de Sardaigne et enfin Élisabeth, la charmante et si touchante Madame Élisabeth dont la Terreur fit une martyre.

Ce destin dramatique de ses enfants, la Dauphine qui ne fut jamais reine n'eut pas à en souffrir. Elle avait trente-cinq ans lorsqu'elle s'éteignit, le 13 mars 1767. Le Dauphin dont elle avait tenu à soigner elle-même la dangereuse variole l'avait précédée dans la tombe deux ans plus tôt...

ENCORE DES RELIQUES!
LE PRINCE DE LIGNE SE MARIE

Si quelqu'un, dans la seconde moitié de ce XVIIIe siècle où se sont épanouies les grâces les plus achevées, a mérité le titre de prince charmant c'est bien Charles-Joseph, prince de Ligne. Comme dans les meilleurs contes de fées, les dames à la baguette magique avaient dû se disputer à qui passerait la première auprès de son berceau. Physique séduisant, charme, esprit, élégance, fortune, rien ne lui manquait. Pas même le nimbe prestigieux d'un grand nom grâce auquel les portes de tous les souverains d'Europe s'ouvraient devant lui avant même qu'il y eût frappé.

Aussi fut-il un prince sans frontière et, avant même que quiconque y eût pensé, pas même lui, un Européen avant la lettre.

« J'aime, disait-il, mon état d'étranger partout : Français en Autriche, Autrichien en France, l'un et l'autre en Russie; j'ai cinq ou six patries, c'est le moyen de se plaire en tous lieux... »

Non seulement il s'y plaisait mais il plaisait, ayant tous les talents, toutes les grâces et se montrant doué en toutes choses mais principalement pour l'amour et l'amitié. Sur ce dernier point, il eut celle de la Grande Catherine, de Frédéric de Prusse, de Talleyrand, de Marie-Antoinette à laquelle il vouait une sorte de vénération ce qui ne l'empêcha nullement d'être l'amant de la Du Barry et l'ami d'une véritable foule de personnages dont la lecture d'un éventuel Gotha de l'époque donnerait une liste assez satisfaisante.

Ses premières années cependant ne lui avaient guère apporté le bonheur dans ce superbe château de Belœil, proche de la frontière belge, où il suffit de pousser une porte pour le retrouver à chaque pas. Son père, Claude-Lamoral, était un terrible petit bonhomme sujet à des crises de fureur tellement intenses qu'elles terrorisaient tout son monde.

« Quand il se mouchait, il avait l'air d'étendre un drapeau; quand il toussait, c'était un coup de canon qui faisait retentir les voûtes; quand il se tournait il faisait rentrer tout le monde sous terre; sa canne avait l'air d'un sceptre ou d'un fouet. Mon père ne m'aimait pas. Je ne sais pourquoi car nous ne nous connaissions pas. Ce n'était pas la mode, alors, d'être bon père ni bon mari. Ma mère avait grand peur de lui. Elle accoucha de moi en grand vertugadin et elle mourut de même quelques années après, tant mon père aimait les cérémonies et l'air de dignité... »

La pauvre Élisabeth de Salm mourut, en effet, âgée à peine de trente-cinq ans, quatre ans après avoir donné le jour à son fils. Outre Charles-Joseph, elle avait également mis au monde deux filles, aussi laides qu'il était charmant, l'aînée surtout, Marie-Christine, gracieusement surnommée « le Grand Diable » mais en qui le père se retrouvait et avec laquelle il avait d'homériques disputes.

A la suite de l'une de ces querelles, il ordonna superbement à Marie-Christine de se retirer dans sa chambre.

« Elle ne veut pas y aller, raconte son frère. Mon père, pour la faire sortir, la traîne avec le fauteuil où elle était et accroche la porte. Et la tête insubordonnée lui dit : " Je savais bien que vous étiez mauvais père, mais vous êtes aussi mauvais cocher. " Cette douce enfant devait mourir chanoinesse de Remiremont... »

Avare à faire rougir Harpagon, Claude-Lamoral tient si

serrés les cordons de sa bourse que, la plupart du temps, Monsieur son fils tire le diable par la queue. Aussi n'émet-il aucune objection lorsque Monsieur son père le fait revenir toutes affaires cessantes de Mons où il tient garnison avec le régiment de Ligne dont il est, naturellement, le plus brillant fleuron. But du voyage : on va marier l'héritier du nom.

A qui? Où? Quand? Comment? Ce sont là des questions qu'aucun garçon soucieux de sa paix intérieure se fût risqué à poser à un tel père. Claude-Lamoral, d'ailleurs, se contente d'indiquer à son fils que l'on part pour Vienne et qu'il ait à faire ses malles en conséquence.

Vienne? Le jeune prince y était deux mois plus tôt ayant définitivement choisi d'y passer les loisirs que lui laissait son service. Il s'y était même bien amusé mais l'idée d'y retourner, flanqué cette fois d'un père si peu récréatif lui souriait infiniment moins. Mais que faire d'autre sinon obéir? D'autant qu'il connaissait, dans l'aristocratie autrichienne plus d'une bien jolie fille dont il se fût parfaitement accommodé comme épouse. Il passa donc tout le voyage à faire des rêves et, en procédant par élimination, à essayer de deviner quelle était celle qui avait réussi l'exploit de se faire agréer par son redoutable géniteur.

Arrivé à destination, on ne lui en dit pas davantage. Claude-Lamoral se rend à la Cour, flanqué de son fils, fait des visites mais sans rien soupçonner de ses intentions. Un soir, les deux hommes s'en vont dîner au palais Kinsky. Grand dîner, beaucoup de monde et pas mal de jeunes filles que Charles-Joseph considère avec une sorte d'avidité. Cette jolie blonde? Ou alors cette brunette?... à moins que cette rousse?... Tout à ses cogitations, il passe le temps du dîner sans parvenir à se faire une opinion. Aussi tombe-t-il des nues quand, une fois rentré au logis, le prince-père lui annonce qu'il sera fiancé dans quelques jours à la princesse Marie-France-Xavière de Liechtenstein...

Au premier abord il ne voit pas du tout de qui il peut

s'agir? Laquelle était-ce donc? Comment cela, laquelle? Mais, sacrebleu, il a soupé à côté d'elle!... La découverte déchaîne une irrésistible hilarité : quoi? cette gamine? Elle ne doit guère avoir plus de douze ans.

« Elle en a quinze et c'est un fort bon âge pour un garçon de dix-huit!... Vous l'épouserez, vous dis-je! »

Pourquoi pas, après tout...

« Huit jours après, j'épousais. J'avais dix-huit ans et ma petite femme en avait quinze. Nous ne nous étions rien dit. C'est ainsi que je fis ce qu'on prétend être la chose la plus sérieuse de la vie : je la trouvais bouffonne pendant quelques semaines et ensuite indifférente... »

Naturellement, le mariage a lieu dans le superbe palais Liechtenstein, construit à la fin du XVIIe siècle, l'un des plus beaux de Vienne, et non moins naturellement avec toute la pompe normale pour une si grande union. C'est le 6 août 1755.

Le soir venu, on se prépare pour la nuit de noces. Les matrones de la famille Liechtenstein sont venues, avant la bénédiction du lit nuptial glisser sous les oreillers quelques reliques familiales particulièrement efficaces afin que Dieu donne vigueur au jeune mari et fécondité à son épouse. Puis le lit est béni en grande cérémonie et la nouvelle princesse de Ligne y est amenée par toutes les femmes de sa parenté tandis que, dans une autre chambre, on prépare Charles-Joseph à entrer dans le sanctuaire.

« On y paraît en robe de chambre et la mienne, au milieu de l'été, était de satin couleur de feu avec des perroquets brodés en or perchés sur une quantité de petits arbres brodés en vert... », écrit-il.

Le malheur, c'est que, cette robe de chambre, il la reconnaît du premier coup d'œil. Elle appartient à son père et elle est loin d'être neuve.

« Quel fut mon étonnement lorsque mon père, avec un air de satisfaction et jouissant de la surprise, me fit passer les bras dans cette vieillerie avec laquelle je lui avais vu essuyer plus de cinquante accès de goutte. Mon père, en revanche, avait l'air du marié et ne portait que des habits brodés sur toutes les coutures... »

Ainsi accoutré et flanqué de Claude-Lamoral ajusté comme un petit-maître, on l'emmène dans la chambre, on l'installe dans le lit où l'attend l'épousée plus morte que vive. On ferme les rideaux, on éteint les lumières et le héros se met à l'ouvrage.

A défaut de beauté, Marie-France avait celle que confèrent quinze printemps et les choses eussent dû se passer normalement. Mais il y avait les reliques! Et le malheur voulut qu'elles se manifestassent de tout autre façon que celle qui leur était habituelle.

Délogés de sous leurs oreillers par le mouvement qu'imprimaient au lit les deux jeunes gens, les reliquaires se mirent à vagabonder dans le lit, s'arrêtant où ils le pouvaient et de préférence sous les reins ou les genoux, ou le dos de Charles-Joseph. Le malheureux ne chassait l'os du métacarpe de saint Jean que pour se retrouver aux prises avec un orteil de saint Gall ou affronté à trois poils de la barbe de saint Joseph bien connu pour la sollicitude avec laquelle il a, de tout temps, veillé sur la conclusion heureuse du mariage.

Le malheureux sortit de là moulu et truffé comme une galantine mais vainqueur. Il en sortit d'ailleurs beaucoup plus tôt qu'il ne le pensait car, à peine venait-il de s'endormir que voilà les matrones, belle-mère en tête, qui reparaissent avec le manque de discrétion inhérent à leurs fonctions. Il ne s'agissait pas d'apporter aux jeunes époux l'agréable café viennois bien chaud qui leur aurait rendu bonne humeur et chaleur mais de leur faire changer de chemises; celles dans lesquelles s'était accompli l'acte majeur de dévirginisation ne devant à aucun prix tomber entre les mains des jeteurs de sorts...

Écœuré, Charles-Joseph choisit d'abandonner le lit, d'enfiler une chemise de jour et, laissant sa femme se rendormir, s'en alla chasser dans la forêt viennoise.

Pendant le voyage de retour à Belœil, il se consola de

cette nuit de noces inconfortable et se dédommagea des charmes un peu simplets de sa princesse en troussant, à Prague, l'une des femmes de chambre de l'hôtel de Waldstein. Puis, une fois Marie-France installée dans les splendeurs du château familial, il s'en alla d'un pas léger voir ailleurs si l'herbe était plus verte.

La guerre de Sept Ans qui allait bientôt éclater lui donnait un prétexte valable pour ne revenir à Belœil que périodiquement, tout juste pour engrosser sa femme à qui cela procurait une saine occupation.

« Étant fort sensible et fort bonne, elle ne gênera personne, pas même moi... »

Il aurait pu dire : surtout moi...

LES NUITS RÉTICENTES

INCONSOMMABLE ROZALA!

S'il avait eu le choix, Hugues Capet, premier roi d'une dynastie destinée à faire quelque bruit dans le monde, eût peut-être préféré un autre genre de fils que celui dont le Ciel l'avait gratifié. Non qu'il ne l'aimât pas ou que le garçon fût malingre ou mal venu. Tout au contraire, à la ressemblance de son père, Robert était taillé pour porter le harnois de guerre : il pliait une barre de fer entre deux doigts comme une vulgaire baguette de coudrier et l'on pouvait espérer d'un tel homme une longue et noble lignée de rois.

Roi, d'ailleurs, Robert l'est déjà depuis un an, en cette année 988, exactement depuis que son père, duc de Neustrie, a été élu roi par les grands. Hugues, désireux d'asseoir sa descendance et peu soucieux de laisser la moindre chance aux vagues résidus carolingiens pouvant surgir ici ou là, a fait couronner son fils peu de temps après lui-même. Malheureusement, le garçon de quinze ans n'a pour la royauté qu'une attirance fort mince et, en dehors de lui, Hugues Capet n'a eu que des filles de son mariage avec Aalis d'Aquitaine. Plus un bâtard qu'il a déjà neutralisé en le confiant à l'Église.

Or, c'est justement l'Église qui attire le plus Robert. Il est pieux (le surnom lui restera), doux, tolérant, aimant la lecture, l'étude et pratiquant l'humilité en toutes circonstances et avec un manque d'à-propos qui met son père hors de lui. Ainsi le garçon ne supporte pas que, pour l'hommage, on s'agenouille devant lui afin de baiser le bas de sa robe ou sa chaussure de lin brodé. Il proclame qu'un roi n'est, après tout, qu'un homme comme les autres et que Dieu seul peut se permettre de voir des hommes prosternés devant lui.

Ces théories, un peu avancées pour les oreilles capétiennes du grand Hugues, valent naturellement à l'imprudent de solides mercuriales paternelles. Robert doit se mettre dans la tête qu'un roi est, d'abord, l'élu de Dieu, son représentant sur la terre et un peu son image. En tout cas au moins autant que les statues. D'ailleurs le peuple ne comprendrait pas qu'il en soit autrement. En conséquence, Robert fera bien de se tenir tranquille la prochaine fois qu'un de ses sujets s'agenouillera devant lui...

Pour ce qui est de la guerre, c'est la même chose : le jeune roi montre beaucoup plus de sympathie au froc noir des moines qu'à la broigne aux écailles d'acier et Hugues se demande ce que fera Robert quand il sera tout seul sur le trône confronté à des vassaux plus que turbulents. Alors il pense que la meilleure chose à faire est de ne pas le laisser seul sur ce trône et qu'en lui donnant pour compagne une femme d'expérience le problème pourrait se trouver résolu. D'autant que l'amour pourrait être un excellent moyen de ramener le garçon dans le cours normal de la vie.

Malheureusement, la « femme d'expérience » qu'il va chercher en a peut-être un peu trop. Un père normalement constitué aurait choisi, pour donner le goût de la vie et de l'amour à un moinillon de seize ans, quelque fillette joliment tournée et en rapport d'âge, ou un peu plus âgée, mais pas beaucoup plus. Or, voulant joindre les intérêts de son fils à ceux du royaume, Hugues s'en va chercher Rozala, fille du roi de Provence et d'Italie du Nord, Bérenger. Rozala est veuve du comte de Flandre, Arnoud II : une jouvencelle de quarante-huit printemps, riche et bien pourvue de terres, certes, mais qui aurait pu sans grand-peine être la grand-mère de son époux. Pour l'expérience, elle n'en manque pas, c'est sûr. Et, naturellement, les flatteurs de la Cour paternelle ne tarissent pas d'éloges sur sa sagesse, son intelligence et son extrême beauté. C'est la Rose de Sâron, le lys dans la vallée, la belle des belles, la rose d'automne plus qu'une autre exquise...

Quand elle arrive à Orléans où doivent se dérouler les noces, on s'aperçoit sans peine que les courtisans – et provençaux encore! – sont déjà ce qu'ils seront toujours : incorrigibles. En dépit de l'apparat qui l'entoure, de la magnificence des robes de soie brodées qui l'emballent et des lourds bijoux qui la parent, la rose d'automne ressemble beaucoup plus à un vigoureux sarment de vigne qu'à une fleur fragile. Par la taille et la naissance c'est vraiment une très haute dame, mais ses charmes ne vont guère plus loin.

A l'aspect de la fiancée, l'impénétrable Hugues Capet se garde bien de laisser paraître son impression. Mais il n'en va pas de même du jeune Hugues, comte de Chalon qui est l'ami d'enfance de Robert.

Les deux garçons se connaissent depuis toujours. Elevés pratiquement ensemble ils ont été aussi camarades d'école, ayant suivi l'un et l'autre à Reims l'enseignement du grand Gerbert, l'ancien berger auvergnat devenu moine dont la science, fantastique pour l'époque, et les idées avancées font chuchoter aux esprits retardataires qu'il a fait un pacte avec le Diable (ce qui ne l'empêchera nullement, par la suite, de devenir pape). Robert et Hugues ont écouté ses leçons avec une véritable passion et pris chez lui le goût de la poésie et des beaux chants liturgiques mais, chez le comte de Chalon, les aspirations sont bien moins mystiques et ils comprend mal l'espèce de fascination que le cloître exerce sur son ami. Un roi, selon lui, ne devrait avoir d'autre ambition que régner, procréer et aimer... mais pas dans les conditions offertes à Robert.

Et Hugues d'aller trouver le roi et de le supplier de se

procurer une autre épouse pour son fils. Cette femme-là, jamais, ne donnera d'enfants. Elle n'en a pas donné à son premier mari et il n'y a aucune raison pour qu'à son âge, elle soit plus féconde. Alors à quoi rime une dynastie sans héritiers?

« Robert aura des enfants plus tard », répond Capet...

Il n'ajoute pas que, dans son idée, Rozala n'est là que pour quelque temps. Il serait bien étonnant qu'elle ne meure pas beaucoup plus tôt que son époux. Et sa dot, elle, sera acquise à tout jamais... Il renvoie donc le jeune Chalon à ses chiens de chasse et s'en va activer les préparatifs du mariage, un mariage qu'il veut aussi chrétien que possible afin qu'au moins la majesté des sacrements inspire à son fils quelque considération et quelque ardeur pour sa femme.

Jamais union ne fut plus consciencieusement bénie. En dehors de la cérémonie où ni l'encens ni les cierges n'avaient été ménagés, on aspergea d'eau sainte tout le contenu de la chambre nuptiale et, naturellement, le lit plus que tout le reste. Puis l'on referma les tentures qui servaient de portes sur les nouveaux époux.

Demeuré seul avec l'imposante dame qui a bien été obligée de déposer ses joyaux et ses soieries, Robert ne sait trop quelle contenance prendre. En tout cas, une chose est certaine : jamais il n'arrivera à investir cette forteresse car il se sent déplorablement privé d'ardeur guerrière. Aussi, après avoir dansé d'un pied sur l'autre pendant un moment en mordillant la chaîne d'or qui lui pend sur la poitrine, il abandonne le combat avant même le premier engagement et, assurant Rozala de son profond respect il s'en va coucher ailleurs, couvrant sa retraite sous l'hypocrite excuse de sa sollicitude pour sa femme. Après une journée aussi épuisante elle a sûrement grand besoin de repos. Il n'ajoute pas « à son âge » mais le cœur y est...

Et il sort tandis que Rozala dépitée essaie vainement de le retenir...

Le lendemain, il se trouve souffrant, et le surlendemain

est un vendredi, jour de pénitence. Et Rozala attend toujours... Avec de moins en moins de patience il faut bien l'avouer. Il lui plaît beaucoup ce jouvenceau couronné et le fait qu'il tarde tant à lui rendre hommage l'indispose. Au bout de trois jours, elle s'en va se plaindre, avec un brin d'aigreur, à un beau-père qui est tout juste un petit peu plus jeune qu'elle...

Hugues Capet est scandalisé et, naturellement, il s'en va toucher deux mots de l'affaire à son garçon :

« Tu l'as épousée, tu dois en faire ta femme, lui dit-il. C'est une question de politesse...

– Mon père, je ne saurais... », se contente de répondre Robert sans entrer plus avant dans les détails de son ignorance. Et le père naturellement s'y trompe. Quelle stupidité de n'avoir pas exigé que Robert fasse quelques gammes avec une servante suffisamment délurée avant de se lancer dans ce concerto pour contrebasse! Bien sûr, le pauvre enfant ne sait pas comment s'y prendre...

Capet s'en va, à son tour, trouver Hugues de Chalon pour lui demander de procurer à son coquebin de fils quelque initiatrice capable de lui apprendre à se montrer galant avec une dame, fût-elle d'âge canonique. Le jeune comte se retient de faire remarquer à ce père entêté qu'il avait bien prévu le désastre mais ne s'en met pas moins aussitôt en campagne, pensant, comme le père, que le plus tôt sera le mieux pour tout le monde et que le vin étant tiré il convient de le boire au plus vite.

Mais il peut aligner indéfiniment proverbes et jolies filles, tout échoue lamentablement : non seulement Robert refuse de toucher à sa femme mais il n'éprouve pas davantage l'envie de toucher aux autres. A croire qu'elles lui font peur. Il suffit d'un sourire un peu alangui, d'un regard un peu appuyé et il pique un fard puis file à la chapelle y chanter vêpres ou complies...

Et cela dura plus de trois ans. Trois ans de refus obstinés de la part de Robert et de bouderies, coupées de scènes de la part de Rozala. Au bout de ce laps de temps, **Hugues**

Capet, de guerre lasse, remercia Rozala et autorisa son fils à la répudier.

« Arrivé à sa dix-neuvième année, écrit le moine Richer, le roi Robert répudia, parce qu'elle était vieille, sa femme Rozala, italienne de nation. Cet acte criminel de répudiation fut censuré alors par quelques hommes d'un esprit sage, mais en secret cependant et il n'éprouva pas d'opposition ouverte... »

L'opposition, elle, n'allait guère tarder à se manifester. Quelques mois après le départ de Rozala, en 993, le jeune Robert tombait amoureux, mais amoureux fou, d'une cousine : Berthe de Bourgogne. Elle était plus âgée que lui, elle était mariée à Eudes, comte de Blois, et elle avait quatre enfants mais, dès qu'il la vit, Robert ne songea plus qu'à une seule chose : s'approprier Berthe. Mais comment? La manière directe, mérovingienne en quelque sorte, eût consisté à faire massacrer Eudes par des sicaires bien entraînés mais les aspirations à la sainteté de Robert ne s'accommodaient pas de ce moyen. Il trouva mieux.

Sur ses terres, Eudes avait à endurer un voisin singulièrement pénible : le comte d'Anjou, Foulques Nerra, une sorte de forban bâtisseur de donjons, noir de poil, noir de peau et encore plus noir de conscience. Sans scrupules, sans pitié et sans autre loi que son bon plaisir, ce joyeux personnage devait passer sa vie à semer autour de lui, outre les donjons, la richesse et la misère, la torture et le sang puis à galoper périodiquement sur la route de Jérusalem pour obtenir le pardon de ses énormes péchés. Après quoi ragaillardi et purifié, Foulques rentrait chez lui et recommençait de plus belle jusqu'au prochain voyage.

Ce fut lui que Robert jeta sournoisement dans les jambes du comte de Blois. Cela donna trois ans d'une guerre meurtrière qui d'ailleurs ne vint pas à bout du comte Eudes. Ce fut une grippe qui s'en chargea. Eudes prit froid, alla se coucher et mourut au moment où l'on s'y attendait le moins. Berthe était veuve.

Il restait à Robert à dédommager Foulques Nerra de ses bons offices, à lui payer un nouveau voyage à Jérusalem... puis à épouser Berthe quelques semaines après la mort d'Hugues Capet.

On sait la suite : le refus de l'Église, puis l'excommunication, l'interdit, l'anathème majeur fulminé contre les coupables enfermés dans un palais où les rares serviteurs passaient à la flamme tous les objets qu'ils touchaient, la terreur à travers le royaume, attisée par l'approche de l'an mille et les bruits de fin du monde, enfin la soumission après deux ans de bonheur maudit, la répudiation de Berthe et le retour à la vie du royaume en 998...

Quatre ans plus tard, Robert, décidé à assurer sa dynastie, épousait Constance d'Arles. Elle était belle mais mauvaise comme la gale et traînait après elle toute une cour de jolis troubadours que Robert, revenu à une intense piété, ne pouvait regarder sans méfiance. Mais quoi? Cette chipie de Constance lui donna cinq enfants et il n'en demandait pas plus. Le vaisseau capétien pouvait continuer hardiment son chemin...

LA NUIT AU DÉBOTTÉ :
HENRI IV ET MARIE DE MÉDICIS

Dans les premiers jours du mois d'octobre 1600, Sully s'en vint déclarer joyeusement à son maître :

« Sire, nous venons de vous marier... »

S'il s'attendait à un écho enthousiaste, il fut déçu : Henri IV «demeura un instant étourdi, puis il se mit à arpenter sa chambre à grands pas, rongeant ses ongles et visiblement en proie à une grande émotion... Enfin, frappant du poing la paume ouverte de sa main gauche, il s'écria, non sans exhaler un énorme soupir :

— « Fort bien donc, s'il n'est pas d'autre remède. Puisque, pour le bien de mon royaume, vous dites que je dois me marier, eh bien, marions-nous!... »

Puis il s'en alla retrouver sa maîtresse, l'insupportable et dangereuse, mais ravissante, Henriette d'Entragues.

En fait, il était déjà légalement marié. A Florence, les contrats venaient d'être signés et, le 5 octobre, le beau duc de Bellegarde, qui avait été l'amant de Gabrielle d'Estrées, épousait par procuration Marie de Médicis, nièce du grand-duc Ferdinand Ier – le méfiant époux de Christine de Lorraine qui avait placé sa nuit de noces sous le signe de l'urinal.

C'était beaucoup à cause de lui qu'Henri IV, alors follement amoureux de la demoiselle d'Entragues, s'était résigné à ce mariage. Ferdinand s'était toujours montré un ami et un allié fidèle. C'était lui qui avait réconcilié l'ancien « parpaillot » avec le Saint-Siège, lui encore qui avait poussé la Sérénissime République de Venise à reconnaître, bonne première, ce roi de France « de hasard, sans sou ni maille [1] », lui enfin qui avait, inlassablement, ouvert sa bourse pour conforter le trône mal cimenté de son ami. A maintes reprises, il avait fourni à Henri les sommes nécessaires à l'entretien de son armée et les circonstances étaient nombreuses où le roi de France avait fait appel à sa bourse. Résultat : en 1600, les dettes d'Henri envers Ferdinand se montaient à la coquette somme de 973 450 ducats d'or qu'il était parfaitement incapable de rembourser.

A vrai dire, ses dettes ne lui causaient aucune insomnie. C'était Sully qui s'en souciait pour lui. Or, un an environ avant la conclusion du mariage, le roi avait dit à son ministre :

« Le duc de Florence a une nièce que l'on dit assez belle; mais étant d'une des moindres maisons de la chrétienté qui porte le titre de prince, n'y ayant pas plus de soixante ou quatre-vingts ans que ses devanciers n'étaient qu'au rang des plus illustres bourgeois de leur ville et de la même race que la reine-mère Catherine de Médicis qui a tant fait de maux à la France et à moi en particulier, j'appréhende cette alliance de crainte d'y rencontrer aussi mal pour moi, les miens et l'État... »

Cette confidence en forme d'hésitation n'était pas, comme l'on dit, tombée dans l'oreille d'un sourd. Une chose était certaine : Marie de Médicis était fort riche. Sa dot pouvait, non seulement éteindre les plus grosses dettes, mais encore procurer à la France les ressources dont elle avait le plus grand besoin. Sourd aux incessantes querelles et raccommodages du roi et de son Henriette dont il avait fait une marquise de Verneuil, laquelle prétendait se faire épouser, Sully, impavide et obstiné, avait poursuivi les tractations en vue du mariage. C'était à présent chose faite et il n'était plus possible de revenir en arrière.

---

1. La maille était une petite monnaie de cuivre.

Le 17 octobre, en effet, la nouvelle reine de France s'embarquait à Livourne à bord d'une galère dont la vue allait laisser les Marseillais pantois quand elle ferait son entrée dans leur port – qui étant alors le seul n'était pas encore Vieux. C'était une énorme machine entièrement dorée, jusqu'à la ligne de flottaison tout au moins, décorée aux armes de France et aux armes de Toscane. Et quelles armes! Celles de France tout en saphirs et diamants, celles de Toscane tout en rubis, émeraudes et saphirs. Derrière ce monument qui fait un peu nouveau riche, il y a seize autres galères portant 7 000 hommes de troupe et deux mille Florentins, familiers, seigneurs ou serviteurs de la princesse : un vrai débarquement! Tout ce monde étale un luxe ébouriffant.

A vrai dire, il faut cela pour que les gens de Marseille se décident à ovationner leur nouvelle souveraine car elle est loin d'être belle et comme elle ne sait pas sourire, elle n'est même pas sympathique.

Elle a « le naturel terriblement robuste et fort », elle est « riche de taille, grasse et en bon point ». Au XXᵉ siècle, la jeunesse populaire voyant passer son équivalent articulerait les mots de « dondon » ou de « mémère » et si Rubens a tiré de son mariage une série de peinture où la luminosité de la chair trouve moyen d'éclater au milieu de la luxuriance des couleurs, il ne lui a tout de même pas fait grâce d'un centimètre et, à vingt-six ans, elle en paraît quarante.

A l'époque, d'ailleurs, les beautés abondantes sont assez prisées. On aime qu'une femme ait de la fesse et du téton. Les Flamandes jouissent, en cette matière, d'une réputation flatteuse, sauf en Provence peut-être où les goûts sont différents. Avec Marie de Médicis, le pinceau courtisan de Rubens a pu s'en donner à cœur joie en exaltant ce qui est passable, en gommant ce qui l'est moins.

Certes « le teint est fort blanc quoiqu'un peu grossier », les bras sont beaux et la gorge opulente. On ne voit pas comment il pourrait en être autrement. Mais – dans une

description honnête de la nouvelle reine il y a beaucoup de
« mais » ou de « quoique » – les traits du visage sont lourds,
les yeux plutôt ronds et sans éclat. « Rarement, écrit
Philippe Erlanger, visage refléta si fidèlement un caractère. Le premier regard suffit à faire comprendre que Sa
Majesté est sotte, orgueilleuse, violente, opiniâtre, indo-
lente et facile à gouverner... » C'est, en fait, très exactement
le caractère qu'elle révélera durant son temps de règne
avec, en outre, une absence totale de cœur, un égoïsme hors
de pair et une tendance marquée à l'ingratitude. Ce n'est ni
une belle femme ni une bonne femme mais elle est
follement riche, elle a le goût du faste et elle s'y connaît
mieux en pierreries – qu'elle adore – qu'un joaillier du
Ponte Vecchio.

De son côté, l'idée d'épouser un homme de vingt ans plus
âgé qu'elle ne lui sourirait guère s'il n'avait l'auréole
prestigieuse de la Couronne. D'abord, elle est amoureuse
d'un des deux frères Orsini, Paolo et Virginiò, qui font
partie de sa suite. Peut-être même des deux... Ensuite elle
n'ignore pas grand-chose des aventures amoureuses de son
futur époux mais elle se croit de taille à mettre bon ordre
dans sa maison. Sa sœur de lait, cette étrange Leonora
Galigaï qui ne la quitte pas, ne lui répète-t-elle pas à
longueur de journée que le Béarnais ne vivra pas
éternellement et qu'elle sera une grande reine?

Le contraste est flagrant entre ces deux femmes que l'on
ne voit jamais l'une sans l'autre. Marie est une grande
génisse blonde, Leonora, noire comme un pruneau avec des
yeux de chat, est presque naine et hystérique mais elle est
d'une dangereuse intelligence. Une intelligence dont elle
animera la marionnette qu'elle s'est donnée pour idole : le
séduisant et vaniteux Concino Concini qui fait, lui aussi,
partie du voyage.

Le mariage doit avoir lieu à Lyon. Depuis plusieurs
semaines Henri IV est en guerre contre le duc de Savoie au
sujet du marquisat de Saluces et la base de ses opérations
est Grenoble. Lyon fera un bon point de jonction entre les

fiancés : l'un venant de Marseille et l'autre des bords de l'Isère.

Avec sa vaste escorte, Marie de Médicis voyage à petites journées paresseuses, en suivant le Rhône, d'abord jusqu'à Avignon où le légat du pape offre à la nouvelle reine une somptueuse réception. Il y a bal au Palais des Papes dont la splendeur est intacte. Puis, les danses terminées, et comme Marie de Médicis songe à se retirer, les grandes tapisseries tendues sur les murs de la grande salle s'abaissent et laissent voir des tables illuminées et toutes servies. Le banquet est digne d'un souverain pontife et, au dessert, chacune des dames reçoit en présent la statue en sucre d'une divinité mythologique...

C'est à regret que la Florentine quitte la cité du Rhône dont la lumière lui rappelle sa ville natale, un regret qui s'accentue quand son cortège, doublé de celui du légat, rencontre le mistral. Il fait froid, soudainement, et il faut bien se rendre à l'évidence : on est en novembre et le temps est de moins en moins beau.

Lorsque l'on arrive aux abords de Lyon, le 9 décembre, il neige et même il gèle. Il y a du verglas et du givre partout ce qui est aussi inhabituel que désagréable. Néanmoins, le château de La Mothe prévu pour y accueillir la reine est aussi confortablement équipé que possible. De grands feux brûlent partout et, dès que le train de la reine est entré, on referme soigneusement toutes les issues et même on relève l'antique pont-levis.

C'est devant ce pont-levis qu'arrive, tard dans la soirée, une troupe de cavaliers transis qui réclament l'hospitalité. Les gardes font la sourde oreille. Et même ils crient aux intrus de passer leur chemin et d'aller se faire pendre ailleurs. Cela pourrait durer longtemps si l'un des cavaliers ne s'avançait et n'ordonnait d'un ton sans réplique d'ouvrir devant lui : c'est le Roi qui a voulu surprendre sa « femme » et la voir sans l'apparat des rencontres officielles.

Aussitôt, c'est le branle-bas de combat. Le pont-levis

s'abat, la herse se relève, les portes s'ouvrent, les porteurs de torches et les valets se précipitent tandis que les chevaux entrent au galop.

Henri IV saute à terre, secouant le givre de ses vêtements et de sa barbe. Où est la reine? On lui dit qu'elle est en train de souper, seule, dans la grande galerie. On veut la prévenir mais il s'y oppose : que l'on n'en fasse rien! Henri entend jeter discrètement son premier coup d'œil.

Pendant ce temps, dans la galerie, Marie fait honneur à la cuisine lyonnaise et ne prend pas garde à l'entrée soudaine de Bellegarde, qu'elle connaît déjà, et de Bassompierre qu'elle ne connaît pas – mais des têtes nouvelles elle en voit tous les jours! -- qui saluent et restent près de la porte et la bouchent en partie. Ce qu'elle mange doit être délicieux car Marie ne s'aperçoit pas de la présence du roi. En effet, caché derrière ses deux amis, Henri observe sa nouvelle épouse et la détaille...

C'est seulement quand elle a fini que celle-ci se rend compte de l'attitude bizarre des deux hommes. Devinant quelque chose d'anormal, elle refuse alors les autres plats qu'on lui présente puis, se déclarant fatiguée, se lève pour regagner sa chambre. Cette façon qu'ont les Français de la regarder ainsi lui déplaît souverainement.

On lui apprend, alors que le Roi vient d'arriver et, avec un cri effarouché, elle n'en bat que plus vite en retraite, pressée de retrouver l'abri, inviolable à son sens, de son appartement particulier.

Si elle pense que le nouveau venu n'en franchira pas le seuil elle se trompe. A peine est-elle entrée qu'un petit bonhomme cuirassé, botté et éperonné se précipite à sa suite, se rue sur elle, la prend dans ses bras et l'embrasse sur la bouche. Tout ce qu'elle a pu voir c'est qu'il a un grand nez rougi par le froid, une barbe grisonnante et que son œil bleu brille à la fois de curiosité et de plaisir anticipé.

Tandis que les dames plongent dans leurs révérences et

que la duchesse de Nemours, première dame, qu'Henri a
saluée courtoisement après ses effusions, s'apprête à servir
de truchement – elle est née Anne d'Este et l'italien est sa
langue maternelle – le roi s'écrie en se frottant les
mains.

« Il fait si froid que j'espère que vous m'offrirez la moitié
de votre lit, Madame, car, étant venu à cheval, je n'ai pas
pu apporter le mien... »

La proposition est si verte que Mme de Nemours
cherche en vain des circonlocutions pour en atténuer la
brutalité. Elle objecte que le mariage n'est pas encore béni
par le légat du pape et que, peut-être, il conviendrait
d'attendre un peu. De son côté, Marie de Médicis qui n'a
pas très bien saisi ce qu'on lui veut mais qui entend faire
preuve de bonne grâce, déclare, sans trop savoir à quoi elle
s'expose, qu'elle n'est venue que pour complaire et obéir à
la volonté du roi... »

La cause est entendue et l'on imagine sans peine le large
sourire du Vert-Galant. Que l'on mette donc la reine au lit!
Pendant ce temps, il ira faire un brin de toilette. Et les
femmes de s'empresser.

Mais Marie qui a enfin compris ce qui va se passer, perd
contenance, ainsi que le rapporte l'un des gentilshommes
de la suite du légat, Agucchi, qui fut témoin de la scène :

« Quand la reine comprit les intentions du roi, elle fut
saisie d'une telle frayeur qu'elle devint froide comme la
glace et que, portée dans son lit, elle ne put s'y réchauffer,
même dans des draps brûlants... »

Tandis que bassinoires et « moines » s'activent pour
réchauffer la reine de France, Henri IV reparaît. Le brin
de toilette a vraiment dû être tout petit pour avoir été aussi
vite troussé!... Tallemant des Réaux prétend que, durant
cette nuit inattendue, Marie de Médicis «quelque bien
garnie qu'elle fût d'essences de son pays, ne laissa pas
d'être terriblement parfumée par l'odeur de gousset de son
époux, au point qu'elle s'en trouva mal... »

Le bon roi Henri, en effet, se lavait peu et son époque fut

sans doute l'une des plus négligées de l'histoire de France. Il sentait mauvais des pieds... et d'ailleurs et, selon un contemporain qui, après tout, était peut-être bien une contemporaine, il « puait le bouc et l'ail ». Habituée à tous les raffinements luxueux de la toilette, à l'usage des parfums les plus rares, Marie de Médicis dut, en effet, trouver l'épreuve pénible.

Au lendemain cependant, elle eut le bon goût de n'en point faire état, se montra, pour une fois, souriante et déclara aimablement « qu'elle était bien aise de l'avoir trouvé (le roi) plus jeune qu'elle ne le pensait et qu'elle ne le pouvait croire d'après sa barbe blanche... »

Quant à Henri, il dit qu'il « avait été attrapé de l'avoir trouvée plus belle et plus gracieuse qu'il ne se l'était persuadé... »

Est-ce le début d'une tendre lune de miel ? En aucune façon. Ce n'est que simple eau bénite de cour destinée aux oreilles du légat et des envoyés de Ferdinand de Médicis. Néanmoins jusqu'à la date du mariage qui eut lieu huit jours après, le 18 décembre, Henri ne quitta guère Marie et lui fit une cour assez convenable.

Mais, à peine mariée, il la plantait là sous prétexte d'affaires urgentes qui le réclamaient à Paris et, voyageant par terre et par eau, il atteignit en deux jours la capitale... qu'il ne fit que traverser pour s'en aller rejoindre à Verneuil son indispensable Henriette d'Entragues. La belle venait d'accoucher et son empire sur Henri était plus puissant que jamais.

Pendant ce temps, Marie avait repris son lent et solennel voyage à travers le royaume et ce fut seulement dans les tout premiers jours de février qu'elle fit son entrée dans Paris, un Paris ébloui par les splendeurs de sa suite et qui lui réserva un accueil encourageant.

Beaucoup plus encourageant, à coup sûr, que celui du Louvre « mi-ruiné, mi-construit, mi-antique, mi-moderne » qui était dans un tel état que la malheureuse crut à une mauvaise plaisanterie : ce n'était, en effet, que peintures sales, tentures déchirées ou montrant la corde et meubles bons pour le rebut. On était vraiment fort loin des merveilles du palais Pitti...

Henri d'ailleurs n'était pas là et la jeune mariée apprit du même coup qu'elle avait une rivale et que cette rivale allait lui en faire voir de toutes les couleurs. Mais ce fut Marie qui l'emporta. Elle avait pour elle la richesse – et le vieux Louvre grincheux s'en aperçut, qu'elle transforma en résidence au luxe tapageur – et la plus ponctuelle des fécondités.

Quand elle en fut à six enfants, la favorite, qui avait été détrônée récemment par la toute jeune et ravissante Charlotte de Montmorency, rendit les armes, fit sa soumission et choisit de l'aider à effacer du siècle un époux qu'elle avait toujours détesté...

LA NUIT DE L'OBÉISSANCE :
LOUIS XIII ET ANNE D'AUTRICHE

Avec ses Italiens arrogants, sa naine hystérique et le beau Concini qu'elle avait fini par épouser, avec ses astrologues, ses mages et ses parfumeurs, Marie de Médicis devenue régente fut un désastre pour la France. Le seul bien qu'elle lui fit — encore que ce fut tout à fait involontaire — fut l'arrivée aux affaires du jeune évêque de Luçon, Armand-Jean du Plessis de Richelieu, qui eut l'habileté de ne pas laisser soupçonner son génie tant que vécut Concini.

Elle eut, entre autres méfaits, une influence néfaste sur la nuit de noces de son fils, le jeune roi Louis XIII, bien que, pour une fois, ses intentions fussent tout à fait louables. Mais c'était une femme qui ignorait pudeur et délicatesse... Le résultat en fut la mésentente tenace qui, au fil des années, s'installa entre le roi et la reine de France.

C'est à Bordeaux, au mois de novembre 1615 qu'a lieu le mariage qui est d'ailleurs un double mariage : Louis XIII va épouser Doña Ana, infante d'Espagne et sa sœur, Elisabeth, va devenir la femme du frère de Doña Ana : Philippe, prince des Asturies, le futur Philippe IV. Ce sont tous des enfants : Louis a quatorze ans, Ana six jours de moins que lui, Elisabeth a treize ans et Philippe dix ans. Mais les choses se font avec un parfait synchronisme car, au jours précis où, dans la cathédrale Saint-André de

Bordeaux, le cardinal de Sourdis marie Madame Elisabeth au prince des Asturies par le truchement du duc de Guise qui tient la place de l'époux, à Burgos, en l'église des Augustins, l'archevêque de la ville royale unit le roi de France, représenté par le duc de Lerma, Premier ministre, à l'Infante.

Et, presque aussitôt après les cérémonies, les nouvelles mariées se mettent en route afin de se trouver au même instant de part et d'autre de la Bidassoa pour y être échangées à la manière des prisonnières politiques qu'elles vont être en fait, mais avec le faste en plus.

Tandis que voyagent les princesses, les princes tuent le temps comme il leur plaît. On ignore ce que fait alors le futur roi d'Espagne mais, pour sa part, Sa Majesté Très-Chrétienne a choisi de s'exercer au noble métier du pâtissier en confectionnant elle-même des massepains dont elle raffole. A d'autres instants Louis XIII fait voler ses oiseaux, joue avec ses soldats qui ne sont pas de plomb mais d'argent... et s'introduit en compagnie des jeunes garnements qui lui tiennent lieu de cour dans la chambre à confitures du cardinal de Sourdis qu'il met joyeusement à sac. Il semble avoir besoin d'un renfort de sucreries pour se remettre du chagrin que lui cause le départ de sa petite sœur Elisabeth qu'il aime beaucoup.

Il réussit surtout à se donner une bonne indigestion. Mais cela a l'avantage de le distraire de soucis plus graves. Il y a cet affreux Concini, devenu le tout-puissant maréchal d'Ancre, qu'il exècre. Et puis il y a le contexte politique et, en cette fin d'automne 1615, il n'a rien de réjouissant... Une fois de plus, la France frise la guerre civile. Il a fallu lever une armée pour tenir en respect les princes brouillons : Condé, Bouillon, Longueville et Mayenne – toujours les mêmes quel que soit le siècle ! – qui rassemblent leurs troupes et publient manifeste sur manifeste. Le prétexte en est, bien sûr, Concini que l'invraisemblable faiblesse de la reine mère a fait scandaleusement riche, mais, en fait, Condé travaille pour lui-même.

Le prince a fait alliance de nouveau avec les huguenots. Il s'efforce de rallumer les guerres de Religion et se pose ouvertement en adversaire des mariages espagnols. Autant de raisons pour Marie de Médicis, qui tient à ces mariages, de presser le mouvement, de raccourcir les distances d'où le choix de Bordeaux. Il faut qu'à la fin de l'année tout soit définitivement réglé afin que tout rentre dans l'ordre...

Pour le jeune roi, l'année qui s'en va vers sa fin a été assez éprouvante. En mars, il a mené le deuil de la reine Margot, première épouse d'Henri IV, morte dans son superbe hôtel de la rue de Seine. Il l'appelait « Maman, ma fille » et l'aimait bien. Aussi l'a-t-il beaucoup pleurée. En juin, il a encore pleuré en posant, sur le Pont-Neuf, la première pierre du socle chargé de supporter la grande statue équestre de son père et, pour finir, en novembre il vient de pleurer beaucoup au mariage d'Elisabeth. Au milieu de toutes ces larmes, une seule vraie joie mais en forme de révélation : M. de Pluvinel, lui ayant donné sa première leçon, lui a dit qu'il était un homme de cheval-né et qu'il serait un grand cavalier... Ce sont de ces choses qui marquent un adolescent et qui lui donnent l'impression d'être bien près de devenir homme tout court.

A présent, il attend l'Infante sans émotion excessive. On lui a dit qu'elle était charmante, mais il ne s'intéresse pas encore à la nature féminine et pense qu'elle sera surtout, et pendant pas mal de temps, une compagne de jeux. Aussi l'attend-il comme il attendrait un camarade : avec une satisfaction mêlée de curiosité.

Mais, lorsqu'il apprend, le 21 novembre, que Doña Ana approche de Bordeaux, il décide d'aller à sa rencontre « incognito » afin de voir à quoi elle ressemble. Il arrive à Castres, à cinq lieues de la ville, juste à temps pour assister au relais et voir l'Infante, qui était allée se réchauffer chez un notable, remonter en voiture et, du fond de son propre carrosse, il l'examine soigneusement mais sans se montrer.

Quand le cortège est reparti, il ordonne à son cocher de

suivre à distance. C'est seulement à deux lieues de Bordeaux qu'il décide de paraître, ordonne que l'on presse l'allure et que l'on remonte le cortège jusqu'à la voiture où se tient la jeune fille que nous appellerons désormais Anne puisqu'elle est en France.

Arrivé à la même hauteur, le cocher royal retient ses chevaux et Louis, se penchant à la portière crie gaiement en se montrant lui-même du geste :

« Io son incognito!... Io son el Rey incognito! »

Un large salut, un grand sourire puis il crie au cocher :

« Touche, cocher! Touche!... »

Et l'attelage royal, lancé au grand galop distance rapidement les voitures de l'Infante, beaucoup plus lourdes avec leurs chargements de bagages. Les deux jeunes époux se reverront le soir même à l'évêché de Bordeaux qui est logis du roi.

Tout de suite, Louis traite Anne en camarade mais avec une nuance de galanterie charmante. Ainsi, le 22 octobre, il se rend chez elle qui est en train de s'habiller, lui présente M. de Souvré, son gouverneur et son médecin Héroard puis bavarde joyeusement. L'Infante a un petit problème : elle cherche une plume incarnate pour la mêler à la blanche de sa coiffure.

« Le Roy, raconte Héroard, lui présente son chapeau où il y avait des deux, luy disant qu'elle en prît ce qu'elle en voudrait : elle le fit et le luy rend. Soudain, il lui dit : " Il faut aussi que vous me donniez un de vos nœuds " qui estoit incarnat. Elle, en souriant le lui donne et il l'applique en façon d'enseigne au pied de sa plume... »

Le 25 octobre, c'est le mariage à la cathédrale. Rarement on a vu couple juvénile mieux assorti. Louis est aussi brun qu'Anne est blonde. Il est tout vêtu de satin blanc brodé d'or, comme un prince de légende. Elle porte le long manteau royal en velours violet fleurdelisé d'or et une couronne étincelante. Elle est charmante avec un teint de fleur et les plus jolies mains du monde.

C'est une cérémonie en forme de conte de fées... à ceci près qu'il a fallu, au dernier moment, remplacer au pied levé le cardinal de Sourdis : l'amateur de confitures n'a rien trouvé de mieux, en effet, que de prendre d'assaut, la nuit précédente, le Château-Trompette pour en extraire un de ses amis de cœur, un certain Hautcastel, condamné à mort pour Dieu sait quelle folie et dont la reine mère a refusé la grâce. Plantant là les pompes royales Son Eminence a choisi la liberté en compagnie de son ami. Il a fallu aller chercher l'évêque de Saintes pour le remplacer...

Le mariage ayant eu lieu à cinq heures de l'après-midi, il n'a pas été prévu de banquet, contrairement à l'habitude. La journée a déjà été suffisamment longue et, en rentrant à l'évêché vers six heures, Louis conduit Anne directement à sa chambre – une belle chambre tendue de rares tapisseries d'or et d'argent représentant l'histoire d'Artémise. Louis la salue, lui souhaite le bonsoir, l'embrasse et rentre chez lui en demandant, tant il se sent fatigué, qu'on le serve au lit.

S'il espère une soirée paisible, il se trompe. Marie de Médicis ne l'entend pas ainsi : pour faire taire Condé et sa bande de trublions, il ne suffit pas que le mariage soit célébré, il faut encore qu'il soit consommé. Ainsi, pour donner d'abord à son fils quelques idées folâtres, lui dépêche-t-elle quelques gentilshommes particulièrement avertis en matière de femmes. Guise, Gramont et deux ou trois autres s'en viennent donc prendre position autour du lit royal et, sous couleur de « donner de l'assurance » au jeune roi entament le chapitre des « bonnes histoires ». Celles de l'époque sont d'une verdeur toute rabelaisienne et, pour un pudique tel que l'est Louis, elles n'ont rien d'encourageant. Il rit un peu, du bout des lèvres. Visiblement cela ne l'amuse guère et il aimerait bien mieux dormir afin d'être dispos pour la chasse du lendemain.

Malheureusement pour lui il ne saurait en être question car voici la reine mère qui fait son entrée.

« Mon fils, dit-elle, ce n'est pas tout d'être marié. Il faut que vous veniez voir la reine, votre femme, qui vous attend... »

Si Louis étouffe un soupir, c'est discrètement. Il a trop l'habitude d'obéir pour oser protester.

« Madame, dit-il poliment, je n'attendais que votre commandement. Je m'en vas, s'il vous plaît, la trouver avec vous. »

On lui donne sa robe de chambre, ses bottines fourrées et le voilà parti, suivi de sa nourrice, de son médecin, du marquis de Souvré et du marquis de Rambouillet. Beringhen, le premier valet de chambre ouvre la marche armé d'un chandelier. Il est alors huit heures du soir.

Anne est déjà couchée, sa nourrice auprès d'elle lorsque le petit cortège pénètre chez elle. La reine mère s'approche du lit et dit :

« Ma fille, voici votre mari que je vous amène; recevez-le auprès de vous et l'aimez bien, je vous prie. »

Elle reste dans la ruelle tandis que Louis se couche. Puis elle se penche sur eux et parle quelques instants, mais si bas que personne ne peut entendre. Pourtant chacun peut voir que les deux enfants ont rougi. Elle les quitte, revient vers le centre de la chambre.

« Allons! dit-elle. Sortons tous d'ici!... »

Qu'a-t-elle dit à ces deux enfants? Quel conseil... ou quel ordre a-t-elle donné avec cette brutalité qui la distingue si souvent? Elle ignore la tendresse et, fréquemment, son comportement a frôlé la grossièreté et la vulgarité. Sans songer à s'encombrer de périphrases elle a dû, fidèle à ses habitudes, appeler un chat un chat et indiquer, en quelques mots sans nuances, ce qu'il convenait de faire. D'où la rougeur des deux visages...

Avant de quitter la chambre, elle ordonne aux deux nourrices de demeurer et de laisser le roi et la reine ensemble pendant environ une heure et demie. En tout cas pas plus de deux heures...

« A dix heures un quart, note le médecin Héroard, il (le roi) revint après avoir dormi environ une heure et fait deux fois, à ce qu'il nous dit. Il y paraissait : le g... était rouge... »

En effet, dès son retour, Héroard, qui aime son jeune maître, l'examine avant de le remettre au lit. Les notes qu'il prend, pour lui-même d'ailleurs, semblent difficiles à mettre en doute. D'autre part, les deux nourrices restées dans la chambre affirmeront l'une et l'autre que le jeune roi a bel et bien consommé son mariage et par deux fois.

Pourtant, il existe une thèse selon laquelle cette « nuit de noces » n'aurait été qu'un simulacre. On aurait « fait semblant » toujours à cause de Condé que l'on savait déjà prêt à attaquer le mariage. Mais faire semblant impliquait un souci de délicatesse envers la pudeur de ces deux adolescents dont Marie de Médicis était bien incapable et dont le ton de l'époque même, l'une des plus grossières de notre histoire, était fort éloigné.

Les conséquences de l'ordre donné par la reine mère porteront loin dans le temps. Les deux enfants que l'on contraint à ce jeu sans nuances sont totalement inexpérimentés. Le jeune roi ne ressemble en rien à son père sur le plan charnel. Les débordements de ce joyeux paillard dont il lui est arrivé d'être le témoin consterné et les drames domestiques qu'ils entraînaient lui ont inspiré une certaine répugnance pour l'amour physique. Pour l'Histoire qui se plaît aux surnoms, il sera d'ailleurs « Louis le Chaste », un sobriquet peu fréquent chez les Bourbons.

Or, voilà que, sans transition, il passe des confitures aux réalités physiques du mariage, des réalités qu'il juge sales et dégradantes et auxquelles il ne se pliera que par devoir et par obéissance...

Le résultat est piètre. Il a dû être très maladroit et, pour la petite reine, l'épreuve fut certainement pénible, en admettant qu'il ait réussi à la déflorer, ce qui n'est pas certain, même après deux tentatives. Les rapports des nourrices, pas plus que les notes d'Héroard ne font mention de l'examen des draps. Quoi qu'il en soit, **Anne** d'Autriche ne se retrouvera pas, au lendemain de ses noces, amoureuse de son jeune mari.

Dans les jours qui suivent, l'entourage royal pourra constater que les jeunes époux n'éprouvent guère de plaisir à se trouver ensemble, qu'ils rougissent et se montrent gênés. De toute évidence, la conclusion hâtive et brutale de leur jour de gloire demeure entre eux. Il faudra beaucoup de temps pour que son souvenir s'atténue suffisamment. Il faudra quatre ans...

C'est seulement le 25 janvier 1619 que Louis entrera de nouveau dans le lit d'Anne. Encore faudra-t-il l'encourager sérieusement à rééditer une expérience qui lui fait peur car, durant ces quatre années, ses connaissances amoureuses en sont restées au même point. Or, la jeune reine est devenue très belle, donc plus impressionnante...

Évidemment, Louis a changé, lui aussi. Depuis deux ans, depuis le coup de pistolet de Vitry qui, sur le pont du Louvre a fait justice de l'infâme Concini, Louis est le maître chez lui. Il serait temps qu'il le devînt aussi auprès de sa femme.

Un double mariage va l'y engager.

Le 11 janvier 1619, le roi et la reine signent le contrat de mariage de Christine de France, sœur de Louis XIII, avec le prince de Piémont, Victor-Amédée de Savoie. Et, à cette occasion, le nonce apostolique glisse respectueusement au roi.

« Sire, je ne crois pas que vous voudriez recevoir cette honte que votre sœur ait un fils avant que Votre Majesté n'ait un dauphin? »

Louis rougit, marmonne qu'il y pensera mais en fait il est très embarrassé. Hypernerveux, il craint comme le feu de rééditer la nuit de Bordeaux. Il lui plairait assez, bien sûr, d'avoir un fils et même de se montrer brillant aux yeux de sa femme afin de lui faire oublier la pénible expérience vécue sous l'œil curieux des nourrices. Mais il sait bien qu'il n'a aucune technique et, d'ailleurs, il ne connaît pas grand-chose au mécanisme d'un corps féminin.

Or, au Louvre, un second mariage se prépare : celui de la demi-sœur du roi par la grâce de Gabrielle d'Estrées, Catherine-Henriette de Vendôme avec le duc d'Elbœuf, Charles II de Lorraine. Et chacun, dans l'entourage de Louis, de l'encourager à bien observer ce qui va se passer.

Pour mieux observer encore, celui-ci, au soir du 20 janvier, assiste au coucher des nouveaux époux comme le veut la coutume mais ne se retire pas avec le reste de la Cour. Il va rester là jusqu'à onze heures du soir afin d'assister à la consommation du mariage et de recevoir ainsi, du nouveau couple, une manière de leçon de choses. Leçon qu'on lui dispense volontiers.

L'époque est toujours aussi peu délicate. En outre, la fille de la Belle Gabrielle, sûre de sa beauté, ne s'encombre d'aucune pudeur superflue. Non seulement elle se prête de la meilleure grâce du monde à la démonstration mais encore, une fois la leçon terminée, elle déclare gracieusement au roi :

« Sire, faites vous aussi la même chose avec la reine et bien vous ferez! »

Louis XIII rentre chez lui tout songeur. Certains espéraient le voir courir aussitôt chez la reine pour mettre en pratique sa science toute neuve mais il n'en fait rien. Il a besoin d'assimiler tout cela et choisit d'aller se coucher. Mais le lendemain, il retourne coucher dans sa chambre, et le surlendemain aussi... et encore le soir d'après. Luynes, son meilleur ami, son mentor même depuis l'exécution de Concini commence à mordre sa moustache : Sa Majesté entend-elle réfléchir encore longtemps?

Le 25 au soir, comme le roi vient de se retirer chez lui avec l'intention évidente de se mettre au lit pour y dire confortablement ses prières, le duc se décide à passer à l'action et à interrompre sans plus tarder les oraisons royales. Il est onze heures du soir. Une très bonne heure pour une visite à la reine. Est-ce que le roi ne pense pas que ce serait une chose à faire?...

Non, le roi ne le pense pas : il a sommeil. Allons! Un petit effort! Il faut en finir avec une situation qui risque à la longue de devenir non seulement embarrassante mais légèrement ridicule!... Eh bien non. Louis est bien dans son lit et il n'a pas la moindre envie d'en bouger... Luynes, alors, d'attaquer sa grande scène et, fin comédien, il y excelle. Et le voilà qui plaide, qui prie, qui supplie et même qui pleure! Le roi ne comprend-il pas qu'il faut un dauphin au royaume et même quelques autres enfants? Alors qu'attend-il pour le mettre en chantier? Que le Parlement vienne en délégation l'en supplier avec les dames de la Halle et ces Messieurs de la Basoche? Que la reine soit hors d'usage et lui-même résolument cacochyme?

Rien n'y fait. Gêné d'abord, Louis s'est peu à peu ému devant les prières de son ami et même il s'est mis à pleurer, lui aussi! Ces larmes éclairent Luynes qui, du coup, essuie ses yeux. Il comprend que le roi a peur. Peur de la reine, peur de lui-même alors que peut-être l'envie ne lui manque pas. Pour s'en assurer, il décide de brusquer ce grand enfant et de tenter le tout pour le tout. Il couchera peut-être à la Bastille mais du moins il aura fait tout ce qu'il pouvait.

Et le voilà qui se penche sur son maître, l'attrape à pleins bras, l'arrache de son lit.

« Beringhen! Le bougeoir! » crie-t-il.

Le premier valet, d'ailleurs prévenu, se précipite pour éclairer la scène et prendre la tête d'un incroyable cortège composé de Luynes portant sur son épaule, comme un simple paquet, son roi qui proteste, gigote et se débat, et de Héroard, le médecin qui ferme la marche en se frottant les mains et en riant dans sa barbe.

Heureusement, le chemin n'est pas long entre la chambre du roi et celle de la reine et Luynes est doué d'une grande force nerveuse. Quelques instants de course et il dépose son royal paquet sur le lit d'Anne d'Autriche qui l'accueille en riant...

Cette nuit-là, Louis XIII restera chez sa femme jusqu'à deux heures du matin, ayant accompli fort convenablement et par deux fois son devoir conjugal avec l'approbation muette de la première femme de chambre de la reine, Mme de Bellière, témoin discret de la scène.

Peu de temps après, Anne se déclarera enceinte mais perdra son fruit par la faute de sa dangereuse amie, la duchesse de Chevreuse. Elle perdra aussi, hélas, l'amour fragile que son époux lui portait après cette folle nuit où M. de Luynes avait joué si gaillardement le rôle de Cupidon. Mme de Chevreuse qui déteste le roi veillera à ce que cet amour ne renaisse jamais et il faudra, à la fois, un gros orage et les prières d'une sainte fille, Louise de La Fayette qui fut le grand amour de Louis XIII, pour que Louis XIV puisse enfin faire son apparition... dix-neuf ans plus tard!

LES NUITS ANGLAISES...
ET BIZARRES

LA NUIT DES CARTES :
HENRI VIII ET ANNE DE CLÈVES

Quand Jane Seymour, troisième épouse du roi Henri VIII, meurt au palais d'Hampton Court, le 24 octobre 1537, douze jours après avoir mis au monde l'héritier tant désiré, le roi fait montre d'une douleur spectaculaire mais exagérée car il n'a qu'une « lueur de chagrin ». S'il pleure, c'est surtout sur lui-même : il se retrouve seul sur son trône et c'est un homme qui a horreur du vide.

Il n'est pas loin de penser que le Ciel lui en veut et entend lui faire payer la guerre qu'il fait au pape... En effet, il n'y a pas dix-huit mois que la tête ravissante d'Anne Boleyn, la « sorcière », est tombée à la Tour de Londres sous la grande épée du bourreau de Calais. Si peu de temps et le voilà veuf de nouveau alors qu'il se croyait bien parti pour un bonheur paisible en compagnie de la chère, très chère Jane, si blonde, si placide et si douce! Qui aurait pu supposer qu'elle mourrait si jeune après n'avoir donné qu'un seul enfant? Henri, qui espérait tant une vaste famille, se retrouve bizarrement abandonné, délaissé et horriblement solitaire...

Pour meubler le temps, il décide de se montrer bon père. Cela consiste essentiellement à tourmenter quotidiennement nourrices, gouvernantes et valets et à paraître à une fenêtre du palais, le bébé dans les bras, en lui faisant des mines afin que le bon peuple de Londres sache quel brave homme il est et s'attendrisse sur son sort...

Mais tout cela ne prend guère de temps et les nuits sont longues dans son vaste lit dont l'immensité déserte lui donne de l'urticaire, sans compter l'ulcère qu'il traîne à une jambe depuis une chute de cheval et ne lui laisse guère de repos. Au moins, chère Jane savait en prendre soin!... Et soupirs et larmes de revenir.

Aussi quand Cromwell, son conseiller le plus écouté – on peut même sans crainte de se tromper dire : son âme damnée – qui le connaît bien vient chuchoter qu'il doit, dès à présent, songer à reprendre femme, Henri le regarde-t-il d'un œil faussement courroucé et mouillé de larmes hypocrites mais déjà intéressé. Il répond au chuchotement par un grand « Hélas!... » mais pose, mine de rien, quelques questions évasives touchant les princesses européennes éventuellement bonnes à marier. Et cela alors même que la chère, très chère Jane n'a pas encore gagné son dernier logis dans la chapelle de Windsor!...

A peine y est-elle déposée qu'il l'oublie pour entamer d'actives discussions avec Cromwell touchant sa remplaçante. Tout naturellement, on pense d'abord à la France, si proche, et Henri suggère sans rire, qu'un choix de princesses lui soit envoyé à Calais afin qu'il puisse les voir et se rendre compte de leurs qualités respectives.

François Iᵉʳ, lui, rit beaucoup d'une telle prétention.

« Il semble, dit-il, que les Anglais agissent avec les femmes comme avec leurs chevaux : ils en réunissent un certain nombre et les font trotter pour choisir ceux qui courent le mieux... »

Il rit... mais il ajoute qu'il ne lui plairait pas que sa fille prît place dans ce genre de concours.

On pense ensuite à la catholique Marie de Guise que le premier protestant anglais n'intéresse pas, puis à Christine de Danemark, veuve du Sforza de Milan. Mais Christine fait répondre que « n'ayant pas de tête de rechange » elle préfère ne pas tenter l'aventure.

Ces deux refus font tout à fait l'affaire de Cromwell car il a déjà sa candidate : une protestante, Anne, fille du duc

Jean III de Clèves qui serait, selon le chancelier anglais, le couronnement de la lutte menée par Henri contre l'Église de Rome.

L'idée ne déplaît pas à Henri mais, avant de se décider, il désire que son peintre, Holbein, aille faire le portrait de la princesse. Tous les visiteurs du Louvre connaissent ce portrait, un très beau portrait mais passablement flatté : le peintre a atténué considérablement la cicatrice en V qui marque le front d'Anne depuis qu'elle est tombée, enfant, sur une paire de ciseaux, et il a totalement gommé les traces de petite vérole du visage. Et Cromwell, au reçu du portrait et s'appuyant sur « certains rapports secrets » d'affirmer hautement qu'Anne de Clèves surpasse Christine de Danemark en beauté « comme l'or du soleil surpasse l'argent de la lune ». Un élan poétique tout à fait inhabituel chez lui et qu'il ne va guère tarder à regretter...

En vérité, les « rapports secrets » sont remarquablement discrets sur la personnalité de la princesse : on sait qu'elle a trente-quatre ans, qu'elle sait lire et écrire mais seulement le bas-allemand, que broderies et travaux d'aiguille n'ont pas de secrets pour elle, pas plus que la science abstraite du blason où elle est capable d'en remontrer au héraut d'armes le plus chevronné. Derniers détails : elle ne boit pas trop de bière et elle commence à apprendre l'anglais.

Henri se contente de cela et, convaincu d'épouser prochainement une vraie beauté, il ordonne de grandes cérémonies et se livre à une véritable débauche de préparatifs. Puis, quand il apprend qu'Anne a quitté Clèves, il dépêche à Calais le comte de Southampton, Fitzwilliam, pour y attendre la nouvelle reine et l'escorter à travers la Manche.

Le mauvais état des routes retarde le cortège de la princesse qui n'arrive à Calais qu'à la fin du mois de décembre 1539. Mais avant de passer la mer, il faut encore attendre une quinzaine de jours car les vents sont contraires. Pour meubler le temps, Fitzwilliam s'occupe

consciencieusement de son précieux dépôt : il lui fait visiter
le port, il organise pour elle des joutes et joue aux cartes
avec elle. La future reine d'Angleterre est déjà d'une assez
belle force à certains jeux mais elle ne connaît pas le
« Cent » qui est le jeu préféré d'Henri VIII. Fitzwilliam se
hâte de le lui apprendre et, en vérité, elle apprend très
vite.

Entre deux parties, le comte envoie message sur message
vantant tous la grâce, la belle allure et la « remarquable
beauté » de la princesse et l'on ne sait trop, à la lumière de
ce qui va suivre, ce qu'il faut en conclure : ou bien le comte
de Southampton boit trop, ou bien il s'est trouvé victime
d'un de ces dangereux coups de foudre comme s'entendent
parfois à en infliger les laiderons confirmés. Mais enfin,
vient le temps de l'embarquement par un temps à peu près
possible : on passe le Channel, on débarque à Douvres et
l'on prend, au milieu des foules rassemblées, le chemin de
Londres.

De Londres où Henri ne tient plus en place. Pour se
montrer galant, il décide soudain d'aller surprendre sa
« Reine » à Rochester où elle doit faire escale, à trente miles
de la capitale. Et il s'embarque secrètement sur un petit
bateau en compagnie de Russel, d'Anthony Browne,
demi-frère de Fitzwilliam, et d'un paquet de superbes
zibelines destinées aux étrennes de sa fiancée.

Quand on atteint Rochester, il envoie Browne en
éclaireur, lui recommandant de revenir au plus tôt lui
donner son impression tout à fait franche. Hélas, quand
celui-ci revient, mal remis de ce qu'il vient de voir, le
malheureux trouve tout juste assez de voix pour annoncer
que la dame attend son seigneur. Et on n'en peut rien tirer
de plus car il se déclare brusquement très souffrant.

Inquiet tout à coup, Henri VIII se dirige à grands pas
vers la chambre où sa future l'attend. Elle est debout, très
droite, les mains sur le ventre, au milieu d'un cercle de
dames qui « ressemblent à des chevaux de Frise » et qui
répondent à des noms aussi mélodieux pour une langue

anglaise que Schwartzenbrock, Brempt, Oosenbruch, Loc et Willik. Et toutes, suivantes et maîtresse sont empaquetées de robes impossibles...

Au seuil de la pièce, Henri reste pétrifié, n'en croyant pas ses yeux. Il est « déconcerté et étonné au possible » et il faut un moment pour qu'il reprenne possession de ses moyens. Enfin il se décide, s'avance vers la princesse qui l'attend avec un sourire béat et lui tend sa joue. Mais, arrivé au pied du mur, l'épreuve lui paraît trop rude. Il bredouille une vague salutation à laquelle la princesse, qui n'a pas compris, répond : « Ja!... Ja!... » avec un large sourire, grommelle quelques paroles inintelligibles accueillies par de nouveaux « Ja!... Ja!... », puis, incapable d'y résister plus longtemps, tourne les talons et sort en oubliant totalement de donner les zibelines. Et c'est seulement quand il se retrouve dans sa barque qu'il explose.

« Je ne vois rien en cette femme qui ressemble au portrait qu'on m'en a fait et je m'étonne que des gens intelligents aient pu en parler comme ils l'ont fait. Votre frère serait-il devenu fou? » jette-t-il à la figure de Browne qui ne sait plus où se mettre. Et moins encore lorsque sa femme, qui a été placée auprès de la future reine, revient en disant qu'elle a des manières et des allures si grossières qu'il est à craindre que le roi ne puisse jamais s'en accommoder.

A Greenwich, l'on se retrouve officiellement et l'on retrouve aussi Cromwell, plus mort que vif quand il peut constater à quoi ressemble en réalité cette future reine qu'il proclamait si belle. Soucieux de détourner la colère qu'il sent venir, il se contente de murmurer :

« Il me semble... qu'elle a le maintien digne d'une reine... »

Le roi pose sur lui un regard qui pèse cinq tonnes.

« C'est vrai. Mais si j'avais été mieux renseigné, jamais elle ne serait venue ici... »

Elle, toujours elle! La pauvre Anne n'a même plus droit à un nom!

« Sire, bredouille le chancelier qui sent une désagréable sueur froide glisser le long de son dos, elle gagne peut-être à être connue. Elle est grande, semble bien faite...

— Quel moyen a-t-on de le savoir avec tous ces harnachements qu'elle porte. Les Français disent qu'avec les robes allemandes n'importe quelle femme serait laide, même si elle était jolie...

— Eh bien... ne faut-il pas espérer que, sans la robe?... »

Mais le roi n'entend pas être calmé. Il tourne comme un ours en cage.

« Si elle n'avait pas fait ce long voyage et si je ne craignais de faire scandale et de pousser son frère du côté de l'empereur et du roi de France, jamais je ne la prendrais! Mais maintenant les choses sont trop avancées... »

Il les trouve même tellement avancées qu'il s'arrange pour retarder le mariage. La pauvre princesse est sur des charbons ardents. Ce mariage est inespéré pour elle, surtout à son âge, et même si Henri ne lui plaît guère – il est beaucoup tros gros! Et puis il y a cet ulcère à la jambe qui n'est pas très engageant! – elle ne veut à aucun prix retourner tirer l'aiguille auprès de sa mère où elle s'ennuie à périr.

Enfin, la résignation vient au roi.

« Allons! finit-il par dire, il n'y a rien à faire. Il faut me mettre sous le joug!... »

Il soupire à faire tomber les murs et le regard qu'il jette à Cromwell est meurtrier. L'autre se demande s'il y survivra.

Le jour du mariage, qui est le 6 janvier 1540, Henri traîne à sa toilette, perd du temps, met les patiences à rude épreuve et quand il autorise enfin Cromwell à annoncer qu'il est prêt à aller chercher sa fiancée, il pousse un nouveau soupir.

« Mon Dieu! Si ce n'était pour satisfaire le monde et mon royaume, je ne ferais jamais ce que je dois faire aujourd'hui... »

Et c'est avec la mine d'un condamné marchant à l'échafaud qu'il conduit Anne de Clèves à l'autel.

Le soir venu, quand on le déshabille avant qu'il n'aille rejoindre sa femme dans la chambre nuptiale, sa mine s'est encore allongée. Ni le banquet ni le bal, qu'il aime pourtant presque autant l'un que l'autre, ne l'ont déridé et l'on ne peut compter ses soupirs. Il ne cesse de marmotter des choses inaudibles qui font dresser les cheveux sur la tête de Cromwell. Pour l'unique fois de sa vie, le chancelier souhaiterait presque être catholique afin de pouvoir brûler un cierge devant un saint quelconque au moment où son maître franchit le seuil fatal.

Il ne dort guère de la nuit et quand, le lendemain, il revient aux nouvelles, il garde le faible espoir que les choses se sont arrangées sur l'oreiller. Et, tout d'abord il le croit. Le roi est en train de prendre son petit déjeuner et il dévore. Cromwell juge la chose de bon augure : si Henri éprouve le besoin de refaire ses forces, c'est qu'il en a dépensées...

Hélas, quand le chancelier se hasarde à demander si la reine plaît davantage au roi, celui-ci explose :

« Non, monsieur! C'est encore pire! Je l'ai laissée pucelle comme devant! D'ailleurs il est impossible qu'elle le soit encore avec des seins et un ventre comme elle en a. Quand je les ai touchés, le cœur m'a tellement manqué que je n'ai pu ni voulu pousser plus avant. C'est une jument des Flandres... Mais, ajoute-t-il plus calmement, elle joue très bien au Cent.

– Au... Cent? Fait Cromwell qui croit avoir mal entendu.

– Parfaitement. Est-il défendu de jouer aux cartes pendant sa nuit de noces?... »

Et plantant là son chancelier abasourdi, Henri s'en va en traînant la jambe et en claquant la porte.

Quelques jours plus tard, chez la reine, quatre de ses dames dont deux parlent l'allemand – Lady Edgecombe et Lady Rutland – lui expriment leur vœu de la voir bientôt enceinte. Anne leur répond qu'elle sait très bien qu'elle ne l'est pas encore. Lady Edgecombe demande alors :

« Comment Votre Grâce peut-elle le savoir?

— Je le sais très bien. »

Petit silence troublé seulement par le léger froissement des soieries que l'on brode puis, à nouveau, Lady Edgecombe :

« Je ne voudrais pas contrarier Votre Grâce mais je crois, moi, qu'elle est toujours vierge. »

Ce qui fait rire la reine.

« Comment pourrais-je être vierge, dit-elle, puisque je couche chaque nuit avec le roi? Quand il entre au lit, il m'embrasse, me prend la main et me dit : " Bonne nuit, mon cœur. " Et le matin, il m'embrasse et me souhaite le bonjour. N'est-ce pas suffisant? »

A son tour, alors, Lady Rutland intervient :

« Madame, il en faut plus, sinon nous pourrons attendre longtemps le duc d'York que tout le royaume désire...

— Non, dit la reine. Je suis contente de n'en pas savoir plus... »

Dit-elle vrai ou force-t-elle une naïveté peut-être toute apparente? Et qui l'arrange? Les cours allemandes de l'époque offraient alors un mélange d'austérité et de grossièreté et il semble difficile de croire que, vivant trente-quatre années dans le cercle étroit d'un burg rhénan plein d'une soldatesque plus que grossière et où il y avait toutes sortes d'animaux, Anne eût gardé les innocences d'une enfant de dix ans. Le secret de cette incroyable candeur tient peut-être dans le fait qu'Henri déplaisait à Anne au moins autant qu'Anne déplaisait à Henri. En revanche, l'état de reine d'Angleterre convenant parfaitement à la jeune Allemande, elle n'avait aucune envie d'y renoncer.

N'est-il pas étrange ce « Je suis contente de n'en pas savoir plus... »? Eût-elle avoué en savoir plus sur les réalités du mariage qu'elle eût été obligée de se montrer offensée de se voir ainsi dédaignée, avec toutes les conséquences possibles d'une telle attitude. Le cher Henri ne s'entendait-il pas à merveille à faire disparaître ceux ou celles – fussent-elles épousées – qui le gênaient si peu que ce soit?

Grâce à ce curieux comportement, Anne de Clèves réussit à s'entendre très bien avec Henri. Beaucoup plus intelligente qu'elle n'avait bien voulu le laisser paraître au premier abord, elle se mit très vite à l'anglais et put bientôt faire montre d'un jugement sain et clair qu'Henri apprécia. En outre, il avait trouvé en elle une adversaire de choix aux cartes et, enfin, Anne eut l'habileté d'aimer entendre son époux chanter en s'accompagnant du luth...

Les choses auraient peut-être pu durer longtemps encore dans le *statu quo* si l'œil avide du roi n'était tombé soudain sur une adorable créature : la jeune Catherine Howard dont il s'éprit de façon foudroyante. Dès lors, il n'eut plus d'autre idée que d'en faire sa femme.

Il ne savait trop comment présenter la chose à cette brave fille dont il s'était fait une amie, mais Anne le connaissait trop à présent pour ne s'apercevoir de rien. Sentant peut-être venir discrètement un petit vent de Tour de Londres, elle facilita la tâche à Henri. A la grande surprise de celui-ci, non seulement elle n'émit aucune protestation mais encore elle se déclara toute disposée à accepter la répudiation, jouant en cela une partie d'une rare finesse. Une partie qu'elle gagna haut la main.

Enthousiasmé par tant de bonne volonté, Henri lui accorda une rente de quatre mille livres par an, lui fit don des châteaux de Richmond et de Blechingley qui comportaient l'un et l'autre de vastes dépendances et des parcs superbes, lui offrit des joyaux, des meubles, de la vaisselle plate, des robes splendides et, pour couronner le tout, prit un décret qui en faisait la « sœur du roi ». Anne devait avoir la préséance sur toutes les autres dames, aussitôt après la reine et les enfants royaux.

Et Anne de Clèves, sortie indemne et très riche d'une

dangereuse aventure, s'installa joyeusement dans une existence qui lui convenait tout à fait et qu'elle partagea d'ailleurs avec un discret gentilhomme.

« Elle est plus joyeuse que jamais, dit la chronique de l'époque, et porte une robe nouvelle tous les jours... »

Ce fut Cromwell qui, décidemment mal inspiré par l'invasion prochaine du clan Howard, paya les tribulations amoureuses de son maître : le 28 juillet suivant, il montait à l'échafaud. Non celui noble et élégant de la Tour de Londres, mais celui du bas quartier de Tyburn, celui des voleurs et des criminels de droit commun.

Ce jour-là, au manoir d'Oatlands Henri VIII épousait la fraîche et ravissante Catherine Howard... qui avait six ans de moins que sa fille Marie. Il avait choisi la campagne pour une nuit de noces qu'il voulait enchanteresse, loin surtout des horreurs de la peste qui s'installait à Londres. Elle ne fut enchanteresse que pour lui et il fut obligé, un triste jour, de s'en rendre compte.

Mais quand, un peu plus d'un an et demi après, le 13 février 1542, il fit décapiter sa trop jolie et trop folle petite reine, ce fut « sa sœur » Lady Anne de Clèves qui vint essuyer les grosses larmes qu'il répandait continuellement...

LA NUIT DU WHISKY :
LE FUTUR GEORGE IV
ET CAROLINE DE BRÜNSWICK

Une autre princesse allemande, montée en graine et pas très belle, est venue en Angleterre pour y vivre une nuit de noces au moins aussi peu orthodoxe que la précédente mais dont les conséquences allaient se révéler beaucoup plus dramatiques.

C'est pour conclure ce mariage, celui du prince de Galles avec la princesse Caroline de Brünswick que, par un jour brumeux et glacé du mois de février 1795, James Harris, Lord Malmesbury s'embarque au pont de Londres. Sans le moindre enthousiasme. Il pense qu'on lui a donné là une fichue commission, tout à fait indigne d'un grand diplomate et qu'on le récompense bien mal des services – fort brillants naturellement – qu'il n'a cessé de rendre à la Couronne anglaise. Ce mariage, en admettant qu'il parvienne à le réaliser, va sûrement le brouiller avec beaucoup de monde, sauf, bien entendu avec le roi. Seulement, le roi George III est fou...

Cela a commencé sept ans plus tôt quand George III, brave homme au demeurant, sage, économe et rangé a commencé à manifester des troubles mentaux d'un genre assez particulier. Victime, de toute évidence, d'une *over-dose* de Shakespeare dont il raffole, il s'est pris subitement pour le roi Lear, a exigé qu'on l'habille de longs vêtements blancs façon druide et s'est mis à son clavecin. Il ne sait pas jouer de la harpe celtique mais, en revanche, c'est un remarquable claveciniste et, aussi passionné de Haendel que de Shakespeare, il s'est mis à en jouer jours et nuits...

Pour combattre cette folie, somme toute assez douce, les médecins ont employé les grands moyens d'un art qui en matière de neurologie n'était guère plus évolué qu'à l'âge des cavernes. Le pauvre roi a été enfermé, ligoté, battu et affamé. Sans obtenir d'ailleurs le moindre résultat. On n'a même pas réussi à le rendre enragé, ce qui est encore une chance...

Or cette thérapeutique barbare a profondément réjoui le tendre fils de ce malheureux roi car il y voyait les signes précurseurs d'une fin prochaine et de sa non moins prochaine accession au trône.

C'est un curieux personnage que le prince George. C'est même un personnage franchement odieux : un libertin criblé de dettes, obèse et cynique, un joueur et un débauché n'aimant guère que lui-même et cette couronne qu'il convoite si âprement. Il pousse même l'absence de cœur jusqu'à singer, pour amuser ses amis après boire, le comportement de son père durant ses crises.

On ne lui connaît qu'une faiblesse sentimentale : la passion égoïste qu'il éprouve, depuis dix ans, pour l'une des plus jolies femmes de Londres : Maria Fitzherbert. Au moyen d'un chantage au sentiment assez lamentable – car la malheureuse a commis l'erreur de s'éprendre de lui – « Georgie » l'a convaincue d'accepter un mariage morganatique, un mariage que l'on cache soigneusement car Mrs. Fitzherbert est catholique et le prince sait bien qu'il ne sera jamais roi si l'on apprend qu'il a épousé une papiste. D'où des démentis, des secrets minables et des brusqueries publiques dont la jeune femme se trouve souvent blessée et qui la rongent.

Or, à la fin de 1794, le roi a réussi à se dégager suffisamment de ses brumes musicales pour constater, avec une stupeur indignée, le genre de vie que mène son fils et le montant astronomique de ses dettes. Et, comme il ignore tout du mariage secret, il propose à « Georgie » une solution qui lui paraît convenable : ou bien il se range en épousant une princesse digne de régner plus tard à ses côtés et l'on paiera ses dettes, ou bien il refuse et on l'abandonne à la meute tenace de ses créanciers qui sont gens tout à fait capables d'envoyer un prince de Galles moisir sur la paille humide de Fleet Street, la prison pour dettes.

Le Parlement joint ses instances à celles du roi : il réglera les dettes du prince de Galles si celui-ci se marie. Or, en Angleterre, c'est le Parlement qui tient les cordons de la bourse et il y a donc tout intérêt à tenir compte de ses « conseils ».

Songeant à l'avenir, Georgie a capitulé. On lui a proposé sa cousine germaine, Caroline de Brünswick : il a accepté sans même demander à voir un portrait car il traite là une affaire comme une autre. Une affaire dont il convient de se débarrasser au plus tôt afin de retourner aux plaisirs habituels et aux compagnons de ces plaisirs : Lord Moïra, Mr. Orlando Bridgeman et surtout l'incomparable Brummell, arbitre des élégances londoniennes et ami de cœur de Georgie.

Pendant ce temps, à Brünswick, une vieille petite ville allemande coincée entre la lande de Lüneburg et la chaîne du Harz, Lord Malmesbury a été mis en présence de la fiancée. C'est une sorte de poulain échappé, une grande fille de vingt-sept ans pas très belle, pas très laide non plus, intelligente mais fantasque, et surtout élevée à la diable dans cette morose petite Cour allemande, entre des parents désunis qui font régner autour d'eux une atmosphère pesante dont leur fille a souffert. Elle n'a pas la moindre éducation et, de plus, extraordinairement populaire, elle se montre avec les petites gens d'une familiarité qui suffoque l'ambassadeur anglais.

Il est de moins en moins ravi de sa mission, Malmesbury. Il souhaitait ramener une fiancée dépourvue d'imagination, froide, indifférente, une sorte de statue de la respectabilité simplement capable de porter couronne et de faire des enfants. Or, cette Caroline qui piaffe, gambade et s'enthousiasme à l'idée de devenir princesse de Galles d'abord, puis reine d'Angleterre ensuite, lui donne froid dans le dos. Quelque chose lui dit qu'il va à une catastrophe. Mais a-t-il le moyen de reculer? Son avis n'a aucune importance...

Sur le chemin du retour, il essaie d'expliquer à la princesse que la discrétion, et même un certain aveuglement, lui semblent un comportement souhaitable. Mais il perd son temps et ses paroles : Caroline ne veut rien entendre. Comment expliquer à cette innocente qui ne cesse de remercier le Ciel que l'homme qu'elle va épouser est fermement décidé à ne rien faire, mais vraiment rien du tout, pour lui plaire?

Encore Malmesbury ignore-t-il ce qui se passe à Londres où l'on s'occupe de constituer la maison de la future princesse de Galles. En effet, c'est à Lady Jersey, sa dernière maîtresse déclarée, que Georgie vient de faire attribuer le poste de dame d'honneur de sa femme.

Lady Jersey est, avant tout, une intrigante. Depuis peu, elle a réussi à supplanter Maria Fitzherbert dans les bonnes grâces du prince et elle n'entend pas en rester là. Ce qu'elle veut, c'est prendre assez d'influence sur son amant pour régner, à travers lui, sur l'Angleterre. Pas plus!

Dans ce but, elle a poussé à la roue du mariage et cela en vertu de deux bonnes raisons : l'argent bien sûr, puisque les dettes vont être payées, et l'élimination totale de la Fitzherbert qu'elle déteste. Jusque-là, elle a parfaitement réussi : Georgie se marie et il a envoyé à la pauvre Maria une lettre, odieuse à force de sécheresse, et dans laquelle il lui exprime froidement son intention de ne plus jamais la revoir. Au reçu de cette lettre, l'épouse morganatique a fait ses malles et elle est partie sur le continent. Cela fait, Lady Jersey a exigé le poste de dame d'honneur afin de garder la haute main sur le nouveau ménage et de pouvoir, tout à son aise, assurer sa domination en détruisant celle, fort hypothétique mais toujours possible, de la nouvelle venue.

En apprenant, par courrier, la nomination de cette mégère, Malmesbury pense vraiment que le Ciel est contre lui : jamais mariage ne s'est annoncé plus mal. Et cette Allemande qui fredonne à longueur de journée!... Il peut s'armer de courage car l'arrivée sera pire encore que tout ce qu'il a pu imaginer.

Tout d'abord, Lady Jersey qui est venue au-devant de la princesse jusqu'à Douvres, comme le veut le protocole, s'arrange pour arriver au château avec un tel retard qu'il s'en faut d'un cheveu que la fiancée ne trouve porte close. Ensuite, comme elle a pris la peine de regarder un portrait et qu'à l'arrivée elle a, en femme à la mode, trouvé fort réjouissante la mise modeste et archaïque de Caroline, elle la fait affubler et coiffer, sous couleur de la mettre au ton de la Cour, d'une manière non seulement peu seyante mais franchement ridicule en dépit des efforts de Lord Malmesbury.

Aussi, quand la pauvre princesse pénètre dans le salon du palais Saint-James où toute la Cour l'attend, essuie-t-elle des sourires et des chuchotements dont le moins qu'on puisse dire est qu'ils manquent de la plus élémentaire politesse. S'il a envie de rire, pourtant, Georgie n'en marque rien et son attitude est d'abord convenable. Peut-être parce que le roi est là!... Il salue gravement sa fiancée, l'embrasse puis, seulement la voit de près (il est myope). Et le léger soupir de soulagement que s'est permis Malmesbury s'étrangle dans sa gorge : Georgie s'est armé de son face-à-main et, après avoir longuement examiné Caroline du haut de sa grandeur, il lui tourne brusquement le dos et réclame :

« Donnez-moi du cognac, Malmesbury!

— Est-ce que Votre Altesse n'aimerait pas mieux un peu d'eau?

— De l'eau? Vous rêvez! J'ai grand besoin d'un cognac! »

Il l'avale d'un trait puis fonce vers la porte et déclarant bien haut qu'il va chez sa mère.

Quand les ondes de la stupeur générale se sont un peu effacées, la princesse demande à l'ambassadeur si son fiancé est toujours aussi désagréable. Il se hâte de lui répondre que non et de mettre au compte de la reine Charlotte [1] qui est souffrante le comportement bizarre d'un fils dont il dépeint soigneusement l'inquiétude... toute fictive d'ailleurs : Georgie est simplement parti continuer sa cure de cognac sous un plafond moins solennel.

« De toute façon, dit alors la jeune fille, je le trouve très gros. Il ne ressemble pas du tout aux portraits que j'ai vus. Et même il est franchement affreux!... »

Prêt à pleurer, Malmesbury accorde alors une pensée pleine de nostalgie à sa chère ambassade de Saint-Pétersbourg où il se trouvait si bien naguère encore. Les Russes, certes, sont des gens à peine civilisés, mais comparée à celles de Georgie et de sa future épouse, leur éducation lui paraît à présent le comble du raffinement.

Trois jours plus tard, le mariage est célébré dans la chapelle de Saint-James. Convenablement habillée, cette fois, d'une robe bien coupée et couverte de diamants, Caroline y entre avec la gravité et le recueillement que commande la circonstance. Georgie, lui, n'est pas là. En retard suivant son habitude, chacun peut constater, quand il se présente enfin qu'il a l'œil fixe et hébété... et la démarche un brin chancelante.

Cela tient à ce qui s'est passé dans la voiture qui l'amenait de sa résidence de Carlton House en compagnie de son ami Lord Moïra. Affreusement triste comme le sont souvent les ivrognes après une nuit bien arrosée, Georgie s'est épanché : il est très malheureux d'avoir perdu sa chère, chère Maria Fitzherbert, la seule femme qu'il eût jamais aimée, « sa » femme, bien que le mariage catholique

---

1. C'est aussi une Allemande : Charlotte de Mecklembourg-Strelitz.

contracté sans le consentement royal ait été dissous.

Devant ce gros chagrin, Moïra lui a, alors, révélé que Maria n'a pas quitté l'Angleterre. Elle se cache à Brighton, dans sa maison où il pourra la retrouver quand il voudra. Du coup, Georgie a jugé urgent d'arroser la bonne nouvelle au moyen d'un flacon de whisky placé dans un compartiment du carrosse et que l'on veille à toujours tenir plein. Le résultat ne s'est pas fait attendre.

Durant toute la cérémonie, sa mine égarée et l'odeur d'alcool qui flotte autour de lui plongent les assistants dans la stupeur. La pauvre Caroline, les yeux pleins de larmes, contemple avec un mélange de tristesse et de dégoût ce gros homme hébété qui, à ses côtés, se lève et s'agenouille à retardement, parfois à contretemps et qu'il faut secouer, au moment crucial, pour qu'il se décide à prononcer le « I will » traditionnel.

Après un tel mariage, la nuit de noces est ce qu'elle doit être : un désastre. Le prince est tellement ivre lorsqu'il déboule dans la chambre nuptiale qu'il lui reste tout juste la force de s'abattre sur le lit. Sur le lit où Caroline est malade à mourir...

En effet, afin de lui « rendre quelque courage », son obligeante dame d'honneur n'a rien trouvé de mieux que de lui administrer, à elle aussi, une ration de whisky mais agrémentée d'on ne sait quelle drogue. Les spasmes de son estomac empêcheront la malheureuse de dormir toute la nuit et finiront par percer l'ivresse de Georgie. Résultat : quand revient le matin, Georgie inspire toujours à sa femme le même dégoût et lui l'a prise en horreur... après l'avoir prise avec une brutalité qui rendrait malade n'importe quelle femme en bonne santé. Sans doute dans l'espoir de mettre un terme à ses nausées...

Dès lors, à Carlton House, où il a bien fallu que Caroline allât s'installer, la vie de princesse héritière devient un cauchemar. Elle doit assister, impassible, aux soupers que donne souvent Georgie et qui tournent régulièrement à l'orgie. Il lui faut voir, sans broncher, son époux boire dans le verre de Lady Jersey et se livrer sur elle à certaines privautés à l'issue desquelles il distribue libéralement à sa maîtresse les bijoux de sa femme. En outre, abusant sans vergogne de ses fonctions, la dame d'honneur ne se gêne pas pour ouvrir le courrier de la princesse, de préférence celui qu'elle échange avec sa famille, et l'apporte à son amant qui en fait des gorges chaudes avec ses compagnons de beuverie.

La patience, très inhabituelle d'ailleurs, de Caroline n'y résiste pas. Balayant les conseils de modération dispensés par Malmesbury, elle se lance courageusement dans la bagarre. Sa langue est agile et elle sait s'en servir, trouvant avec un art consommé les mots les plus susceptibles de blesser son mari. Quant à Lady Jersey, un peu surprise tout de même, elle s'entend soudain traiter comme elle le mérite : avec un maximum de mépris et des sarcasmes qui la démontent bien souvent. Enfin Caroline trouve plaisir à dauber sur les amours de son mari avec la Fitzherbert qu'elle traite de « grasse blonde quadragénaire ». Dans de telles conditions, le ménage ne peut pas marcher.

Pourtant, une chance de salut se présente bientôt : si ahurissants que soient les rapports des deux époux, la princesse de Galles se trouve bientôt enceinte et met tous ses espoirs dans la venue de l'enfant annoncé pensant que peut-être son entrée en scène incitera son père à une vie plus honorable.

Malheureusement il n'en est rien et quand naît, le 7 janvier 1796, une jolie petite fille que l'on prénommera Charlotte, Georgie laisse entendre qu'il se considère désormais comme délié de toute obligation envers sa femme : il est sous le coup d'une nouvelle flambée de passion pour Maria Fitzherbert à laquelle il lègue, à la suite d'un accident de santé qui lui a fait très peur, la totalité de ses biens. Pour un peu il lui léguerait les joyaux de la Couronne!

Aussitôt après ce testament larmoyant, il écrit à **sa**

femme, en présent de relevailles, une lettre dans laquelle il lui signifie poliment leur rupture.

Dignement, la princesse répond qu'elle communique cette lettre au roi « comme à son souverain et à son père », mais ce recours à George III ne change rien à la décision de Georgie : Caroline doit quitter Carlton House et chercher refuge dans sa propriété de Blackheath, présent du roi. Un refuge où l'on ne lui permet pas d'emmener sa fille, seconde à présent dans la ligne de succession au trône.

Le peuple anglais prend sa défense. La rupture lui déplaît profondément et plus encore le fait que le prince vit ouvertement avec sa maîtresse. Dès lors, tandis que la princesse de Galles recueille partout, sur son passage, hommages et ovations, son époux et la favorite ne peuvent plus sortir sans déchaîner des bordées d'insultes et des huées.

Naturellement, ce fut à Caroline que le mari s'en prit. Non seulement il lui fit interdire de voir sa fille mais encore il donna des ordres pour que l'enfant fût élevée dans la haine et le mépris de sa mère. Sur ce point, il échoua complètement : en grandissant Charlotte se mit à adorer sa mère et à détester un père qui non seulement l'en privait mais osait vivre au grand jour avec une concubine.

Le peuple, cette extraordinaire expression du chœur antique, encourageait d'ailleurs l'enfant dans ces sentiments. Quand elle sortait en voiture avec sa gouvernante, les passants lui criaient :

« Aimez bien votre mère, mignonne! »

En revanche, si le prince apparaissait, les mêmes passants lui jetaient :

« George! Où est votre femme?... »

Pour tromper sa faim maternelle, Caroline s'occupa d'enfants abandonnés dont certains, il est vrai, furent d'assez mauvais sujets. Georgie en profita pour faire courir le bruit d'enfants adultérins, allant jusqu'à demander que l'on fît une enquête sur la vie privée de la princesse de Galles.

Quand le vieux roi sombra définitivement dans la folie, Caroline, ayant perdu son meilleur défenseur, quitta l'Angleterre. Son époux s'était arrogé le titre de prince régent, et elle ne trouvait plus qu'outrages et insultes dans son entourage. Elle vécut en Europe, principalement à Naples où elle fut la proie de gens sans grands scrupules, et fit même un pèlerinage en Terre sainte. Allant d'extravagance en extravagance, elle semblait avoir pris à tâche de couvrir de ridicule son titre de princesse de Galles.

Mais en novembre 1817, un terrible choc fit brusquement cesser toutes ses folies : sa fille Charlotte qui avait épousé par amour, son cousin Léopold de Saxe-Cobourg-Saalfeld [1], mourut en couches. Le cœur de la mère se brisa. Elle décida de rentrer en Angleterre.

Ce fut pour y faire face à un effarant, un ignoble procès en adultère intenté par le prince régent. N'ayant pas osé la faire assassiner comme il l'avait si souvent pensé, il tentait de la détruire par voie de justice. Il n'y réussit pas. Mais, en 1820, le roi George III étant mort, son détestable fils devint roi d'Angleterre. Caroline était reine mais, naturellement, George lui en refusa farouchement le titre et les prérogatives.

Le jour du couronnement, non seulement elle n'eut pas le droit de figurer dans l'église mais encore on lui en interdit l'entrée sous un incroyable prétexte : elle n'avait pas de carton d'invitation!... Pourtant son vrai couronnement, elle allait le recevoir du peuple anglais plus vite qu'elle ne l'imaginait.

Quelques semaines après la cérémonie, en effet, le 7 août 1821, elle mourut, épuisée. Exultant de joie, George IV, lui refusant la sépulture royale, ordonna que son corps fût embarqué sur une frégate et ramené à Brünswick. Encore le cercueil devait-il rejoindre la Tamise par un chemin

---

1. Il sera plus tard le premier roi des Belges, Léopold Iᵉʳ.

détourné, en faisant le tour de la Cité afin d'éviter toute manifestation de sympathie.

Les gens de Londres ne l'entendirent pas ainsi. Dans la nuit précédant le départ, des barricades surgirent sur l'itinéraire tracé par le roi lui-même et, sachant de quoi il était capable, des piquets se formèrent pour les garder.

A l'aube, fou de rage, George envoyait des troupes, ordonnait même à la cavalerie de charger la foule. Celle-ci tint bon et quand parut le corbillard portant les initiales C.R. (Carolina Regina) et les armes d'Angleterre, le peuple, à genoux, jalonna pour lui la voie royale de la Cité dont sonnaient toutes les cloches tandis que tonnaient les canons de la Tour. Sur le cercueil, une plaque d'argent avait été posée par une main inconnue. Elle portait, gravée : « Caroline, reine outragée d'Angleterre ».

Les canons de l'escadre prirent le relais de ceux de la Tour quand le vaisseau, lentement, descendit la Tamise, défilant devant les navires aux pavillons en berne. Au bout du voyage, la terre natale allait reprendre celle qui ne l'avait quittée que pour souffrir, mais ce couronnement-là, voulu par tout un peuple, valait bien la pompe dérisoire de Westminster.

Neuf ans plus tard, George IV mourut à son tour mais ses funérailles ne ressemblèrent en rien à celles de sa femme. Non seulement le peuple ne s'agenouilla pas sur son passage mais ce fut tout juste s'il ne pavoisa pas. Des brochures satiriques coururent les rues de Londres racontant avec un grand luxe de détails ses amours scandaleuses. Et l'on rédigea même son épitaphe, donnant la pleine mesure de la tendresse qu'on lui portait :

> *Il eut une carrière noble et infâme*
> *Vil et répugnant avec magnificence*
> *C'était le premier gentilhomme du monde*
> *Et il rendit ce titre odieux...*

Ainsi disparut le « vainqueur » de Napoléon. Son frère

Guillaume lui succéda. Pas pour longtemps : sept ans plus tard, pour le plus grand bien de l'Angleterre, une petite jeune fille de dix-huit ans devenait reine. Elle s'appelait Victoria et elle allait porter plus haut qu'elle ne l'avait jamais atteint la grandeur de l'Angleterre...

LES NUITS ENTHOUSIASTES

DE LA NUIT DE TOBIE
À L'ESCALIER DE SERVICE :
LE MARIAGE DE SAINT LOUIS

Jamais repas de noces n'avait été plus lugubre et, seuls, les jeunes époux ne s'en apercevaient pas car ils ne voyaient qu'eux-mêmes. Ils étaient tellement occupés à se regarder, à se sourire et à se tenir la main que tout le reste du monde disparaissait pour eux. Mais il n'en allait pas de même pour les autres convives dont les regards inquiets convergeaient tous sur un seul visage, sévère, austère, rébarbatif à souhait : celui de la reine mère, Blanche de Castille qui, depuis la veille, arborait une mine proprement funèbre...

On était le 27 mai 1234, dans la bonne ville de Sens et l'on venait d'y célébrer les noces du jeune roi Louis, neuvième du nom, dix-neuf ans, et de la petite Marguerite de Provence, fille du comte Raymond-Bérenger, âgée de quatorze ans. Ces deux enfants, beaux et charmants, encore que dans un genre tout à fait différent, étaient tombés amoureux l'un de l'autre avec ensemble et spontanéité lorsque, le 26 mai, leurs cortèges – celui qui avait mené le roi depuis Paris, celui qui conduisait Marguerite depuis Forcalquier – s'étaient rejoints et mêlés. Et personne ne comprenait pourquoi, devant l'éclatant succès de ce mariage qu'elle avait combiné, cherché, voulu, Madame Blanche faisait la tête...

Personne? Voire!... Dans la brillante assemblée, il y avait au moins trois personnes qui savaient à quoi s'en tenir grâce au souvenir encore cuisant de la scène dont les avait régalées la reine mère aussitôt après la rencontre : c'étaient Gilles de Flagy, premier ambassadeur dépêché en Provence pour observer les filles de Raymond-Bérenger, et les deux envoyés qui, sur sa recommandation, étaient allés chercher la fiancée pour la conduire en France : Gautier Cornu, évêque de Sens, et Jean de Nesle.

« Je vous avais chargés, leur dit en substance la Castillane, de faire choix d'une princesse pieuse, dévote même, bonne, douce, vertueuse...

— Madame Marguerite est tout cela, dit Flagy; fort pieuse, très bonne et pleine de vertus. Tous les gens de Provence chantent ses louanges avec tendresse en dépit de son jeune âge...

— ... et sans doute aussi cette folle troupe de ménestrels, de chanteurs, de troubadours et de jolies filles à la mine bien trop éveillée qu'elle traîne après elle? En outre, j'avais recommandé que la fiancée ne fût pas trop jolie afin que ses soins ne détournassent point le roi de ses graves devoirs et ne risquassent point de le faire tomber dans le péché. Et c'est tout juste ce qui se passe : il ne la quitte plus des yeux. Quelle sottise venez-vous de nous faire faire là!... »

L'évêque s'en était mêlé. La moutarde commençait à lui monter au nez en entendant la reine mère lui reprocher de n'avoir pas rompu les négociations en constatant la beauté de Marguerite.

« Le roi est jeune, fort pieux et bien attaché à ses devoirs. Il faut qu'il donne au royaume belle et nombreuse descendance. Quel mal y a-t-il à ce qu'il y prenne quelque plaisir? J'ajoute : plaisir légitime et tout à fait permis par Dieu! Le feu roi Philippe, dont Dieu ait l'âme, s'était fort préoccupé de la beauté de Votre Majesté lorsqu'il l'a fait demander en Castille... »

Ce rappel à son propre mariage n'avait pas calmé Madame Blanche. Chacun voyait midi à sa porte et feu Philippe Auguste n'était jamais apparu à personne comme un parangon de vertu. Pour sa part, Blanche s'entêtait à

considérer le mariage de son fils avec cette petite Proven-
çale brune, fraîche, dorée comme un brugnon, « une vraie
petite caille » selon l'expression gourmande de Paul Guth,
comme une véritable catastrophe dont il fallait limiter
sévèrement les conséquences.

Elle allait s'y employer activement.

« Les duretés que la reine Blanche fit à la reine
Marguerite, écrit Joinville, furent telles que la reine
Blanche ne voulait pas souffrir, autant qu'elle le pouvait,
que son fils fût en la compagnie de sa femme si ce n'est le
soir quand il allait coucher avec elle... »

Et encore! De toute façon nous n'en sommes pas encore
là...

Le « joyeux banquet » terminé, tandis que les dames
conduisaient la jeune épousée à sa chambre, le jeune roi
était allé dire un bout de prière à la chapelle afin de
remercier Dieu de lui avoir fait un si joli cadeau. Cela fait,
il déclara joyeusement à ses deux frères, Robert et
Alphonse, qu'il s'en allait rejoindre sa femme, sans
imaginer un seul instant à quel point l'entreprise pouvait
se révéler périlleuse.

En effet, au lieu de rencontrer, au seuil de la chambre
fleurie, l'aimable cohorte des jeunes filles couronnées de
roses, chargées de le conduire au paradis de l'amour, c'est
sa mère qu'il trouve devant la porte close qu'elle barre, au
surplus, de toute sa haute personne. Jamais l'Espagnole
n'a été aussi espagnole! Jamais ses yeux noirs n'ont été
aussi sombres! Et c'est d'une voix qu'elle s'efforce de faire
paisible et grave qu'elle explique : le mariage est un
sacrement et pas une partie de jambes en l'air! Avant
d'aborder le lit qui doit être traité comme une sorte d'autel
(autrement dit, il ne convient pas de s'y attarder), il faut s'y
préparer longuement par la prière. La mine réjouie et
quelque peu gourmande que montre Louis est profondément choquante. A la chapelle, sire! Et tâchez d'y bien
prier!...

A la chapelle? Mais il en vient. Qu'importe, il doit y

retourner afin que Dieu consente à bénir ce mariage...
Louis aime trop Dieu pour ne pas accéder à l'injonction
maternelle. Il veut bien retourner à la chapelle. Mais pour
combien de temps? Trois nuits, pas moins! Pour qu'un
mariage soit saint, il convient de consacrer à Dieu les trois
premières nuits de la vie conjugale et de lui offrir l'ardeur
réfrénée des époux. On appelle cela les nuits de Tobie, en
hommage à ce jeune Juif qui, durant la grande captivité de
Babylone, fut mené au mariage par l'ange Raphaël en
personne et, ayant observé l'abstinence des trois nuits obtint
ainsi de Dieu la guérison de la cécité paternelle. Selon la
reine mère on observait beaucoup cette coutume en
Castille.

Le futur saint avait bien trop l'habitude d'obéir à sa mère
pour entrer en conflit avec elle. Étouffant ses soupirs, il
retourna à la chapelle et entreprit d'y passer la nuit.
Satisfaite, Blanche de Castille rentra chez elle, en omettant
toutefois de prévenir sa belle-fille et, dans sa chambre-
jardin, Marguerite attendit en vain. D'abord calmement,
puis nerveusement et, finalement, en pleurant à gros
sanglots qui finirent d'ailleurs par l'endormir d'épuise-
ment. Elle qui croyait avoir plu à son jeune seigneur blond,
voilà qu'il la dédaignait!

Le lendemain, bien sûr, on lui explique, on l'apaise.
C'est une coutume. On aurait dû la prévenir mais, autant
qu'elle le sache, il y a encore deux nuits du même genre à
passer...

Marguerite est loin d'être sotte. L'œil vaguement
triomphant de sa belle-mère l'incite à penser qu'on a bien
pu exhumer cette bizarre coutume tout juste à son usage et,
comme elle aime déjà de tout son cœur son jeune mari, elle
décide de mettre les rieurs de son côté.

Et, la nuit venue, tandis que Louis agenouillé dans la
chapelle s'abîme dans la prière et tente de fermer ses sens
aux doux parfums qui montent de la campagne, il a la
surprise de voir arriver Marguerite.

« Nous prierons ensemble, mon doux seigneur, dit-elle

avec un sourire courageux, puisque c'est la coutume!... »

Lorsqu'un peu plus tard la reine mère vient s'assurer de la présence de son fils dans la chapelle, elle reçoit un choc. Agenouillés tous les deux devant l'autel illuminé comme durant la cérémonie de leur mariage, la main dans la main, Louis et Marguerite prient à haute voix... Ne sachant trop que penser, elle va se retirer sur la pointe des pieds quand elle se heurte presque au connétable Imbert de Beaujeu qui passait par là.

« Encore une nuit d'amour comme celle-là, lui décoche le vieux soldat, et le roi s'endormira en plein conseil!... »

En dépit de son courage, Marguerite finit par s'endormir au milieu de ses oraisons et Louis la fit porter, tout doucement, chez elle en recommandant bien de ne pas l'éveiller. Puis il se remit à prier...

Le surlendemain, enfin, les voilà réunis. Les guirlandes et les bouquets de la chambre ont été changés. La nuit est encore plus belle qu'au premier soir... D'ailleurs pleuvrait-il à plein temps que Louis et Marguerite la trouveraient tout de même plus belle. Ils ont commencé par se parler, par se dire tout ce qu'ils n'ont pas réussi à se dire sous l'œil de granit de la reine mère... Marguerite est d'un pays où la poésie enveloppe toutes choses, où l'accomplissement de l'acte d'amour ne saurait se passer d'une foule de tendres préliminaires. Et les jeunes époux en sont encore à ces préliminaires qui sont découvertes et émerveillements réciproques... lorsque quelques coups énergiques sont frappés à la porte, les ramenant sur la terre un peu brutalement. Qui ose?... Doux Jésus! Qui veulent-ils que ce soit? Mais Blanche de Castille, bien sûr! Elle leur apprend qu'il y a deux heures qu'ils sont ensemble, qu'ils ont largement eu le temps de faire ce qu'ils étaient censés faire et que ça suffit comme ça! Pour faire bonne mesure, elle ajoute que, vu l'âge encore tendre de la jeune reine, il ne saurait être question de recommencer tous les soirs.

D'ailleurs Louis sait quelles sont les obligations religieuses en matière de nuits conjugales.

Peu de chose en vérité : il ne saurait être question d'aimer pendant l'Avent, ni bien sûr pendant les quarante nuits du Carême, ni les veilles et jours de fêtes et pas davantage le vendredi et le samedi. Il sait tout cela, le pauvre Louis IX mais, ce soir, il aimerait bien ne rien savoir du tout... Marguerite, naturellement le pousse à la révolte. Mais il y a toujours ce respect filial... et aussi le fait que, pour quelques mois encore, Blanche est régente de France. Tant qu'il n'aura pas atteint la majorité, Louis n'est roi que de nom. Il n'en est encore qu'à l'entraînement...

Quand on regagne Paris, le 8 juin, l'accueil de la ville est si chaleureux que Marguerite s'en trouve réconfortée. Il faut au moins cela pour compenser l'aversion grandissante que lui inspire sa belle-mère. Blanche surveille le jeune couple jour et nuit. Plus le temps passe et plus le tête-à-tête devient difficile. Alors, comme un collégien aux prises avec un pion trop attentif, Louis ruse, cherche les coins sombres et les couloirs déserts pour y rencontrer quelques instants Marguerite.

Malheureusement, la reine mère semble douée d'un flair tout particulier pour dénicher les cachettes des amoureux. Elle a le pied singulièrement silencieux et, leur tombant dessus comme la foudre, elle les sépare aussitôt d'une main vigoureuse en faisant rouler son accent espagnol :

« Que faites-vous ici? Vous employez mal votre temps! Vous êtes dans le péché... »

Les nuits ne sont pas meilleures. On leur accorde quelques instants mais jamais toute la nuit...

Un beau jour, ils pensent avoir trouvé la solution. Le jeune frère de Louis, Robert, vient gentiment lui faire cadeau de son petit chien. Un petit chien qu'il ne peut pas garder car il a de curieuses manières : du plus loin qu'il aperçoit Madame Blanche, il aboie jusqu'à s'en étrangler. Il suffit même qu'il la sente dans les parages...

Hélas, le charmant expédient ne dure pas longtemps. Un matin, on trouve le petit chien mort, peut-être d'avoir été trop gourmand... peut-être d'autre chose. Marguerite pleure, Louis aussi... Il décide alors, pour se changer les idées, qu'un séjour au château de Pontoise ferait du bien à tout le monde. Ayant passé là une bonne partie de son enfance, il en connaît les moindres recoins et sait qu'il y a peut-être un parti intéressant à tirer d'un certain escalier...

A Pontoise, en effet, les choses vont tout à coup beaucoup mieux. Blanche de Castille a beau continuer à patrouiller dans les couloirs, à fouiller les buissons et à multiplier les arrivées surprises tantôt chez sa belle-fille, tantôt chez son fils, elle ne trouve rien. Et pour cause : la chambre de Marguerite et celle de Louis sont situées juste au-dessus l'une de l'autre mais, pris dans l'épaisseur de la muraille, un petit escalier secret les relie. Sous couleur de donner à son service plus de majesté, le roi a fait installer à sa porte comme à celle de sa femme, des huissiers à verge, personnages graves et pompeux mais nantis d'un bâton, insigne de leur fonction, qui leur sert à annoncer les visiteurs. En l'occurrence, lesdits bâtons servent surtout à taper à tour de bras sur l'une ou l'autre porte quand un habile téléphone arabe signale l'approche de la reine mère. Et celui qu'elle honore de sa visite a le temps, grâce à ce système, de quitter le petit escalier et de se réinstaller à ses occupations.

Ce n'est pas un endroit bien confortable que cet escalier mais, en dépit de ses toiles d'araignées et de son obscurité, Louis et Marguerite le trouvent le plus merveilleux endroit du monde. Malheureusement, il ne peut être question de passer l'hiver à Pontoise. Il faut bien rentrer à Paris où n'existe aucun escalier complice.

Les pauvres tourtereaux essayèrent bien de reprendre les parties de cache-cache dans les couloirs mais, un soir, la terrible belle-mère les découvrit, serrés l'un contre l'autre, derrière une tapisserie qui cachait un recoin de débarras.

Elle se laissa emporter par une si violente colère que la petite reine éclata en sanglots et piqua une crise de nerfs. Alors, pour la première fois, Louis osa se dresser contre sa mère :

« Je suis le roi, dit-il sévèrement, et vous oubliez la foi que vous me devez! »

Le ton était royal en effet et Blanche comprit que l'adolescent faisait place à l'homme, un homme bon et tendre mais qui saurait se faire obéir. D'ailleurs, déjà, d'un mot gentil – Marguerite avait eu peur et il ne pouvait supporter qu'elle eût peur – il atténuait l'effet trop brutal. L'orage n'eut donc pas de suite mais Marguerite vaincue par tant d'émotions, et par les courants d'air, tomba malade... Blanche en profita pour interdire sa chambre à tout ce qui n'était pas médecin ou femme de service. Le roi lui-même se vit consigner la porte, sous prétexte d'une contagion possible. Sa mère lui conseillait de prier; ce serait bien meilleur que ses visites pour le rétablissement de la jeune reine.

Prier, Louis ne s'en privait pas, mais il était inquiet et un soir, il passa outre la défense maternelle et se fit ouvrir la porte de Marguerite. Il venait juste d'entrer quand Blanche accourut et, tout de suite elle se fâcha, voulut l'obliger à sortir.

« Venez-vous-en! Vous n'avez rien à faire ici... »

Alors Marguerite à nouveau éclata :

« Mon Dieu, madame, s'écria-t-elle avec désespoir, ne me laisserez-vous voir mon seigneur ni morte ni vive?... »

Cette fois, Blanche dut capituler. L'éclat avait fait quelque bruit et, par la ville, on blâmait son attitude abusive. Elle comprit qu'elle allait trop loin, relâcha un peu sa surveillance. Oh! pas beaucoup. Cela lui tenait trop à cœur. Il fallut attendre le 25 avril 1236, jour où s'achevait sa régence pour qu'enfin le roi et la reine de France puissent entamer sérieusement la série de onze enfants (dont huit seulement vécurent) qui allait donner des ancêtres, non seulement aux grandes maisons souveraines françaises, Valois, Bourbon et Orléans, mais encore à toutes celles de l'Europe...

LA NUIT DU RECORD :
CÉSAR BORGIA

Il fallut au moins deux générations aux habitants de Chinon pour oublier, si peu que ce soit, l'entrée fracassante que fit, dans leur bonne ville, le seigneur César Borgia le 18 décembre 1498. Jamais on n'avait rien vu de pareil! C'était tellement fabuleux qu'on se demanda un moment si d'aventure ce personnage ébouriffant n'était pas le Grand Turc. Renseignements pris, c'était seulement le fils d'un pape et un cardinal tout fraîchement défroqué.

Mais pour un beau spectacle, c'était un beau spectacle! Brantôme qui tirait sa description d'un poème populaire a dépeint la scène. Venaient d'abord deux douzaines de mules caparaçonnées de satin jaune et rouge, couleurs que César avait adoptées comme siennes puis vingt-deux autres couvertes de satin jaune ou de drap d'or. Ensuite, seize chevaux superbes tenus en main par des pages et portant des housses de drap d'or rouge ou d'or jaune. D'autres pages encore, bien montés ceux-là, seize d'entre eux en velours cramoisi, et deux en drap d'or « grossier », six mules tenues en main et vêtues de velours cramoisi brodé d'or précédant deux autres mules harnachées d'or et portant des coffres peints et dorés.

Derrière ce « menu train » s'avançaient trente gentils-hommes habillés de drap d'or ou de drap d'argent mais tous portant au cou de lourdes chaînes d'or. Ensuite une troupe de ménestrels, de tambourinaires, de joueurs de rebec ou de trompette habillés, comme tout le monde, d'or et de cramoisi mais leurs instruments étaient d'argent et ils en jouaient avec ardeur. Vingt-six laquais mi-partie de satin jaune et mi-partie de satin cramoisi venaient ensuite précédant César qui chevauchait en s'entretenant avec le cardinal de Rohan...

Les yeux des assistants commençaient à se fatiguer mais ils se réveillèrent à l'aspect du Borgia.

« Quant audit duc [1] il était monté sur un beau et noble coursier, très richement caparaçonné, vêtu d'un pourpoint mi-partie de satin noir et de drap d'or, embelli de pierres précieuses et de grosses perles. Sur son chapeau qui était à la mode française, figuraient deux rangées de cinq à six rubis de la dimension d'un gros haricot qui étincelaient brillamment. Il y avait aussi quantité de pierres précieuses sur la bordure de son chapeau, entre autres une perle aussi grosse qu'une noisette tandis que, même sur ses bottes, on voyait abondance de cordelières d'or bordées de perles.

> « *Et un collier, pour en dire le cas,*
> « *Qui valait bien trente mille ducats.* »

Ainsi harnaché, César qui devait ressembler furieusement à un arbre de Noël, récolta plus de sourires que d'admiration, notamment de la part du roi Louis XII. De sa fenêtre, celui-ci assistait à la fabuleuse entrée de cirque, mais il se contenta de dire que c'était un peu trop pour un petit duc de Valentinois. Sa cour, d'ailleurs, était modeste et plutôt austère. Quant aux gens de Chinon, habitués à plus de retenue, ils n'apprécièrent pas davantage : les gens des pays de Loire, cela est bien connu, sont plus sensibles à la mesure et à l'élégance qu'à l'étalage écrasant d'un parvenu.

Mais le roi n'avait pas le choix : il lui fallait faire bonne figure à ce mirliflore dont il venait de faire un duc français,

---

1. **Louis XII** l'avait fait duc de Valentinois.

s'il voulait en obtenir la bulle d'annulation de son premier mariage avec la pauvre Jeanne de France, fille de Louis XI et affreusement disgraciée physiquement, qu'il avait été contraint jadis d'épouser. Cette annulation était indispensable à son remariage avec Anne, duchesse de Bretagne, vouve de son prédécesseur le roi Charles VIII. Louis espérait bien que César l'apportait dans ses bagages...

Poussé par son fils, Alexandre VI avait marchandé cette bulle comme un maquignon, y mettant d'autant plus d'ardeur qu'il souhaitait vivement voir s'éloigner de Rome le meurtrier impuni de son fils aîné, Juan, duc de Gandia, qu'il aimait chèrement. Rendu à la vie civile, César avait exigé un duché et entendait se marier en France. Mais pas avec n'importe qui : il lui fallait une princesse de sang royal...

Il avait eu le duché – et même, en prime, le comté de Die – il lui fallait maintenant la femme et il entendait bien ne pas lâcher la fameuse annulation tant qu'il n'aurait pas obtenu satisfaction... On devine sans peine quel mal se donnait Louis XII pour qu'il obtînt satisfaction.

Au château de Chinon, il installa César et la bande de hautains coupe-jarrets qui lui servait d'escorte dans la tour de Boissy, proche de la chapelle où avait prié Jeanne d'Arc, il lui donna aussi sa propre garde et le confirma dans les titres déjà reçus. Une indiscrétion lui ayant appris que César apportait bel et bien la fameuse annulation, force fut au Valentinois de la donner avant d'avoir reçu l'assurance d'être marié. Mais Louis XII était un homme qui tenait à sa parole : le temps d'épouser sa petite Bretonne et il se mettait en devoir de marier l'encombrant César.

On avait d'abord pensé à Carlotta d'Aragon, fille du roi de Naples, qui faisait partie des demoiselles d'honneur de la reine Anne. Ferdinand, son père, n'aimait pas les Borgia et ne souhaitait guère ce mariage mais, pensant que César réussirait peut-être à séduire la jeune fille, Louis, un soir, les plaça côte à côte à table.

Cela ne donna rien du tout. Avec une belle franchise, Carlotta déclara que le seigneur Borgia ne lui plaisait pas, qu'elle n'avait aucune envie d'attraper sa maladie [1] et qu'enfin elle ne voulait à aucun prix s'exposer à être appelée un jour « la Cardinale »... Elle n'ajouta pas qu'elle aimait profondément le jeune Guy de Laval parce que c'était vraiment superflu...

C'était la catastrophe, d'autant que le Borgia passait pour rancunier. Il prit très mal l'affront, se jura que les Napolitains lui paieraient cela tôt ou tard et commença ses bagages : si on ne l'avait fait venir que pour l'humilier, il allait rentrer chez lui se plaindre au pape, faire du scandale... et Louis XII pourrait enterrer pour toujours ses prétentions sur le duché de Milan...

Affolé, le roi fit donner la garde : on offrit à l'offensé de choisir entre deux autres demoiselles de la reine Anne : sa nièce, Catherine de Foix ou Charlotte d'Albret, sœur du roi de Navarre et fille d'Alain d'Albret, duc de Guyenne. Le choix fut vite fait : ce serait Charlotte d'Albret pour une raison fort simple : on l'appelait « la plus belle fille de France » et elle était ravissante.

Mais si César se déclare d'accord, le futur beau-père l'est moins. Il joue aussi les marchands de tapis, celui-là discute la dot pied à pied, fait monter les prix. Le roi promet une dot de 120 000 écus d'or – dont d'ailleurs il ne paiera jamais un centime. Alain d'Albret alors ouvre sa bourse pour 30 000 écus mais demande à examiner le bref de sécularisation de l'ancien cardinal. Cela fait du temps qui passe et César s'énerve...

On finit tout de même par tomber d'accord et l'on établit une convention aux termes de laquelle César est déclaré « très honnête et bon personnage, sage et discret... ». On croit rêver!... Et l'on prépare le mariage... au grand chagrin de la fiancée. Elle n'est pas du tout ravie, Charlotte

---

1. Il était atteint d'une vérole qui l'obligeait parfois à porter un masque.

d'Albret! Outre qu'il est un « ancien prêtre », César perd beaucoup de sa splendeur quand son mal se manifeste, lui couvre le visage de pustules qui l'obligent à se promener masqué. C'est très romantique, un masque... à condition de ne pas savoir ce qu'il y a dessous. Enfin ce n'est rien d'autre qu'un bâtard et, pour Charlotte, un mulet même couvert d'or et de pierreries sera toujours un mulet. Elle ne se prive pas de le dire. Mais quoi? Quand arrive l'autorisation paternelle, il faut bien se résigner à obéir. Charlotte y a d'ailleurs été doucement mais fermement engagée par Jeanne de France, l'ex-épouse de Louis XII, retirée à présent à Bourges, et qui a sur elle une grande influence. La sainte créature – elle sera canonisée par Pie XII – n'est que pardon et obéissance. Charlotte doit, elle aussi, pratiquer ces rudes vertus...

Le 12 mai, au château de Blois, où les travaux sont achevés et où la Cour se réinstalle pour la belle saison, César Borgia épouse Charlotte d'Albret. Le roi mène lui-même à l'autel, où attend le cardinal d'Amboise, la fiancée, merveilleusement belle dans une robe de satin blanc entièrement brodée d'or avec un long manteau d'or frisé bordé d'hermine. Des émeraudes, des perles et des diamants étincellent à sa gorge et à sa coiffe de satin, mais chacun peut voir qu'elle est très pâle et qu'elle ne regarde guère son époux. Il est beau, pourtant, César, dans un pourpoint d'écarlate tissé d'argent avec une profusion de diamants. Celui qui attache la plume blanche à son toquet est gros comme un œuf de pigeon et chacun en reste stupéfait d'admiration.

Après les festivités habituelles, Anne de Bretagne prend la tête du cortège qui mène la mariée, qu'elle tient par la main, jusqu'au lit nuptial. Un peu plus tard, le roi amènera lui-même César... et les portes se refermeront. Personne n'assistera à cette nuit de noces dont l'écho, pourtant, ira jusqu'à Rome car, dès le matin, César dépêche à son père un messager avec une lettre écrite en espagnol dans laquelle il proclame sa victoire sur la **plus** belle fille de France. Brutalement, il écrit qu'il a « couru huit postes » *(hizo ocho viajes)*.

Se vantait-il? Comment était-il parvenu à imposer, à une fille qui ne l'aimait pas, une telle performance, c'est ce que l'on ne saura jamais. Peut-être César usa-t-il de brutalité, pour commencer, et l'on peut supposer qu'à la fin Charlotte était exténuée et peut-être assez mal en point; sept assauts après une défloration ne pouvant guère entraîner le plaisir chez une fille neuve...

Mais une autre version circulait qui a été rapportée par Henri Estienne d'abord, puis par Jean Lucas-Dubreton. Selon cette version César « ayant demandé à un apothicaire des pilules pour festoyer sa dame, on lui en bailla de laxatives tellement que toute la nuit il ne cessa d'aller au retrait, comme les dames en firent le rapport au matin... »

Qui croire? Tandis que le pape faisait pratiquement placarder sur les murs de Rome le bulletin de victoire de son fils, les nouveaux époux recevaient les cadeaux et les félicitations de la Cour de France. Charlotte écrivait à son beau-père pour lui dire qu'elle était « enchantée de son mari ». Louis XII investissait César du grand collier de Saint-Michel et, finalement, le couple, emportant un fabuleux déménagement allait s'installer, pour la lune de miel, au château de la Motte-Feuilly, près de Bourges.

On y passa la plus grande partie de l'été jusqu'à ce matin du début de septembre où César monta à cheval pour rejoindre Louis XII qui s'en allait conquérir son cher duché de Milan... et pour se conquérir à lui-même un royaume.

Quand retomba la poussière du chemin, César Borgia avait disparu. Charlotte, duchesse de Valentinois et déjà enceinte de sa fille, Louise, ne devait jamais le revoir...

LA NUIT INESPÉRÉE :
LOUIS XII ÉPOUSE MISS ANGLETERRE

Le bon roi Louis XII qui s'était donné tant de mal pour épouser Anne de Bretagne, veuve de son prédécesseur Charles VIII, se retrouva un beau matin veuf à son tour. Sa chère Bretonne trépassait, le 9 janvier 1514, presque sans préavis, d'une crise de gravelle qui la fit beaucoup souffrir. Elle n'avait que trente-huit ans et sa mort, courageusement supportée, fut des plus pénibles mais elle le fut presque autant pour un époux qui se retrouvait seul, vieux avant l'âge – il n'avait que cinquante-deux ans mais en accusait facilement quinze de plus –, malade car il souffrait de fréquentes hémorragies internes et, de plus, sans le moindre héritier mâle pour coiffer après lui la couronne de France. D'héritier en ligne directe s'entend car, depuis des années, un certain jeune cousin piaffait à sa porte : François d'Angoulême, et surtout sa mère Louise de Savoie qui ne vivait que pour lui, respiraient, ou ne respiraient plus, au rythme des grossesses incessantes de la reine, souvent interrompues d'ailleurs par des fausses couches.

La mort d'Anne de Bretagne constituait pour eux la meilleure des nouvelles. Louis XII restait avec deux filles, Claude et Renée, exclues naturellement du trône, et son délabrement avancé laissait espérer qu'il ne ferait pas attendre trop longtemps son successeur. Le chagrin qu'il éprouvait n'arrangeait rien. Le veuf était l'image même de la désolation, ne voulant se laisser approcher par personne et ne demandant plus qu'à mourir.

« Allez, disait-il, allez, faites le caveau et le lieu où doibt estre ma femme assez grand pour elle et pour moy, car devant que soit l'an passé, je seray avec elle et luy tiendrai compagnie... »

Ces plaintes sont douce musique pour les Angoulême car, en outre, la reine, en mourant a confié sa fille aînée Claude et l'administration de ses biens à la comtesse d'Angoulême, son ennemie de toujours pourtant. Cela veut dire que François va pouvoir épouser Claude et prendre, de ce fait, rang de dauphin.

Les noces, les plus lugubres que l'on puisse voir car la mariée y est en noir, ont lieu le 18 mai à Saint-Germain. C'est une cérémonie d'une grande discrétion car le roi, qui mène un deuil spectaculaire n'entend pas être distrait de son chagrin. François lui-même, toujours si élégant, si somptueux dans ses habillements, se contente d'une simple robe de damas noir brodée de velours. La seule note blanche, dans tout cela, est apportée par les rideaux de damas blanc dont la fiancée a garni elle-même, le lit nuptial apporté par celui qui a pris le titre de duc de Valois.

On a rarement vu couple plus mal assorti. Claude a quinze ans et elle ressemble beaucoup à sa mère mais elle est « bien petite et d'étrange corpulence ». Elle boite des deux hanches. Pourtant, elle possède un charme infini, fait de douceur et d'affabilité. « Sa grâce de parler, écrit un ambassadeur, supplée beaucoup de la faulte de beauté. »

François, lui, est superbe : deux mètres de haut et taillé en conséquence. Il suffit d'aller contempler son armure au musée des Invalides pour s'en rendre compte. Il est « blanc et vermeil, les cheveux bruns... », toujours gai, toujours aimable, toujours courant les filles qui ne savent guère lui résister. La douce Claude, qui passera à la postérité en donnant son nom à la plus succulente des prunes, ne lui résistera pas davantage. Il y a longtemps qu'elle **est** amoureuse du beau cousin et elle le sera toute sa vie. Lui, de son côté, ne lui ménagera ni la tendresse ni le respect, mais la trompera abondamment.

Or, durant l'été qui suit le mariage, une effroyable nouvelle vient troubler la quiétude béate de Louise de Savoie qui attend la mort de Louis XII en faisant embellir son château favori de Romorantin : le veuf inconsolable serait sur le point de se remarier! Et avec qui? une gamine de seize ans, fraîche comme une fleur, vive comme une gazelle et pourvue, d'après les cancans londoniens, d'un tempérament de feu : Mary d'Angleterre, la propre sœur du jeune roi Henri VIII. Une fillette qui porte tellement de vie en elle que ce serait bien le diable si elle ne réussissait pas à la transmettre! Et Madame d'Angoulême de se revoir attendant dans l'angoisse le résultat des grossesses royales...

Mais d'abord, tout cela est-il vrai? Eh bien oui, tout est vrai. L'artisan de ce mariage effarant, c'est un prisonnier de guerre : Louis de Longueville, marquis de Rothelin, qui tuait le temps à Londres en jouant à la paume avec Henri VIII. Sa raquette habile lui a rapporté d'abord sa rançon et ensuite cette étrange idée, qui est une bonne idée d'ailleurs, car elle mettra fin à toutes les bisbilles avec les Anglais et pour longtemps, surtout si l'Anglaise donne un héritier. Les souverains britanniques renonceraient peut-être alors à cette déplorable manie qu'ils ont gardée de s'intituler toujours « rois de France » au jour de leur sacre...

Et, de prisonnier, Longueville s'est retrouvé ambassadeur. Bien mieux, le 13 août, c'est lui qui épouse, par procuration, la jeune princesse anglaise en la chapelle du château royal de Greenwich, puis accomplit, dans sa chambre, le simulacre de consommation.

« ...au soir, la jeune épousée, déshabillée, fut mise au lit en présence de nombreux témoins. Le marquis de Rothelin, en robe de chambre, chaussé de bas couleur de pourpre mais avec une jambe nue, entra dans le lit et toucha la princesse de sa jambe nue. Le mariage fut alors déclaré consommé... »

Restait à gagner la France où se préparaient les autres cérémonies. Louis XII a décidé que ces cérémonies auraient lieu à Abbeville et, aux premiers jours d'octobre, les chemins qui mènent en Picardie se couvrent de litières et de cavaliers car le roi a mandé tous les gentilshommes de son royaume pour faire honneur à la nouvelle reine. Et Louise de Savoie de soupirer amèrement :

« Le 22 septembre, le roy Louis XII, fort antique et débile, sortit de Paris pour aller au-devant de sa jeune femme... »

En fait, il ne paraît plus si antique le futur époux. Non seulement il ne pleure plus et il a remisé ses crêpes funèbres, mais l'idée de prendre prochainement livraison d'une épouse jeune et jolie dont il pourra espérer un héritier l'émoustille et le ravigote. Il sent renaître quelque peu en lui le galant et bouillant duc d'Orléans qu'il fut jadis.

De son côté Mary quitte Londres avec une suite imposante. Elle est sous la garde d'une respectable douairière, la duchesse de Norfolk, et de « bons et vieils personnaiges des plus estimés qui sont en Angleterre », au milieu desquels se perd un autre « personnaige » qui n'a rien de « vieil », qui est même singulièrement séduisant : l'amant de la princesse, le duc de Suffolk.

Pour ne pas trop terrifier les Français, il y a tout de même quelques jolies filles parmi lesquelles Marie Boleyn dont la jeune sœur Anne fera un jour quelque bruit dans le monde. Le 2 octobre tout ce beau monde aborde à Saint-Valéry puis se met en route pour Abbeville à petites étapes de deux ou trois lieues par jour.

Les uns après les autres – le duc de Vendôme d'abord, puis le duc d'Alençon, les grands seigneurs français viennent au-devant de leur reine. Le dernier apparaît, le duc de Valois qui ne peut plus guère s'intituler dauphin.

Ce n'est pas d'un cœur joyeux que François, flanqué de son ami Fleuranges, s'en vient accueillir celle qui devient sa belle-mère mais son goût des femmes reprend bien vite le dessus et, quand il s'incline devant Mary il oublie complètement qu'il a décidé de la détester. Le seul sentiment qu'il éprouve c'est une vague jalousie envers le vieux roi qui va posséder cette merveille. Car c'en est une! Grande, bien faite, le teint éblouissant des Anglaises, des cheveux d'or et de grands yeux d'azur, Mary a tout ce qu'il faut pour séduire François. Mais il doit se rendre à l'amère évidence : elle n'est pas pour lui...

A Abbeville pendant ce temps, Louis XII « monta sur un grand cheval bayart, qui sautoit, et avecques tous les gentilshommes et pensionnaires de sa maison, et sa garde, et en moult noble estat, vint recevoir sa femme, et la baisa tout à cheval. Et, après ce, embrassa tous les princes d'Angleterre, et leur fit très bonne chère; et à l'aborder, pour mieux resjouir toute la compagnie, avoit plus de cent trompettes et clairons... »

Le lendemain ont lieu les épousailles, non dans une église mais au logis du roi dans une grande salle tendue de drap d'or. Pour un roi réputé avare, Louis XII a bien fait les choses...

Le cardinal de Prie célèbre le mariage. La nouvelle reine qui n'est pas encore couronnée à Saint-Denis « est toute deschevellée » ce qui veut dire que ses beaux cheveux tombent librement sur ses épaules mais « elle avoit un chapeau de pierreries sur son chef, le plus riche de la chrestienté ». Le duc de Valois sert de garçon d'honneur au roi, sa femme assiste la reine et le bavard Fleuranges, à qui l'on doit la relation minutieuse de la cérémonie, ne peut s'empêcher de la plaindre. « Et scai bien que ladite dame Claude avoit un merveilleusement grand regret, car il n'y avoit guères que la reine sa mère estoit morte... »

Jusqu'à la nuit, on festoya puis « la nuit vinct et se couchièrent... » en présence de toute la Cour naturellement. Pourtant, en apercevant les cheveux dorés de Mary répandus sur l'oreiller de satin ce ne fut pas à la couronne de France, en si grand danger de lui échapper, que songea François de Valois, tandis que toujours flanqué de Fleuranges, il se retirait en s'efforçant de se remonter le moral. Comment « l'antique et fort débile » Louis XII réussirait-il à venir à bout de cette triomphante jeunesse?

Il s'attendait à apprendre que le roi avait eu besoin de secours durant cette nuit et ne dormit guère. Or, il n'en est rien. Quand Louis XII reparaît le lendemain, il est tout changé. Jamais on ne l'a vu si gai, on pourrait presque dire si frétillant.

« Suis tout vaillant! répète-t-il en se frottant les mains, Suis vraiment tout vaillant! »

Et de clamer à tout vent « qu'il avoit faict merveilles... »

Pour sa part François n'en croit rien.

« Adventureux, confie-t-il deux jours plus tard à Fleuranges que l'on surnommait le jeune Aventureux, je suis plus ayse que ne suis de l'année car je suis sûr, on ne m'a fort bien menty, qu'il est impossible que le roy et le royne puissent avoir enfant, qui est ungne chose qui viendrait fort à mon désavantage... »

Le roi et la reine, c'est bien possible... mais la reine et quelqu'un d'autre? ce séduisant Suffolk par exemple qu'Henri VIII a autorisé sa sœur à « emporter dans ses bagages » avec mission de pallier la défaillance éventuelle du roi de France! Le roi d'Angleterre qui craint comme le feu François de Valois entend donner à la France un roi de son cru.

Louise de Savoie qui est venue assister au couronnement de la reine s'épouvante de cette présence intempestive et met son fils en garde : chacun sait que Suffolk est l'amant de Mary; si elle continue « son commerce » avec lui, François peut dire adieu à la couronne.

Il prend aussitôt des dispositions judicieuses : sa femme, Madame Claude, ne bougera de la chambre de la reine quand celle-ci ne sera pas avec le roi, Mme d'Aumont, sa dame d'honneur l'accompagnera partout et, de toute façon, couchera dans sa chambre. Quant à Suffolk, François lui trouvera de l'occupation dès que les fêtes qu'il offre fastueusement pour le couronnement de la reine – entre autres un prodigieux tournoi aux Tournelles – seront achevées.

Six semaines passent ainsi en fêtes diverses. Puis les seigneurs et les dames d'Angleterre prennent congé et, comblés de présents, rentrent chez eux. Seul demeure Suffolk, l'inquiétant Suffolk...

Pour s'en débarrasser, François l'emmène chasser à Amboise où le sanglier pullule. Suffolk, chasseur impénitent, ne sait pas résister à l'appel d'une trompe de chasse. Et puis, depuis quelques jours, il se sent du vague à l'âme : la reine n'est plus la même avec lui. Elle est distraite et, de toute évidence si satisfaite d'être reine de France qu'elle souhaite beaucoup le rester. Et elle mitonne son vieux mari avec une constance qui exaspère l'Anglais.

Après la chasse, François offre une fête au cours de laquelle il présente Suffolk à une ravissante indigène des bords de Loire, Marie Babou de la Bourdaisière qui est sa maîtresse depuis pas mal de temps. Pour écarter l'Anglais de Mary il lui sacrifierait jusqu'à sa propre épouse si elle était plus attrayante. La belle Babou sait prendre un homme et, deux jours plus tard, lui ayant confié son duc anglais, François délivré d'un gros souci, rentre aux Tournelles à francs étriers.

Or, s'il court si vite, c'est moins pour retourner veiller au grain que pour se rapprocher de Mary. Elle l'attire comme la flamme attire le phalène et, depuis le fameux tournoi où il a porté ses couleurs, elle le regarde avec une complaisance troublante. Entre ces deux tempéraments ardents il suffirait d'une étincelle facile à provoquer car subitement Louis XII s'est mis à décliner. Soumis jusqu'à son mariage à un régime sévère et à une vie réglée, il a bousculé tout cela, mangeant à des heures variées, se couchant tard. En outre, il a « trop faict du gentil compagnon avecque sa femme ». Pour leur part, les clercs de la Basoche, à Paris, qui savent toujours tout, parient entre eux que « le roi d'Angleterre a envoyé une haquenée au roi pour le porter plus tôt et plus doucement en enfer ou en paradis... »

Louis XII n'est plus bien loin de sa fin, en effet, et voilà que ce fou de François est en train de se laisser séduire par Mary, qu'il lui fait une cour pressante, ouverte?... A cette nouvelle Louise de Savoie sent le cœur lui manquer. Après tout le mal qu'elle s'est donné, ce grand imbécile ne va tout de même pas tomber dans le panneau? Ne comprend-il pas que tout ce que veut Mary c'est qu'il lui fasse l'enfant dont le mari a été incapable, l'enfant qui lui permettra de rester en France? Va-t-il se donner à lui-même un roi?...

La scène qu'elle fait à son fils – la seule qu'elle fera jamais à ce fils adoré qu'elle appelle orgueilleusement « mon César! » – est si violente qu'elle laisse François pantois. Jamais il n'a vu sa mère à ce point déchaînée. Mais cette violence porte ses fruits, François a compris. Il évitera Mary...

Les choses d'ailleurs se précipitent. Dans les derniers jours de décembre, Louis XII ne quitte plus son lit. Il est presque impotent. Se sentant mal, il fait venir François et lui dit qu'il n'en réchappera pas. Pourtant, il lutte désespérément contre la mort. Le 1er janvier 1515, c'est la fin. Vers dix heures et demie du soir alors que Paris courbe le dos sous une violente tempête de neige, il s'éteint... Alors, à travers les bourrasques, Fleuranges, Bonnivet et les autres compagnons de François courent vers l'hôtel de Valois criant, hurlant, braillant : « Vive le Roi!... Vive François Ier!... »

Louise de Savoie peut dormir enfin tranquille. Le règne du Roi-Chevalier qu'éclairera, en fin d'été, le soleil de Marignan peut commencer...

Au fait, le peut-il vraiment? Enfermée à l'hôtel de Cluny selon la tradition, ensevelie sous le deuil blanc des reines de France, Mary fait courir le bruit qu'elle est

enceinte. Brantôme se charge de rapporter ce bruit qui a
encore chaviré le cœur de Madame d'Angoulême.

« La reine Mary faisait courir le bruict, après la mort du
roy, tous les jours, qu'elle estoit grosse; si bien que ne
l'estant poinct dans le corps, on dit qu'elle s'enfloit par le
dehors avec des linges peu à peu... »

Certains chroniqueurs prétendent que la mère de
François découvrit elle-même le pot au roses, d'autres, plus
vrais sans doute, que François alla en personne demander
à la reine blanche « s'il pouvait se faire sacrer roi... »

Mary, alors, abandonna le jeu.

« Sire, je ne connais point d'autre roi que vous... »,
murmura-t-elle en plongeant dans sa révérence.

Le rêve était fini pour elle. Après si peu de mois – à
peine un automne! – la couronne de France lui échappait.
Il lui restait le cher, très cher Suffolk, échappé des jolies
mains de Marie Babou, et dont le goût lui revenait. Elle
l'épousa et repartit avec lui pour l'Angleterre.

Pourtant, il semblerait que François Iᵉʳ ait un instant
songé à répudier Claude de France pour garder la belle
Anglaise, croyant qu'elle l'aimait. Honnête, Mary aurait
alors avoué qu'elle n'avait jamais aimé d'autre homme que
son duc anglais...

LA NUIT D'UNE CENDRILLON POLONAISE

Elle avait vingt-deux ans, elle était charmante et elle n'avait pratiquement pas de chemise quand un portrait, mis presque par inadvertance sous les yeux d'un roi qui n'avait pas seize ans, fit d'elle une reine de France. L'une des moins connues! Car naturellement c'est l'étrange destin de ces épouses royales capables d'assumer leur rôle dans toute sa grandeur vertueuse, charitable et pieuse, de se voir délaissées par l'historien au profit des maîtresses singulièrement plus tapageuses que leur infligeaient leurs volages époux. A l'habituelle formule « les gens heureux n'ont pas d'histoire » on pourrait ajouter « les gens convenables n'intéressent pas l'Histoire ». Ce fut à de rares exceptions près le sort de Claude de France, d'Éléonore d'Autriche, de Marie-Thérèse, de Marie Leczinska et de quelques autres; leur seul titre à l'intérêt général semblant tenir uniquement au fait d'avoir été abondamment et publiquement trompées. Pourtant, la charmante histoire du mariage de Louis XV vaut bien celle de sa rencontre avec la sémillante épouse du fermier général Lenormand d'Étiolles dont il allait faire la Pompadour, et l'emblème tout-puissant de son siècle... C'est, à la lettre, un conte de fées...

Il était une fois, donc, dans une modeste demeure de Wissembourg, en Alsace, une jeune princesse polonaise qui vivait presque misérablement entre son père et sa mère. Le père s'appelait Stanislas, la mère s'appelait Catherine. Ils avaient été roi et reine mais un rival heureux les avait chassés, pourchassés même avec un acharnement impitoyable à travers la Posnanie, la Suède, la Poméranie et l'Allemagne en général. Ce rival, l'Électeur de Saxe, était tout-puissant car, à ses propres forces, se joignaient celles de l'immense Russie, son alliée. Et les aventures angoissantes n'avaient pas été ménagées à ce roi, à cette reine en exil et à leur petite fille Marie.

Un jour, par exemple, alors qu'elle était encore toute petite, au château de Posen, les Russes étaient arrivés pendant une absence de son père. Ils avaient enfoncé toutes les portes et l'on avait fait fuir l'enfant par une fenêtre donnant sur le jardin. Elle avait couru jusqu'au village où un brave paysan l'avait cachée dans son four à pain...

Finalement, la malheureuse famille avait échoué sur les bords du Rhin. Là, les représentants du roi de France lui avaient offert de se choisir une ville résidentielle et l'avaient assurée qu'une pension lui serait servie car elle n'avait plus rien : les biens polonais, toute la fortune avaient été confisqués par Auguste de Saxe. Stanislas choisit alors Wissembourg et s'installa dans cet hôtel de Weber qui n'était pas loin d'être une masure.

On y avait vécu petitement car la fameuse pension n'était pas payée bien régulièrement. Peu ou pas de serviteurs et trois amis fidèles : la marquise d'Andlau, le marquis du Bourg et le cardinal de Rohan qui s'efforçaient, spasmodiquement, d'entretenir l'illusion d'un semblant de cour. Un autre ami, à Paris celui-là, s'efforçait de veiller aux intérêts de ses illustres et misérables amis : c'était le chevalier de Vauchoux. Alors, le père et la fille s'étaient rapprochés l'un de l'autre, trouvant une grande douceur à leur mutuelle tendresse. La reine Catherine, dont le caractère était aussi raide que l'échine, se contentait de veiller à l'intendance et s'en acquittait par toute la rigueur d'un sergent-fourrier. Quand elle ne veillait pas à la maison, elle priait, laissant tout loisir au père et à la fille de s'entretenir de leurs rêves et de leurs espoirs.

Stanislas Leszczynski n'ayant pas les moyens d'offrir à

sa petite Marie les maîtres qui lui eussent orné l'esprit, s'en chargeait lui-même avec bonheur. Il était cultivé, philosophe, artiste aussi et l'instinct, bien polonais, de l'adolescente la portant tout naturellement vers la musique elle sut chanter, danser et jouer du clavecin sans qu'on le lui eût appris vraiment.

Quand on en vint à cette année 1725 qui allait avoir tant d'importance pour l'avenir de la famille, Marie était une jeune fille accomplie. Grande, très bien faite, d'une blondeur de lin, elle n'était pas réellement belle, mais elle était peut-être mieux que cela grâce à la vivacité de son regard, au charme de son sourire et à l'éclat sans rival de son teint. Un vrai teint de Polonaise : neige et roses...

Telle qu'elle était, elle avait gagné le cœur d'un jeune officier qui avait tenu garnison à Wissembourg : le marquis de Courtanvaux, petit-fils de Louvois qui, en regagnant Versailles, était devenu colonel des Cent-Suisses. Hélas, si misérable qu'il fût, Stanislas n'oubliait pas qu'il avait été roi. Courtanvaux n'ayant pas pu obtenir le duché-pairie qui l'eût rapproché un peu de Marie s'était vu refuser sa demande.

A Paris, cependant, il se passait d'étranges choses. Le Régent était mort, le pouvoir était tombé aux mains de Monsieur le Duc : autrement dit le duc de Bourbon, chef de la maison de Condé et son pire ennemi. Or Monsieur le Duc et son égérie la marquise de Prie étaient hantés par un cauchemar : si le jeune roi Louis XV venait à mourir sans avoir eu le temps de faire un enfant, la royauté reviendrait à celui qui était alors son héritier : le duc d'Orléans.

Ce duc d'Orléans, Louis, que l'histoire surnommerait le Génovéfain, n'avait ni la grandeur et les vices de son père le Régent ni les vices sans grandeur de son petit-fils le futur Philippe Égalité. C'était un garçon plutôt terne, pieux, gourmand et sans malice, mais la seule idée de le voir escalader le trône de France donnait de l'urticaire à son cousin et rival Bourbon.

Certes, le roi est fiancé. Depuis plus de trois ans, on lui avait mis à couver une petite infante mais qui n'a pas encore atteint sa septième année ce qui la rend totalement inapte à la consommation. Quand Louis XV tombe brusquement malade et se retrouve en danger, voilà les deux complices aux cent coups.

« S'il en réchappe, il faudra le marier! » dit Monsieur le Duc.

Il a si peur, qu'il cherche fébrilement une épouse. Mais, quand le roi guérit, il n'en a pas trouvé. C'est alors que Mme de Prie se souvient de certain portrait d'une certaine princesse pauvre que lui a un jour porté le chevalier de Vauchoux. On avait pensé un moment la marier à Monsieur le Duc lui-même mais, après tout, pourquoi ne ferait-elle pas l'affaire du roi? D'autant qu'une fille si misérable ne pourrait éprouver que la plus substantielle reconnaissance pour la personne qui l'aurait tirée de sa misère... Et la rusée s'en va, son portrait sous le bras, trouver le jeune roi... Et le jeune roi s'emballe : quelle fraîcheur, quel charmant sourire, quels jolis yeux! C'est celle-là qu'il lui faut! Elle a six ans et demi de plus que lui? Aucune importance!...

Évidemment, il y a bien l'Infante mais, en face des angoisses de Monsieur le Duc, elle ne pèse pas lourd. On la renvoie poliment à son Espagne natale. Son père, Philippe V (le petit-fils de Louis XIV) prend très mal la chose et va se jeter dans les bras des Habsbourg. Ce renvoi est une lourde défaite politique mais de cela Monsieur le Duc se moque éperdument : il lui faut, tout de suite, une reine et un dauphin!...

Quelques jours plus tard, à Wissembourg, Marie qui travaille avec sa mère dans sa chambre voit soudain entrer son père, une lettre à la main. Il paraît si heureux que les deux femmes s'étonnent. Qu'y a-t-il donc?

« Ah, ma fille, s'écrie Stanislas, tombons à genoux et remercions Dieu!

— Quoi! Mon père, seriez-vous rappelé au trône?

— Le ciel nous accorde mieux encore : ma fille, vous êtes reine de France!... »

Le roi Stanislas devait dire plus tard que l'on « étouffait de joie »...

« Pas un instant, écrit Pierre de Nolhac, la princesse Marie n'hésita à accepter la grâce qui lui était envoyée et qui apportait la consolation à ceux qu'elle aimait. Son jeune cœur s'attachait déjà de toute sa force au bel adolescent royal dont les estampes lui avaient fait connaître les traits et pour le bonheur de qui elle avait souvent prié, en retour de l'hospitalité reçue par les siens... »

Lui aussi pensait à elle. Le dimanche 27 mai, à son petit lever, Louis XV déclarait hautement :

« Messieurs, j'épouse la princesse de Pologne. Cette princesse qui est née le 23 juin 1703 est fille unique de Stanislas Leczinsky, comte de Lesno, ci-devant staroste d'Adelnau puis palatin de Posnanie, ensuite élu roi de Pologne au mois de juillet 1704, et de Catherine Opalinska, fille du castellan de Posnanie, qui viennent l'un et l'autre faire leur résidence au château de Saint-Germain-en-Laye avec la mère du roi Stanislas, Anne Jablanoruska, qui avait épousé en secondes noces le comte de Lesno, grand général de la Grande Pologne... »

Ayant fini son petit cours d'histoire, sa jeune majesté expédia le duc de Gesvres propager la nouvelle dans le reste du palais et ne s'occupa plus que des préparatifs.

Chose étrange, la nouvelle fut très mal prise, non seulement par la Cour qui voyait dans ce mariage baroque une insoutenable mésalliance, mais encore par le peuple qui, à ses heures, se révélait plus royaliste et surtout plus snob que le roi. Il est vrai que la faction d'Orléans, affreusement déçue et mécontente, se chargea des clabaudages. Et quels clabaudages! Il n'est pas de sottise, si énorme soit-elle qui ne courut les rues : on disait que la princesse était affreuse, qu'elle avait les doigts de pieds palmés, qu'elle était épileptique et qu'elle souffrait « d'humeurs froides ».

> *On dit qu'elle est hideuse,*
> *Mais cela ne fait rien*
> *Car elle est vertueuse*
> *Et très fille de bien...*

Seul le roi était ravi et plein d'impatience...

Et Marie quitta la triste maison de Wissembourg, où elle avait parfois eu faim et froid, escortée de plusieurs brigades de carabiniers royaux, dans une superbe voiture où ses parents prirent place avec elle, pour gagner Strasbourg où devait se faire le mariage par procuration. Quand elle y entra, elle entendit pour la première fois le canon tonner, les cloches sonner en son honneur tandis que les premiers magistrats de la ville venaient lui offrir leurs hommages, Mais ce fut chez l'amie des jours difficiles, la comtesse d'Andlau, qu'elle choisit de s'installer de préférence au palais du gouvernement.

Le 15 août, vêtue de brocart d'argent garni de dentelles d'argent et semé de roses, Marie Leczinska pénètra dans la cathédrale de Strasbourg, entre son père et sa mère, suivie de Mlle de Clermont, sœur de Monsieur le Duc, qui a été chargée de la ramener à Paris. Pour la première fois, la splendeur des pompes royales l'entourait Le roi a envoyé une partie de sa maison, les gardes du corps, les Cent-Suisses (et leur colonel le pauvre Courtanvaux!), les nouvelles dames d'honneur et les dames du palais. Et ce fut au son des grandes orgues et des chants religieux que celle qui devenait reine de France vint s'agenouiller... auprès de Mgr le duc d'Orléans qui aurait bien préféré être ailleurs...

Et puis ce fut le long voyage vers l'époux réel, un voyage qui ouvrit, devant Marie, les cœurs des Français. Son sourire, sa gentillesse, sa gaieté les lui gagnaient tous et, surtout, son inépuisable charité. Elle qui n'avait jamais eu un sou à elle découvrait la joie de pouvoir donner sans compter, de soulager autant de misère qu'il s'en montrait à elle et les vivats mêlés de bénédictions suivaient à la trace le long cortège qui prenait les allures d'un triomphe.

Un cortège qui eut des aventures. A mesure que l'on avançait, le temps se détériorait et l'état des chemins s'aggravait. De temps à autre, un carrosse s'enlisait, tel celui du duc d'Antin : le gentilhomme et les siens se retrouvèrent dans un champ avec de la boue jusqu'aux genoux. Mais le bouquet fut pour l'avant-dernier soir : la pluie devint torrentielle et tous les carrosses s'embourbèrent avec un bel ensemble aux approches de Montereau, sans espoir de pouvoir se tirer de là.

Monsieur le Duc, qui se trouvait à Montereau, envoya du secours aux naufragés. On put mettre la reine dans la voiture de Mlle de Clermont qui était plus légère que la sienne, mais les autres s'arrangèrent comme ils purent de charrettes de paille et de fourgons à bagages délestés. Les arrivées burlesques de duchesses en grand habit trempées comme des soupes et de seigneurs crottés jusqu'aux sourcils mirent en joie, toute la nuit, les habitants de Montereau qui n'avaient jamais rien vu de pareil... et la reine qui décida d'en faire faire un tableau.

Heureusement, au matin du 4 septembre, prévu pour la rencontre des jeunes époux, le temps était redevenu doux et clair. Il y avait même un bel arc-en-ciel quand, à quatre heures, le cortège de Marie aborda les hauteurs de Froidefontaine où Louis XV attendait avec les équipages de la Cour, des détachements de sa maison « et tout le populaire du pays à quinze lieues à la ronde ».

C'est au son des violons que l'on a disséminés un peu partout que la reine descend de son carrosse et va s'agenouiller, selon la tradition, devant le roi. Mais il la relève avant que ses genoux n'eussent touché le tapis et l'embrasse à plusieurs reprises avec une joie si visible que tout le monde l'applaudit. Jamais on n'a vu Louis XV aussi gai, aussi joyeux. Il rayonne littéralement à la grande stupeur de la Cour. Se pourrait-il qu'il soit à ce point amoureux de sa Polonaise ?

Mais oui, il est amoureux et on va bien s'en apercevoir!

Le lendemain, au château de Fontainebleau où a lieu la cérémonie définitive, il se précipite chez Marie avant même qu'elle ne commence sa toilette. Cette toilette de la mariée est un événement, bien sûr, et de nombreuses personnes y assistent mais ce n'est pas l'usage que le roi s'y montre. On doit presque le mettre à la porte tandis qu'entrent Monsieur le Duc suivi du garde du Trésor qui vient déposer deux bourses de pièces d'or sur la toilette. Paraît ensuite le duc de Mortemart flanqué de l'intendant de l'Argenterie qui apportent la couronne de la reine : un chef-d'œuvre de diamants fermé par une double fleur de lys qui va être posé sur ses cheveux. La robe de la mariée est de velours violet et d'hermine avec un déluge de pierreries mais, quand le roi apparaît, il ressemble au soleil : habit de brocart d'or, manteau de point d'Espagne d'or et, fulgurant à son chapeau à plumes blanches, le Sancy...

La toilette dure trois heures et le roi s'est énervé pendant tout ce temps et d'autant qu'il n'est pas au bout de ses peines. Il faut à présent aller à la chapelle. Marie s'y rend menée d'un côté par Monsieur le Duc et de l'autre par le duc d'Orléans et elle n'imagine certes pas à quel point ces deux-là se détestent : ils ne sont que sourires.

Une fois de plus, c'est le cardinal de Rohan qui officie, mais pontificalement et flanqué des évêques de Soissons et de Viviers.

La cérémonie est superbe mais fatigante. En dépit de la sainteté du lieu, Louis XV ne tient pas en place. Ce puceau (on assure qu'il l'est!) n'a qu'une hâte, c'est de se libérer de cette encombrante distinction... mais la journée n'est pas finie!

Il y a ensuite le dîner au grand couvert, puis la première distribution de cadeaux que la reine fait aux dames, princesses et dames d'honneur. Elle le fait avec une joie d'enfant.

« Voilà, dit-elle, la première fois de ma vie que j'ai pu faire des présents. »

Elle en fera d'autres le lendemain pour les serviteurs plus modestes mais, pour l'heure, il est temps d'aller... voir la comédie de Molière! Après le théâtre, on soupe, puis il y a encore le feu d'artifice tiré au bout du parterre du Tibre. Louis XV ne dissimule plus qu'à peine son impatience, d'autant que le spectacle est médiocre. Il souhaite, visiblement, une intimité dont le sépare encore, hélas, une assez longue étiquette car il doit d'abord procéder à son propre coucher, tout seul, et recevoir les compliments de ses gentilshommes. L' « enfin seuls! » tant attendu ne viendra-t-il donc jamais?...

Si! Il arrive enfin le moment bienheureux où Chérubin peut aller rejoindre sa dame! Il n'y va pas, il y court, bousculant le cérémonial dans sa hâte d'arriver plus vite après avoir littéralement sauté à bas de son lit. Il est onze heures du soir. Marie est assez fatiguée mais lui pas du tout! Il bondit auprès de sa jeune femme et, avec un grand sourire qui est en lui-même un congé, il souhaite le bonsoir à la compagnie. Comme il est le roi, personne ne peut espérer s'éterniser et l'un après l'autre, longues robes à traînes et souliers à talons rouges glissent sur le parquet de la chambre royale dont les gardes du corps referment les vantaux. Cette fois, Louis et Marie sont bien seuls.

Le lendemain, quand les ducs de Bourbon, de Morte-mart et de La Rochefoucauld entrent dans la chambre pour les compliments du matin, ils sont accueillis par un double et rayonnant sourire et ils peuvent contempler à leur aise un couple d'amoureux, spectacle assez rare dans une chambre royale.

« Ils montraient l'un et l'autre, écrit le maréchal de Villars, une vraie satisfaction de nouveaux mariés. »

Quant au duc de Bourbon, il prétendait en savoir plus que tout le monde grâce à des informations de première main qu'il se hâtait de communiquer à Stanislas.

« Le mari a donné à sa femme sept preuves de sa

tendresse. C'est le roi lui-même, précise-t-il, qui, dès qu'il s'est levé, a envoyé un homme de sa confiance et de la mienne pour me le dire et qui, dès que j'ai entré chez lui me l'a répété lui-même en s'étendant infiniment sur la satisfaction qu'il avait eue de la reine... »

Pour un innocent, c'était entamer de triomphante manière une carrière amoureuse qui allait faire le bonheur des chroniqueurs présents et futurs. Ce fut le début d'une charmante période pleine de gaieté pour les deux époux, et aussi la mise en train d'une longue suite de grossesses pour la reine Marie qui allait avoir la joie d'accoucher dix fois pour le bonheur de son cher époux...

Le mariage était en tout point réussi. Tout le monde était content... sauf Voltaire qui blâmait le programme de comédie donné le soir des noces : *Amphytrion* et *le Médecin malgré lui*... « ce qui, dit-il, ne parut pas très convenable... »

Il est vrai que l'on avait refusé de jouer un petit divertissement qu'il s'était donné la peine de préparer lui-même...

LA NUIT À LA HUSSARDE DE NAPOLÉON

Napoléon attendant sa fiancée autrichienne ressemblait beaucoup à un gamin qui espère, du Père Noël, son premier train électrique. Il avait beau jouer à l'esprit fort, déclarer à qui voulait l'entendre, avec une grossièreté voulue rappelant le style du lieutenant Bonaparte : « J'épouse un ventre... », il n'en « espérait » pas moins son arrivée avec un curieux mélange de vanité, d'anxiété, de curiosité et d'excitation. Et, à partir du 13 mars 1810, date du départ de Marie-Louise pour la France, il ne tint plus en place.

Continuellement partaient des messagers, porteurs de lettres ou de présents pour la voyageuse et, chaque fois que l'un d'eux revenait il passait au crible.

« Voyons, parlez-moi franchement! Comment avez-vous trouvé l'archiduchesse Marie-Louise?

— Sire, très bien.

— Très bien ne m'apprend rien. Voyons, quelle taille a-t-elle?

— Sire, elle a la taille... à peu près de la reine de Hollande.

— Ah! c'est bien : de quelle couleur sont ses cheveux?

— Blonds. A peu près comme ceux de la reine de Hollande.

— Bon. Et son teint?...

— Fort blanc et des couleurs très fraîches, comme la reine de Hollande.

— Elle ressemble donc à la reine de Hollande?

— Non, Sire, et cependant, dans tout ce que vous me demandez je vous ai rapporté l'exacte vérité... »

Talleyrand, qui rapporte la scène dont il fut témoin, ajoute qu'après avoir laissé partir le jeune aide de camp qu'il venait d'interroger, Napoléon hocha la tête et marmotta :

« J'ai de la peine à leur arracher quelques mots. Je vois que ma femme est laide car tous ces diables de jeunes gens n'ont pu prononcer qu'elle était jolie. Enfin! Qu'elle soit bonne et me fasse de gros garçons, je l'aimerai comme la plus belle... »

Mais toute cette fraîcheur unanimement proclamée le hantait. Il avait grand hâte de juger par lui-même de ce qu'il en était au juste.

Le 20 mars avant de quitter Paris pour Compiègne qui sera la première résidence impériale de la fiancée, il lui écrit encore :

« Madame, j'ai reçu votre portrait. L'Impératrice d'Autriche a eu l'attention de me le faire remettre. Il me semble y voir l'empreinte de cette belle âme qui vous rend si chère à tous ceux qui vous connaissent et justifie toutes les espérances que j'ai mises en Votre Majesté. Vous aimerez, Madame, un époux qui veut avant tout votre bonheur et dont les droits ne seront jamais fondés que sur votre confiance et les sentiments de votre cœur. Je pense que vous êtes bien près de la France et je vous attends avec bien de l'impatience... »

C'est plus que de l'impatience, c'est de la fièvre. Pourtant, lui non plus ne s'extasie pas sur sa beauté. Il lui parle de « sa belle âme » et comme il sait que les peintres de cour usent et abusent parfois de la flatterie, il est de moins en moins rassuré.

Constant, son valet de chambre, raconte comment, en attendant, il se cherche des raisons d'aimer l'inconnue lui qui a tant aimé Joséphine, ce chef-d'œuvre de grâce et d'élégance.

« Il ne tient pas en place, va voir les appartements préparés pour la nouvelle impératrice où, déjà, l'attendent robes, lingeries, chaussures exécutées sur des modèles envoyés de Vienne. Un jour, il se saisit d'un soulier remarquablement petit et m'en donne un coup sur la joue en forme de caresse.

« – Voyez, Constant, voilà un soulier de bon augure. Avez-vous vu beaucoup de pieds comme celui-là? C'est à prendre dans la main... »

En outre, pour charmer l'attente et les soirées de Compiègne, il décide de se remettre à la danse. Un exercice qu'il n'a pas pratiqué depuis l'École militaire et où, d'ailleurs, il n'a jamais été brillant; mais il pense qu'épousant une Viennoise il lui faut se mettre au courant. Et c'est, curieusement, à la reine Hortense, la propre fille de Joséphine la Répudiée, qu'il demande de lui apprendre la valse car elle est, selon sa propre expression « notre Terpsichore ».

Hortense fait ce qu'elle peut mais le résultat est piteux.

« Je suis trop vieux, déclare l'Empereur. D'ailleurs, ce n'est pas par là que je dois chercher à briller... »

Les leçons de danse servent, au moins, à user le temps, ce temps qu'il trouve interminable.

La rencontre avec la voyageuse est prévue pour le 28 et doit se dérouler à Pontarcher, un village qui se trouve à deux lieues et demie de Soissons, sur la route de Compiègne. A Soissons, où elle aura passé la nuit, Marie-Louise aura eu tout le loisir de se « faire belle » et de se préparer pour le premier coup d'œil. Mais, le 27, Napoléon est à bout de patience. Aux environs de midi, il décide d'aller au-devant de la nouvelle impératrice et quitte Compiègne en calèche accompagné du seul Murat. Il verra sa femme vingt-quatre heures plus tôt et sans préparatifs.

On ne peut pas dire que le temps soit agréable, surtout passé Soissons : il pleut à plein temps. Pour comble de bonheur, un peu au-delà de Braine, l'équipage impérial, dont une roue vient de se briser, manque d'envoyer le fiancé dans un fossé boueux. Heureusement on est au petit village de Courcelles et c'est sous le porche de l'église que Napoléon, toujours flanqué de Murat qui se fait un souci du diable pour son beau chapeau à plumes – il a le génie des panaches gigantesques – va se réfugier pour attendre le cortège qui ne doit plus être loin.

En effet, le voilà. Une longue file de voitures précédées de cavaliers bleus et mauves apparaît sur la route. Alors, oubliant la pluie, Napoléon se jette au milieu de la route, s'y plante... Les hussards de tête reconnaissent la silhouette si familière, la redingote grise, le chapeau noir, et retiennent leurs chevaux.

« L'Empereur! Voilà l'Empereur! »

Le cri est repris par le chambellan qui suit immédiatement M. de Seyssel. Mais Napoléon n'entend rien, ne voit rien que certaine grande berline, tirée par huit chevaux et vers laquelle il court, comme un jeune homme. Il ouvre la portière sans attendre l'aide de personne. Deux femmes sont à l'intérieur et l'une d'entre elles s'écrie :

« Sa Majesté l'Empereur!... »

C'est sa sœur Caroline, la reine de Naples qui a été chargée d'amener la fiancée. A côté d'elle, une grande fille blonde et rose aux yeux globuleux mais d'un joli bleu d'azur et qui semble d'ailleurs passablement effrayée par cette première rencontre avec l'Ogre qu'elle n'attendait pas si tôt. Ses lèvres lourdement ourlées tremblent quand elle s'efforce de sourire. Elle a dix-neuf ans et elle a la fraîcheur de son âge mais ses yeux bleus n'ont guère d'expression et elle est un peu trop potelée. En outre, elle est fagotée dans un manteau de velours vert qui à la rigueur pourrait passer s'il n'était accompagné d'un étrange couvre-chef : une toque garnie de plumes de perroquet multicolores qui ressemble à un plumeau.

Mais Napoléon ne voit rien de tout cela, ni le nez trop long, ni les yeux à fleur de tête, ni la fameuse lèvre Habsbourg qui au contraire le charme : c'est la marque de fabrique... Sa voix claironne joyeusement.

« Madame, j'éprouve à vous voir un grand plaisir! »

Et là-dessus, sans se soucier du fait qu'il est mouillé comme un barbet, le voilà qui escalade le marchepied, prend l'archiduchesse dans ses bras et l'embrasse à plusieurs reprises avec un enthousiasme qui arrache un sourire crispé à la reine de Naples. Puis il s'installe entre les deux femmes et crie au chambellan demeuré debout au milieu de la route :

« Maintenant vite à Compiègne! Et que l'on brûle les étapes!

— Mais, Sire, proteste Caroline, nous sommes attendues à Soissons où l'on a préparé le souper, le coucher...

— Ils mangeront leur souper sans vous. Je désire que Madame soit dès ce soir chez elle... »

Et l'on part, laissant Murat s'arranger comme il voudra de la voiture accidentée...

A Soissons, en effet, le cortège passe en trombe sous l'œil ébahi et quelque peu scandalisé du sous-préfet, du conseil municipal et des autorités militaires qui ont attendu des heures sous les parapluies pour le seul plaisir de voir l'Empereur leur filer sous le nez.

Mais, soudain, à la sortie de la ville, on s'arrête. Les rares observateurs que le mauvais temps n'a pas chassés peuvent voir la portière de la grande berline s'ouvrir pour livrer passage à une dame vêtue de velours gris et coiffée d'une charmante capote à plumes mauves et roses. Une dame qui, le pas énergique et la mine offensée, va s'installer dans la seconde voiture. C'est Caroline que son frère vient de prier aimablement de le laisser seul avec « sa femme »...

Et l'on repart pour Compiègne où l'on arrive à la nuit close et aux flambeaux après avoir mené un train d'enfer.

Et chacun de se demander ce qui fait courir si vite Napoléon...

Vers les dix heures du soir, c'est le branle-bas de combat au château à la suite de l'arrivée essoufflée d'un page abondamment crotté qui annonce le cortège. Tout s'anime comme sur un coup de baguette magique. Des laquais en livrée verte, portant des torches, s'alignent sur le vaste perron. Les fenêtres se peuplent d'une foule brillante, les terrasses des toits sont envahies. Un orchestre s'installe sur la galerie qui domine les grilles, un autre prend position quelque part sur la place, un troisième aux fenêtres d'un grand hôtel particulier. De partout jaillissent des flambeaux... Le perron se garnit de tapis, se couvre de femmes en robes à traîne dont les diadèmes jettent des feux multicolores et d'hommes en uniformes chamarrés. Enfin, dans un grand tumulte de cris que dominent les orchestres jouant, plus ou moins ensemble, *Veillons au salut de l'Empire!* paraissent les voitures, une première à six chevaux, puis une autre. La berline impériale à huit chevaux vient ensuite. Portée dirait-on par l'enthousiasme populaire, elle franchit les grilles, décrit une courbe pleine d'élégance et vient s'arrêter devant le perron. Les valets de pied se précipitent, les porteurs de torches lèvent leurs flammes bien haut, les tambours battent tandis que, sur le perron, les révérences courbent les satins et les brocarts des toilettes de cour.

On peut voir alors Napoléon sauter à terre puis se tourner, rayonnant vers celle qui est encore dans la voiture pour l'aider à descendre avec tous les soins et toutes les tendres précautions d'un amant attentif. Chacun peut constater, non sans une certaine stupeur amusée, que l'archiduchesse est rouge comme une pivoine, que sa toilette semble quelque peu dérangée et que son absurde chapeau à plumes de perroquet donne fortement de la bande. De plus son attitude est bizarrement gênée. Plus d'une mauvaise langue en conclura que la berline vient de servir de vestibule à la chambre à coucher...

Quand le couple monte le perron on s'aperçoit que Marie-Louise a une demi-tête en plus que Napoléon.

« J'ai vu, écrit le prince von Clary und Aldringen, courrier diplomatique autrichien, l'impératrice sauter assez lestement à bas de sa voiture, embrasser immédiatement toute la famille et monter l'escalier conduite par son petit mari. Comme elle a une demi-tête de plus que lui, elle avait vraiment bon air... »

C'est un avis autrichien. Quand la nouvelle venue embrasse les femmes de la famille, la ravissante Pauline cache à peine son envie de rire en contemplant le fameux chapeau. Incontestablement les Bonaparte ont de l'allure. Il y a la sage Elisa et son sévère profil de Minerve; Pauline, reine des élégances déjà nommée; la beauté brune de la reine d'Espagne, ex-Julie Clary; la grâce blonde de la reine Hortense dont la robe de soie blanche, les perles et l'élégance sans défaut jurent effroyablement avec la vêture de Marie-Louise. Il y a Caroline, enfin, extraite du carrosse où elle s'était vue reléguée.

Dans le château, Napoléon entraîne Marie-Louise au pas de charge vers ses appartements. On lui présente sa dame d'honneur, la duchesse de Montebello, veuve de Lannes, qui va devenir son intime amie. Marie-Louise lui confie aussitôt :

« L'Empereur est bien charmant et bien doux pour un homme de guerre si redoutable; il me semble maintenant que je l'aimerai bien... »

Le fameux sourire Bonaparte a fait des siennes et si l'Ogre l'a quelque peu lutinée dans l'ombre complice de la voiture, elle ne semble pas lui en tenir rigueur. D'autant moins qu'en arrivant dans sa chambre, elle trouve des attentions charmantes : il y a là son canari qu'elle pensait ne jamais revoir, son petit chien venu avec sa femme de chambre favorite et même une tapisserie qu'elle avait laissée inachevée.

Il y a aussi une table toute servie pour trois personnes :

le nouveau couple soupe avec la reine de Naples. Le souper est très gai mais, quand il s'achève, chacun pense que l'Empereur va se retirer pour s'en aller coucher à l'hôtel de la Chancellerie où tout est préparé pour le recevoir. Mais il n'en a pas la moindre envie...

Au lieu de partir, il s'en va trouver son oncle, le cardinal Fesch et lui pose la question qui lui brûle les lèvres : est-il marié? Autrement dit, est-ce que le mariage par procuration de Vienne est valable et lui permet d'user, dès ce soir, de ses droits d'époux? Le cardinal qui connaît bien son neveu est embarrassé : ce n'est pas l'usage. La bonne règle veut que, pour la nuit de noces, on attende que les noces officielles aient été célébrées. L'Empereur doit se rappeler que son mariage civil sera célébré le 1ᵉʳ avril à Saint-Cloud et son mariage religieux le lendemain dans le Salon Carré du Louvre. En outre, l'archiduchesse doit être fatiguée de ce long voyage...

Il perd son temps. Napoléon n'a qu'une idée en tête : goûter tout de suite à son dessert viennois. Et quand le cardinal parle de prendre conseil, de discuter, il refuse d'entendre : il n'a pas le temps. En désespoir de cause l'oncle Fesch propose de demander à l'intéressée elle-même ce qu'elle en pense. Et Napoléon s'en va trouver Marie-Louise pour lui demander si, en la quittant, son père lui a fait quelque recommandation.

« Il m'a dit, répond la jeune fille, qu'aussitôt seule avec vous j'aurais à faire absolument tout ce que vous me diriez et que je devrais obéir à tout ce que vous pourriez exiger!... »

On ne peut être plus claire et il n'est pas difficile d'imaginer le large sourire de Napoléon. Il s'approche de sa jeune femme et murmure :

« Quand vous serez seule, je viendrai vous trouver... »

Au fond c'était pure courtoisie de sa part d'aller demander son avis au cardinal! Dans la berline, il n'avait pas demandé de permission pour entamer les préliminaires. Et le voilà, tout ravi, qui court procéder à une minutieuse toilette de nuit tandis que Caroline se croit obligée de jouer les grandes sœurs et de donner à Marie-Louise les conseils d'usage. Mais elle n'a rien à apprendre à la mariée. A Vienne « on lui avait tout dit... »

Un moment plus tard, Napoléon s'inonde d'eau de Cologne avec une impériale générosité (c'est Jean-Marie Farina qui, sans le savoir, embaumera la nuit de noces) puis, nu, il enfile sa robe de chambre et s'en va chez Marie-Louise...

A Sainte-Hélène, il confiera à Gourgaud :

« Je vins, et elle fit tout cela en riant... »

« Le lendemain au matin, raconte Constant, l'Empereur me demanda à sa toilette si l'on s'était aperçu de l'accroc qu'il avait fait au programme. Je répondis que non, au risque de mentir. En ce moment entra un des familiers de l'Empereur qui n'était pas encore marié. Sa Majesté lui dit :

« – Mon cher, épousez une Allemande. Ce sont les meilleures femmes du monde, douces, bonnes, naïves et fraîches comme des roses...

« A l'air de satisfaction de Sa Majesté il était facile de voir qu'Elle faisait un portrait et qu'il n'y avait pas longtemps que le peintre avait quitté le modèle.

« Après quelques soins donnés à sa personne, l'Empereur retourna chez l'Impératrice et, vers midi, il fit monter à déjeuner pour elle et pour lui, se faisant servir près du lit par les femmes de Sa Majesté. Tout le reste du temps, il fut d'une gaieté charmante... »

L'aventure du mariage autrichien commençait bien dans la gaieté et dans la joie. L'accueil de Compiègne, un peu improvisé, avait été suffisamment enthousiaste. Il n'en alla pas de même de celui de Paris. Écoutons la reine Hortense qui partageait une voiture avec Julie Clary et le grand-duc de Wurtzbourg.

« Sous l'Empereur, les cérémonies furent toujours belles

et imposantes. L'arc de Triomphe de l'Étoile, déjà commencé, avait provisoirement été achevé en bois... Sur notre route, le peuple me parut assez froid. Il ne témoignait pas de plaisir à voir une Autrichienne... »

Ce fut surtout quand le cortège, sortant des Champs-Élysées, traversa la place de la Concorde pour pénétrer aux Tuileries que le froid se fit sentir. Parmi les assistants, ils étaient encore nombreux ceux qui, seize ans et demi plus tôt, avaient vu tomber, sur cette même place, la tête de la reine Marie-Antoinette. L'arrivée en France de sa nièce réveillait bien des mauvais souvenirs. Seule l'aristocratie se montrait enthousiaste.

« La société de Paris, écrit la reine Hortense, qui s'était réunie tout entière dans la galerie du Louvre, laissa éclater l'enthousiasme le plus vif, les uns par d'anciens et chers souvenirs, les autres par l'espoir d'une paix solide, ou enfin par cette émotion que communique la vue de ce qui est puissant et brillant... »

Napoléon est si heureux qu'il écrit au vaincu de Wagram cette lettre débordante de reconnaissance dont le traitement ne laisse pas d'être amusant puisqu'il y appelle l'empereur François « Monsieur mon frère et beau-père » :

« ... la fille de Votre Majesté est depuis deux jours ici. Elle remplit toutes mes espérances et, depuis deux jours, je n'ai cessé de lui donner et d'en recevoir des preuves des tendres sentiments qui nous unissent. Nous nous convenons parfaitement. Je ferai son bonheur et je devrai à Votre Majesté le mien. Qu'elle me permette donc que je la remercie du beau présent qu'elle m'a fait et que son cœur paternel jouisse des assurances de bonheur de son enfant chérie... »

Marie-Louise, pour sa part se déclare enchantée.

« Je ne puis assez remercier Dieu de m'avoir accordé une aussi grande félicité... »

Une félicité qu'elle oubliera bien vite quand viendra le temps des revers, quand s'effondrera le grand Empire, quand disparaîtra de sa vue l'homme qu'elle prétendait aimer si tendrement. Et aussi simplement qu'elle avait accepté l'époux qu'on lui ordonnait de satisfaire, son cœur accommodant acceptera l'amant chargé de lui faire oublier jusqu'à ses devoirs de mère...

LES NUITS DRAMATIQUES

LA NUIT MORTELLE D'ATTILA

Une fois de plus Attila quittait le Ring – sa ville de bois et de feutre – pour s'en aller combattre. Mais le cœur n'y était guère... C'était le printemps 453 et le Chan-Yu [1] commençait à sentir le poids des années. Il se sentait las et vaguement dégoûté car derrière lui il devinait l'impatience de ses six fils principaux (il en avait plus de soixante que lui avaient donnés ses quelque deux cents femmes) qui brûlaient de se partager son empire. Seul Ellak, l'aîné et le préféré, était sûr car il espérait bien succéder entièrement à son père et garder tout. Mais les autres... Avec la soixantaine venue, le conquérant comprenait qu'il ne pourrait plus endiguer longtemps leurs appétits.

Il y avait aussi le poids de sa première défaite, subie deux ans plus tôt aux champs Catalauniques sous les coups d'Aétius, son exact contemporain et son compagnon d'enfance, ce qui ne l'avait pas rendue moins amère. Et pour la première fois, Attila s'était sauvé, levant le camp pendant la nuit afin que la débâcle ne devînt pas désastre.

Certes, il avait pris ensuite, sur son rival, une éclatante revanche, détruisant Aquilée puis s'emparant tour à tour de Concordia, de Vérone, de Padoue, chassant devant lui les Venètes qui cherchèrent refuge sur quelques îles

1. Équivalent chinois du Duce ou du Führer.

défendues par une lagune malsaine et stérile dont ils n'allaient plus bouger. Ensuite ce furent Milan, Pergame, Brescia, Crémone. Rien ne semblait plus devoir arrêter le flot enragé des Huns qui roulait vers Rome quand, monté sur une mule blanche, un majestueux vieillard tout de blanc vêtu vint vers eux au milieu d'une troupe de prêtres qui chantaient des cantiques...

Le Hun était allé vers ce vieillard – le pape Léon – traversant à cheval pour le rejoindre le fleuve Mincio et pendant quelques instants, il l'avait écouté parler mais jamais personne ne saurait ce que « le vieux lion à crinière blanche » lui avait dit. C'était son secret à lui... A l'étonnement de ses hommes, il avait retraversé le fleuve et puis il était parti, emmenant la horde sauvage où personne ne se fût avisé de lui poser la moindre question...

Durant l'hiver de 452 il s'était occupé de reconstituer une armée, quelque peu réduite tout de même par les dures campagnes précédentes, annonçant aux Huns qu'au printemps il attaquerait l'Empire d'Orient dont l'empereur Marcianus lui avait refusé le tribut.

Quand vint le printemps il était prêt et, pour mettre ses hommes en appétit, s'en alla passer une tournée d'inspection punitive chez certains de ses vassaux germains dont quelques-uns avaient osé, après les champs Catalauniques, se proclamer indépendants. Ayant mis la main sur eux, il ordonna de les exécuter.

Mais l'un d'entre eux, dont l'Histoire n'a pas conservé le nom, avait une fille et cette fille, qui se nommait Ildico, était d'une éblouissante beauté. C'était l'une de ces longues Germaines aux cheveux de lin soyeux, au corps délié, aux larges prunelles d'azur pâle et nombreux déjà étaient les guerriers qui l'avaient demandée à son père, plus nombreux encore ceux qui s'étaient entre-tués pour elle bien qu'elle n'en regardât aucun. Mais, pour tenter de sauver son père, elle vint aux genoux d'Attila...

Prosternée sur les tapis qui garnissaient la yourte noire du Mongol, Ildico priait, suppliait, implorait, osant à peine lever les yeux sur l'homme terrifiant qui la regardait sans mot dire, accroupi sur une sorte d'estrade garnie de zibelines. Même pour une fille des temps barbares, le Fléau de Dieu n'avait rien de rassurant. Pas très grand, il paraissait presque difforme ainsi accroupi sur ses fourrures avec son torse disproportionné pour la longueur de ses jambes, sa tête puissante aux yeux fendus obliquement sur quelque chose qui ressemblait à de la pierre. Il avait un teint foncé, de fortes lèvres, un nez plat d'Asiate, de hautes pommettes, des cheveux raides et gris et une longue moustache assortie. Auprès de lui, caressant de temps en temps la poignée de la longue lame dentelée passée à sa ceinture, un colosse encore plus laid qui lui se tenait debout : Dahkhan, son bourreau...

Quand, à bout de larmes et d'arguments, la jeune fille se tut, Attila ne répondit rien. D'un geste, il ordonna qu'on emmène la suppliante, d'un autre il confirma la sentence de mort du père. Ildico avait prié pour rien : elle vit tomber la tête de son père et, quand on se saisit d'elle, la première pensée qui dut lui venir fut qu'elle allait subir un sort semblable. Il n'en fut rien : on l'emballa comme un objet précieux, on la hissa sur un cheval et quand Attila leva le camp pour retourner au Ring, elle apprit qu'on l'emmenait pour devenir la dernière épouse du Chan-Yu...

Aucun chroniqueur ne s'étant penché sur les états d'âme de cette malheureuse, on en est réduit aux conjectures touchant ce qu'elle pouvait penser tandis que s'apprêtaient pour elle des noces aussi redoutables qu'inattendues. Les femmes qui l'entouraient s'extasiaient sans doute, non sans jalousie, sur sa chance et comment ne pas se méfier de Kreka, la première épouse, que la venue de cette trop jolie fille ne devait guère enchanter? Et puis il y avait le futur époux : l'idée d'être livrée à ce gnome sanguinaire qui avait quarante ans de plus qu'elle et la tête en moins n'avait rien d'épanouissant. Il n'était jusqu'au décor, inhabituel et vraisemblablement déroutant pour une fille des forêts et des montagnes de Bavière.

Le Ring, que les Germains nommaient Etzelburg – le château d'Attila – se dressait au bord du Danube dans la plaine de Pannonie. C'était un immense agglomérat de maisons de bois, de tentes de feutre et de chariots qui se groupaient en cercles autour d'emplacements où s'allumaient les feux. Au milieu de tout cela, sur une colline se dressait, entouré d'une haute palissade où ne se voyait qu'une seule porte, le palais d'Attila, vaste construction de cèdre couverte de tuiles à la mode romaine qui affectait des allures de villa et groupait plusieurs bâtiments dont le plus orné était la maison des femmes.

Toutes les nations européennes, ou à peu près, étaient représentées dans cet immense camp retranché car les éléments purement mongols n'étaient pas les plus nombreux s'ils étaient les plus puissants. Chaque peuplade vaincue fournissait une troupe, des prisonniers, des esclaves. En outre, les fuyards de tous ordres étaient certains de trouver asile et nourriture à Etzelburg à condition qu'ils respectassent la règle du jeu, faute de quoi ils trouvaient aussi une mort particulièrement longue à venir. Des aventuriers grecs, des transfuges romains, des Gaulois chevelus y côtoyaient des rebelles bretons, des déserteurs goths, des otages wisigoths, des Alains, des Vandales et même, parfois, de longues robes de soie raidies de lourdes broderies qui signalaient des envoyés de Constantinople alors capitale de l'Empire romain d'Orient comme Ravenne était celle de l'Empire romain d'Occident. Et ce monde bigarré n'avait, en fait qu'un seul lien : le barbare de génie, le guerrier foudroyant dont les chevauchées fantastiques avaient soumis un empire et contraint les autres à lui payer tribut...

Tout cela s'activait aux préparatifs de la noce car le bruit courait qu'Attila, très épris de la jeune Germaine, retrouvait une nouvelle jeunesse, prometteuse de nouvelles conquêtes, de nouveaux profits...

Le jour venu, les noces sont célébrées avec une exceptionnelle splendeur. Attila les a voulues dignes de la beauté de sa nouvelle épouse. Après les invocations des chamans et le simulacre d'enlèvement rituel, la longue file des chefs de tribus vient déposer devant le couple les présents de noces : des chevaux, du koumys, le lait de jument fermenté que les Huns affectionnent, des bijoux d'or, ou d'argent, ou de jade, des fourrures précieuses, des soies brodées. Et puis, comme partout ailleurs on passe à table avec l'intention ferme d'y rester le plus longtemps possible.

Pendant des heures, on dévore, on bâfre, on boit. Et pas seulement du lait de jument mais aussi du vin. La vaisselle est d'or et d'argent, sauf pour le maître qui, sa vie durant, n'a jamais accepté d'autre vaisselle qu'un gobelet et une écuelle de bois.

C'est un banquet très gai. On chante, on danse, on admire des bouffons danseurs, des jongleurs, on se défie aux boules – on ignore s'il s'agit de la « longue » ou de la pétanque – ou au lancement du poignard. Et puis on reboit, on remange et on recommence à boire. Il y a déjà quelques invités qui ronflent sous les tables quand, le soir venu, Attila saisit Ildico par le bras pour l'entraîner dans la chambre nuptiale.

Il a beaucoup mangé, lui aussi, et bu plus encore. Non pour se donner du courage mais parce qu'il est heureux et qu'il veut montrer à sa bien-aimée qu'il est, en tout, le meilleur et le plus fort. Et tandis que les autres continuent à festoyer, tous deux sortent suivis par les encouragements, fort gaulois pour des Huns – de ceux des convives qui ont encore les idées nettes.

La chambre nuptiale n'est pas grande. Un vaste lit couvert de fourrures blanches y tient presque tout l'espace libre. Pressé à présent, Attila y jette Ildico, arrache les voiles et la tunique dont elle est couverte... Et l'on ne sait rien de plus.

Au matin, quand le jour se lève, les convives les plus solides sont encore à table. On s'étonne de n'avoir pas vu revenir Attila. Normalement il aurait dû venir rendre compte aux amis de la dévirginisation de la Germaine. Or, il n'est pas revenu et la porte de sa chambre est toujours close.

Le soleil est déjà haut qu'elle ne s'est pas encore ouverte et qu'aucun bruit ne se fait entendre de l'autre côté du vantail. Ce n'est pas naturel. Attila, même amoureux, faisant la grasse matinée cela ne s'est jamais vu... Son plus fidèle serviteur, Edécon, s'inquiète. Il faut aller voir. Et il va voir. Et il frappe à la porte, doucement d'abord puis de plus en plus fort mais sans obtenir de réponse...

Cette fois, on appelle les fils du Chan-Yu. Ils accourent et toute une foule avec eux. La porte est toujours fermée et ne peut s'ouvrir. Alors Ellak saisit une hache et l'abat.

Le spectacle que tous découvrent est effrayant. Attila est là, couché à plat ventre et les bras en croix, nu sur la fourrure blanche inondée de sang... Ildico est là, elle aussi; tapie dans un coin dans ses voiles déchirés elle tremble et pleure. On la secoue, on la questionne, pour un peu on la tuerait mais elle est frappée de terreur et ne peut répondre. A-t-elle tué le meurtrier de son père?

Non. Quand on examine le corps du défunt, on ne trouve aucune blessure et, à l'odeur du corps, les médecins affirment qu'il n'y a pas trace de poison. Tout ce sang qui souille le lit a jailli de la bouche d'Attila. C'est lui qui l'a étouffé après les excès de nourriture et de boisson auxquels il s'est livré.

Alors on emporte le corps pour le laver et l'étendre dans la grande salle sur un lit de parade. L'un des conseillers annonce au peuple, qui hurle à la mort réclamant l'assassin, que le maître a succombé à une cause naturelle et déjà les cavaliers parcourent la cité pour inviter les guerriers aux jeux funèbres...

« Au centre de la plaine, écrit Marcel Brion, on avait dressé une tente de soie sous laquelle reposait le corps d'Attila. Les ministres et les officiers accroupis autour de la tente pleuraient... Soudain, le silence se fit; les poètes chantèrent les louanges du roi... Les jeux des cavaliers alternèrent avec les chants... Dans l'espace laissé libre entre la tente et les spectateurs, ils s'élançaient au galop, tendaient leurs arcs vers le ciel, faisaient tourner les haches et siffler les lassos. Les flèches se croisaient au-dessus de la tente...

« Au moment où le soleil couchant atteignant l'horizon posa un dernier reflet sur la tente brillante, l'agitation cessa tout à coup et le silence immobilisa la foule... »

L'heure était venue de conduire le Chan-Yu à sa dernière demeure. On dispersa la foule et même on l'obligea à regagner ses foyers car l'ensevelissement d'un conquérant n'était pas fait pour les yeux du vulgaire. Seuls demeurèrent les notables qui enlevèrent la tente de soie laissant voir ce qu'elle contenait : le corps d'Attila étendu sur des tapis et entouré d'un énorme trésor fait, d'abord des couronnes et des insignes de commandement des rois vaincus et des dépouilles superbes de tant d'églises, de temples et de lieux sacrés pillés par la Horde : des reliquaires, des vases sacrés, des joyaux... Mais, de chaque côté de la tête deux objets tout simples : un arc avec ses flèches d'une part, une écuelle de bois de l'autre.

A la nuit close les guerriers les plus valeureux creusèrent la fosse, une vaste fosse dans laquelle le corps fut déposé. Puis sur lui on jeta pêle-mêle tout le trésor qu'il combla. Alors seulement on remit la terre qui, bientôt, forma un grand tumulus.

« Vers minuit la tâche fut achevée. A ce moment, les cavaliers qui avaient sollicité l'honneur de suivre le mort dans l'au-delà firent, au galop, une dernière fois, le tour du tumulus. Puis on les égorgea, on tua les chevaux et on les dressa debout sur des pieux autour du tombeau. Assis sur leur selle, tenant dans leur main l'arc et le carquois, ils formaient un cercle de figures terribles dont les visages regardaient tous les points de l'horizon... »

Avec le temps, les cavaliers morts tombèrent en poussière. Le tumulus devint colline, se couvrit d'herbes, entra dans le paysage qu'allaient encore fouler, au cours **des** siècles, tant de pieds de guerriers, tant de galops de chevaux. Et nul, jamais, n'a retrouvé le tombeau d'Attila...

Nul ne sait non plus, ce que devint la belle Ildico...

LA NUIT ENSORCELÉE
DE PHILIPPE AUGUSTE

Le royaume de France, et singulièrement son roi Philippe II que l'on disait déjà Auguste, fondaient de grands espoirs sur le nouveau mariage que le roi allait contracter; des espoirs qui se teintaient de curiosité car, jusqu'à présent, on n'avait pas encore vu de Danoises sur le trône de France. Or, celle que Philippe attendait à Amiens, en ce mois d'août 1193 se nommait Ingeburge et, fille de Valdemar le Grand, roi de Danemark, elle était la sœur de Knut, le roi actuel. Ajoutons qu'outre son auréole d'exotisme la princesse était précédée d'une réputation d'extraordinaire beauté.

Veuf depuis trois ans de l'exquise et touchante Isabelle de Hainaut, la petite reine des pauvres gens, morte à vingt ans, Philippe Auguste n'avait pas réellement besoin de se remarier : avant de s'en aller reposer dans Notre-Dame inachevée, Isabelle lui avait donné un fils, beau et vigoureux et qui atteignait ses six ans. Simplement, il en avait envie. Rester célibataire à vingt-huit ans est difficile, surtout lorsque l'on aime les femmes et le jeune roi souhaitait vivement épouser cette Ingeburge que l'on disait si belle. Et puis, du point de vue politique, l'alliance avec le Danemark présentait des avantages certains car, outre la possession de navires et de guerriers dont la réputation, depuis les Vikings, n'était plus à faire, les souverains danois pouvaient arguer de certaines prétentions sur la couronne anglaise.

Or, la couronne anglaise était singulièrement mal portée à cette époque : Richard Cœur de Lion dont le plus grand tort avait toujours été de préférer les exploits sportifs et les beaux coups d'épée à la sécurité de son royaume, croupissait dans une forteresse autrichienne et son frère affectionné, le prince Jean qui assurait la régence, faisait de son mieux pour balayer définitivement le roi légitime. N'ayant que fort peu d'estime pour Jean, Philippe Auguste, qui ne tenait d'ailleurs pas plus que lui à voir Richard sortir de sa prison, pensait qu'avec l'aide danoise il n'aurait guère de peine à balayer le gêneur, à récupérer les possessions anglaises de l'hexagone et, peut-être à coiffer la couronne des Plantagenêts...

Lui et Richard avaient été compagnons de jeunesse, jadis, et même amis mais la croisade pour laquelle ils étaient partis ensemble d'un cœur si joyeux ne leur avait guère réussi. Tout avait commencé à se gâter durant cet hiver passé ensemble en Sicile à attendre les vents favorables. A cause d'une femme : Jeanne d'Angleterre, veuve du roi de Sicile et sœur de Richard.

Elle plaisait à Philippe qui l'eût volontiers épousée. Richard s'y était opposé et le Capétien n'avait pas digéré l'offense. Il avait gagné la Terre sainte de son côté mais les deux rois s'étaient retrouvés sous les murs de Saint-Jean-d'Acre où Philippe s'était battu avec la fougue et la passion d'un simple chevalier, payant de sa personne autant et parfois plus que Richard lui-même. Tout l'enchantait : le pays, la couleur intense du ciel et des murailles rousses, l'odeur de la terre brûlée, l'étrangeté des choses et des gens et jusqu'à l'ennemi, ce Saladin chevaleresque et magnifique dont la vaillance et la courtoisie étaient dignes d'un paladin...

Et puis il y avait eu l'inexplicable maladie, cette suette miliaire (on ignorait alors totalement ce que cela pouvait bien être) qui les avait abattus l'un et l'autre, brûlant leurs corps sous les morsures de la fièvre, les pelant ensuite, faisant tomber leurs cheveux et leur énergie. Richard s'était remis plus facilement mais Philippe avait compris qu'il était un homme mort s'il restait dans ce pays malsain. Il était assez sage aussi pour comprendre qu'il ne viendrait jamais à bout de Saladin et qu'il avait beaucoup mieux à faire en France où le royaume avait besoin de lui. Et laissant l'autre s'arranger comme il l'entendrait, il était reparti, heureux de retrouver l'air vif d'Ile-de-France et l'odeur de ses grandes forêts, heureux de retrouver la vie...

Aussi quand son entourage, avec beaucoup de précautions oratoires, commença d'insinuer qu'un trône est un meuble bien austère si le sourire d'une reine ne vient l'éclairer, Philippe tendit l'oreille avec quelque complaisance. Le reste avait été assez vite grâce à un personnage étonnant : Guillaume, chanoine de Sainte-Geneviève qui vivait au Danemark et, en attendant la canonisation, s'occupait à fonder des abbayes dans le cadre d'une mission évangélique.

Guillaume fréquentait beaucoup la Cour danoise et c'est lui qui, le premier, suggéra le mariage avec Ingeburge dont il admirait, en tout bien tout honneur, la beauté. Il vint en France pour présenter son projet et, en homme avisé, y prit langue avec l'un des confidents du roi, le frère Bernard de Vincennes qu'il n'eut aucune peine à convaincre : une jolie femme pourvue d'une dot intéressante c'était exactement ce qu'il fallait à Philippe. Et quand Guillaume repartit pour le nord, ce fut entouré d'une belle ambassade composée de l'évêque de Noyon, Étienne de Tournay, du sire de Montmorency et du comte de Nevers : ils étaient chargés de négocier les conditions du mariage et de ramener la princesse que leur maître se mit à attendre avec une impatience grandissante.

Il y avait pourtant en France quelqu'un que ce mariage n'enchantait pas. C'était Adèle de Champagne, la mère de Philippe Auguste, veuve du roi Louis VII dont elle avait été la troisième épouse. Femme énergique, autoritaire même – Philippe avait eu quelque peine à lui arracher le pouvoir qu'elle prétendait exercer en compagnie de son frère Guillaume, archevêque de Reims – mais non dépourvue d'intelligence, Adèle, qui était une belle-mère au moins aussi redoutable que le serait plus tard Blanche de Castille, avait pris ses renseignements, en mère avisée, sur les antécédents de sa future belle-fille et ce qu'elle avait appris l'avait laissée soucieuse.

Non qu'il y eût quelque chose à reprendre à la réputation de la jeune fille. Elle était sans reproche et, s'il en était allé autrement, le bon chanoine Guillaume ne l'eût pas proposée. Mais celle de sa mère, Sophie de Polotsk, une Russe, était effroyable. Cette femme était à l'origine d'un drame atroce dont avait été victime son propre frère, le prince Burisius.

Ce malheureux s'était épris follement de la sœur de Valdemar le Grand, Christine. Son amour ayant été payé de retour, les deux jeunes gens s'étaient laissés aller à leur passion, adultère d'ailleurs car Christine était mariée. Malheureusement pour elle, Sophie la haïssait et, ayant découvert le pot aux roses elle s'était fait un plaisir de le rapporter à son époux. Le résultat fut abominable : Christine périt sous le fouet. Quant à Burisius, après l'avoir fait témoin de la mort de sa maîtresse, on lui creva les yeux, on le châtra et, comme le châtiment semblait encore un peu faible, on lui coupa une main et un pied.

« La suite, rapporte le duc de Levis Mirepoix, mériterait d'être chantée parmi les plus pathétiques témoignages d'amour que donnèrent les romans de la Table Ronde. Elle eût arraché des larmes d'admiration aux Tristan et aux Lancelot! L'estropié obtint de se retirer dans le monastère où fut ensevelie sa bien-aimée. Et tous les jours, soutenu par un bras charitable, il allait se pencher sur le tombeau de ses amours... »

Après la mort de son époux, l'odieuse Sophie se remaria, cette fois avec le landgrave de Thuringe qui ne la supporta que deux ans et la renvoya chez elle à la suite d'on ne sait trop quel exploit. Ce fut également le sort d'une de ses filles, fiancée au fils de Frédéric Barberousse et que l'on retourna avant le mariage.

Tout cela n'était guère encourageant pour une mère. Le chanoine Guillaume avait beau jurer qu'Ingeburge était la douceur et la charité incarnées, Adèle se demandait, non sans quelque raison, où, avec de tels géniteurs, elle avait bien pu prendre de telles vertus.

Naturellement, Philippe n'avait rien écouté de tout ce qu'elle avait pu dire : on lui avait promis une sorte de sirène aux cheveux de flammes et aux yeux couleur de mer et il la lui fallait... Adèle se garda d'insister : depuis son retour de croisade le roi se montrait nerveux, lunatique même, plus obstiné que jamais mais aussi plus violent. Il devenait dangereux de le contrarier. Adèle se résigna donc à faire comme lui : elle attendit.

On en est là, ce matin d'août éclatant de soleil quand un coureur couvert de poussière entre en trombe dans la ville, se rue au palais archiépiscopal où loge le roi et vient s'abattre plus qu'il ne s'agenouille aux pieds de celui-ci : le cortège de la future reine approche de la ville...

Philippe ne perd pas une seconde : il va courir au-devant d'elle! Quelques minutes plus tard, le casque couronné d'or en tête, il mène à travers champs l'assaut furieux d'un escadron aussi joyeux que chamarré.

Ingeburge de Danemark a vu venir de loin le nuage de poussière qui grossit d'instant en instant en jetant des éclairs et qui révèle bientôt un groupe de cavaliers. Celui qui galope en tête porte au casque une couronne et le cœur de la jeune fille bat un peu plus vite sans doute. Le roi! Elle va enfin voir cet homme que le chanoine Guillaume lui a appris à connaître et dont, en toute innocence, elle rêve depuis qu'elle sait qu'elle doit être sa reine.

Philippe saute à terre à quelques mètres d'Ingeburge. Il remet son casque aux mains d'un page et s'approche, tête nue. La jeune fille rougit de le trouver si semblable à son espoir avec cette haute stature, ce visage énergique et ouvert, ce regard clair et dominateur et jusqu'à cette demi-calvitie, souvenir de sa récente maladie et qui fait refluer vers l'arrière la couronne des cheveux roux. Quant à Philippe, la beauté qu'il découvre le suffoque et, sur le moment, il ne trouve rien à dire...

Non seulement le chanoine Guillaume n'a rien exagéré mais il serait plutôt resté en dessous de la vérité car Philippe n'a jamais contemplé beauté pareille à celle-là. Ingeburge est grande et svelte mais son corps élégant, serré dans une robe écarlate, est déjà épanoui. Son visage, entre des tresses couleur de feu et grosses comme un bras d'enfant, est d'une irréelle pureté : pas un trait qui ne soit la perfection même. La peau est d'une idéale blancheur et fait ressortir des yeux immenses, d'un vert de mer et si transparents que leur regard paraît vide. Il est difficile à supporter ce regard et le roi ferme les yeux un instant, comme s'il avait regardé le soleil en face. En fait, Ingeburge a la beauté sans défaut d'une statue, celle de la déesse de la mer... C'est un peu angoissant.

La première surprise passée, Philippe tend les bras pour aider sa fiancée à descendre de sa monture et lui souhaite la bienvenue. Elle sourit sans paraître comprendre puis murmure quelques mots dans une langue assez rude. Philippe s'étonne : est-ce qu'elle ne parle pas du tout le français? Non, elle parle seulement un peu latin... mais, ajoute l'évêque de Noyon, son intelligence est vive et elle apprendra vite...

Qu'importe! On s'arrangera du latin. Philippe entend se marier sur l'heure. Il avoue sans honte sa hâte de faire sienne cette merveilleuse créature et si quelqu'un élève de vagues objections, elles sont vite balayées. Direction : la cathédrale! Demain Ingeburge sera sacrée.

Quand on lui traduit les paroles du roi, la Danoise devient aussi rouge que sa robe mais ne proteste pas. Elle sait qu'elle est là pour se soumettre. D'ailleurs, il est visible que le roi lui plaît. Et le double cortège se remet en marche.

Tandis que l'on revient vers la ville, Philippe, qui

chevauche entre sa fiancée et Étienne de Tournay, s'entretient avec ce dernier. Il est heureux de voir sa future épouse mais les conditions du mariage l'intéressent aussi. A-t-on obtenu la cession des droits à la couronne d'Angleterre? Eh bien... rien n'est encore décidé mais les choses sont en bonne voie! Au moins, les Danois sont prêts à aider en cas de débarquement sur le sol anglais... Pas tout à fait. Le roi Knut aimerait, en contrepartie, que son beau-frère français s'engage à combattre pour lui l'empereur d'Allemagne...

Philippe Auguste fronce le sourcil. Combattre l'empereur? Son allié? L'homme qui tient Richard en son pouvoir? Il ne peut en être question! A quoi ont pensé ses négociateurs? La belle humeur du roi est en train de fondre au soleil d'août. L'évêque s'en rend compte et pour effacer la mauvaise impression se hâte d'avancer que lui et les autres ambassadeurs ont demandé une dot énorme : dix mille marcs d'or.

Du coup, le roi retrouve le sourire. C'est une somme! Et naturellement, ils sont là, ces dix mille marcs?... Une partie tout au moins car, étant donné l'importance du chiffre il a bien fallu consentir quelques délais...

Cette fois, Philippe est tout près de se mettre en colère mais il regarde Ingeburge et se calme. Une fille pareille vaut bien quelques sacrifices. En outre, le roi a grande confiance en sa diplomatie personnelle : il saura bien remettre les choses en ordre un peu plus tard. Pour le moment présent, il ne veut songer qu'à l'amour.

Aux portes d'Amiens, Adèle de Champagne attend sa belle-fille entourée d'une suite nombreuse. Les deux femmes se saluent avec tout le cérémonial compassé de rigueur en pareil cas et l'on se dirige vers la cathédrale qui apparaît au bout de la principale rue, dans toute la blancheur de sa nouveauté.

Le cérémonial habituel se déroule suivi du festin qu'animent les chansons, les danses et les jongleurs. Autour du palais toute la ville est en liesse. On fait ripaille partout. Des tonneaux sont mis en perce à tous les carrefours. On danse des caroles en se promettant encore plus de plaisir demain, après le sacre. C'est une aubaine pour Amiens que ce mariage royal... Pendant ce temps, Philippe regarde Ingeburge. Il n'a qu'une hâte : être seul avec elle et il sourit, déjà heureux, quand les dames, conduites par Adèle, emmènent la mariée pour la dévêtir...

Quand tous les rites sont accomplis, il la rejoint dans la chambre jonchée de fleurs. Il est plein d'ardeur, plein de désir... et pourtant!... Quand il rejette les draps, quand il contemple sans voiles, sans ombre, toute la splendeur de la beauté d'Ingeburge, il sent fuir le désir. Sans ombre? Justement, il n'y a pas assez d'ombre, pas la plus petite ombre d'humanité sur cette perfection. Avec sa peau de lait et ses grands yeux trop clairs, la princesse n'a pas l'air vraiment vivante et la barrière du langage dressée entre les époux n'arrange rien. Que faire de quelques mots de latin pour animer une statue sous les caresses des mots? Les caresses, Ingeburge les attend, passive bien sûr, mais Philippe ne peut se résoudre à les lui dispenser. Par trois fois, il se relèvera, reviendra s'étendre auprès d'elle, la prendra même dans ses bras, mais sans parvenir à briser la glace qui l'enveloppe tout entier, se glisse dans ses veines comme une sorte de mort, le paralyse... Cette femme est trop belle.

« Son désir, écrit Levis Mirepoix, est comme égaré dans un désert de beauté... »

Alors Philippe se croit ensorcelé et prend peur. Ce corps inaccessible pour lui, en vient à lui inspirer peu à peu une sorte d'horreur et, finalement, il s'en éloignera le plus qu'il pourra pour tenter de dormir. Toute la nuit, les chandelles brûleront dans la chambre royale, à la grande inquiétude de la reine-mère qui n'a pas dormi elle non plus et qui regarde ces lumières, de son appartement.

Au matin, qui est le 15 août, fête de la Vierge Marie, alors que la ville se prépare pour le sacre de la reine, un huissier à verge vient frapper par trois fois au battant de la chambre royale. La porte s'ouvre alors découvrant le couple royal assis sur un lit de parade. Tous deux sont vêtus uniformément d'une tunique de satin rouge et d'une robe de toile d'argent. Ils sont superbes mais chacun peut voir que le roi, habituellement coloré de visage et l'œil vif, est pâle comme un spectre tandis que ses yeux bleus, d'une bizarre fixité, regardent devant eux sans paraître rien voir. Quant à la reine, il est plus que visible qu'elle a pleuré...

Au milieu d'un brillant cortège et d'une ville en délire, le couple gagne la cathédrale et vient s'agenouiller devant l'archevêque de Reims, Guillaume de Champagne, qui officie.

Frère d'Adèle, Guillaume de Champagne connaît bien son neveu et il n'a pas besoin de le regarder deux fois pour comprendre que quelque chose ne va pas. Ces deux-là n'ont certes pas la mine d'un jeune couple tout frais émoulu de sa nuit de noces. Mais il n'en faut pas moins que les choses suivent leur cours...

Les douze évêques qui assistent l'achevêque font de grands efforts pour avoir l'air de ne rien remarquer mais, soudain, c'est le drame : au moment de l'onction du saint chrême, comme deux diacres dénouent respectueusement les lacets d'or qui ferment certaines ouvertures de la tunique de la reine pour permettre d'oindre son corps, Philippe devient encore plus pâle. Les yeux agrandis d'horreur, il se cramponne soudain à la chape d'or frisé de son oncle et tremble en contemplant la jeune femme. Ses lèvres blêmes murmurent quelque chose sans qu'aucun son sorte de sa bouche et comme Guillaume de Champagne secoue doucement sa chape pour lui faire lâcher prise, Philippe a, vers Ingeburge qui ne peut retenir ses larmes, un geste des deux mains, un geste d'effroi qui repousse...

Dans l'église chacun retient son souffle. Tous les regards sont posés sur l'archevêque dont la main, enduite d'huile sainte demeure en l'air... Il hésite visiblement. Puis, soudain, il se décide : sa main descend, se pose sur le front du roi, s'y appuie fortement dans un appel désespéré à la réalité... Philippe a un frisson mais les couleurs, peu à peu lui reviennent. Il regarde Guillaume et pousse un profond soupir auquel fait écho celui de l'archevêque. La cérémonie reprend son cours, lente, solennelle, interminable...

Après l'action de grâces, le roi et la reine quittent la cathédrale au chant des cantiques et prennent le chemin qui les ramène au palais au milieu de folles acclamations qui font renaître un sourire dans les yeux et sur les lèvres d'Ingeburge... Hélas, elle n'a guère le temps de se conforter dans ce courage qui lui revient. A peine aperçoit-il les imposants bâtiments que Philippe, comme un cheval qui sent l'écurie, prend le mors aux dents, presse l'allure entraînant le cortège au pas de course et, à peine franchie la porte, plante là Ingeburge effarée sans lui adresser ni mot ni regard et se précipite chez lui, réclamant d'urgence ceux de son conseil.

Ils accourent, bien sûr, l'archevêque de Reims, le chancelier Guérin l'Hospitalier, Étienne de Tournay et les autres. Ils trouvent le roi assis dans son haut fauteuil de bois sculpté. Il a retrouvé ses couleurs. La panique dont il a été victime tout à l'heure s'est dissipée mais elle a fait place à la colère, une colère froide où se retrouvent ses déboires de mâle frustré et ses déceptions touchant les négociations de la dot. Il y a là aussi son médecin, le moine Rigord, et son chapelain, Guillaume Le Breton qui tous deux ont rapporté la scène.

En fait, Philippe ne réclame point conseil. Il raconte, il se raconte : la nuit désastreuse, le maléfice qui lui a « noué l'aiguillette » en face de cette femme dont la beauté inhumaine ne peut venir que du Diable. Il est ensorcelé, il le sait, et il ne peut tolérer l'idée de le rester. Cela ne peut être bon ni pour lui-même ni pour le royaume...

Alors pourquoi n'avoir rien dit avant le sacre?... Pourquoi avoir laissé Ingeburge recevoir l'onction sainte?... Eh bien, justement parce qu'il comptait sur la puissance du sacrement pour abattre le maléfice. Dans sa foi de chrétien, il pensait que Dieu balayerait le Diable mais Dieu ne l'a pas voulu! Philippe l'a bien compris quand la terreur s'est emparée de lui au moment où l'on ouvrait, si peu pourtant, la robe d'Ingeburge sur son corps démoniaque. Il est impossible qu'il continue à vivre avec cette femme. Il faut la renvoyer. Il faut qu'elle reparte avec ceux qui l'ont amenée! Au point de vue politique le dommage ne sera pas grand puisque l'on n'a rien obtenu de ce que l'on espérait. Et il fait dire aux envoyés danois que la princesse va leur être remise afin qu'ils la ramènent à son frère.

On devine comment ceux-ci prennent la nouvelle. La seule idée de ce que leur dira Knut lorsqu'ils lui ramèneront sa sœur, et surtout de ce qu'il pourrait leur faire, leur donne des battements de cœur : le jeune roi n'est pas plus tendre que son père et ses réactions peuvent être fort désagréables. On l'a bien vu quand on lui a rendu tour à tour sa mère et sa sœur...

Cette fois, d'ailleurs, l'échappatoire est plus facile et les Danois ne la manquent pas : il n'y a plus d'Ingeburge de Danemark. Elle est non seulement mariée mais sacrée et ils n'ont plus rien à voir avec une reine de France qui, elle, n'a plus rien à faire au Danemark. Et, pour être bien sûrs que ces Français tortueux ne vont pas leur opposer quelque astuce de leur façon, les Danois plient bagages et reprennent, à grande allure, le chemin de leur pays...

Reste Ingeburge. C'est l'interprète habituel, le chanoine Guillaume, qui est chargé de lui expliquer ce qui se passe. Une corvée qui lui met les larmes aux yeux mais il faut bien qu'il s'exécute.

Or, à sa grande surprise, Ingeburge ne réagit absolument pas comme il s'y attendait. Certes, elle commence par pleurer lorsqu'il lui apprend la décision de Philippe – qui n'en ferait autant à sa place? – mais lorsque le chanoine ajoute que les envoyés danois ont reçu l'ordre de la ramener à son frère, elle se calme et c'est avec beaucoup de fermeté qu'elle fait entendre son point de vue : le roi de France l'a épousée...

« Oui, coupe le chanoine, mais il nous a dit s'être trouvé dans l'impossibilité de consommer le mariage.

— Qu'appelez-vous consommer? Nous avons couché ensemble...

— Sans doute mais cela ne suffit pas et...

— Moi cela me suffit. En outre, j'ai reçu la couronne qui m'est remise au nom de Dieu. Je suis reine de France et rien ni personne ne m'y fera renoncer... »

Guillaume a beau plaider, prier, représenter qu'il peut être dangereux d'exciter la colère de Philippe Auguste, rien n'y fait : Ingeburge s'en tient à ce qu'elle a dit. Reine elle est, reine elle restera! Le Danemark ne doit plus être, pour elle, qu'un souvenir...

Il ne reste plus au bon chanoine qu'à venir rendre compte de son ambassade en se demandant avec angoisse comment le roi va prendre tout cela... La réponse vient d'elle-même : très mal! Et c'est pire encore qu'il ne le craignait : d'une voix que la colère fait trembler, Philippe ordonne que la malencontreuse Ingeburge soit sur l'heure conduite au couvent des Dames de Saint-Maur tandis que lui-même regagne, à bride abattue, son palais de la Cité à Paris.

Au jour du mariage, il avait constitué en douaire pour la nouvelle reine, les terres de Crécy, Châteauneuf-sur-Loire, Neuville-aux-Bois ainsi que la prévôté d'Orléans, mais il ne saurait être question de l'envoyer occuper une de ces terres : elles sont à la reine de France et il ne veut plus d'Ingeburge dans ce rôle.

A Paris cependant les langues commencent à marcher : c'est une ville où les nouvelles ont toujours galopé la poste, même quand il n'y avait pas encore de poste. Le peuple s'émeut des bruits étranges venus d'Amiens et y cherche une explication. On murmure déjà que la Danoise a jeté un charme sur le roi, qu'elle lui a noué l'aiguillette et c'est une chose qui fait horreur à une époque où l'on craint le Diable plus que le feu. Le bruit prend facilement, d'ailleurs, car le souvenir de la reine Isabelle n'est pas encore effacé. On était prêt, bien sûr, à accueillir joyeusement la nouvelle reine que l'on disait si belle mais à la seule condition que le roi y trouve le bonheur car lui aussi on l'aime autant pour son courage et son bon sens que pour son énergie. On l'aime aussi pour le soin qu'il prend de la capitale : les rues, infects bourbiers jusqu'à ce temps, reçoivent peu à peu une vêture de gros pavés ronds, les murailles sont restaurées, agrandies, la forteresse du Louvre s'élève et une police active s'efforce de faire régner l'ordre et la sécurité. Enfin le roi sait se mêler au menu peuple. Les bains de foule sont assez son fait et il n'est pas rare de le rencontrer, vêtu simplement, baguenaudant par les rues, écoutant les propos, participant aux conversations, soulageant une misère...

Sur la Montagne Sainte-Geneviève où sont les collèges, des bagarres éclatent entre étudiants danois et étudiants français. Cela crée une effervescence dont il faut tenir compte ainsi d'ailleurs que d'autres bruits alarmants : on dit que Richard d'Angleterre a payé sa rançon, qu'il revient animé d'intentions belliqueuses... Il n'y a évidemment rien d'autre à attendre de ce foudre de guerre qui n'a jamais rêvé que plaies et bosses mais on dit aussi que le roi de Danemark, gravement offensé, est prêt à lui venir en aide avec ses navires pour envahir la France... On dit, on dit... que ne dit-on pas quand l'imagination brode sur ce que l'on ne sait pas clairement?

Enfermé chez lui, Philippe oppose un mutisme absolu à tous ces bruits. Lèvres serrées au seul nom d'Ingeburge, il refuse d'entendre quoi que ce soit. Une seule solution pour lui : la rupture d'un lien odieux et il ne cesse de presser l'archevêque de Reims et le collège des évêques de lui donner satisfaction.

Très ennuyé, Guillaume de Champagne atermoie, palabre, tente de raisonner son neveu. Il a essayé de lui faire entendre que les séquelles de sa maladie nerveuse ont pu causer chez lui une carence momentanée et que, peut-être, avec un peu de patience... Philippe lui a répondu en le regardant de travers et en prenant trois maîtresses coup sur coup. Voilà pour la carence!

L'archevêque s'en va alors trouver sa sœur. Adèle n'est pas plus satisfaite que lui des événements. Le fait que ses noirs pressentiments se trouvent vérifiés ne lui cause aucune joie et elle aimerait trouver une solution à cette situation invraisemblable. Aussi, un matin, après avoir longuement conféré avec Guillaume et certains conseillers de Philippe, elle entraîne son frère chez le roi...

Aux premières paroles qu'elle prononce, Philippe se cabre : on a entendu sa volonté, il attend à présent qu'on l'exécute. Guillaume de Champagne intervient alors. Que le roi consente au moins à une seconde tentative!

« Allez voir la reine, dit-il. Donnez cette preuve de bon vouloir à l'Église qui vous a bénis, au royaume et même au roi de Danemark... »

Peut-être l'étrange aversion du premier soir disparaîtra-t-elle? Qui peut savoir? Mais au cas où elle persisterait, lui, Guillaume archevêque de Reims s'engage à instruire immédiatement le procès d'annulation. Mais qu'au moins le roi fasse un effort! On ne peut, sur une seule nuit manquée, engager l'avenir d'un royaume...

C'est à la fois la sagesse et l'espoir. Philippe a trop de bon sens pour ne pas en convenir. Soit! Il essaiera encore... et même il va essayer tout de suite! Dès le lendemain, flanqué de son oncle, d'Étienne de Tournay et du chanoine Guillaume qui donnerait cher pour être ailleurs, il monte à cheval et se rend à Saint-Maur où l'arrivée tumultueuse de cette troupe d'hommes sème la panique chez les nonnes...

Dans un grand envol de robes blanches et de voiles, les saintes filles éperdues et rougissantes s'égaillent comme une volée de mouettes quand le pas de Philippe résonne sur les dalles de leur cloître. On sait – ou l'on devine – quelle

étrange cérémonie risque de se passer dans l'une des
cellules et il y a de quoi mettre en émoi toutes ces femmes
vouées à la chasteté. Dans leur imagination le roi, oint du
Seigneur, redevient l'homme et traîne après lui une odeur
de soufre fort troublantee.

Prévenue, Ingeburge attend Philippe dans sa chambre.
Quand il paraît, flanqué du chanoine Guillaume, celui-ci
explique à la recluse que le roi vient animé des meilleures
intentions et qu'elle doit s'efforcer de lui faire bon accueil.
A Philippe, il chuchote qu'Ingeburge est remplie de crainte
et qu'un peu de douceur, peut-être... Pour toute réponse,
Philippe le prend par les épaules et le met à la porte. Il n'a
que faire d'un chanoine pour vaincre cette créature
anormale. Il a tort, sans doute, car la barrière du langage
demeure et lui ne voit, dans cette entrevue, qu'un combat à
mener...

Le temps passe, mortel pour ceux qui attendent, dans le
jardin, le résultat de cette curieuse démarche en un tel
lieu... Au bout d'une demi-heure qui paraît un siècle, la
porte s'ouvre enfin et chacun retient sa respiration...

Hélas, quand le roi sort il est frémissant de rage et
derrière lui la porte retombe avec fracas. Pas assez fort
cependant pour que l'on ne puisse entendre des sanglots...
A ceux qui attendent, Philippe lance que le maléfice
demeure et qu'ayant tenu sa promesse, il attend d'eux, à
présent, qu'ils tiennent la leur. Il ne peut pas approcher
cette femme : elle lui fait horreur... Et il le répète plusieurs
fois : horreur, horreur, horreur!... Il veut qu'on l'en
débarrasse...

Mais Ingeburge refuse toujours de s'en aller. Au milieu
d'un torrent de larmes, elle jure qu'à Saint-Maur comme à
Amiens elle a bien appartenu à Philippe mais elle est
incapable de s'expliquer plus clairement là-dessus. Excès
d'innocence sans doute, bien compréhensible chez une
jeune fille non avertie. Une chose est certaine : elle veut
rester reine de France parce que... eh bien, parce qu'elle
aime Philippe!

Cela n'arrange rien. Devant cette impasse Guillaume de Champagne réunit à Compiègne, le 5 novembre, l'assemblée des prélats et des grands feudataires afin de trancher le débat. Ingeburge est appelée à comparaître. Fière et calme, mais les yeux rougis, elle vient s'asseoir au milieu du cercle de ces hommes qui l'observent gravement. Les débats durent longtemps. Pourtant elle ne se départit pas un seul instant de sa ligne de conduite : elle est la femme de Philippe Auguste, la reine de France et elle entend le rester...

Qui croire? Naturellement, l'assemblée penche davantage vers le roi qui n'a aucune raison de faire si hautement étalage d'impuissance même momentanée. Et comme il faut, par décence, trouver autre chose que la non-consommation, on déniche un vague lien de parenté prohibitif entre les époux et, là-dessus, l'archevêque de Reims prononce la dissolution du mariage.

Quand on lui traduit le verdict, Ingeburge se lève, soudain furieuse.

« Mala Francia! s'écrie-t-elle Roma! Roma! [1]

Guillaume de Champagne étouffe un soupir. Si cette entêtée en appelle à Rome, les ennuis ne sont pas finis! Mais il est impossible de l'en empêcher.

Et, en effet, les ennuis ne font que commencer. C'est une lutte de près de vingt années qui commence entre Ingeburge et Philippe, une lutte étrange, épuisante et pleine de péripéties.

Pour commencer, le roi ordonne que l'entêtée soit conduite au couvent des Augustines de Cysoing, près de Tournai, c'est-à-dire hors de France, en terre d'Empire, chez le pire ennemi du roi de Danemark. La pauvre créature va y séjourner plusieurs années dans un dénuement à peu près total car Philippe ne pousse pas la grandeur d'âme jusqu'à payer sa pension : Ingeburge vendra peu à peu tout ce qu'elle possède, y compris ses

---

1. « Mauvaise France! Rome! Rome! »

robes de princesse. Évidemment, si elle souhaite en finir avec cette triste condition elle en a le moyen. Mais ce moyen, justement elle ne l'emploiera jamais. Seules consolations dans sa solitude : les visites fidèles d'Étienne de Tournay et du chanoine Guillaume qui ne cessent de se reprocher de l'avoir entraînée dans cette galère matrimoniale.

Comme elle l'avait annoncé, la reine reniée s'est plainte à Rome où le pape Célestin III a refusé de reconnaître le jugement de divorce mais sans lancer la moindre foudre canonique. C'est un vieillard de plus de quatre-vingts ans et il a grand besoin du roi de France qui d'ailleurs s'en soucie comme d'une guigne. Il a mieux à faire...

Trois ans après la nuit d'Amiens, Philippe, en effet, accueille une nouvelle épouse. Elle se nomme Agnès de Méran, ou de Méranie. Elle est la fille d'un frère d'armes, un ancien compagnon de croisade, Berchtold, duc de Méran, de Dalmatie et autres lieux. Elle est aussi brune qu'Isabelle de Hainaut était blonde et Ingeburge rousse et, quand il l'accueille, sur la route de Compiègne, Philippe reste un instant frappé de stupeur... à la grande terreur de l'entourage : est-ce l'affaire d'Amiens qui va recommencer? Non. C'est très différent cette fois : ce n'est plus l'étonnement quasi paralysant en face d'une beauté presque surnaturelle, c'est le plus humain, le plus brutal des coups de foudre en face d'une créature exquise. Et qui mieux est, le coup de foudre est réciproque : Agnès s'éprend de Philippe à l'instant même où il tombe amoureux d'elle. Cette nuit de noces-là sera une réussite absolue et le simple prélude d'une passion digne d'une chanson de geste. C'est l'amour d'Aude pour Roland, celui de Tristan pour Yseult, celui de Lancelot pour Guenièvre... c'est l'aurore d'un grand bonheur d'où naîtront deux enfants : une fille et un garçon...

Un bonheur trop court car les choses vont se gâter très vite quand meurt le vieux et débonnaire Célestin III en janvier 1198. Malheureusement pour Philippe Auguste, celui qui le remplace n'est pas, et de loin, aussi facile à vivre et il n'y a guère de chance qu'il consente à quitter ce monde rapidement car il n'a que trente-huit ans. C'est le cardinal Lothaire de Segni, un Romain de grande race qui se métamorphose soudain en Innocent III, l'un des plus grands mais aussi des plus redoutables papes de l'Histoire.

Quand il monte au trône pontifical, il est déjà décidé à faire plier le roi de France, encouragé d'ailleurs par les incessantes suppliques d'Ingeburge et les réclamations du roi de Danemark. La lettre qu'il écrit pour annoncer son avènement est, sans doute, paternelle à souhait mais n'en laisse pas moins prévoir de gros ennuis si Philippe ne renvoie pas Agnès sur l'heure pour reprendre, au moins momentanément, l'indésirable Ingeburge. Rome, en effet, a cassé le jugement rendu par les prélats français et le roi, considéré comme bigame, doit se soumettre à la loi commune.

Pour lui faire avaler la pilule, Innocent ajoute qu'il ne refusera pas d'examiner l'affaire, d'autres annulations ayant été prononcées dans des conditions bien plus épineuses mais, conscient de ce que le roi a bafoué l'autorité pontificale, le pape exige, avant de procéder à quelque examen que ce soit, que les choses reviennent où elles en étaient après Amiens.

Mais Philippe Auguste dont la puissance grandit de jour en jour n'est pas un petit sire et il le sait. A la prose pontificale, il oppose le silence et les astuces de sa politique, ne fût-ce que pour gagner du temps et tenter d'amadouer Innocent III. Le pape, il le sait aussi, a besoin de lui, de son appui dans la querelle qui l'oppose à l'empereur et il entend bien le lui faire payer...

Cela marcherait peut-être avec un autre. Avec Innocent cela ne prend pas. Il envoie en France un légat, Pierre de Capoue, avec des instructions précises : le roi se soumettra et reprendra Ingeburge jusqu'à nouveau jugement ou bien il sera frappé d'excommunication avec sa complice et si cela ne suffit pas, ce sera l'interdit jeté sur la France...

Ce nouveau jugement que l'on agite devant son nez comme une carotte, Philippe n'y croit pas. Il n'a aucune confiance et, en dépit des trésors de diplomatie que dépense Pierre de Capoue, des promesses qu'il ne ménage pas, il demeure intraitable : il aime Agnès, il la gardera!

Chose étrange, le plus malheureux des deux, c'est le légat. Il aime et respecte profondément le grand souverain qu'est le Roi de France. Il l'estime à sa juste valeur et donnerait beaucoup pour qu'il accepte d'entendre raison. Devoir le condamner le rend malade mais allez donc raisonner un homme aussi passionnément amoureux que l'est Philippe! D'autre part, le légat ne peut prendre le risque de désobéir au pape et, le 6 décembre 1199, il réunit un concile à Dijon. Il y a là les archevêques de Reims – bien contre son gré celui-là! – de Bourges, de Vienne, dix-huit évêques, l'abbé de Vézelay, ceux de Cluny, de Saint-Rémy, de Saint-Denis « et beaucoup d'autres ecclésiastiques venus des côtes de Bretagne et jusque des sommets des Alpes... » Durant sept jours on délibère et, finalement, l'Interdit, le terrifiant Interdit qui frappe de mort spirituelle le royaume tout entier, est fulminé...

Mais, même cela ne fait pas plier Philippe. Sa colère s'abat sur les évêques du royaume qui ont osé prononcer sa condamnation, et aussi sur Ingeburge naturellement. Si Agnès ne le suppliait pas, il la ferait tuer. Il se contentera de l'arracher, de nuit, à son couvent et de la faire enfermer dans un lieu tenu soigneusement secret. Agnès lui est si chère qu'il est prêt à tout pour la garder.

Celle-ci le comprend si bien qu'elle va se sacrifier. L'amour de Philippe l'a faite reine et elle ne veut pas que le royaume souffre par elle. L'Interdit est une punition inhumaine, injuste car elle ne frappe que des innocents. Dans l'arsenal des punitions de l'Église il est le pire des châtiments mais il est aussi, sur l'Église, une tache parce que ce n'est rien d'autre qu'un ignoble chantage et le déni absolu de toute charité chrétienne. Le 1ᵉʳ septembre 1200

Philippe Auguste cédera aux prières de celle qu'il
aime.

Il fait venir le légat et lui dicte les conditions de sa
reddition : Agnès partira pour le château de Poissy tandis
qu'il recevra Ingeburge à Saint-Léger-en-Yvelines, mais il
entend qu'après six mois le procès en nullité soit ouvert et...
conclu comme il l'entend. L'ambassadeur papal tente bien
de discuter : c'est Paris qui doit accueillir la reine mais
Philippe est intraitable : c'est cela ou rien!

On s'en tient là. D'ailleurs les instructions d'Innocent III ordonnent de ménager le roi s'il fait preuve de
bonne volonté. Le lendemain Agnès quitte son époux pour
Poissy avec une suite nombreuse et Adèle qui s'est attachée
à elle. Quelques jours plus tard, Ingeburge amaigrie et
changée mais toujours belle reparaît. Visiblement l'aversion qu'elle inspire au roi est intacte et sa politesse glacée
est de pure commande mais l'Interdit est levé. Le royaume
va revivre. C'est l'essentiel.

Incapable de reprendre la vie commune avec la Danoise,
Philippe la fait conduire dans un couvent confortable où
elle recevra tous les honneurs dus à une reine mais il
s'attache surtout à faire ouvrir le procès qui le libérera
complètement d'elle...

Un concile s'ouvre enfin à Soissons et le roi fonde sur lui
les plus grandes espérances, ignorant qu'Ingeburge a
encore écrit à Rome pour se plaindre, du légat cette fois,
qu'elle a trouvé trop attentif à plaire à Philippe. Le
résultat ne se fait pas attendre : Innocent envoie un autre
légat, un bénédictin austère et cassant, le cardinal de
Saint-Paul, qui cherche tant de tracasseries au roi que
celui-ci décide d'en finir avec un concile qui tremble
visiblement et de le couvrir de ridicule : montant à cheval, il
galope jusqu'au couvent où réside Ingeburge, l'enlève
littéralement en criant bien haut que puisque le concile est
incapable de dire si elle est sa femme ou non, il va la
garder...

Vexé le cardinal de Saint-Paul regagne Rome où le pape

trouve que l'affaire a assez duré. Il n'a aucun intérêt à rendre fou le roi de France et, cette fois, il envoie le légat Octavien avec ordre de réunir un nouveau concile... et à cette occasion de libérer le Capétien!

Hélas, le concile est à peine réuni qu'Agnès, qui vient de donner le jour à un petit garçon, Tristan, qui ne vivra pas, meurt en couches...

La douleur de Philippe est terrible. Le concile, terrifié, se sépare en hâte. Il est devenu sans objet et craint fort les représailles, mais c'est Ingeburge qui fait les frais de la colère royale car Philippe la tient pour responsable de la destruction de son bonheur. Enfermée au château d'Étampes, elle y sera traitée en prisonnière. Elle y demeurera douze ans...

Elle n'y mourra pourtant pas. Elle aura même finalement, le dernier mot. En 1213, comme, avec la cinquantaine proche, le poids des années se fait sentir et que son entourage le harcèle pour que cesse un état de fait pénible pour tous, Philippe la libérera, la rappellera auprès de lui et lui rendra les honneurs royaux. Au fond tout cela n'avait plus d'importance à ses yeux puisque Agnès l'attendait ailleurs...

Mais jamais la Danoise ne sera sa femme selon son cœur ni selon la chair...

Le couple est superbe : une double image de missel sous les voûtes sonores de la cathédrale de Valladolid. Pierre Ier de Castille a dix-huit ans, Blanche de Bourbon, nièce du roi de France Jean II le Bon, n'en a pas quinze mais tous deux sont blonds, tous deux sont beaux, tous deux sont l'image même de la jeunesse sous leurs robes identiques, de brocart d'or fourré d'hermine. Et le peuple de la ville qui se presse aux portes sous le soleil de ce jour de septembre 1352, préparant ses acclamations pour la sortie, est persuadé qu'il assiste à l'éclosion d'un roman d'amour. Depuis la nuit des temps, les peuples ont aimé croire au bonheur de leurs princes...

A l'intérieur de l'église, la cérémonie s'achève au grand soulagement du chancelier de Castille, Juan Alphonse d'Alburquerque dont ce mariage est l'œuvre. Cette fois, tout est dit : il n'y a pas à y revenir mais jusqu'à l'instant des consentements, Albuquerque s'est vraiment demandé si cette union, si soigneusement préparée, n'allait pas tourner à l'aigre et se changer en guerre avec la France. C'est que le jeune roi n'a montré jusqu'à présent à sa fiancée que la plus offensante indifférence. Il ne l'a même pas regardée...

Le jour où la princesse a franchi la frontière de Castille, seul Albuquerque s'est trouvé là pour l'accueillir : le roi chassait dans le sud de l'Espagne en compagnie de sa maîtresse et n'avait pas daigné se déranger. Il avait fallu des trésors de diplomatie pour expliquer la chose aux Français. Pour empêcher les épées de voir le soleil, le chancelier a prétexté une indisposition de son maître, ajoutant qu'il était naturel qu'un fiancé souhaite se montrer sous son meilleur jour et les choses se sont arrangées... A présent, Dieu en soit loué, tout est terminé et il n'y a aucune raison pour que le reste ne se passe pas au mieux : Blanche de Bourbon est ravissante, bien assez jolie pour retenir auprès d'elle un époux de dix-huit ans, même amoureux d'une autre...

En évoquant le charmant visage de Maria de Padilla, que lui-même a jadis poussée dans le lit de Pierre, Albuquerque soupire de nouveau, mais de regret cette fois. Il a cru bien faire en donnant une maîtresse à un jeune maître dont la violence, les ardeurs sauvages et la précoce cruauté l'inquiétaient. Non sans raison...

Quand, deux ans plus tôt, Pierre a pris possession du trône laissé vacant par son père, Alphonse le Vengeur, mort de la peste devant Gibraltar, son premier soin a été d'assouvir férocement tout ce qu'il croyait avoir de vengeances à exercer. La première, la maîtresse du feu roi, la belle Leonor de Guzman qui lui a donné plusieurs fils bâtards, les Trastamare, a été sauvagement assassinée sur l'ordre de Pierre au château de Medina Sidonia. Ensuite, plusieurs des anciens conseillers d'Alphonse, dont Juan Nuñez de Lara, ont payé de leur vie leur attachement au roi défunt et les quelques conseils qu'ils ont eu l'audace de donner à ce roi de seize ans. Albuquerque, après avoir assisté à ce débordement de sauvagerie, a compris que son tour pourrait bien venir s'il n'offrait pas une diversion à Pierre et, bien qu'il eût déjà entamé les pourparlers avec la France en vue du mariage, il a pris le risque de lui présenter, un soir au retour de la chasse, une éblouissante créature qui était un peu sa pupille : Maria de Padilla.

Le succès a été foudroyant : les cheveux noirs, les yeux clairs et le corps charmant de la jeune fille, de deux ans seulement son aînée, ont séduit Pierre au point que, dès ce premier soir au château de Sahagun, il l'a entraînée dans sa chambre. Le lendemain en repartant pour Valladolid, il l'emmenait avec lui mais s'arrêtait à Tordesillas et s'enfermait avec elle, durant des semaines... L'entourage royal pouvait respirer. D'ailleurs les exécutions sommaires cessèrent.

Albuquerque espérait une simple diversion mais il avait déchaîné une véritable passion et les difficultés recommencèrent quand on reparla mariage. Pierre ne voulait rien entendre : Maria venait de lui donner une fille et il était heureux auprès d'elle, passant le plus clair de son temps dans son Alcazar de Séville qui était sa résidence préférée, chassant et festoyant entouré d'une cour de Maures et de Juifs qui étaient ses serviteurs favoris. Il y vivait dans un luxe oriental et les gazes translucides, perlées ou brodées seyaient à la beauté de Maria. Chaque jour, pour le plaisir du maître, la « sultane » se rendait à la piscine des anciennes sultanes almohades, y prenait son bain en public afin que chacun pût admirer sa beauté, après quoi ceux que Pierre distinguait ou qui souhaitaient lui faire leur cour, venaient recueillir dans le creux de la main, pour la boire, un peu de l'eau sacralisée d'où sortait la maîtresse royale.

Un soir Pierre piqua l'une de ces rages dont il était coutumier : un officier de sa garde s'était refusé à la galante libation. Sa tête faillit voler mais l'homme ne perdit pas son sang-froid :

« Je craindrais, après avoir goûté la sauce, dit-il, d'être tenté par le perdreau... »

Le roi éclata de rire. L'insolent était sauvé.

La tête d'Albuquerque, elle aussi, avait été fort en danger quand il avait insisté pour la conclusion du mariage français. Pourtant il avait tenu bon et Pierre, devant la raison d'État, finit par s'incliner...

A présent, la cérémonie est terminée. Se tenant par la main, Pierre et Blanche marchent, dans le tonnerre des cantiques, vers le soleil de la place où les attendent deux mules jumelles. Mais, avant même que l'on ait atteint le portail, le jeune roi laisse tomber la main de son épouse et, sans plus s'en occuper monte sur sa mule pour prendre la tête du cortège. Il est si raide, si glacial que sa mère, Marie de Portugal, s'inquiète. Quel genre de nuit de noces va connaître cette petite Blanche dont le regard, déjà tendre, a suivi la silhouette de l'époux ? Et plus Albuquerque, tout à la joie de voir dûment béni ce mariage difficile, se rassure, plus la reine mère se tourmente.

Elle n'a pas tort. A peine achevé le festin rituel et tandis qu'elle conduit Blanche à la chambre nuptiale, Pierre disparaît... Chacun pense qu'il est en train de se préparer dans son appartement mais, chez la jeune reine, une longue attente commence, interminable, bientôt angoissante. C'est seulement quand Marie de Portugal, non sans inquiétude car elle connaît ses réactions, se rend chez son fils qu'elle apprend la vérité : dès la fin du repas, Pierre s'est fait seller un cheval et il a quitté la ville.

Il n'est pas difficile d'imaginer où il est allé : au château de Montalvan, chez Maria de Padilla.

La jeune femme l'a accueilli avec un mélange de joie et de crainte. De joie parce qu'elle l'aime et qu'aucune femme amoureuse n'aime se voir supplantée par une autre; de crainte parce que l'attitude de Pierre est une offense cruelle pour le roi de France qui pourrait chercher à en tirer vengeance. Aussi, dès le lendemain, le supplie-t-elle de retourner auprès de sa femme. Il faut que les seigneurs français qui ont accompagné Blanche le voient auprès d'elle afin qu'ils puissent repartir rassurés.

Pierre admet que le raisonnement est sage et il retourne à Valladolid. Il y passera deux jours, pas un de plus : le temps de réexpédier les Français mais aucune force humaine ne lui fera franchir le seuil de la chambre de Blanche. Bien qu'il ne soit pas, et de loin, l'homme de la fidélité, bien que ses appétits sexuels soient exigeants et que la Française soit belle, il n'y touchera pas. Et s'il l'emmène avec lui à Séville, ce n'est certes pas pour l'installer à l'Alcazar où Maria l'a précédé sur son ordre : il la laisse à la garde de l'évêque de Séville qui a ordre de l'empêcher de sortir et qui en répond sur sa tête.

Et quand la pauvre petite reine lui demande timidement ce qu'elle va faire dans cette maison inconnue, il lui ordonne méchamment de lui broder une bannière : « le fond couleur de son sang et la broderie couleur de ses larmes... » Et puis il s'en va.

Il va l'oublier là pendant près d'une année. Il est même décidé à l'oublier tout à fait et, pour bien marquer cette volonté, il oblige l'évêque de Salamanque à annuler son mariage avec Blanche, déclare qu'il envoie la princesse à Cadix pour la faire embarquer à destination de la France... et, en fait, la fait enfermer sous bonne garde dans la forteresse de Medina Sidonia, entre Jerez et Algesiras. C'est, au milieu d'un pays de landes incultes, une demeure sans grâce et sans agrément mais qui a déjà servi à Pierre : c'est là qu'il a fait enfermer, puis assassiner Leonor de Guzman...

De son côté Maria de Padilla ne cesse de protester contre son comportement et cela lui déplaît. Alors, pour qu'elle comprenne bien qu'elle n'est pas l'unique, il décide brusquement de se remarier. Il épouse une certaine Juana de Castro, une belle Sévillane qu'il délaisse d'ailleurs presque aussitôt.

Mais l'horizon se couvre pour Pierre le Cruel. L'Aragon, l'éternel ennemi de la Castille lui déclare la guerre. Cela tombe mal : le Trésor est à sec. Pour se procurer de l'argent, le roi pressure un peu ses amis juifs mais surtout il pille, sans la moindre vergogne, les tombeaux de ses ancêtres afin de récupérer les bijoux et l'or qui parent leurs dépouilles. Il dépouille aussi la chapelle de la Vierge sans un battement de cil : n'est-il pas plus musulman que catholique? Cela lui rapporte quelque deux mille pierreries : saphirs, émeraudes et topazes plus le rubis, gros comme un œuf de pigeon qui ornait le pommeau de l'épée du roi Ferdinand.

Ainsi renfloué, il entreprend d'assurer ses arrières. Leonor de Guzman a laissé cinq fils illégitimes. Pierre les fait assassiner l'un après l'autre, à coups de masse par ses arbalétriers maures qui lui rapporteront leurs têtes à l'arçon de leur selle. Même l'aîné, Don Fadrique avec qui le roi prétendait entretenir de bons rapports, est abattu comme il pénètre dans l'Alcazar et son cadavre est apporté à Pierre qui achève de souper et à qui cette vue ne coupe pas l'appétit. Pourtant, il ne sera jamais tranquille car l'un des infants lui a échappé et c'est le plus dangereux : Henri de Trastamare, réfugié en Aragon, s'est assuré l'aide du roi mais il garde, en Castille, des partisans, et des partisans qui passent de fort mauvais moments. Chaque fois que l'on peut mettre la main sur l'un d'eux, il est brûlé, écartelé, coupé en morceaux... Malheur aussi aux habitants des 00llages suspects d'avoir laissé passer Henri; les gens de Miranda sont là pour en témoigner : on a jeté tous leurs notables dans de grandes chaudières et on les a fait bouillir vivants...

La guerre civile à présent fait rage. Un instant, Pierre est pris par l'ennemi qui l'enferme à Toro mais il parvient à s'évader et à rejoindre son armée.

Toute cette sanglante agitation jointe à la bigamie du roi ne pouvait guère laisser le pape indifférent. Indigné des procédés de Pierre, Innocent VI a, d'Avignon, lancé contre lui l'excommunication majeure qui délie ses sujets de l'obéissance. Cela ne sert strictement à rien avec un mécréant comme Pierre mais Maria de Padilla est non seulement bonne catholique mais très pieuse. Tout cela l'épouvante et à son tour elle s'enfuit, gagne un couvent dont Pierre viendra bientôt la tirer de force. A nouveau elle se retrouve enceinte.

Cette fois c'est un garçon et le roi décide qu'il sera son héritier. D'ailleurs, à présent, il veut épouser Maria et comme il ne peut, tout de même, encourir une nouvelle fois les foudres papales, il faut qu'il se débarrasse de Blanche de Bourbon...

Un soir du printemps 1361, Blanche, qui prie dans la chambre haute où elle vit dans le plus grand dénuement et qu'elle ne quitte jamais, voit entrer l'un des arbalétriers maures de Pierre. A la main, il tient une lourde masse d'armes.

Elle comprend très vite, la malheureuse, que c'est sa mort qui vient d'entrer. Alors, elle pleure et le poète traduira sa plainte :

« Ô France, mon noble pays, ô mon sang de Bourbon! Je viens d'avoir dix-sept ans aujourd'hui. Le roi ne m'a point connue. Je m'en vais avec les vierges. Castille, dis-moi, que t'ai-je fait?... »

Elle n'en dit pas plus. L'homme a levé sa masse. L'arme s'abat, fracasse la tête blonde dont le sang éclabousse les murs... Pierre le Cruel peut se croire libre : il vient en fait de signer son arrêt de mort car la France du roi Charles V lui demandera compte de cette mort.

Il n'en tirera pas davantage de bonheur. Maria de Padilla, épouvantée, s'est retirée dans le couvent de Santa Clara qu'elle a fondé mais elle se relève mal de ses couches. Une fièvre puerpérale se déclare et, dans les premiers jours de juillet, elle meurt à son tour laissant le Cruel en proie à un désespoir comparable à ce que sera un jour celui de Jeanne la Folle. Les funérailles de la favorite sont célébrées avec une pompe royale, tandis que le corps de la reine assassinée n'a eu droit qu'à une hâtive et nocturne sépulture.

Mais Pierre n'échappera pas à la malédiction divine. Deux ans plus tard, le fils de la Padilla meurt. C'est déjà un châtiment mais ce n'est pas le dernier : le roi va devoir faire face à la plus redoutable des invasions : celle des Grandes Compagnies qu'en 1367 le roi de France lui envoie sous le commandement de Bertrand Du Guesclin. Le terrible Breton escorte Henri de Trastamare, le seul survivant des enfants de Leonor de Guzman. Il porte aussi avec lui la colère de son roi qui l'envoie venger le sang innocent d'une fille de France.

Pierre que les siens, recrus d'horreur, abandonnent, se jette alors dans les bras des Anglais. Le fameux Prince Noir lui promet son aide et, à Navarette, Du Guesclin, trahi par l'un des chefs des Grandes Compagnies dont il a voulu débarrasser la France, est fait prisonnier.

Ce n'est qu'un mince répit. L'énorme rançon exigée par le Prince Noir qui estime le Connétable à sa juste valeur est rapidement payée et Du Guesclin, sorti de Bordeaux, se jette à nouveau sur la Castille. A la bataille de Montiel, près de Tolède, il écrase définitivement Pierre le Cruel.

Il faut lui reconnaître cette qualité : Pierre Ier est loin d'être un lâche au combat. Il se bat bien mais la mort glorieuse sous une vaillante épée lui est refusée. Il ne le regrette guère d'ailleurs : la vie a du bon et, vaincu, il lui faut s'éloigner au plus vite pour tenter de refaire une armée. Au soir de la bataille, sautant à cheval, il tente de s'enfuir mais se trompe de chemin et tombe droit dans le camp des Français.

Amené devant la tente du Connétable, il en voit sortir un homme qui tient au poing une dague nue : Henri de Trastamare, son demi-frère, l'homme qui le hait le plus au monde. Un instant les deux princes se mesurent du regard puis, sans un mot, Pierre tire sa dague et se rue sur Henri. Les deux hommes roulent à terre, noués l'un à l'autre, embrassés, soudés dans une lutte à mort... Des chevaliers se précipitent, veulent les séparer. Un geste de Du Guesclin les arrête :

« Laissez! C'est à Dieu de juger... »

La sentence divine ne se fait pas attendre. Quelques instants seulement et Pierre le Cruel, la gorge tranchée, expire dans le sable qui boit son sang. Celui qui se relève, poudreux et sanglant, va être le roi Henri II de Castille. Il a vengé ses frères, sa mère et les nombreuses victimes d'un règne dont les siècles n'oublieront pas l'horreur. Le malheur est qu'à son tour il succombera à la tentation du pouvoir despotique et sera presque aussi cruel que son frère...

LA NUIT MONSTRUEUSE :
MARIE-LOUISE D'ORLÉANS
ET CHARLES II D'ESPAGNE

Le 17 septembre 1678, la France de Louis XIV et l'Espagne de Charles II signaient la paix de Nimègue qui mettait fin à la guerre de Hollande. En pareil cas il était fréquent qu'un mariage vînt renforcer l'accord tout neuf conclu entre les anciens belligérants, tout au moins si les circonstances s'y prêtaient.

On ne manqua pas à la règle. Le jeune roi Charles II allait atteindre ses dix-sept ans. Il était donc bon à marier en dépit d'un physique désastreux et d'une santé totalement délabrée due au fait qu'il était le résultat de huit mariages consanguins. Quant à Louis XIV, s'il n'avait pas de fille à marier, il avait une nièce : Marie-Louise d'Orléans, dite Mademoiselle, fille de Monsieur, son frère, et de sa première épouse Henriette d'Angleterre. Une nièce qu'il aimait beaucoup... avec peut-être la meilleure raison du monde. Nombreux étaient, à la Cour, ceux qui se souvenaient encore de la romance passionnée qui avait, dès son mariage, jeté la nouvelle Madame dans les bras de son beau-frère. Nombreux étaient ceux qui voyaient en la charmante Marie-Louise le résultat de cette romance...

Car elle était charmante. A seize ans, Mademoiselle possédait d'opulents cheveux noirs, de jolis yeux, une bouche fraîche marquée de fossettes et un teint de camélia. De sa mère, elle tenait son charme et son caractère décidé, de son père – quel qu'il fût ! – une beauté qu'il ne serait venu à l'idée de personne de refuser au roi ou à Monsieur. Elle ne manquait d'ailleurs pas d'adorateurs dont le plus convaincu était le prince de Conti. Malheureusement, elle ne leur prêtait aucune attention étant amoureuse, comme on l'est à cet âge, de son cousin Louis, le Grand Dauphin, fils de Louis XIV, personnage lent, lourd, endormi, grand amateur de chasse, de concerts et de siestes qui, d'ailleurs, ne devait jamais être attiré que par des femmes laides. C'est dire qu'il ne s'intéressait pas du tout à sa jolie cousine...

Le 2 juillet 1679, le roi fait savoir au marquis de Los Balbazes, ambassadeur d'Espagne, qu'il accorde à son roi la main de Mademoiselle d'Orléans. Bien sûr, il en a d'abord entretenu son frère et Monsieur n'a pas fait preuve d'un grand enthousiasme : il aurait préféré voir sa fille épouser le Dauphin. En outre le portrait du roi Charles avec son long visage blême, ses lèvres épaisses et ses cheveux raides n'a rien d'engageant.

« Et comme c'est un portrait de Cour, il doit être encore pire! » déclare Madame, ex-princesse Palatine, qui a son franc-parler, même devant Louis XIV dont elle est d'ailleurs toujours secrètement amoureuse.

« Il est le maître du second royaume de la chrétienté », coupe son beau-frère qui, non sans raison, s'attribue la première place. « Que signifie un visage plus ou moins beau quand il s'agit de régner?

— Cela signifie, fait Madame, logique, qu'on ne couche ni avec un principe ni avec une couronne... »

Louis XIV sait bien qu'elle a raison mais sa nièce sur le trône d'Espagne c'est déjà la mainmise de la France sur l'empire de ce Habsbourg dégénéré que l'on dit impuissant, que l'on surnomme l'Ensorcelé et qui, d'ailleurs, a déjà subi cinq ou six exorcismes. Il n'est qu'épileptique pourtant mais, à l'époque, ce mal constituait la signature la plus certaine du Malin. Et le roi de France s'en va dire à Mademoiselle :

« Ma nièce, vous allez être reine d'Espagne! »

S'il s'attend à de la reconnaissance, ou même à de la simple obéissance, le Grand Roi va déchanter. La fille d'Henriette d'Angleterre a de la défense : elle refuse tout net puis, quand on lui présente le portrait de son « prétendu » elle éclate en sanglots. Le Grand Dauphin est loin d'être un prix de beauté mais l'Espagnol lui paraît impossible.

Longtemps, Louis XIV plaide, explique avec une patience qu'il n'aurait eue avec personne d'autre. Finalement il lui dit – et c'est presque un aveu :

« Je ne pouvais faire mieux pour ma fille...

– Vous pouviez faire mieux pour votre nièce », riposte la jeune fille...

Mais elle sait bien qu'elle est vaincue. On n'a jamais dit « non » à Louis XIV.

La signature du contrat a lieu à Fontainebleau, le 30 août. Marie-Louise, que son oncle et son père couvrent de toilettes somptueuses et de bijoux, y paraît « en habit de couleur, en broderie d'or et d'argent que couvrait une mante de gaze rayée d'or ». Son père lui tient une main, le Grand Dauphin tient l'autre et la pauvre amoureuse a bien du mal à retenir ses larmes en pensant qu'il aurait pu la lui tenir en d'autres circonstances. Mais Monseigneur ne s'est jamais aperçu de cet amour. Bien mieux, tandis qu'il marche lentement auprès de la pauvre princesse, il se penche vers elle et murmure, badin :

« Vous m'enverrez du touron ma cousine?... »

Quelle horreur! Il lui réclame des sucreries quand elle brûlait de se donner à lui!

Le jour du mariage par procuration que célèbre le cardinal de Bouillon, c'est au tour d'un autre de souffrir. En effet, le roi a désigné le prince de Conti pour représenter le roi d'Espagne. Encore un amoureux qui devra se contenter d'un simulacre mais qui donnerait cher pour avoir le droit de marcher sur l'Espagne à la tête d'une armée!

Enfin, le 20 septembre, c'est le jour du départ. Le roi s'approche de sa nièce et lui fait ses adieux :

« Je souhaite, Madame, vous dire adieu pour toujours car, souvenez-vous-en bien, le plus grand malheur qui pourrait vous arriver serait de revoir la France... »

Il peut être tranquille, elle ne la reverra pas et pourtant le plus grand malheur lui sera arrivé.

Une suite nombreuse accompagne la nouvelle reine qu'entourent la duchesse d'Harcourt et la maréchale de Clérambault, plus sa dame d'atours, Mlle de Grancey. Mais parmi les hommes, Marie-Louise voit soudain caracoler le chevalier de Lorraine.

« Quoi? s'écrie-t-elle. Celui qui a empoisonné ma mère?... »

Décidément Louis XIV a toutes les attentions, mais la jeune reine peut se rassurer : le chevalier n'ira pas jusqu'à Madrid. Monsieur, qui a beaucoup plus de chagrin qu'il ne veut le montrer, tient à accompagner sa fille le plus longtemps possible : il fera route avec elle pendant une semaine et, à l'instant de la séparation, il ne pourra cacher ses larmes. Mais il remmènera l'indésirable chevalier.

Le long voyage à travers la France automnale se poursuit, navrant pour celle qui part sans retour et sans l'espoir de trouver l'amour au bout du chemin. Pourtant, d'après une légende, un homme aurait suivi le cortège de la nouvelle reine, un simple roturier qui était l'un de ses maîtres – de musique ou de peinture – et qui, l'aimant passionnément n'aurait pu se résoudre à la perdre définitivement. L'aventure est peut-être vraie mais ce sont de ces secrets que l'Histoire survole et que l'historien ne peut jamais percer.

Par un jour de Toussaint froid et triste, on atteint enfin la Bidassoa, la rivière des « échanges » que l'infante Marie-Thérèse a franchie, une vingtaine d'années plus tôt, mais dans l'autre sens pour devenir reine de France. Là, Marie-Louise voit venir à elle les envoyés de son époux.

Le premier contact est pénible. L'Espagne, à bout de souffle au point de vue financier aussi bien qu'au point de

vue militaire, stérilisée par l'or des Amériques, cache mal
une misère déjà endémique. Les seigneurs espagnols,
arrogants, pleins de morgue, portant de sombres velours
râpés sous de fabuleux joyaux ne cèlent guère, comme
jadis, leur mépris et leur mauvaise humeur en face de la
somptuosité des ambassadeurs français que mènent le
comte de Villars et le duc d'Harcourt. Ils sont si sombres et
si peu avenants que la malheureuse princesse sent ses
craintes lui revenir. Et quand, à la nuit tombante et à la
lumière des torches, on lui fait franchir la rivière, escortée
seulement d'une petite partie de sa suite, celle qui est
autorisée à l'accompagner jusqu'au bout, elle éclate en
sanglots désespérés.

La rencontre qu'elle fait, dans une maison située sur
l'autre rive, de la Camerera Mayor, duchesse de Terranova qui va désormais régler son existence n'arrange rien.
La duchesse est le prototype de la duègne : une vieille
femme sèche, raide et compassée sous son vertugadin
funèbre et qui, de sa vie, n'a dû savoir sourire. De toute
évidence, elle est là pour « dresser » sa nouvelle souveraine,
cette fille de France qui est, comme chacun le sait, le pays
du laisser-aller. Victor Hugo a fait un sort illustre à ses
recommandations incessantes :

« Madame, une reine d'Espagne ne rit pas... Madame,
une reine d'Espagne ne chante pas... Madame, une reine
d'Espagne ne regarde pas par la fenêtre ou par la
portière... Madame, une reine d'Espagne n'adresse pas la
parole à n'importe qui... »

Tant et si bien qu'au bout de quelques jours, la jeune
reine aux prises avec cet épouvantail poussiéreux a pris en
grippe la duchesse de Terranova... Mais bientôt, entre les
Français et les Espagnols qui se regardent en chiens de
faïence, une dispute éclate. Par l'indiscrétion d'une suivante, les ambassadeurs de Louis XIV apprennent que la
cérémonie nuptiale, dont on leur avait dit qu'elle aurait
lieu dans la cathédrale de Burgos, est prévue dans un
modeste village, situé à seize kilomètres de la ville :

Quintanapalla... C'est là que le roi doit venir à la rencontre de sa fiancée et c'est là qu'il l'épousera.

La raison de ce choix étrange est simple et tient tout entière dans l'état désastreux des finances espagnoles : lorsqu'une ville sert de théâtre à un mariage royal, elle est exemptée d'impôts pour une année et, lorsqu'il s'agit d'une ville aussi importante que Burgos, la perte est sévère pour le Trésor. Un village de quelques feux a beaucoup moins d'importance.

Ce choix, qu'ils jugent injurieux, indigne les ambassadeurs français d'autant qu'ils apprennent en même temps qu'ils ne seront pas admis à la cérémonie faute de place. Effectivement, Quintanapalla est loin d'être une métropole et l'église est toute petite. Néanmoins, ils se mettent à la recherche du duc de l'Infantado qui conduit la délégation espagnole.

Or, voyant soudain passer, sur un âne garni de pompons, la Camerera Mayor qui se hâte vers la modeste maison de la reine, ils lui courent après pour lui faire leurs doléances et, comme elle refuse de les entendre, ils saisissent l'âne par la queue tout en couvrant la duègne d'injures variées qui s'achèvent par un solide coup de houssine appliqué sur le derrière de l'âne qui file comme un zèbre.

« Allez dire à votre maître, crie Harcourt, que si nous n'assistons pas à ce mariage, le roi, notre maître, en demandera raison à l'Espagne! »

Plus morte que vive et passablement secouée, la duchesse atterrit plus qu'elle ne s'arrête devant la maison de la reine et se hâte d'informer le duc de l'Infantado des désirs de ces « maudits Français ». Celui-ci promet de faire le nécessaire et presse la dame d'aller habiller la reine car le roi ne va pas tarder à arriver en compagnie de l'archevêque de Tolède.

Tant bien que mal, on surcharge Marie-Louise de brocarts, de joyaux et d'un énorme manteau doublé d'hermine dont le poids la fait vaciller. On la coiffe et on essaie de la maquiller mais c'est là une tâche impossible : la

jeune fille, épouvantée de l'approche de ce mari dont elle a
si peur, pleure tellement que la poudre et les fards se
délayent, formant sur son charmant visage de tragiques et
grotesques rigoles.

Hors d'elle, la Camerera Mayor tance si vertement la
malheureuse – Madame, une reine d'Espagne ne pleure
pas... – qu'elle réussit à tarir les larmes et à plâtrer
littéralement cette figure désolée qui, dans ses brocarts
dorés, finit par prendre l'aspect figé d'une idole. Mais
enfin, elle est prête et il était plus que temps.

Quelques instants plus tard, Charles II, dans un
costume de velours noir tellement brodé d'or qu'il brille
comme un reliquaire, se précipite dans la chambre en
s'écriant :

« *Mi reina! Mi reina!...* [1] »

Il le répète dix fois, vingt fois, entrecoupant ses
exclamations d'embrassements frénétiques tandis que
Marie-Louise, réellement figée cette fois mais d'épouvante,
le regarde avec un mélange de pitié et d'horreur car ce
qu'elle voit est pire encore que ce qu'elle craignait. Ce
garçon de dix-huit ans est un avorton blême aux cheveux
raides, légèrement bossu. Il a un long nez toujours humide,
le menton en galoche des Habsbourg mais tellement
accentué que la lèvre supérieure est très en retrait de la
lèvre inférieure ce qui l'oblige à garder la bouche continuellement entrouverte. Dans son enthousiasme, il tremble
et même il bave... C'est un personnage digne de la plume
d'Edgar Poe.

Pour la malheureuse, livrée par la politique à ce
dégénéré royal, la rencontre tient du cauchemar plus que
du roman rose. Pétrifiée, Marie-Louise ne parvient même
pas à répéter les quelques paroles que lui souffle la
duchesse de Terranova et c'est Villars qui, avec l'habileté et
la politesse de Versailles, traduit « l'émoi » de la fiancée de
façon acceptable pour l'orgueil espagnol.

1. « Ma reine! Ma reine! »

La cérémonie nuptiale a lieu sur l'heure dans l'église du village hâtivement décorée de draps et de tentures à crépines d'or. Cela fait, et les angoisses du Trésor espagnol dûment apaisées, on quitte enfin Quintanapalla au grand soulagement de Marie-Louise qui avait craint un instant de devoir passer la nuit de noces sur les matelas de paille de la maison où elle a rencontré le roi. Mais on fait la route à toute allure car le roi est pressé de coucher avec cette jolie fille dont il porte autour du cou le portrait depuis des semaines.

A Burgos, où les notables font un peu la tête, on trouve tout de même l'accueil et le logis auxquels peut prétendre une reine d'Espagne. Les souverains s'installent au Palais de l'Archevêché, la fameuse « Maison du Cordon » que connaissent bien les touristes du XXᵉ siècle.

Là, ses femmes accommodent la reine pour la nuit qu'elle ne voit pas approcher sans épouvante. Va-t-elle vraiment devoir subir ce malheureux monstre qui bave en la regardant?...

L'attente est brève car l'époux est pressé. A peine Marie-Louise est-elle installée dans son lit que Charles apparaît. Il est en robe de chambre mais pour faire plus martial, il a l'épée au côté. Et surtout il est encombré d'un singulier déménagement : les yeux arrondis de stupeur, la jeune reine constate qu'il transporte à la fois une grosse lanterne allumée, un bouclier rond... et un vase de nuit.

Cette apparition grotesque et inattendue a, au moins, un heureux résultat : la reine oublie sa peur et éclate de rire. Un rire qui, selon les observateurs attentifs de ce mariage ahurissant, durera une partie de la nuit. Jamais reine n'a tant ri au cours de sa nuit de noces mais c'est un rire nerveux, plus triste peut-être que les larmes et qui s'achèvera en syncope, une bienheureuse syncope qui évitera à Marie-Louise d'Orléans le plus pénible d'une défloration maladroite. Car, si Charles II est incapable de procréer, il n'est pas impuissant et la beauté de sa jeune femme l'inspire : il faudra, au matin, l'arracher de sur elle pour le rendre à ses devoirs d'État.

Le lendemain, Burgos offre à sa reine, dont le fard dissimule la mine pâle, une réception digne du temps de Charles Quint avec un fastueux banquet au monastère de Las Huelgas. Puis l'on se met en route, très lentement, pour Madrid.

On va mettre six semaines pour atteindre la capitale, six semaines que Marie-Louise passera assise à côté du roi, dans un carrosse de cuir noir, gai comme un corbillard, et ouvert à tous les vents glacés de la sierra afin que le peuple puisse contempler à son aise ses souverains. Le tout sur des routes présentant plus de nids-de-poule et d'ornières que de surfaces sablées. A l'étape, on se couche de bonne heure : le roi n'entend pas perdre une seconde d'une intimité conjugale qui rend sa femme malade. Si raide qu'elle soit, la duchesse de Terranova n'est ni aveugle ni tout à fait inhumaine. Elle pense qu'à ce régime la jeune femme n'atteindra pas Madrid et, chaque soir, elle lui fait prendre une tasse de chocolat additionné d'un somnifère. Elle lui en fera prendre ainsi pendant quelque temps, singulièrement pendant la lune de miel passée dans le charmant palais du Buen Retiro et jusqu'à ce que s'apaise un peu, pour raison de santé d'ailleurs, la frénésie amoureuse de Charles.

A Madrid, autre épreuve : la nouvelle reine doit faire la connaissance de la reine mère, Marie-Anne, ex-archiduchesse d'Autriche, dévorée par un cancer du sein et qui ne quitte jamais l'habit monastique. Elle est le centre d'une coterie autrichienne dont la tête a longtemps été le jésuite Nithard qui vient de mourir après avoir régné pratiquement sur l'Espagne grâce à la reine. Il est remplacé par le prince Colloredo-Mansfeld mais tous ces gens ont, de tout temps et définitivement, voué à la France une haine mortelle.

Dans ces conditions, aucune sympathie n'est possible entre les deux femmes et Marie-Louise s'aperçoit bientôt que la surveillance de la Camerera Mayor ne fait que doubler celle de la reine douairière.

Dans tout cela, elle finit tout de même par trouver un ami dans le chef du parti pro-français, le cardinal Portocarrero qui assume les fonctions de Premier ministre. Grâce à lui, elle parvient à se créer une existence supportable tout en restant compatible avec l'oppressante étiquette. Ainsi, le cardinal lui apprend que les couvents sont des lieux où une reine d'Espagne peut se rendre autant qu'elle le veut et que certains d'entre eux, beaucoup plus mondains que religieux, offrent des séjours assez agréables pour que l'on ait envie de les renouveler et plus gais que ceux des palais royaux, sombres, sinistres, aussi éloignés de l'éclatant Versailles et du ravissant château de Saint-Cloud, que Monsieur vient d'achever, que la terre de la lune. On y trouve aussi des distractions plus raffinées que les perpétuelles corridas, ces boucheries, ou les abominables autodafés où l'Inquisition, toujours active, traînait de malheureux Juifs ou chrétiens soi-disant coupables d'impiété.

Il était aussi plus aisé d'en sortir que des formidables alcazars où s'étiolait la royauté espagnole...

Quel rôle jouèrent-ils, ces couvents, dans la vie quasi momifiée de la reine Marie-Louise? On l'ignore, mais quand, après dix ans de cauchemar, la reine mourut subitement, le 12 février 1689 d'un « flux de ventre », on chuchota que la reine-mère et le prince Colloredo-Mansfeld l'avaient fait empoisonner. Mais on dit aussi que le roi avait donné l'ordre fatal dans une crise de jalousie furieuse car, dans cette mort étrange, une chose était certaine; épouse d'un roi incapable de procréer, la reine d'Espagne était enceinte...

Sa mort n'éteignit pas la passion du misérable prince auquel on l'avait livrée. Souvent, même quand on l'eut remarié à Marie de Neubourg, une Allemande hystérique, Charles se rendit dans le caveau de l'Escorial où Marie-Louise reposait. Il se faisait ouvrir le cercueil, embrassait, comme jadis Jeanne la Folle, le corps à demi défait de la charmante princesse venue de France et restait là long-temps, répétant, avec des larmes, les premiers mots qu'elle avait entendus de lui :

« *Mi Reina!... Mi Reina!...* »

LA NUIT DE LAEKEN
S'ACHÈVE À MAYERLING...

A l'aube du 5 février 1875, l'une des sentinelles chargées de veiller sur les superbes serres du palais royal de Laeken, près de Bruxelles, qui comptent parmi les plus belles du monde, entend tout à coup, non sans surprise, l'écho de soupirs et de sanglots qui semblent venir de l'orangerie.

Inquiet et ne sachant trop que faire car c'est un tout jeune soldat, il se décide à aller voir, ouvre une porte, fait quelques pas, le cou tendu, l'oreille au guet, l'arme à la main se guidant sur le bruit qui grandit. Et soudain, à la lueur d'une bougie posée à même le sol, il découvre sous un oranger une jeune fille blonde en robe de chambre, ses cheveux en désordre croulant sur ses épaules en somptueuses vagues d'or et qui pleure désespérément, à demi couchée sur un banc, et le visage caché sous ses bras repliés.

Elle pleure tellement qu'elle ne sent même pas le courant d'air qu'a libéré la porte entrouverte. Le jeune soldat se hâte d'ailleurs de la refermer puis revient, ne sachant trop que faire. Il est déjà étrange de trouver une jeune fille en larmes au petit matin dans une serre royale mais quand cette jeune fille, qu'il n'a eu guère de peine à reconnaître, n'est autre que la fille aînée du roi, la princesse Louise que l'on a mariée la veille même à un prince étranger, cela dépasse les facultés d'assimilation d'une honnête sentinelle et risque même de toucher au secret de l'État.

Le jeune homme n'ose pas s'approcher. Il faudrait même qu'il regagne son poste, mais il pense tout à coup que les orangers ne vont pas s'en aller tout seuls et que personne ne lui reprochera un abandon momentané de sa garde : il n'est pas possible de laisser la princesse abandonnée dans cette serre, pleurant comme n'importe quelle servante congédiée. Et le voilà qui prend ses jambes à son cou, rentre au palais, grimpe jusqu'aux appartements de la reine Marie-Henriette, fait réveiller la dame d'honneur de garde et lui demande humblement la permission d'entretenir la souveraine d'une affaire grave ne souffrant aucun retard.

Élevée à la dure école des archiduchesses d'Autriche, la reine Marie-Henriette est une femme calme, assez froide même et douée d'une grande faculté de contrôle sur elle-même. Elle vient tout de suite, écoute ce que dit le garde, le remercie, demande un manteau et suit le jeune homme.

Quelques instants plus tard, Louise qui pleure toujours voit entrer sa mère et, sans autre explication, se jette dans ses bras pour y pleurer de plus belle.

« Oh, Maman!... C'est affreux!... C'est trop affreux!... »

La reine laisse passer le plus gros de l'orage et, tout en berçant sa fille, essaie de comprendre car, pour l'instant, Louise est incapable d'en dire plus. Marie-Henriette sait, d'expérience personnelle, que la recherche du bonheur des filles du Trône ne préoccupe guère les chancelleries et n'entre jamais dans les négociations d'un mariage royal, mais le désespoir de sa fille l'inquiète parce que rien, jusqu'à présent, ne laissait prévoir pareille fin de nuit de noces. Louise est normalement gaie, bien vivante, saine et jamais elle n'a montré pareil désarroi. Le mariage avec le prince Philippe de Saxe-Cobourg, officier dans la garde hongroise de l'empereur François-Joseph, semblait même lui plaire beaucoup...

En effet, quand son père, le roi Léopol II lui a **présenté** son cousin Philippe comme un époux éventuel, Louise n'a manifesté ni répugnance ni hostilité, au contraire. Bien qu'il soit son aîné de quatorze ans, Philippe est grand, de belle prestance, brun avec de beaux yeux myopes (il porte des lunettes, c'est le seul défaut) et une barbe soyeuse. C'est un homme du monde, un excellent cavalier, un grand chasseur et il jouit, à la cour de Vienne, d'une situation privilégiée.

A Bruxelles il a séduit tout le monde. D'abord le roi, dont il est deux fois cousin : la mère de Léopold d'Orléans, fille du roi Louis-Philippe, étant sœur de Clémentine d'Orléans, mère de Philippe, puis par les pères, tous deux des Saxe-Cobourg. Ensuite ce fut la reine, heureuse de penser que sa fille aînée allait vivre dans cette ville de Vienne dont elle a toujours gardé la secrète nostalgie. Enfin, Louise elle-même : très romantique, la jeune fille a vu dans cet élégant militaire le chevalier de légende dont elle a toujours rêvé. En outre, elle a très vite découvert les joies de l'état de fiancée. Les toilettes et les bijoux de sa corbeille de mariage l'ont transportée de joie car Louise, très coquette, n'appréciait guère la mode austère à laquelle on la soumettait.

Le mariage, dans un Bruxelles en fête, a été magnifique. Louise rayonnait sous d'admirables dentelles auprès d'un Philippe superbe dans son magnifique uniforme et, visiblement, très amoureux de sa blonde fiancée. Et quand les portes de la chambre nuptiale se sont refermées sur eux chacun pensait qu'une nuit agréable se préparait. Et voilà qu'au bout de cette nuit, Louise, au lieu de dormir paisiblement dans les bras de son époux, sanglote dans l'orangerie comme une enfant abandonnée.

Au bout d'un moment, la reine relève doucement le visage tuméfié de sa fille.

« Peux-tu me dire à présent? Qu'est-ce qui est si affreux? »

Tout! Tout est affreux! Le mariage, cet homme... cette brute plutôt! Et Louise d'expliquer comme elle peut l'affreuse aventure de sa nuit : le tendre fiancé changé soudainement en satyre déchaîné se jetant, complètement nu – même les lunettes avaient disparu – sur sa proie. Il l'a littéralement violée après lui avoir arraché sa chemise de nuit. Il l'a brutalisée : ses épaules, ses bras, sa gorge portent les traces de l'assaut. L'homme élégant s'est changé par une sorte d'affreux sortilège en une bête qui grognait, une bête qui a fait mal à Louise et qui avant de s'abattre enfin en travers du lit pour y ronfler a recommencé par trois fois ses horribles agissements...

Cette fois la reine a compris. Le malheur veut que son gendre soit un homme habitué, depuis l'adolescence, à la vie de garnison, aux plaisirs et aux filles faciles. La trentaine atteinte il est devenu incapable de faire la différence entre une adolescente de dix-sept ans et une courtisane. Le désir, évident que lui inspirait sa fiancée a fait le reste et, à présent, le mal est fait...

Souhaitant qu'il ne soit pas irréparable, Marie-Henriette essayera, patiemment, de recoller les morceaux de ce ménage déjà prêt à sombrer. Elle s'efforcera d'expliquer à sa fille combien une première nuit peut être décevante, plaidera de son mieux la cause d'un mari trop pressé, tentera d'expliquer la part de sauvagerie que le désir peut déchaîner chez un homme, surtout quand il a bu peut-être un peu trop. Enfin, elle parlera devoir : Louise est mariée devant Dieu et devant les hommes. C'est une situation irréversible et elle doit tenter, honnêtement l'expérience de la vie conjugale...

Son plaidoyer achevé, la reine ramène sa fille chez elle et dans la journée, elle aura un entretien avec son gendre, s'efforçant de lui faire comprendre que des ménagements seraient de mise. Philippe a commencé par tourner la chose en plaisanterie mais, devant la mine grave de sa belle-mère, il a promis de faire attention à l'avenir...

Mais c'est là un serment d'ivrogne et, en quittant Laeken pour l'Autriche, Louise, en dépit des encouragements maternels, sait déjà qu'elle n'aimera jamais l'homme qu'elle a épousé et que le devoir conjugal sera toujours pour elle ce qu'il est : un devoir, justement, et fort désagréable...

Au Palais Cobourg, à Vienne, comme dans les domaines hongrois de Philippe, la vie s'organise tant bien que mal. Cynique, viveur, brutal et foncièrement égoïste, le mari a vite oublié les promesses d'un lendemain de noces. Il ne voit guère dans sa jeune femme qu'un joli animal qu'il a plaisir à retrouver le soir dans son lit quand toutefois il ne passe pas la nuit chez les Tziganes, chez Sacher, ou chez l'une de ses nombreuses maîtresses. Ce dont d'ailleurs Louise se soucie peu ayant plutôt tendance à bénir lesdites maîtresses qui la débarrassent momentanément de son bourreau.

Mais comme il veut qu'elle lui fasse honneur, Cobourg a entrepris de donner à Louise une éducation d'un genre particulier, indispensable à son sens pour tenir dignement sa place à ses côtés. Louise apprend à demeurer des heures à table, à distinguer un bourgogne d'un bordeaux, à boire sans rien perdre de sa dignité et à supporter d'un front serein les plaisanteries souvent salées de son seigneur et maître. Il l'initie à la bonne chère et aux lectures... bizarres mais cela ne l'empêche pas d'être jaloux et, pour deux valses dansées avec le même cavalier à un bal, il lui fait une scène affreuse.

Ce n'est pas la seule et, à ce régime, le caractère, naturellement gai et aimable de Louise, s'affermit : elle apprend à se défendre et même à attaquer.

Pour se consoler, car elle n'aura jamais le goût des beuveries, Louise découvre les joies de l'élégance. Très dépensière de nature, elle montre bientôt une passion véritable pour les toilettes, les chaussures et les accessoires qu'elle assortit soigneusement à ses robes, mais surtout pour les fourrures et les bijoux. Naturellement pingre, Philippe n'en est pas moins obligé de payer pour ne pas abîmer son image de marque, auprès de l'Empereur d'une part, mais surtout du prince héritier, l'archiduc Rodolphe qui est devenu, une fois l'âge adulte atteint – il a exactement le même âge que Louise – son compagnon le plus habituel de plaisir et de chasse : les deux hommes se sont rencontrés un beau soir chez Sacher et Cobourg s'est fait, bien volontiers, l'initiateur de son jeune cousin pensant ainsi se l'attacher par le lien des souvenirs pour le jour où il sera empereur...

Or, si Rodolphe apprécie les talents de chasseur et de fêtard de son cousin, il s'est pris d'une assez tendre affection pour Louise. La maternité – elle a deux enfants, Louise et Dorothée, fruits inconscients des désastreuses nuits conjugales – l'a épanouie. Elle a l'éclat d'un Rubens sans en avoir encore les débordements de chair, et son élégance, que l'on cite partout, en font l'une des femmes les plus séduisantes de Vienne. Des plus courtisées aussi et Rodolphe joue sa partie dans ce concert masculin. Comme il ne manque pas, lui non plus, de charme, il est possible ?000l ait été celui qui réconcilia Louise avec l'amour. Sans qu'il y ait jamais eu de preuves, mais la suite de l'histoire l'indique assez clairement.

En 1880, quand il est question de marier l'archiduc, c'est Louise qui influence le destin.

« Va voir ma sœur. Elle me ressemble. Elle te plaira... »

Il faut qu'elle soit bien certaine de ce qui peut plaire ou ne pas plaire au prince... A Laeken, en effet, le roi Léopold a encore deux filles : Stéphanie et Clémentine dont la première approche l'âge du mariage. La seconde, Clémentine, en est encore loin, bien plus loin même qu'on ne pourrait le penser car elle devra attendre des années et des années, jusqu'après la mort de Léopold II, pour épouser l'homme qu'elle aime : un proscrit, le prince Victor Napoléon.

Le conseil de Louise séduit Rodolphe et, avec l'accord de son père, il se rend en Belgique où, effectivement, il demande la main d'une gamine de quinze ans ce qui permet à Léopold II d'ajouter à l'éclat des fêtes du Cinquantenaire de la Belgique en annonçant les prestigieuses fiançailles de sa fille avec l'héritier d'Autriche-Hongrie. Quant à l'impératrice Élisabeth, la célèbre Sissi qui chasse le renard en Angleterre, elle apprendra la nouvelle par un simple télégramme et, comme on lui fait remarquer que ledit télégramme n'annonce aucun malheur, elle se contente de soupirer, toujours optimiste : « Pourvu que cela n'en devienne pas un!... » Elle reviendra tout de même assister au mariage.

Celui-ci a lieu le 10 mai 1881, au milieu de la pompe fabuleuse habituelle aux Habsbourg. La petite Stéphanie porte une robe et une immense traîne tissées d'argent, des dentelles de Bruxelles et des bijoux somptueux : entre autres la fameuse parure d'opales et de diamants que portait Elisabeth au jour de son mariage avec François-Joseph.

Ce grand mariage met la princesse Louise à une place d'honneur et elle s'efforce de rassurer sa petite sœur, qui fait un peu moineau effrayé en face de ce déploiement de faste si éloigné des habitudes belges. Au moment où le jeune couple, qui doit passer sa nuit de noces à Laxenburg, à quelques kilomètres de Vienne, se dispose à partir, elle murmure, consolante par avance :

« Courage, Steffie! Ce n'est qu'un mauvais moment à passer... »

Elle croit plaisanter. Rodolphe n'est pas une brute comme Philippe. Et pourtant...

Stéphanie est recrue de fatigue quand on arrive à destination. Elle n'a que seize ans et la journée a été écrasante. Aussi souhaite-t-elle trouver la maison paisible, douillette et feutrée dont rêvent tous les couples de jeunes mariés.

Malheureusement Laxenburg n'a rien d'un nid d'amoureux. Pas de confort. Des pièces froides, hostiles dans leur solennité... Pas une fleur! On s'est contenté apparemment de faire le ménage sans rien ajouter qui puisse embellir une nuit de noces. Et encore! L'ambiance de Laeken, toujours abondamment fleuri grâce aux serres, son confort moderne et sa propreté belge sont loin!...

Rodolphe, d'ailleurs, a commencé à grogner en arrivant. Il a houspillé les serviteurs, réclamé à souper. Un morne souper où les deux époux, trop fatigués, ne trouvent pas trois mots à se dire. Stéphanie se raidit, corsetée par son éducation de princesse royale, pour ne pas montrer sa déception. Où est passé le tendre compagnon des fiançailles qui lui faisait donner la sérénade?

Quand on se lève de table, Rodolphe se contente de déclarer, avec un sourire il est vrai :

« Je vais fumer un cigare dans la salle de billard. J'irai vous rejoindre tout à l'heure... »

Les heures qui suivent ne sont pas plus réussies. Habitué, comme Philippe, à des maîtresses averties, Rodolphe a trouvé sa petite Belge charmante mais trop couventine. Il aurait fallu beaucoup de douceur et de patience pour amener cette enfant affolée à l'instant crucial où la jeune fille devient femme. Mais Rodolphe n'a aucune patience et, surtout, il n'est pas amoureux. Cette nuit n'est pour lui qu'une formalité et il s'en acquitte assez cavalièrement.

Au matin, Stéphanie n'ira pas pleurer dans la serre mais elle a découvert que son époux ne lui porte qu'un sentiment fort tiède alors qu'elle en est vraiment éprise... En fait, elle n'arrivera jamais à le comprendre, ni à être comprise de lui, mais qui pourrait lui en faire le grief?

Instable, d'une intelligence certaine mais tournée vers l'impossible, Rodolphe que sa mère, à dix-sept ans, a mené chez Louis II de Bavière et qui s'en est engoué, a le goût de la mort, de la violence aussi et il déteste d'instinct tout ce que Stéphanie a appris à admirer : la royauté, le devoir, les principes rigides, les convenances. Ses idées avancées, révolutionnaires même inquiètent l'Empereur autant que ses fréquentations, ses trop nombreuses maîtresses ainsi que son goût pour certains vices. Il y a en lui un perpétuel désir de tuer qui s'assouvit continuellement sur le gibier passant à portée de son fusil. Et à Laxenburg déjà il se livre, sous les yeux horrifiés de sa jeune femme, à de véritables hécatombes.

Deux ans après le mariage, Stéphanie accouchera d'une fille mais restera fragile et, vraisemblablement, ne pourra plus avoir d'enfant. Le ménage s'en ira lentement à vau-l'eau en dépit des efforts de Stéphanie qui accepte, sans jamais se plaindre, toutes les corvées de cour que refusent son mari et sa belle-mère. Cela lui vaudra l'affection de François-Joseph. Elle est, comme lui, une bonne ouvrière du Trône et il admire en silence le courage de cette jeune femme en face d'un protocole écrasant et de manifestations fastidieuses. Stéphanie essaiera aussi de rapprocher Rodolphe de son père mais sans y parvenir. Son influence sur son époux est nulle et les scènes entre eux sont fréquentes : un soir Rodolphe, qui boit comme une éponge, lui proposera de se tuer avec lui...

Parfois, une éclaircie se produit dans les relations du ménage. Ainsi ce jour de 1886 ou, en compagnie de Louise et de Philippe, le couple inaugure, dans l'intimité, le nouveau pavillon de chasse de Mayerling, aux environs de Vienne. Ce jour-là, tout le monde est gai, détendu. Rodolphe est charmant. Philippe est aimable. Ce pourrait être, pour les deux couples, le beau temps : ce n'est qu'une éclaircie...

Le comportement de Rodolphe, dont elle est toujours très proche, inquiète Louise. Et plus encore lorsqu'il noue une intrigue bientôt connue de tout Vienne, avec la jeune baronne Vetsera pour laquelle il se prend d'un caprice violent mais qui, pourtant, ne lui fait pas délaisser ses autres maîtresses. Entre autres l'actrice Mitzi Kaspar avec laquelle il passe souvent ses nuits. La jeune Marie éclate d'orgueil et affiche sans vergogne son triomphe en face de Stéphanie qui le supporte mal.

Pourtant, Louise ne la croit pas si dangereuse cette Marie. Rodolphe, elle le sait, a de plus graves soucis : ses relations avec la Hongrie, au bord de la révolte, sont étroites et Philippe, qui a des terres là-bas, y est mêlé. Est-ce pour cela que l'archiduc vient souvent au palais Cobourg où il s'attarde auprès de Louise quand le mari n'est pas là? Il a même dit un jour à sa cousine, en lui désignant discrètement Marie Vetsera :

« Ah! si quelqu'un pouvait m'en débarrasser! »

C'est néanmoins celle-ci qu'il emmène secrètement à Mayerling quand il y part, avec Philippe de Cobourg et le comte Hoyos, le 26 janvier 1889, pour une partie de chasse qui s'achèvera, le 30, de la manière que l'on sait.

Quand la nouvelle de la double mort arrive à Vienne, portée sur les plus folles hypothèses, Louise de Cobourg est encore au lit. On vient alors lui dire que son mari a tué l'archiduc dans une crise de jalousie. Et elle va y croire... La première version qui court, en effet, est celle de l'assassinat et vingt noms de maris trompés voltigent. Dont celui de Philippe... qui, pourtant, la dernière nuit, n'était pas à Mayerling officiellement.

Sans doute Louise ne croira pas longtemps au meurtre commis par son époux mais l'énigme de la double mort ne va pas moins achever de relâcher les liens conjugaux entre la princesse et le prince de Cobourg. Philippe, en effet, sait la vérité mais il refusera toujours de la révéler à sa femme.

« L'Empereur m'a fait jurer de ne jamais rien révéler... »

Louise trouve cette attitude commode. Puérilement peut-être, elle s'obstinera à voir quelque chose de suspect dans le rôle joué par son époux dans cette sombre affaire. Mais une chose est certaine : elle sera fort utile à Philippe de Cobourg quand sera venu le temps du combat ignoble et inhumain qu'il livrera, durant ses années, à sa femme...

Six ans après Mayerling, en effet, Louise qui a perdu beaucoup de son goût de vivre rencontre, au Prater, un beau cavalier, un officier de hussards croate, le comte Mattachich, qui se fera présenter à elle, quelque temps après, à Abbazia, chez Stéphanie.

C'est le début d'une grande passion, d'un étonnant amour romantique et obstiné auquel rien ne manquera :

les poursuites, les enlèvements, les duels, l'internement de Louise dans plusieurs maisons de fous, le tout avec la bénédiction de François-Joseph qui n'a rien à refuser au prince de Cobourg puisque celui-ci détient le secret de Mayerling.

Durant des années, Cobourg refuse le divorce pour l'excellente raison qu'il escompte l'héritage de Léopold II, devenu grâce au Congo le roi le plus riche d'Europe. Il faudra qu'il soit bien certain que Louise est déshéritée par un père aussi inhumain que lui, pour renoncer. Mais ceci est une autre histoire...

Saint-Mandé, 7 juillet 1982.

BIBLIOGRAPHIE SOMMAIRE

G. CONTENAU : *La Vie quotidienne à Babylone et en Assyrie*, Hachette, Paris, 1953.

E. DHORME : *La Littérature babylonienne et assyrienne*, Paris, 1937.

J.-G. FRAZER : *Le Rameau d'Or*, Robert Laffont (« Bouquins »), Paris, 1981.

Ch. de BARTILLAT : *La Civilisation aux ailes de briques*, Albin Michel, Paris, 1980.

J. HUREAU : *L'Égypte d'aujourd'hui*, Éd. J.A., Paris, 1980.

L. COTTRELL : *Les Épouses des Pharaons*, Robert Laffont, Paris, 1968.

Jean DUCHÉ : *Histoire du Monde*. Tome I. *L'Animal vertical*, Flammarion, Paris, 1958.

– *La Mythologie racontée à Juliette*, Robert Laffont, Paris, 1971.

Mario MEUNIER : *La Légende dorée des dieux et des héros*, Club français du Livre, 1960.

La Première Fois. Divers auteurs. Ramsay, Paris, 1981.

P. MIQUEL : *Les Faiseurs d'Histoire*, Fayard, Paris, 1981.

Janine ASSA : *Grandes Dames romaines*, Le Seuil (« Le Temps qui court »).

René GUERDAN : *Vie, Grandeur et Misère de Byzance*, Plon, Paris, 1954.

Charles DIEHL : *Impératrices de Byzance*, Livre Club du Libraire, 1960.

Jean HÉRITIER : *Catherine de Médicis*, Fayard, Paris, 1963.

Jacques SAINT-GERMAIN : *Louis XIV secret*, Hachette, Paris, 1970.

Philippe ERLANGER : *Louis XIV*, Arthème Fayard, Paris, 1965.

– *Le Massacre de la Saint-Barthélemy*, Gallimard, Paris, 1960.

- *Monsieur, Frère de Louis XIV*, Hachette, Paris, 1970.
- *La Monarchie Française, du Roi-Chevalier au Roi-Soleil*, Gallimard, Paris, 1955 et Tallandier, Paris, 1975.

Charles TERRASSE : *François Ier, le Roi et le Règne*. T. I, Grasset, 1945. T. II, Grasset, 1948.

J.B. MOLIER : *Rituel du mariage en France du XIIe au XVIe siècle*, Beauchesne-Croit.

Ivan CHARLES : *Catherine de Médicis*, Fayard, Paris, 1979.

Maurice ANDRIEUX : *Les Médicis*, Plon, Paris, 1958.

Maurice DONNAY : *La Reine Margot*, Fayard, Paris, 1946.

BRANTOME : *Les Dames galantes*, Livre de Poche, 1975.

Princesse PALATINE : *Une Princesse allemande à la Cour de Louis XIV*, 10/18, Paris, 1962.

Duc de CASTRIES : *Maurice de Saxe*, Fayard, Paris, 1963.

Claude PASTEUR : *Le Prince de Ligne*, Librairie Académique Perrin, Paris, 1980.

G. DUBY : *Le Chevalier, la Femme et le Prêtre*, Hachette, Paris, 1981.

G. LENOTRE : *La Petite Histoire « Femmes »*, Grasset, Paris, 1933.

F. HACKETT : *Henri VIII*, Payot, Paris, 1930.

J. CASTELNAU : *La Reine Margot*, Payot, Paris, 1930.

G. SLOCOMBE : *Henri IV*, Payot, Paris, 1930.

G. BORDONOVE : *Les Rois qui ont fait la France : Henri IV, Louis XIII*, Pygmalion, Paris, 1980 et 1981.

Louis VAUNOIS : *Vie de Louis XIII*, Grasset, Paris, 1943.

Armand BASCHET : *Le Roi chez la reine*, Plon, Paris, 1866.

André CASTELOT : *Les Battements de Cœur de l'Histoire*, Le Livre Contemporain, Paris, 1960.
- *Napoléon Ier*, Librairie Académique Perrin, Paris, 1968.

Jacques LEVRON : *Le Maréchal de Richelieu*, Librairie Académique Perrin, Paris, 1971.

Paul GUTH : *Saint Louis, roi de France*, Bloud et Gay, 1961.

Duc de LEVIS MIREPOIX : *La France féodale*, Tallandier, Paris, 1974.
- *Les Trois Femmes de Philippe Auguste*, Librairie Académique Perrin, Paris.
- *Le Roi n'est mort qu'une fois*, Librairie Acédémique Perrin, Paris, 1965.

Historia (hors série n° 44) « Le Roman du mariage ».

Alfred FRANKLIN : *La vie privée au temps des premiers Capétiens*, Émile Paul, 1911.

Edmond FARAL : *La Vie quotidienne au temps de saint Louis*, Hachette, Paris, 1938.

Jean LUCAS-DUBRETON : *Les Borgia*, Arthème Fayard, Paris, 1952.

J. COLLISON-MORLEY : *Histoire des Borgia*, Payot, Paris, 1934.
Maria BELLONCI, *Lucrèce Borgia*.

Charles YRIARTE, *César Borgia, sa vie, sa mort*, J. Rothschild, 1889.

J. RODOCANACCHI : *Une cour princière au Vatican*, Hachette, Paris, 1923.

Pierre de NOLHAC : *Louis XV et Marie Leszczynska*, Calmann-Lévy, Paris, 1904.

Pierre GAXOTTE : *Le Siècle de Louis XV*, Arthème Fayard, Paris, 1966.

Pierre RICHARD : *La Vie privée de Louis XV*, Hachette, Paris, 1954.

Maréchal de VILLARS p.p. de VOGUE, S.H.F., 1891.

Mémoires de Constant, Albin Michel, Paris, 1909.

Mémoires de la Reine Hortense, Paris, 1927.

Frédéric MASSON : *Napoléon et les femmes*, Paris, 1921.
– *Napoléon et sa famille*, Paris, 1907.

Charles KUNSTLER de l'Académie française : *Napoléon et l'Empire*, Hachette, Paris, 1969.

Jules BERTAUT : *Marie-Louise, Impératrice de France*, Tallandier, Paris, 1972.

F. ALTHEIM : *Attila et les Huns*, Payot, Paris, 1952.

Marcel BRION : *Attila*, Gallimard, Paris, 1959.

Alain DECAUX de l'Académie française, *Histoire des Françaises*, Librairie Académique Perrin, Paris, 1972.

RIGORD (le moine) : *Gesta Philippi-Augusti*, Paris, 1854.

DELISLE Catalogue des Actes de Philippe-Auguste, Paris, 1896.
Slatkine Reprints, Genève, 1975.

Guy BRETON : *Histoires d'Amour de l'Histoire de France*. 12 vol., Presses de la Cité, Paris, 1973.

Paule HENRY-BORDEAUX, *Louise de Savoie*, Plon, Paris, 1954.

FLEURANGES (Robert de la Marck, sire de) : *Histoire des choses mémorables advenues du règne de Louis XII et François I ᵉʳ*, Petitot, Paris, 1826.

Robert COURAU : *Histoire pittoresque de l'Espagne*, T.I et II, Plon, Paris, 1962.

Jean DESCOLA : *Histoire d'Espagne*, Fayard, Paris, 1959.

François PIETRI : *Pierre le Cruel, le vrai et le faux*, Plon, Paris, 1961.

Prosper MÉRIMÉE : *Histoire de Don Pedro I ᵉʳ, roi de Castille*, Charpentier, Paris, 1848.

Pierre de GORSSE : « Une maîtresse royale à la cour de Castille »,

Histoire pour tous, n ° 160.

Morel FATIO : *Histoire d'Espagne des XVI' et XVII' siècles,* Paris, 1879.

John de STUERS : *La Dynastie des Habsbourg,* Genève, 1946.

Princesse Louise de BELGIQUE : *Autour des trônes que j'ai vus tomber,* Albin Michel, Paris, 1921.

Comtesse LARISCH : *Les Secrets d'une maison royale,* Payot, Paris, 1949.

Gerty COLIN : *Les Châtelaines de Laeken,* Robert Laffont, Paris, 1963.

Comte Egon CORTI : *Elisabeth d'Autriche,* Payot, Paris, 1936.

Henri VALLOTON : *Elisabeth d'Autriche, l'impératrice assassihée,* Fayard, Paris, 1939.

Guy CLAISSE : *Les Suicidés de Mayerling,* Les Amis de l'Histoire, 1968.

Michel GEORIS : *Les Habsbourg,* Rencontre, Lausanne, 1962.

Dominique AUCLÈRES : « Louise de Cobourg, la princesse captive », *Histoire pour tous,* n ° 97.

Arnaud CAFFANJON : *Histoires de familles royales,* T. I et II, Ramsay-Images, Paris, 1980.

– *Grandes Familles de l'Histoire de France,* Albatros, Paris, 1980.

– *Napoléon et l'Univers impérial,* Serg, 1963.

Paul MORAND : *La Dame blanche des Habsbourg,* Laffont, Paris, 1963.

Georges POISSON : *Cette curieuse famille d'Orléans,* Librairie Académique Perrin, Paris, 1976.

TABLE DES MATIÈRES

Achevé d'imprimer
le 22.7.83
par Printer Industria
Gráfica S.A.
Provenza, 388   Barcelona-25
Sant Vicenç dels Horts   1983
Depósito Legal B. 25649-1983
Pour le compte de
France Loisirs
123, Boulevard de Grenelle
Paris

Numéro d'éditeur : 8206
Dépôt légal : juillet 1983
Imprimé en Espagne